FINAL JUDGMENT

The House of Lords, for over 300 years the UK's highest court, was transformed in 2009 into the UK Supreme Court. This book provides a compelling and unrivalled view into the workings of the Court during its final decade, and into the formative years of the Supreme Court. Drawing on over 100 interviews, including more than 40 with Law Lords and Justices, and uniquely, some of their judicial notebooks, this is a landmark study of appellate judging 'from the inside' by an author whose earlier work on the House of Lords has provided a scholarly benchmark for over 30 years.

The book demonstrates that appellate decision-making in the UK's final court remains a social and collective process, primarily because of the dialogues which take place between the judges and the key groups with which they interact when reaching their decisions. As the book shows, the forms of dialogue are now more varied, yet the most significant dialogues continue to be with their fellow Law Lords and Justices, and with counsel. To these, new dialogues have been added, namely those with foreign courts (especially Strasbourg) and with judicial assistants, which have subtly altered the tenor and import of their other dialogues.

The research reveals that, unlike the English Court of Appeal, the House of Lords in its last decade was only intermittently collegial since Lord Bingham's philosophy of appellate judging left opinion writing, concurrences and dissents largely to individual preference. In the Supreme Court, however, there has been a marked shift to team working and collective decision-making bringing with it challenges and occasional tensions not seen in the final years of the House of Lords. The work shows that effectiveness in group decision-making in the final court turns in part on the stages when dialogues occur, in part on the geography of the court and in part on the task leadership and social leadership skills of the judges involved in particular cases. The passing of the Human Rights Act and the expansion in judicial review over the last 30 years have dramatically altered the two remaining dialogues—those with Parliament and with the Executive. With the former, the dialogue has grown more distant, with the latter, more problematic, than was the case 40 years ago. The last chapter rehearses where the changing dialogues have left the UK's final court. Ironically, despite the oft applauded commitment of the new Court to public visibility, the book concludes that even greater transparency in the dialogue with the public may be required.

Final Judgment

The Last Law Lords and the Supreme Court

Alan Paterson

·HART·

OXFORD · LONDON · NEW YORK · NEW DELHI · SYDNEY

HART PUBLISHING

Bloomsbury Publishing Plc

Kemp House, Chawley Park, Cumnor Hill, Oxford, OX2 9PH, UK

1385 Broadway, New York, NY 10018, USA

29 Earlsfort Terrace, Dublin 2, Ireland

HART PUBLISHING, the Hart/Stag logo, BLOOMSBURY and the Diana logo are
trademarks of Bloomsbury Publishing Plc

First published in Great Britain 2013

First published in hardback, 2013
Paperback edition, 2021

A catalogue record for this book is available from the British Library.

ISBN: HB: 978-1-84946-383-6
PB: 978-1-50995-715-6
ePDF: 978-1-78225-278-8
ePub: 978-1-78225-279-5

Typeset by Compuscript Ltd, Shannon

To My Family

Foreword
by
Lord Hope of Craighead KT

Seen from outside, public buildings tell one very little about what goes on inside them. Not much more is revealed by the names and titles that are given to them and to the people who work there. One has to go inside, to see and to listen if one is to get some idea of their purpose and character. But even then the impression one gets is likely, at best, to be superficial. However open-minded one tries to be, it is hard to overcome pre-conceptions and to avoid misunderstandings that the names and titles themselves are apt to create. The only way to overcome these obstacles is to meet and speak to the people who really know what is going on. But a casual conversation here or there will not do. That too is apt to mislead. It is only when contributions are obtained across a much wider and deeper canvas that the true picture begins to emerge.

Professor Paterson has devoted much of his professional life to studying the work of those who have been privileged to sit in the nation's highest courts. His method has been to base his research to a very large extent on interviews. That in itself was no easy task. He had first to win the confidence of those whom he was seeking to interview. There is no doubt that this was made a little easier this time round by the fact that he had been able to do that at a much earlier stage in his career when he was conducting his original study of the Law Lords, based on interviews with the judges and counsel, 40 years ago. I have never known it to be suggested that their confidence in his integrity in the use of that material was misplaced. This experience gave him an inestimable advantage, on which he was able to build on this occasion as he probed deeper into the inner workings of these courts as seen by its users and by those at all levels who worked and who still work there. But he still had to reassure those whom he wished to interview that they could properly speak to him. It is much to his credit that he was able to persuade so many people to join with him in conducting this very sensitive exercise.

The period to which this phase of his research has been devoted gives it an added significance. His theme is that the process of collective appellate decision-making which we enjoy in this country is a social process. As such, it is apt to be much influenced by the characters of those who take part in it. Inevitably, as people change the character of the institution changes too. But this process was limited in the House of Lords by the long-established rules and conventions that, as members of the House, the Appellate Committee had to work to. There was little room for fresh initiatives. The extent to which this was so was not, I think, fully appreciated until the Law Lords were removed from the House in the summer of 2009 and given the task of setting up a court of their own design on the other side of Parliament Square, to be known as the Supreme Court of the United Kingdom. This was a remarkably liberating experience, as the Justices found when they set about working out a new system for themselves. They had to achieve everything by consensus, as no-one was in a position to give them orders or instruct them as to what they should do. That the social process of which Professor Paterson writes was able to achieve this so amicably and in such a short space of time was quite an achievement. It is still open, however, to further development in the light of experience.

That is the context in which the way appellate judges at the highest level behave to each other, to counsel, with other branches of government and with other courts is brought under closer scrutiny in this book than ever before. It is scrutiny with a light touch, as the author's aim for the most part is not to criticise but rather to describe, analyse and explain what he has found. The remarkable width and depth of his examination is supplemented throughout by extensive and very well-informed footnotes. This has resulted in a work of real scholarship, which all those who are interested in how appellate courts work all over the common law world will find especially valuable.

But this is not just a historical record. The book as a whole will provide a basis for further discussion of the kind that the author permits himself to engage in as he sets out his final reflections. The Justices themselves are, of course, well aware that the way that their comparatively young and vigorous court can improve itself lies in their own hands. Discussion about the way forward, and the risks that making changes or declining to change may give rise to, goes on there all the time. The author's reflections will, however, act as a guide to those who will be watching what they do with this new freedom from the outside. And the work as a whole should also lead to a deeper understanding of how the collective system of justice in that court works. The reader may well feel, at the end, that this study has shown beyond question that the vital task of maintaining the rule of law in a modern democratic society could not be in better hands.

David Hope   7 October 2013

Preface and Acknowledgments

In many ways the aetiology of this work stems back to over 40 years ago when I first began to study the House of Lords as a judicial body as a DPhil student at Oxford. Anyone who is familiar with the publication to emerge from that research, *The Law Lords* (Macmillan, 1982), will recognise that this work draws in part on material taken from that book (for which I gratefully acknowledge the permission of Palgrave Macmillan), as well as examining similar issues. In 2008, prompted by the impending demise of the House of Lords and its replacement by the new Supreme Court in October 2009, and fortified by the generous support of the Nuffield Foundation (a charitable trust that funds research and innovation in social policy), I returned to my original task of describing, analysing and explaining in terms which are hopefully intelligible to lawyers and laypersons alike, how appellate judicial decision-making in the United Kingdom's top court works. I was intending to draw comparisons between the final years of the judicial House of Lords, which had been largely dominated by Lord Bingham, and the court presided over by his great predecessor as senior Law Lord, Lord Reid, which I had studied in the 1970s. As before, the fieldwork lasted far longer than anticipated, in part because of the huge responsiveness of those whom I approached for interviews this time round. As a result the working title for the project—the Last Law Lords—had to be abandoned when it became clear that despite not interviewing nearly as many counsel as in the first project, I was going to end up with many more judicial interviews. As my publishers wisely advised, a work which emerged several years after the establishment of the Supreme Court would not only be slighted dated, it would miss the wonderful opportunity of comparing the House of Lords with the early years of the Supreme Court. Accordingly, I commenced further interviews with the early Justices of the Supreme Court and with the generous assistance of the Leverhulme Trust (which funds research and education), which provided a Fellowship for 18 months, I was enabled to complete the fieldwork (including, for the first time, the scrutiny of judicial notebooks from the top Court) and the bulk of the writing up in 2012–2013.

A work with a gestation period of five years in its modern iteration, inevitably owes much to many. In addition to the many interviewees and advisers listed in *The Law Lords*, there is a modern cohort of individuals whose invaluable assistance with the project has ensured that this book has not only seen the light of day, but has done so with new material, even in an area that is as well scrutinised by scholars as our top court. Those whom I interviewed were often disarmingly candid, invariably tolerant in the face of intrusive questions and never less than generous with their time, with sessions ranging from one to three hours. In this connection I sincerely and gratefully acknowledge the assistance of Lord Bingham, Lord

Brown, Lord Carnwath, Lord Carswell, Lord Clarke, Lord Collins, Lord Dyson, Lady Hale, Lord Hoffmann, Lord Hope, Lord Hutton, Lord Kerr, Lord Lloyd, Lord Mackay, Lord Mance, Lord Millett, Lord Neuberger, Lord Nicholls, Lord Phillips, Lord Reed, Lord Saville, Lord Scott, Lord Steyn, Lord Sumption, Lord Walker, Lord Wilson, Lord Woolf, Dame Mary Arden, Sir Terence Etherton, Sir Jack Jacob, Sir John Mummery, Sir Stephen Sedley, Sir Philip Sales, Sir Rabinder Singh, Michael Beloff QC, Jonathan Crow QC, Sir Sydney Kentridge QC, Lord David Pannick QC, David Perry QC, Gordon Pollock QC, Victoria Ailes, Charles Banner, Corinna Ferguson, Nicholas Gibson, Matthew Hancock, Francesca John, Louise Di Mambro, Brendan Keith and James Vallance White.

My original supervisor for the doctoral thesis, Sir Neil MacCormick, prior to his untimely death, urged me to revisit my scrutiny of the House of Lords and Sharon Witherspoon, Director of the Nuffield Foundation and Anna Grundy, Grants Manager of the Leverhulme Trust, also provided helpful encouragement to the author as the project unfolded. Lady Bingham kindly permitted me to publish data derived from a scrutiny of a range of Lord Bingham's judicial notebooks and Lord Hope was unfailingly tolerant of my many intrusions on his time, ranging from a request for a Foreword, to providing access to Lord Bingham's notebooks and permission to approach a selection of former judicial assistants. Others with whom I have discussed the project have included Sir Jack Beatson, John Blackie, Michael Browde, Simon Chester, Brice Dickson, Jim Ellis, Dame Hazel Genn, Simon Halliday, Chris Hanretty, William Holligan, James Lee, Kate Malleson, Joanna Manning, Neil McIntosh, Duncan Murray, Philip Petchey, Thomas Poole, Avrom Sherr, Roger Smith, Lindsay Stirton, Richard Susskind, Adam Tomkins and Neil Walker. Several more took time to read and comment on parts of the book including Emma Boffey, Michael Browde, David Feldman, Lord Hope, Sarah McConnell, Kenny Miller, Richard Moorhead, Chris Paterson, and Lord Reed. To all of them grateful thanks are due.

I am also obliged to Andrew Burrows and several Justices in the Court for graciously allowing me to read chapters from A Burrows et al (eds) *Judge and Jurist* (OUP, 2013) whilst it was at the proof stage and to Finola O'Sullivan for similarly permitting me to draw on material which had earlier been published in chapter four of A Paterson, *Lawyers and the Public Good* (Cambridge University Press, 2012).

In the last few years I have made many visits to the House of Lords and the Supreme Court and all of the staff—security, receptionists and secretaries have been unfailingly helpful. Specific thanks however are due to Brendan Keith, Jenny Rowe, Grainne Hawkins, Jackie Sears and Ben Wilson for help with different aspects of the research.

Those who provided the support function throughout the project are owed a special debt of gratitude: Michael Cannon, Sharon Ennis and Craig Grant of Strathclyde University; Dot Kirkham, Eileen Ritchie and Carol Hutton for producing the interview transcripts; and above all my long suffering but immensely valuable research assistants, Danielle McLaughlin, Darren Murdoch, Emma

Boffey, Sarah McConnell and Paul Ferrie. Without them the book would never have been written.

Lastly, but no means least, I owe a major debt of thanks to my publishers and to all those who have been involved in the production of the book to very tight timescales—Richard Hart, Mel Hamill, Tom Adams, Charlotte Austin and Emma Swinden.

One final point. In a work such as this, which has benefitted from external funding and where so many of the participants in the research project have been identified, it is peculiarly incumbent on the author to stress that he, and he alone, is responsible for the material presented. The theme, content and conclusions of the book, are mine. I am profoundly grateful to all who have contributed in one way or another to this work, but none of them must be taken to agree necessarily with all or any of the arguments which follow.

Contents

Table of Cases

Table of Legislation

United Kingdom

International Treaties and Conventions

European Union Legislation

1

Introduction, Context and Methodology

RESEARCH INTO THE judiciary in the United Kingdom has taken on a new lease of life in the last few years. Unsurprisingly, the demise of the House of Lords and the retirement of Lord Bingham was marked by a stream of anthologies.[1] Penny Darbyshire has produced her highly impressive participant observation study of the English and Welsh judiciary, *Sitting in Judgment*[2] and Cheryl Thomas and Hazel Genn have launched the first UK Judicial Insitute at UCL. Several appellate judges on the international stage have produced heavyweight commentaries on judicial decision-making from the inside,[3] reminiscent of the reflections of Benjamin Cardozo in *The Nature of the Judicial Process*.[4] We have even seen the first few attempts since Robertson[5] to study the attitudes and values of Law Lords and UK Supreme Court Justices.[6] In the United States, political science-based attitudinal studies have now been embellished by a focus on strategic decision-making.[7] This endeavours to harness the scrutiny of the value preferences of the US Supreme Court Justices with practical politics, namely an

---

[1] L Blom-Cooper, B Dickson and G Drewry, *The Judicial House of Lords 1876–2009* (Oxford, Oxford University Press, 2009); J Lee (ed), *From House of Lords to Supreme Court* (Oxford, Hart Publishing, 2011); M Andenas and D Fairgrieve (eds), *Tom Bingham and the Transformation of the Law* (Oxford, Oxford University Press, 2009).

[2] Oxford, Hart Publishing, 2011.

[3] R Posner, *How Judges Think* (Cambridge MA, Harvard University Press, 2008), EW Thomas, *The Judicial Process* (Cambridge, Cambridge University Press, 2005). See also the series of articles by the Australian High Court Justice J D Heydon, eg 'Limits to the Powers of Ultimate Appellate Courts' (2006) 122 *LQR* 399–425; 'Judicial Activism in Common Law Supreme Courts' (2008) 124 *LQR* 706–12; 'Threats to Judicial Independence: The Enemy Within' (2013) 129 *LQR* 205; 'Varieties of Judicial Method in the Late 20th Century' (2012) 34 *Sydney Law Review* 219.

[4] B Cardozo, *The Nature of the Judicial Process* (New Haven CT, Yale University Press, 1921).

[5] David Robertson, *Judicial Discretion in the House of Lords* (Oxford, Clarendon Press, 1998).

[6] C Hanretty, 'The Decisions and Ideal Points of British Law Lords' (2013) 43 *British Journal of Political Science* 703; TT Arvind and L Stirton, *Lawyers and the Legal Model: Judicial Ideology, Judicial Professionalism and Institutional Strategy Among the Law Lords* (14 May 2012) available at: extranet. isnie.org/uploads/isnie2012/arvind_stirton.pdf. See also Rachel Cahill-O'Callaghan, 'The influence of personal values on legal judgments' *Journal of Law and Society* (forthcoming) on psychological values and the Supreme Court.

[7] T Hammond et al, *Strategic Behaviour and Policy Choice on the US Supreme Court* (Stanford, Stanford University Press, 2005), and L Epstein and J Knight, *The Choices Justices Make* (Washington DC, CQ Press, 1998). See generally the discussion in R Posner, *How Judges Think* (Cambridge, MA, Harvard University Press, 2008) in chapter 1.

awareness that in order to get the court to move in the direction favoured by a Justice, it may be necessary for the Justice strategically to temper his or her actual views to achieve tactical and ad hoc alliances with those of less extreme views. Understandably, some within the federal appellate judiciary have responded to these attempts to attribute their judicial decisions to their political philosophy and their understanding of Machiavelli, by a focus on collegiality or team-working to show that values can be overridden by a group think.[8] Unfortunately for judicial scholars (and the federal judiciary), with the exception of the US Supreme Court which has been favoured with the notebooks and papers of various retired and deceased Justices, the study of team-working in appellate courts is quite hard to do, since by the nature of things it takes place behind the purple curtain.

Tempting though it may be to focus on the attitudes and values of the judges in the final appeal court of the UK, in this work the focus, as 40 years ago,[9] will be on appellate judicial decision-making as a social process.[10] It will be argued that the key to understanding judicial decision-making in the UK's final court of appeal lies in studying the dialogues which take place between the judges and those with whom they interact most frequently when making their decisions. These range from the traditional—with counsel, to the novel—with judicial assistants, from the near (the Court of Appeal) to the far (other supreme courts), from the theoretical (with academics) to the practical (the law reporters), from the open (with Parliament) to the forbidden (with Government). The range and content of these dialogues has changed over the last 40 years, but the following four chapters in this work focus on a set of dialogues which has remained central to understanding decision-making in the final court for many years, namely, the dialogue between the final court and counsel and the dialogue within the court itself. In the first we examine how counsel, at different stages in the process, seek to constrain the court to reach decisions favourable to their clients, and how the court responds to such overtures. In looking at the dialogues between the judges themselves the focus is again on the scope for dialogues at different stages of the decision-making

---

[8] HT Edwards, 'The Effects of Collegiality on Judicial Decision-Making' (2003) 151 *University of Pennsylvania Law Review* 1639.

[9] This work builds on my original study of the Law Lords in the 1970s (based on interviews with the judges and counsel) which concluded that appellate judicial decision-making is best understood as a social process. A Paterson, *The Law Lords* (London, Macmillan, 1982).

[10] Attitudinal and value studies of appellate judges are necessarily reductive in their approach. That does not mean that they do not have insights even in a court such as the UK Supreme Court, which does not sit en banc. Nor do I accept the arguments of scholars such as Kavanagh who consider that greater transparency over the roots of judicial decision-making may undermine public confidence in the judiciary. A Kavanagh, 'From Appellate Committee to United Kingdom Supreme Court: Independence, Activism and Transparency' ch 3 in J Lee (ed), *From House of Lords to Supreme Court* (Oxford, Hart Publishing, 2011). However, as David Robertson showed in his study of the House of Lords, *Judicial Discretion in the House of Lords* (Oxford, Clarendon Press, 1998) the fact that if Lord Templeman was on an Appellate Committee in a Tax case HMRC's chances of winning improved by 60% does not explain *why* this occurred. Even if Templeman's antipathy to tax avoidance explained his vote, what explained those of his colleagues? Some understanding of group decision-making in the House is required to explain Templeman's successes in such cases.

process, the factors which affect the efficacy of such dialogues and how such dialogues impact on swing voters and voting patterns on the court. Thereafter the work moves from an examination of the older dialogues (with the Court of Appeal and with academics) to a scrutiny of the new dialogues (with Scotland, with courts overseas and with judicial assistants). In the penultimate chapter the focus is on the dialogue with the other two arms of government—Parliament and the Executive. The concluding chapter draws together the threads from the earlier parts of the book against a backdrop of the final dialogue—that with the public.

SOURCES AND METHODOLOGY

In *The Law Lords*, the emphasis was on judicial decision-making as a social process viewed through the prism of role analysis. This time, the focus remains on social processes but with an even greater emphasis on the interactions as dialogues which, as in role analysis, are influenced by expectations. Information on the dialogues between judges in the final court of appeal and those with whom they interact was gleaned from a range of sources: observation, judgments, lectures, media interviews, documentaries, other research, judicial notebooks and personal interviews. In the last 40 years information about the workings of the final appeal court has been easier to come by. The Supreme Court is far more accessible than ever the House was. Not only can visitors drop in on oral hearings but they can watch them on Sky broadcasts and, on cause shown, obtain videocopies of past hearings. This enables researchers to access not only what was said in the dialogues between counsel and the judges but how it was said. This is a major advance on the situation in the House of Lords where transcripts were hard to obtain[11] and law reporters focused more on counsel's arguments than on the exchanges with the Law Lords. Access to judgments is also easier since they are all freely available on the Supreme Court website along with a summary for the media.[12] They are also freely available and searchable on the BAILII website. This is a major improvement on the situation 40 years ago when there were no electronic databases, free or otherwise.

The increased transparency of the Supreme Court is matched by the willingness of its judicial members to deliver regular public lectures on aspects of judicial decision-making, which are also accessible on the Court website. Moreover, there have been several documentaries made about the new Court with lengthy interviews with the Justices which provide valuable information on the decision-making process. Although the Law Lords did give public lectures, it was not with the same frequency and there were no TV documentaries on the Law Lords.

---

[11] In *The Law Lords* I criticised the lack of availability of transcripts for researchers because it deprived them of the opportunity to study how much the oral hearing contributed to the outcome of the case (n 9 above, at 82).

[12] YouTube now carries clips of the judgments being handed down.

Judicial Notebooks

There is also much more research into Bingham's[13] House of Lords and the new Supreme Court than was the case with the House of Lords 40 years ago. Moreover, for the first time it has been possible to have access to judicial notebooks compiled by Law Lords. Such sources have been available to scholars of the US Supreme Court for decades but for whatever reason,[14] until comparatively recently no Law Lord's notebooks had been preserved for posterity. The first to emerge were those of Scott Reid who donated 104 of his notebooks from his 26 years on the Court to the Parliamentary records. Five boxes of notebooks are available, including almost every one of the major cases in which Lord Reid sat or presided. Not only do they contain details of counsel's arguments, more importantly they almost always contain Lord Reid's notes of the dialogue between the Law Lords which took place in the first conference at the end of the hearing, and frequently an indication as to how the votes were cast. Unlike their American counterparts the notebooks do not contain observations about counsel or his fellow judges or examples of the exchanges between Law Lords and counsel.

The second set of notebooks belonged to Lord Bingham.[15] In his time in the Lords he sat in 240 cases but the 96 House of Lords notebooks that survive relate exclusively to the period of mid-2000 to late 2004 when he sat in 118 cases. Unfortunately, almost none of the notebooks from Lord Bingham's major cases (whether between 2000–04 or later) seem to have survived, even the most important of all, *Belmarsh*.[16] There is a surprising degree of similarity with Lord Reid's notebooks. Lord Bingham does not (obviously) record interventions by his colleagues during the oral arguments or the answer by counsel to such interventions. Neither does he indicate his views on the oral arguments he is hearing, or on counsel, or on his colleagues. Nor does he indicate at any stage what his views of the case are. Thus, unlike Lord Reid, it is rare[17] for his notebooks to contain any notes of his proposed contribution to the first conference after the hearing is over. However, like Lord Reid, the notebooks will sometimes contain handwritten draft judgments[18] which, in Lord Bingham's case bore a very close resemblance to that which appeared in the Law Reports. Finally, they almost all contain Bingham's notes of the contributions of his colleagues (but not his own) to the first conference

---

[13] Lord Bingham was the iconic senior Law Lord who presided magisterially over the House of the Lords between 2000 and 2008.

[14] Lord Hope in 'Lord Rodger's notebooks' in A Burrows, D Johnston and R Zimmermann (ed), *Judge and Jurist: Essays in Memory of Lord Rodger of Earlsferry* (Oxford, Oxford University Press, 2013) notes that most Law Lords threw out their notebooks along with the voluminous papers from appeals, in order to prevent their offices from becoming over-cluttered.

[15] I am greatly indebted to Lady Bingham for generously permitting me to draw on the material contained in these notebooks for this publication.

[16] *A and others v Secretary of State for the Home Department* [2004] UKHL 56, [2005] 2 AC 68. The first really big terrorism case to reach the Lords after 9/11.

[17] Only seven of the 96 contain such notes.

[18] Thirteen of the 96 notebooks contain such draft judgments.

and usually an indication as to how they voted. It is thus sometimes possible to identify switches of vote between the first conference and the date when judgment was handed down. This provides the best evidence available to historians as to how often Law Lords changed their minds between the first conference and the final judgment. In my interviews with 40 Law Lords over the years, all of them have been happy to discuss this issue, but none, understandably, has been able to provide much by way of a numerical estimate of the frequency with which such changes occur. These records also provide some indirect evidence as to the length of time these conferences last.

In keeping with its greater commitment to transparency, there are signs that efforts may be made to retain some judicial notebooks from the UK Supreme Court. A few of Lord Rodger's Supreme Court notebooks have been kept for posterity,[19] and, in time, some of Lord Hope's notebooks may also become available.

Elite Interviews

However, the most substantial source of information for this project has come from elite interviews. In the original research for *The Law Lords* in the early 1970s I conducted interviews with 15 current or former Law Lords and 46 counsel,[20] who had appeared in the leading cases in the 15 years prior to the interviews. For this study, with the invaluable assistance of initially the Nuffield Foundation and latterly the Leverhulme Trust, I have had the privilege[21] and good fortune to interview 27 Law Lords and Justices of the Supreme Court,[22] six members of the Court of Appeal,[23] nine leading counsel,[24] six judicial assistants, two Principal Clerks of the Judicial Office and one Registrar of the Supreme Court. The willingness of those approached to be interviewed was a testament to the openness

---

[19] See Lord Hope, 'Lord Rodger's Notebooks' ch 9 in A Burrows, D Johnston and R Zimmermann (eds), *Judge and Jurist: Essays in Memory of Lord Rodger of Earlsferry* (Oxford, Oxford University Press, 2013).

[20] By the time of the interviews some 'counsel' had been promoted to the High Court or even the Court of Appeal. Of course, several of them went on to become Law Lords after *The Law Lords* had been published.

[21] My experience of elite, 'off the record' interviews both 40 years ago and now attests to the levels of trust that many interviewees are prepared to repose in an academic researcher that they may hardly know.

[22] Some of them on several occasions. Lord Neuberger was interviewed in the House of Lords and again when he became President of the Supreme Court, Lord Phillips in the House of Lords and again when he retired from the Supreme Court and Lord Carnwath in the Court of Appeal and again when elevated to the Supreme Court. Only Lord Sumption was interviewed as leading counsel and again as a Justice in the Supreme Court.

[23] One of whom, Lord Justice Carnwath, was then appointed to the Supreme Court.

[24] Two of whom have since been appointed to the High Court, Philip Sales and Rabinder Singh QC, and one, Jonathan Sumption QC, to the Supreme Court.

and transparency of today's lawyers and judges, something that Darbyshire[25] had already experienced. All were unfailingly patient and tolerant of an interviewer who came to them with no introduction or sponsor,[26] but an insatiable curiosity with respect to judicial decision-making.[27] Contrary to my approach in *The Law Lords*, it was relatively uncommon for me to use a third party introduction or the snowball technique of elite interviewing, ie, using one interviewee to put me in touch with another. However, I adhered to the orthodoxy of a standard set of questions[28] administered in a semi-structured way, following leads offered by subjects and being prepared to ask the questions in any order. All of the interviews were tape recorded under strict terms of confidentiality and all were on the basis that they remained 'off the record' until and unless the interviewee had cleared the transcript or parts of it for subsequent publication. This undoubtedly led to many very candid discussions. Occasionally, an interviewee would indicate that certain matters were 'off limits' in our conversations but this was relatively uncommon.

The Drawbacks of Oral History

Although undoubtedly a socio-legal research project in its conception and execution, this study of decision-making in the UK's final appeal court could equally well be described as an exercise in oral history.[29] Relying very substantially on a swathe of elite interviews to enhance the picture painted by basic statistical data on the final court is a research strategy which is not without its drawbacks.[30] Quite apart from the challenges posed by malfunctioning digital recorders,[31] are

---

[25]   P Darbyshire, *Sitting in Judgment* (Oxford, Hart Publishing, 2011).

[26]   Although some interviewees were known to me personally, many were not. As with the original interviews I did not seek the endorsement of the Senior Law Lord, the President of the Supreme Court or the Lord Chief Justice: first, because Law Lords and Justices are not line managed by anyone; and secondly, because sponsorship by the senior judiciary has in the past—although it seems not to have been the case with *Sitting in Judgment* (above, n 25, ch 1)—sometimes come with strings attached about independence and editorial control. I did have permission to approach the judicial assistants from the Law Lord responsible for them at the time, Lord Hope.

[27]   The interviews ranged from one hour to three hours.

[28]   I almost never sent a questionnaire in advance of the interview, although I would give an indication of possible topics for conversation in the initial letter.

[29]   Defined as: 'Tape-recorded historical information drawn from the speaker's personal knowledge; the use or interpretation of this as an academic subject' (*New Shorter Oxford English Dictionary*). One of the ironies of Lord Rodger's celebrated antipathy to socio-legal research—he left a legacy of £2,000 to Glasgow University Law School on condition that 'not one penny can be spent on the study of sociology or criminology' (*The Herald*, 22 September 2012)—was that he was an excellent historian, as evidenced by his D Phil research in Roman Law and his lectures on the Free Church disruption: Lord Rodger of Earlsferry, *The Courts, The Church and the Constitution* (Edinburgh, Edinburgh University Press, 2008). Yet the line between social history and descriptive sociology is a fine one.

[30]   See generally, Paul Thompson, *Voices of the Past: Oral History*, 3rd edn (Oxford, Oxford University Press, 2000) ch 4 'Evidence'.

[31]   In my original tape recordings a malfunctioning cassette recorder 'lost' a significant part of my interview with Lord Reid. In the more recent interviews two digital recorders nearly escaped and one became incapable of recording without distortion.

the problems caused by the difference between the spoken and the written word.[32] Lord Rodger's peerless account of the infelicities and ungrammatical nature of oral or extempore judgments applies equally well to interview transcripts:[33] 'Tidying the transcript to make it even vaguely presentable is an exercise in forgery that is as time consuming as it is uncongenial'.

Like all forms of oral history there is the risk of distortion caused by memory flaws. Lord Wilberforce in an incomplete autobiography referred to the work as 'a work of creative fiction given the effect of memory'.[34] More scientifically, Schacter in *The Seven Sins of Memory*[35] adverted to the dangers of:

— Transience—with the passing of time the particulars fade and the opportunities multiply for interference generated by later, similar experiences to blur recollections;
— Absent-mindedness—due to a failure of memories to embed properly in the memory;
— Misattribution—assigning memory to the wrong source;
— Suggestibility—memories implanted by leading questions; and
— Bias—the impact of current knowledge and beliefs on how we remember the past.

In my interviews I found most judges and counsel had very impressive levels of recall. Even though Law Lords and Justices take part in around 40 cases[36] a year between the House of Lords and the Privy Council, most experienced little difficulty in providing detailed illustrations in response to my questions. That said, the examples tended to come from most recent cases unless the interviewee was prompted by specific reference to actual cases from an earlier era. I did encounter occasional examples of transience and misattribution, but hopefully such examples were minimised as a result of operating a policy of seeking corroboration for every factual statement of any significance. This policy threw up relatively few discrepancies of any note.

The second risk associated with oral history is partial disclosure or limited candour due to a lack of trust on the part of the interviewee. This was an occasional problem with my initial interviews 40 years ago. So far as I can tell it has been rather less of a problem this time round. First because the fact that almost all of the available Law Lords and Justices were interviewed enabled corroboration to be obtained as to many of the key aspects of judicial decision-making in the final court, including accounts of some of the most significant cases in the last 15 years. Although some judges were more guarded than others, a refusal or an

---

[32] See Marshall McLuhan, *The Medium is the Message* (Harmondsworth, Penguin Books, 1967).
[33] Lord Rodger, 'The form and language of judicial opinions' (2002) 118 *LQR* 226, 231.
[34] Lord Wilberforce, *Reflections on My Life* (Durham, Roundtuit Publishing, 2003) 1ff.
[35] D Schacter, *The Seven Sins of Memory: How the Mind Forgets and Remembers* (New York, Houghton-Mifflin, 2001).
[36] Typically in a full year a judge of the final court will sit in 30 cases in the House or the Supreme Court and 12 in the Privy Council.

inability to discuss actual cases was quite unusual where the judge was still sitting in the final court. Indeed far more often the judges, having been assured that every interview was off the record until they had had a chance to examine the transcript and decide what could then be done with it, became remarkably frank in their answers. Inevitably, as a result, much time was spent on negotiating the use of parts of the transcripts as background, attributed to 'a Law Lord or Justice' or to the judge by name in the book.[37] Once again a policy of seeking corroboration appeared to be the best tactic for damage limitation of misconceptions attributable to respondent reticence.[38]

A third problem is that, unsurprisingly, it turns out that very few Law Lords or Justices have a very accurate picture of decision-making data such as the frequency with which they are on the winning or losing side where the court is sharply divided, their agreement rates with other judges, the proportion of judgments that are single, majority judgments, or whether their share of the lead judgment allocations is above or below the average for the Court. Even more intuitive statistics such as the Justices' dissent rates, the average time taken between the hearing and judgment being handed down, and the average success rate for permission to appeal petitions or for full appeals, are matters where the Law Lords and Justices' 'guestimates' may be considerably off the mark. Similarly, they find it difficult to reach consensus as to the average length of the first conference which takes place at the end of the oral hearing. This is, in part, because the length of these conferences can vary dramatically. Asking interviewees for their thoughts on such matters in order to establish the true facts, is therefore likely to be an exercise of limited utility. The primary purpose of such questions is to gauge whether the judges' behaviour can be influenced by the judges' perceptions of what the actual statistics are. Indeed there are positive dangers in discussing such matters since the interviewer is likely to be asked for an outline of the true facts—which risks an equivalent of the Heisenberg 'observer effect'.

The fourth and final feature of oral history as the primary research method is that judges are social actors just as much as other human beings. Reality is socially constructed for them, just as it is for others. This includes such vexed questions as how unhappy the Court was in 2011–12 when the dissent rate was very high, the level of single majority judgments fell sharply, and public exchanges took place between some of the Justices. The President and others denied that the Court was an unhappy environment at the time and firmly believed this to be the case. However, anyone conducting in-depth interviews with Justices at the time was left in no doubt that the congenial atmosphere which prevailed in the House of Lords

---

[37] Understandably, the interviews produced a reasonable amount of information—usually relating to other judges or counsel—which fell into the 'cannot be used in its current form' category.

[38] There is potential for another form of bias in interviews, namely social response bias—saying what the audience wants to hear or the speaker wants to them to hear. The frankness of most of my interviews did not suggest to me that that form of bias was a significant problem in these interviews.

in the final Bingham years had dissipated more than a little. Several Justices made pointed references in their interviews to the disparity between the esprit de corps of the Court of Appeal and the mood of the Supreme Court at the time. However, debating as to how unhappy the Court was at that time would be a somewhat fruitless exercise. Reality in this case was in the eye of the beholder.

DEFINITIONS

In this work a number of terms are used with meanings which may not always accord with the technical meaning that they have in certain forms of academic or judicial discourse. These have been set out below.

Dialogue

A discourse or conversation between two or more persons. Distinguishable in the first place from a monologue or competing monologues. Distinguishable in the second place from the technical use of dialogue by constitutional scholars to discuss the discourse with Strasbourg or Parliament. In this work it will be argued that the dialogues in the final court of appeal which most influence judicial decision-making in that court are those with counsel, with fellow judges, with other courts, with Scotland, with judicial assistants, with academics, with Parliament, with the Executive and with the public. These dialogues can take various forms eg oral and written—and have a range of dimensions:

— Proximity, eg face to face, phone, email, written materials for an appeal, opinion circulation or letter;
— Timing, eg contemporaneous, sequential or asynchronous;
— Duration
— Directness
— Real versus virtual or symbolic
— Effectiveness.

The argument in this work will be that the key optic through which to understand judicial decision-making in the final court of appeal in the UK is the study of the dialogues which take place between the judges and others. On this view judicial decision-making is a social activity,[39] with the dialogues set out in the succeeding chapters lying at the heart of it. These dialogues are many and varied. Most are with the living, though when considering precedents, they may be with the dead; some are with the future eg a dissent, whilst other are with the past. Some dialogues are more symbolic than real, eg with Parliament or the Executive, although where Parliament passes legislation to overturn a decision of the final

---

[39] As I argued in *The Law Lords*, n 9 above.

court, the effect can be all too real. Dialogues are affected by issues of context (ie, where they occur—surprisingly in final courts, geography matters),[40] stage in the case (ie, when they occur) and the mode of communication. As McLuhan argues, the medium affects the message and a face to face communication may have a different impact than an email or a printed case. Oral and written advocacy, whether by counsel[41] or a judge,[42] are different skills and lead to dialogues which may differ in terms of immediacy and impact. Again, some judges are more effective at certain dialogues than others. Lord Atkin often failed to convince his colleagues because of his style of judicial advocacy—they did not feel he was open to persuasion in return—yet he was much more successful with his family[43]—or with posterity.[44] Some dialogues therefore are more fruitful than others—statistically the symbolic dialogue with Parliament is rarely effective. Parliament appears to have a selective form of deafness.[45] While some dialogues fail, other dialogues never begin, eg direct engagement with colleagues' judgments in the Lords (until the Bingham era) or direct engagement with the Executive. Further dialogues which might have been include counsel choosing not to run certain arguments in the hope of nudging the court to decide the case on another point or the Executive not engaging with the Law Lords about the decision to abolish the Lord Chancellor.

Appeal Committee

Committee in the House of Lords which heard or dealt with petitions for leave to appeal.

Appellate Committee

Committee in the House of Lords which heard appeals to the judicial House of Lords.

Close Call

Case in which two or more judges in the final court dissent from the majority outcome, as distinct from a split case (*q v*) where there is at least one dissent.[46]

---

[40] See chapters 3 and 4 of this volume below.
[41] See chapter 2 of this volume below.
[42] See chapter 4 of this volume below.
[43] See chapter 2 of this volume below at fn 112.
[44] See chapter 4 of this volume below.
[45] See chapter 7 of this volume below
[46] Definition derived from B Dickson, 'Close Calls in the House of Lords' ch 13 in J Lee (ed), *From House of Lords to Supreme Court* (Oxford, Hart Publishing, 2011).

Composite Judgment

Single judgment which is the work of two or more judges on the Court. It can be either in the majority or in a dissent. Some composite judgments are attributed to the whole Court. In the House of Lords such judgments might be written by one or several Law Lords. In the UK Supreme Court composite judgments of the Court are very rare however, single majority judgments in the name of one Justice are very common (60 per cent of cases in the first third of 2013 were single majority judgments). Nevertheless, such judgments are almost always a collective work product of most of the Justices in the case, unlike the normal position in the Privy Council.

Concurrence

In this work it means an opinion or judgment which is not a lead or majority judgment of the court but one which either simply agrees with the majority judgment(s) or adds some thoughts on a particular aspect of the appeal, or which reaches the same result as the lead or majority judgment but for different reasons. The third form of concurrence can be tactical and disguise what is nearer to a dissenting opinion. Authors who wait for the lead or majority judgment to emerge and then write a concurrence, know that they are writing a concurrence—at least at the outset. However, if there is no agreed lead judgment at the outset, anyone who writes a judgment may find that it becomes the lead or a majority judgment or it may end up as a concurrence or even a dissent.

Conference

The term used for formal meetings of the panel hearing a case which take place after the end of the oral hearing. In most cases in the House of Lords there was only one case conference—described in this work as the *first conference*. There are a few more cases a year in the UK Supreme Court where there are second or third case conferences but they are still very much in the minority.

Court

In this work 'Court' refers to the final appeal court of the UK, which was the House of Lords and is now the UK Supreme Court.

Deference

This concept has acquired a quasi-technical meaning in public law circles as referring to the recognition by the courts that certain matters are beyond their institutional competence and best left to other, more democratic institutions to decide.[47] However, it is used in this work to denote the tendency for the individual judges in the final court to give additional weight to the opinion of another judge in the Court on the grounds of seniority or, more usually, specialist expertise in a particular field of law. In such situations the 'deferring' judge will think twice before disagreeing with the other judge, although he or she may nonetheless choose in the end to do so.

Dissent

In standard usage this refers to a reasoned judgment which disagrees with the outcome to an appeal which is supported by the majority of the judges hearing the case. However, although the overwhelming majority of dissents fall into this category, in this work it will include also judgments which agree on the outcome favoured by the majority but whose reasoning is radically different from that of the majority. An example was Lord Hoffmann's judgment in *Belmarsh*.[48] It is not unknown, as we shall see, for judgments which start out as the lead judgment to become dissents and vice versa.

Dubitans *or* Dubitante *Judgment*

(From the Latin for hesitant or doubting). One in which the author is sorely tempted to disagree with the outcome reached by the rest of the Court but goes along with it because he or she is insufficiently sure about the matter to produce a formal dissenting judgment. A *dubitans* judgment can resemble a tactical concurrence, but can be differentiated by the fact that it tends to be shorter and to focus on the fact that the author is in doubt.

ECHR

European Convention on Human Rights.

ECtHR

European Court of Human Rights, based in Strasbourg—generally considered to be the ultimate arbiter of the correct interpretation to be given to the standards laid down in the Convention.

Hard case

In legal philosophy a case that falls within the penumbra of a rule or where the judge has an element of choice or discretion. In this work it refers to a case in

---

[47] J Jowell, 'Judicial Deference: servility, civility or institutional capacity' [2003] *Public Law* 592.

[48] *A and others v Secretary of State for the Home Department* [2004] UKHL 56, [2005] 2 AC 68, [97].

which two or more judges in the final court disagree on the outcome, and either outcome would be regarded by some other final appellate judges as correct or 'better' than any of the alternatives. On this definition all close calls (*q v*) are hard cases, but not all hard cases are close calls.

Judicial Committee

In this work only refers to the Privy Council. There has never been a judicial committee of the House of Lords. Appeals to the House of Lords between 1950 and 2009 were heard almost always by the Appellate Committee of the House of Lords. Petitions for leave to appeal were heard by the Appeal Committee (*q v*).

Judgment

Formal ruling of the court (or of its members) including the UK and US Supreme Courts. In the judicial House of Lords they were known as opinions or speeches (since in constitutional theory they were speeches in the upper chamber of the UK parliament).

Justice

Judicial member of the UK or US Supreme Court.

Law Lord

Judicial member of the House of Lords who sat in appeals to that court.

Lead or Leading Judgment

Originally the judgment which sets out the facts of the appeal in the most detail. Over time this has become elided with the concept of the most important judgment in the Court on the majority side. This will usually be the majority opinion (*q v*) in the case. The lead judgment is not necessarily the first to be circulated. In the House of Lords it was not necessarily the first to appear in the law reports— since they were published in order of seniority. In the UK Supreme Court the lead judgment is usually the one that is printed first in the Report. Where the lead judgment changes hands because of vote switches in the Court after the first conference, the detailed statement of the facts may remain in the original lead judgment which may have become a dissent. Particularly in the House of Lords, but even in the UK Supreme Court in the early years there were cases where there was no single lead opinion but several of them.

Majority Judgment

The judicial opinion in an appeal which is agreed to by more than half of the members of the Court. Occasionally there may be more than one such judgment.

It is sometimes regarded as a failing of the judges on the deciding panel, and of the presiding judge in particular, if a majority judgment is not forthcoming. However, another school of thought takes the view that some decisions benefit from a multiplicity of lead opinions provided there is sufficient common ground between them to establish the *ratio* of the decision.

Obiter

Short for *obiter dicta*. Legal propositions discussed in a case which form no part of the *ratio* (*qv*) of the case.

Plurality Judgment

This refers to the situation in which there is no majority judgment in the Court. In that situation the judgment which receives the most support is sometimes referred to as a plurality judgment.

Ratio

Short for *ratio decidendi*. The legal proposition(s) on which the decision of the court is based.

Split case

Case in which there is at least one dissent.

Unanimity

Literally, 'of one mind'. Used to describe the outcome to a case where all members of the panel hearing the case are agreed as to the outcome. Often used in contrast to univocality (*qv*), which applies to a more restricted range of cases where the Court is agreed not only as to the result but also as to the reasons for the outcome (even where there is more than one judgment).

Unit of analysis

Generally speaking, in this work 'appeals' and 'cases' will be used as interchangeable terms. However, it is not uncommon for appeals which raise the same question of law to be heard together or 'conjoined' at the same hearing. In such situations the overall hearing will be treated as one 'case' although it may deal with several appeals. When it comes to calculating the rates at which judges dissent, or write judgments or concurrences the fairer approach appears to be to focus on 'cases' rather than 'appeals' because of the distorting effect that multiple appeals can have. Thus, if a Law Lord dissents on his own in a 'case' with five conjoined 'appeals', this will be counted as a single dissent, not five dissents.

Univocal

Literally, 'of one voice'. Describes an outcome to a case where all the judges are agreed both as to the outcome and as to the reasons leading to that outcome.

2

The Dialogue with Counsel[1]

INTRODUCTION

FORTY YEARS AGO the key to understanding judicial decision-making in the final court of appeal lay in studying the dialogues which took place between the judges and those with whom they interacted most frequently when making their decisions.[2] The thesis of this book is that although the nature and content of the dialogues may have changed, they remain the key to understanding judicial decision-making in the UK's final court (the Court) today. Then the final court was the House of Lords (to be precise, its Appellate Committee) and its judges were the Lords of Appeal in Ordinary (referred to in this work as 'Law Lords'). Now, the final court is the Supreme Court of the United Kingdom (UK Supreme Court),[3] and its judges are Justices. There can be little doubt—given our adversarial system—that the two principal dialogues are those (1) between the judges and counsel and (2) between the judges themselves. This chapter will focus on the former dialogue, and examine how it has changed over the last 40 years. The next three chapters will focus on the dialogue between the judges themselves.

In *The Law Lords*[4] it was argued that the dialogue with counsel had a considerably greater impact than had been commonly recognised at the time on the Law Lords' decisions, not simply because of their advocacy but also because of their ability to impose constraints on the court's decision-making. These constraints included: counsel's influence on the selection and timing of appeals going to the Lords, their ability to constrain the points of law for decision by the court through concessions or simply a refusal to run certain arguments,[5] the shared understanding between Bench and Bar that the points of law which determine an appeal must be raised by, or at least put to, counsel and the understanding that counsel could not run points of law in the Lords which they had not run in a lower court.[6] However,

---

[1] This chapter is based substantially on A Paterson, 'Does Advocacy Matter in the Lords?' ch 12 in J Lee (ed), *From House of Lords to Supreme Court* (Oxford, Hart Publishing, 2011).

[2] A Paterson, *The Law Lords* (London, Macmillan, 1982).

[3] Which opened in October 2009.

[4] Above, n 2, at 31.

[5] Of course the Law Lords have always possessed, and exercised, a considerable capacity to decline to hear argument from counsel.

[6] See *The Law Lords*, above, n 2, ch 3.

it is clear from my interviews over the last few years that while a few of these constraints retain considerable force, most of them have lost some of their potency. On the other hand the interaction between Bench and Bar is a two-sided one and the chapter will also show how the judges in the final court use the dialogue to constrain the arguments of counsel (most graphically, when refusing leave/permission to appeal but also through imposing and policing time-limits on their arguments, and indicating what areas of the case they would find it helpful and not helpful to hear argument on), as well as to interrogate counsel (through testing counsel's arguments, putting their own thoughts to counsel and or simply clarifying what counsel's argument is).

THE CONTEXT OF THE DIALOGUE BETWEEN COUNSEL AND THE JUDGES IN THE FINAL COURT

The constraints which counsel can impose on the dialogue with the final court reflect in part the power of repeat players with repeat-player clients[7] and in part the strength of the shared understandings between counsel and the final court of appeal. Each of these forms part of the context or background in which the dialogue takes place. In this sense the dialogue between counsel and the final court does not begin in the courtroom, but long before. For the counsel who *address* Britain's final court of appeal are typically senior barristers and advocates or Queen's Counsel.[8] As such they will have gone through the same socialisation process as the judges themselves did while at the Bar, with respect to the constraining conventions as to the conduct of appeals at the higher levels of the adversarial system, including which propositions of law may be relied on and the types of argument that carry weight in the final court.[9]

Conventions aside, counsel have the advantage (unless they are brought in for the first time at the highest level)[10] that they can plan their approach to the contested terrain which is a final appeal case, well in advance, possibly long before the judges first encounter it, probably at the permission for leave to appeal stage. This advantage today is more imagined than real since in the last 30 years the

---

[7] Marc Galanter in his seminal article 'Why the "Haves" come out ahead' (1974) 9 *Law and Society Review* 96, draws the distinction between litigants who are 'repeat-players' who are involved in litigation on a regular basis such as insurance companies, creditors, the Government and recidivists, and 'one shotters' who are typically private individuals or small businesses who are rarely involved in litigation. Repeat-players, he argues, will generally gain advantages denied to a one-shotter through knowing the ropes. Lawyers, especially counsel who appear frequently in the final court, are a special type of repeat-player who may gain some advantages in terms of judicial tolerance and susceptibility from their familiarity with the court and the judges, especially where the judges have learned to trust and respect them.

[8] Junior barristers appear in all appeals before the final court but in most cases there will be a senior counsel who does the oral argument. The principal exceptions are 'Treasury devils'—elite junior counsel instructed by the Government who are in many respects like QCs in the first place.

[9] See A Paterson, *The Law Lords*, above, n 2, 20–21 and 38–49.

[10] Like J Crow QC in *R (on the application of Bancoult) v Secretary of State for Foreign and Commonwealth Affairs* [2008] UKHL 61, [2009] 1 AC 453.

	1970–72	1980–82	1990–92	2000–02	2003–05	2006–08	2009–13
Criminal	28 (23%)	36 (23%)	32 (22%)	39 (24%)	36 (18%)	26 (14%)	14 (6%)
Human Rights	2 (2%)	8 (5%)	10 (7%)	15 (9%)	32 (16%)	34 (19%)	35 (14%)
Public	14 (11%)	18 (11%)	31 (21%)	25 (15%)	31 (16%)	38 (20%)	63 (26%)
Private/ Commercial	53 (43%)	71 (44%)	58 (40%)	70 (43%)	75 (38%)	71 (38%)	105 (43%)
Family	8 (6%)	4 (3%)	3 (2%)	6 (4%)	6 (3%)	8 (4%)	15 (6%)
Tax	18 (15%)	23 (14%)	11 (8%)	9 (5%)	18 (9%)	11 (6%)	7 (3%)
Total Cases	123	160	145	164	198	188	246

Table 2.1: Caseload by case type in the House of Lords and UK Supreme Court in selected years.

Court's caseload, and the routes by which it comes to the final Court, have been completely transformed.[11] First, the final court has gained far greater control of its caseload than it did 30 years ago. Now 83 per cent of its cases come to them with permission from the Court, then it was 17 per cent.[12] Perhaps, in part, because of this the type of case which now predominates is radically different, as can be seen from Table 2.1:[13] tax,[14] shipping and criminal law cases have declined, whilst public law and human rights cases have dramatically increased.[15]

Although in theory counsel and clients with a series of potential cases in, say, tax or shipping law, might many years ago have sought to influence the order in which those cases came to the Lords,[16] today only the central Government and the

---

[11] See S Shah and T Poole, 'The Impact of the Human Rights Act on the House of Lords' LSE Working Paper 8/ 2009, now available at (2011) 74 *Modern Law Review* 79–105.

[12] B Dickson, 'The processing of appeals in the House of Lords' (2007) 123 *Law Quarterly Review* 571, 572 and Gavin Drewry et al, *The Court of Appeal* (Oxford, Hart Publishing, 2007) at 146.

[13] Any case classification contains room for quibbles. Many cases now contain human rights points, but where they are obiter, I have not classified them as human rights cases. Here I can do no better than quote from Louis Blom-Cooper and G Drewry, *Final Appeal* (Oxford, Clarendon Press, 1972) at 244. 'Any subject-classification we construct is essentially arbitrary, and the assignment of marginal cases to particular categories is extremely difficult'.

[14] Which between 1952 and 1968 represented 30% of the civil caseload, *Final Appeal*, ibid, at 145. By 2005 it was down to 8% G Drewry et al, *The Court of Appeal*, above, n 12, at 147.

[15] From 4% in 1952–68 to 38.4% by 2005. G Drewry et al, *The Court of Appeal*, above, n 12, at 147.

[16] This could have occurred in the *Three Rivers* litigation during the first decade of the 21st century, but there is nothing to indicate that it actually did. See (*Three Rivers District Council v Governor and Company of the Bank of England* [2000] UKHL 33, *Three Rivers District Council v Governor and Company of the Bank of England* [2001] UKHL 16) *Three Rivers District Council v Bank of England* [2004] UKHL 48.

Crown (and certain other frequent interveners) now appear with great regularity before the Court.[17] Whilst Treasury counsel might hypothetically seek to influence the order in which certain appeals involving the Government or the Crown come to the final court, in practice, given the vicissitudes of litigation (including the need to get leave/permission to appeal from the final court) this an unlikely scenario. True, they could choose to intervene systematically in appeals where the Government is not a party which raise matters of strategic importance to the state, but there is no entitlement to intervene[18]—it is at the discretion of the final court. Secondly, they are more often being taken to the Court rather than doing the taking (and thus have little say in the timing of the case).[19] Thirdly, they could embrace the nuclear option of an accelerated hearing to alter the sequence of appeals to the court but such a step is not without danger if the date allocated does not suit Treasury counsel. It should not surprise us therefore if even the most experienced counsel reaches the conclusion that there is little point in seeking to influence the course by which appeals reach the final court.[20]

Again, as repeat-players in the final Court the main Government Ministries have, at least in theory, possibilities to play for rules, that is to decide to settle or to fight cases depending on the balance of perceived advantage in terms of favourable rule outcomes.[21] As David Pannick QC put it,[22]

> I think if you're appearing for the Secretary of State or for some other public body your client, and therefore you, may have an interest in doing more than winning the case.

---

[17] In the period between September 2009 and March 2013, central government or the Crown Prosecution Service/Crown Office appeared a total of 89 times (out of a total of 207 cases), all using their own select panels of counsel.

[18] There are no available statistics on what percentage of applications to intervene are granted, but the great majority are. Nevertheless, in 35% (73 of the 207) cases disposed of in the Supreme Court (up until the end of March 2013) permission was granted for one or more interveners. The most frequent intervener, however, was central Government or the Crown (in 16% of all cases and 47% of cases in which there was an intervener).

[19] In the first three years of the Supreme Court, central Government or the Crown Prosecution Service/Crown Office acted as respondent in 78% of the cases they appeared in (58 times out of the 74 cases).

[20] '[Where] you have a number of cases at the lower level there may ... be some tactical consideration by counsel as to which is the appropriate test case to go to the Lords. Those decisions are then affected by non-scientific factors, for example, the personality issue that everybody wants their own case to go to the Lords. In any event the courts may not co-operate with any wish that you may have, other cases may be listed first, leave to appeal may be granted [in another case] before your case can be considered. So it's very difficult to manipulate the system in that sense'. Interview with David Pannick QC, 2009.

[21] Marc Galanter in 'Why the "Haves" Come Out Ahead' (1974) 9 *Law and Society Review* 96, 100 observes: 'Repeat-players can ... play for rules in litigation itself, whereas a "one-shotter" is unlikely to ... Because his stakes in the immediate outcome are high and because by definition a "one-shotter" is unconcerned with the outcome of similar litigation in the future, the "one-shotter" will have little interest in that element of the outcome which might influence the disposition of the decision-maker next time around. For the repeat-players, on the other hand, anything that will favourably influence the outcomes of future cases is a worthwhile result. The larger the stake for any player and the lower the probability of repeat play, the less likely that he will be concerned with the rules which govern future cases of the same kind'.

[22] Interview with the author, 2009.

You're concerned about the way in which the case is decided because of its implications for the future. Indeed you may know, albeit that it's not explored in argument, that to have the case decided in a particular way may be very damaging to the interests of that Department of State for reasons that may simply be not known to the Law Lords or indeed not known to your opponent. Therefore you may well have that in mind, you may well be seeking to nudge the Law Lords in a particular direction. Far, far less common if you're appearing for a private party whose main concern, and normally their only concern, is to win the case.

The failure of the British Government to intervene at Strasbourg in the *Salduz*[23] case (relating to whether a suspect held in a police station for questioning should be entitled to have access to a lawyer), given its potential to cause a major disruption of the Scottish criminal justice system, highlights graphically the dangers of not monitoring ECHR developments in the domestic courts and Strasbourg. The history of *Al Khawaja*[24] and *Horncastle*,[25] (cases in which there was a dialogue between Strasbourg and the Supreme Court)[26] and the growing signs that the Supreme Court (and the Government) wish to loosen the shackles of Strasbourg,[27] only reinforce the value of Government lawyers adopting a proactive stance where human rights cases are concerned. Not surprisingly, there are some indications that that is what the Government has been doing, first by trying to track significant human rights cases as they move through the courts, even if the Government is not a party; and secondly by liaising with interested Ministries to co-ordinate the Government response (either as a party or an intervener) to developments in the human rights jurisprudence. As one of the counsel involved observed, if you get a policy area where the Government has a major interest that the system as a whole should work smoothly, but the parties in the case have no such interest, the Government will be inclined to seek to intervene to try to prevent a result which the Government would find very difficult to live with. The same counsel indicated that part of the difficulty confronting the Government in such human rights cases is that it has to face in two directions.

> It has to deal with the internal legal system so it doesn't want that to be thrown out of kilter because that would cause huge problems but also it knows that it's going to be sued in Strasbourg by an individual who begins a claim here and so it has an interest to try to educate the Lords as to, in a sense, what position it feels it can maintain in Strasbourg with reasonable prospects of success.

However, apart from the Government there are few, if any, parties with the opportunity and the inclination to 'play for rules' in this way. In the past counsel in the House of Lords who were seeking a ruling on a particular point of law might concede or eschew certain points of debate in order to focus the argument before

---

[23] *Salduz v Turkey* (2009) 49 EHRR 19.
[24] *Al-Khawaja and Tahery v United Kingdom* (2012) 54 EHRR 23.
[25] *R v Horncastle and Others* [2009] UKSC 14, [2010] 2 AC 373.
[26] See chapter 6 of this volume below.
[27] See chapter 6 of this volume below.

the final court,[28] yet few of my recent interviewees recognised the phenomenon.[29] It seems therefore that today's counsel see little scope for imposing constraints on judicial decision-making in the final court of appeal through the use of such tactics. In their eyes the opportunities for strategic planning of the initial phases of the dialogue with the final court present themselves relatively infrequently.

Expectations which Constrain

The fact that the justice system in the United Kingdom has traditionally been, and remains, essentially adversarial in nature inevitably influences the context within which dialogues between judges of the final court and counsel take place. Thus amongst counsel whom I have interviewed in the last 40 years, there has been a high degree of consensus on one point. Even at the level of the House of Lords or Supreme Court they do not consider it appropriate for the judges to decide appeals on points of law which have not been argued by counsel or at least put to them for comment.[30] In the Sixties both counsel and most of the Law Lords held a strong version of this expectation, as Lord Denning found this out to his cost in his first case as Law Lord, *Rahimtoola v Nizam of Hyderabad*.[31] Believing that the House should take a broader approach to developing the law than the lower courts could, he devoted the better part of his summer vacation to research on points not raised by counsel.[32] Viscount Simonds, who was presiding, went out of his way to indicate in his judgment that he should not be taken as assenting to Lord Denning's views 'in regard to which the House has not had the benefit of the arguments of counsel or of the judgment of the courts below'.[33] Lords Reid, Cohen and Somervell expressed their entire agreement with Viscount Simonds' remarks on this point, which were perceived by Lord Denning as a reprimand from his new colleagues. Such evidence as we have suggests that most of the Law Lords of that era shared the normative expectation of counsel that they should confine their propositions of law to matters covered by the arguments of counsel.[34] Twenty years

---

[28] See eg *The Law Lords*, above, n 2, 44–45.

[29] In part, perhaps, because the statement of facts and issue for decision in the Supreme Court, whilst drafted by the appellant, has to be agreed with every respondent (Rule 22, Rules of the Supreme Court).

[30] Counsel may well accept that, particularly at the level of the Supreme Court, if counsel get the law wrong, the public will rightly expect that the Justices should correct them. However, that does not weaken in any way the expectation that in an adversarial system, counsel—who are under a professional obligation to bring all the relevant authorities to the attention of the Court, and not just those that suit their book—should have the opportunity to respond to and debate any points of law on which the judge wishes to rely in reaching his or her decision.

[31] *Rahimtoola v Nizam of Hyderabad* [1958] AC 379.

[32] He subsequently asserted that he took more pains with that case than any other in which he had taken part *Thai-Europe v Government of Pakistan* [1975] 3 All ER 961, 966f.

[33] *Rahimtoola v Nizam of Hyderabad* [1958] AC 379, 398.

[34] Paterson, *The Law Lords*, above, n 2, 38–45.

later whilst counsel remained strong in their belief that this should be the position, the Law Lords were less unanimous.[35]

> I think it most unfair if a judge in the House of Lords puts forward a proposition of law which has never been advanced either in the courts below or in counsel's arguments ... and its most unsatisfactory. (Lord Guest)

Others were less convinced. 'Usually, but not necessarily' (Lord Hailsham) or 'You couldn't make a formula of this, I don't think you could lay down a rule' (Lord Kilbrandon). However, in *Spring v Guardian Assurance*[36] Lord Goff indicated that if there is something that occurs to the court which counsel did not argue, it would be appropriate to invite counsel to address it, even if only in writing, and to the extent that the court does indulge in judgments unaided by the submissions of counsel, their pronouncements should be treated with limited authority.[37]

In the Bingham court[38] the great majority of Law Lords (including Lord Bingham) accepted the force of the convention whether the new issue arose through additional research by the Law Lords or their Judicial Assistants—or subsequent decisions of the ECtHR, which emerged after the hearing but before the judgments had been delivered.[39] The few dissenters such as Lords Steyn and Millett were conspicuous in their belief that the expectation was an old fashioned notion. Today, relatively little appears to have changed. Counsel remain as supportive of the expectation as before. As one indicated,

> [If that happened] I would be absolutely stunned and I would look at it to see if there was anything one could do about it because that would be so grossly unfair since there is no recourse beyond the House of Lords.

However, counsel largely accept that whilst it may be inappropriate for the Court to decide an appeal on an *issue* that has not been put to counsel, relying on new *material or cases* in relation to an issue that has been debated by counsel is generally thought to be unproblematic. This, of course, merely shifts the ground of debate to 'when is the material so new that it constitutes a new issue?'.

As for the Justices of the Supreme Court the balance has remained very much as it was in the Bingham era. Only Lord Phillips and Lady Hale were sceptical as to the strength of the convention, when interviewed. However, Lord Reed told me,[40]

---

[35] With Lords Cross, Edmund-Davies, Gardiner, Guest and Pearson supporting it and Lords Diplock, Hailsham, Kilbrandon, Simon and Wilberforce more ambivalent on the point. See *The Law Lords*, above, n 2, 38–45.

[36] *Spring v Guardian Assurance plc and Others* [1995] 2 AC 296.

[37] Ibid, 316.

[38] Lord Bingham was senior Law Lord in the House of Lords from 2000 to 2008.

[39] As in the *Doherty* case (see n 63 below) when *McCann v United Kingdom* [2008] LGR 474 was published after the oral argument in *Doherty* had been completed, but judgments had not been handed down.

[40] Interview with the author, 2012.

I think it applies less than it used to. You are still essentially looking at the arguments that are being presented. Working on the judgment you will see other angles, or perhaps a way of developing the argument to be put. I suppose it is a question of judgement what you decide to do.

Another Justice encapsulated the views of most of them when faced with a new issue after the oral argument has finished, by indicating that there are only two options in that situation,

> [First] … 'well there was no argument about this but I have reflected on it and I have some doubts about it for the following reasons' and you set them out very briefly so at least there is a torch for somebody to pick up in another case. That is fine if you do that because you are not deciding anything. You are just saying 'Well I am concerned about this and here it is and somebody else might want to pick it up on another occasion'. Alternatively, you can say 'On reflection I think this is the fundamental point of this case … this case was decided on a fundamentally false basis and we have got to reconvene to have a fresh argument'. That is another way of doing it. What you can't do is just decide the thing. It seems to be contrary to natural justice.

The differences between the Justices in relation to the expectation surfaced in several cases decided in 2011. Thus, Lord Dyson, not known for ducking challenges, having bravely[41] taken on the lead judgment in the *Lumba* appeal,[42] then observed that Lord Phillips had breached the convention,

> In my view it is not appropriate to depart from a decision which has been followed repeatedly for almost 30 years unless it is obviously wrong (which I do not believe to be the case), still less to do so without the benefit of adversarial argument.[43]

Again, Lord Walker impliedly criticised Lady Hale's dissent in the *McDonald* case[44] for breaching the convention,

> Having expressed the view that the appeal has focused on a narrow issue which is not a point of law of general public importance, [Lady Hale] makes some strongly-worded observations on an issue … which was not referred to in the agreed statement of facts and issues, and was not argued by Miss McDonald's counsel,

leading Lady Hale to reply in her judgment[45] that 'there is ample precedent for this court addressing itself to an important point which has not been argued by the parties (see, for example, *Granatino v Radmacher (formerly Granatino)*'.[46]

---

[41] Bravely, because the case—a fearsomely complex deportation appeal—involved multiple issues on each of which Dyson as lead writer would have to set a lead that a majority of the Court would be prepared to follow. It took him 169 paragraphs, the longest judgment he could recall writing, and a second conference, to retain his majority on every issue. See p 199 in chapter 5 below.

[42] *Walumba Lumba (Congo) v Secretary of State for the Home Department* [2011] UKSC 12.

[43] Ibid, para 25.

[44] *McDonald v Royal Borough of Kensington and Chelsea* [2011] UKSC 33, para 28. A case where it would be fair to say that relations between the Justices were somewhat strained. See chapter 4 below.

[45] Ibid, para 61.

[46] *Granatino v Radmacher (formerly Granatino* [2010] UKSC 42, [2011] 1 AC 534.

Curiously, however, it is understood that in *Flood v Times Newspapers*[47] there was a major disagreement between several of the panel over the issue of the role of appellate courts when considering first instance decisions on points of evidence. In the end the point was left over for another day. Lord Phillips, contrary to his earlier position on the expectation observed,[48]

> How, and in particular [the issue] should be addressed is a matter on which I would wish to hear oral argument in a context where it mattered before reaching any conclusion. We have heard no oral argument on such points. In these circumstances I do not consider that this Court should lay down any general principle as to the approach to be adopted by an appellate court to an issue of *Reynolds* privilege.

These cases seem to indicate that whatever else may have changed with the advent of the Supreme Court, the constraining effect of the expectation that the Justices should stick to points of law that they have at least put to counsel has not greatly diminished. This was demonstrated spectacularly in the *Assange*[49] case (concerning the attempt to extradite Julian Assange, the founder of Wikileaks, to Sweden) about whether a Swedish public prosecutor could be a 'judicial authority' for the purposes of the Extradition Act 2003. When judgment was being handed down in the case, Assange's counsel, Dinah Rose QC, surprised the Supreme Court with the following,

> Dinah Rose QC:
> My Lords, my Lady … there is one matter which causes us considerable concern on our initial reading of the decision. And that is that it would appear that a majority of the members of this court have decided the point either principally or solely on the basis of the interpretation of the Vienna Convention on the Law of Treaties, a point with respect [which] was not argued during the appeal and which we were given no opportunity to address …
>
> Lord Phillips:
> You must consider the judgment at proper leisure and if you wish to make an application we will afford you the opportunity to do so.

Not the least of the ironies in the case was that it appears that the Justices had written to counsel involved in the appeal after the hearing to ask for their observations on another point[50] that had not emerged in the hearing. Assange's legal team considered that nonetheless the majority of the Supreme Court panel had decided the case on a point relating to the Vienna Convention that had not been put to them at any stage. A week after the *Assange* judgments were handed down, Dinah Rose QC made an 18-page submission to the Court. The Supreme Court,

---

[47] *Flood v Times Newspapers Ltd* [2012] UKSC 11.
[48] [2012] UKSC 11, para 106.
[49] *Assange v Swedish Prosecution Authority* [2012] UKSC 22, [2012] 2 WLR 1275.
[50] On the extent of the incorporation of European Treaties into domestic law, see Lord Mance in *Assange v Swedish Prosecution Authority* [2012] UKSC 22, para 208.

however, surprised the watching world by dismissing the submission within two days in a tersely worded page with five short paragraphs. They did not deny the existence of the expectation, nor did they assert that the *issue* of what was a 'judicial authority' had been argued by counsel[51] and that the Supreme Court had simply relied on new *material*, namely the Vienna Convention, to interpret the meaning of 'judicial authority'. Rather they asserted that Assange's team had got it wrong, Lord Brown had put the point to her during the argument and that Dinah Rose had now accepted this and accordingly her submission had been without merit. The actual exchange was revealing,

Dinah Rose QC:
The next question is about events subsequent to the implementation of the Framework Decision and the [2003 Extradition] Act. The first point I make is, of course, one has to proceed with considerable caution because the task of this Court is to construe a provision in the 2003 Extradition Act in accordance with the obligations on the state pursuant to the Framework Decision and events subsequent to both the Framework Decision and 2003 Act are of questionable significance in relation to that task.

Lord Dyson:
That's a rule we're well familiar with in domestic interpretation but if we're focusing on interpreting the Framework Decision itself it is legitimate, isn't it, to look to see what happened afterwards, to see whether it does shed light on the true meaning of the decision?

Dinah Rose QC:
My Lord, I don't suggest you shouldn't look at it, but I do submit that when one does look at it one doesn't gain an enormous amount of assistance for reasons that I'm going to elaborate.

Lord Dyson:
Well that's a different point.

Dinah Rose QC:
But I do submit that you need to be a bit careful about how much weight should be put upon it. This is very much a secondary area compared with those we've looked at, namely the context in which the decision was first made, the evolution of the decision and the language of the decision. These are secondary considerations.

Lord Brown:
But surely the Vienna Convention allows subsequent events, and the way it's been interpreted and applied, to operate in terms of [construing] the ... Framework Decision. *But I'm not sure that then it can bear similarly on the interpretation of the 2003 Act* (emphasis added).

Dinah Rose QC:
Quite, my Lord.

---

[51] It had not been argued by the respondents.

Lord Brown:
I'm not sure that isn't pulling oneself up by one's own bootstraps.[52]

Dinah Rose QC:
Yes, and there's a further difficulty because of the inherent ambiguity in the way in which different states have implemented the Framework Decision because one doesn't know if they are in breach of the Framework Decision. Indeed, it isn't even as straight forward as being in breach of the Framework Decision. The point is this, there is nothing in the Framework Decision that prohibits a state from designating a non-judicial authority to issue a European arrest warrant. The point is simply that, if a non-judicial authority issues a European arrest warrant, there is no obligation under the Framework Decision for another state to execute that warrant ... Now that's why the construction of the 2003 Act is important because the 2003 Act very clearly does not go any further than permitting the execution of a warrant which has been issued by a judicial authority because if it hasn't been issued by a judicial authority, it's not a valid warrant.

In fact, the majority of the Court in *Assange* had indeed reached their decision principally on the interpretation of Article 31.3(b) of the Vienna Convention on the Law of Treaties which allowed subsequent state practice to be used as an aid in the interpretation of the Framework Decision on the European Arrest Warrant provided that agreement between the parties has been established in relation to the interpretation of the Framework Decision.[53] As such, the majority of the Supreme Court held the view that a 'judicial authority' under section 2(2) of the Extradition Act was to be given the same meaning as in the Framework Decision and thus a public prosecutor could indeed be an issuing judicial authority.

This episode, probably as embarrassing for the Supreme Court as it was for Assange's team, threw up a number of unresolved issues related to the expectation. Thus journalists and blog writers[54] speculated extensively as to whether the decision whether the hearing should be re-opened should be taken by a new panel of Justices—as in the *Pinochet (No 3)* case[55] and whether, if the panel considered that there was any merit in Dinah Rose's application, she would be permitted a further hearing before the Supreme Court or only to submit further written arguments on the Vienna Convention point. The practice of the House of Lords in relation

---

[52] This transcript, taken from the videotape of the hearing, indicates that Lord Brown's raising of the topic of the Vienna Convention was rather more tentative than the Justices' apparent recollection of it. It is unclear whether the Justices checked the videotape as opposed to their notebooks when responding to the submission that the point had not been put to counsel.

[53] The point took up less than 10 minutes of a two-day hearing.

[54] Carl Gardner, 'Supreme Court Judgment: Assange v Swedish Prosecution Authority', Head of Legal Blog for TheLawyer.com, www.thelawyer.com/supreme-court-judgment-assange-v-swedish-judicial-authority/1012802.article; Carl Gardner, 'Could Assange apply to set aside the Supreme Court judgment?' Head of Legal Blog for TheLawyer.com, www.headoflegal.com/2012/05/30/could-assange-apply-to-set-aside-the-supreme-court-judgment/; Owen Bowcott, 'Julian Assange loses appeal against extradition', *The Guardian*, 30 May 2012, www.guardian.co.uk/media/2012/may/30/julian-assange-loses-appeal-extradition; Katy Dowell, 'Blackstone silk fails to stop Julian Assange extradition', *The Lawyer*, 30 May 2012, www.thelawyer.com/blackstone-silk-fails-to-stop-julian-assange-extradition/1012798.article.

[55] *R v Bow Street Metropolitan Stipendiary Magistrate ex parte Pinochet Ugarte (No 3)* [2000] 1 AC 61.

to the last issue varied. If the point was a substantial one, the House would re-convene for further argument from counsel, as they did in *Regis Property Co v Dudley*,[56] *Rookes v Barnard*,[57] *Oppenheimer v Cattermole*,[58] *Pepper v Hart*,[59] *Linden Gardens Trust Ltd v Lenesta Sludge Disposal Ltd and others*,[60] *Melluish v BMI (No 3) Ltd*[61] and *Clarke v Kato*[62] but this was cumbersome, inconvenient and expensive, so on most occasions they simply asked counsel to submit further arguments in writing. The practice of the final court in recent times when it concludes that the convention is in play has also varied—but mostly counsel will be invited to make additional submissions in writing.[63] Reconvened hearings caused by new issues arising between the end of the hearing and the delivery of the judgment are relatively rare[64] (occurring once every few years).[65] Most counsel indicated that they had never encountered an example of the final court deciding an appeal on an issue not debated by counsel, although two of them referred to different appeals in which a new issue had been raised by the Appellant's counsel for the first time in their Reply which was ultimately the point on which the appeal was decided. Neither felt that they had had an adequate opportunity to respond to the new point and both accordingly felt somewhat aggrieved by this.

---

[56] *Regis Property Co v Dudley* [1959] AC 370.

[57] *Rookes v Barnard* [1964] AC 1129.

[58] *Oppenheimer v Cattermole* [1976] AC 249.

[59] *Pepper v Hart* [1993] AC 593. It is thought that there was a re-convened hearing in this case because Lord Griffiths insisted on it. He had discovered after the original hearing that in that case MPs had considered the very point in issue in the case and this was in *Hansard*. He considered that it would be manifestly unfair not to let counsel argue the point. As he noted at the end of his judgment on p 619 'I was in a judicial minority of one at the end of the first hearing of this appeal. It was as a result of the discovery that the Parliamentary history of the legislation gave conclusive support to the construction I preferred that your Lordships agreed that the matter should be reargued to determine whether it was permissible to use the Parliamentary history as an aid to the interpretation of the legislation'.

[60] *Linden Gardens Trust Ltd v Lenesta Sludge Disposal Ltd and Others* [1994] 1 AC 85. It is understood that in this case shortly before the House was going to give its decision Lord Browne-Wilkinson who had written the main judgment, encountered Lord Mustill in the corridors of the House. On hearing the facts of the appeal the latter pointed to the applicability of a shipping case *The Albazero* [1977] AC 774 which had not been raised by counsel. The oral argument was re-opened to enable counsel to address the Court on the case and Lord Browne-Wilkinson and his colleagues were able to distinguish the applicability of *The Albazero*.

[61] *Melluish v BMI (No 3) Ltd* [1996] AC 454.

[62] *Clarke v Kato* [1998] 1 WLR 1647.

[63] As in *Doherty (FC) and others v Birmingham City Council* [2008] UKHL 57, and indeed it would seem in the *Assange* case itself in relation to another issue. The example of *Pepper v Hart* [1993] AC 593 (see ch 5 below) might suggest that in order to persuade the Court to grant a reconvened hearing rather than additional submissions in writing requires a determined champion within the ranks of those sitting on the panel. This was certainly true of *Elder Dempster & Co Ltd v Paterson Zochonis & Co Ltd* [1924] AC 522 where Lord Sumner forced a re-argument by threatening to resign unless this were done. See Lord Roskill, 'Law Lords, Reactionaries or Reformers' in (1987) 37 *Current Legal Problems* 247 at 250.

[64] Eg *Sempra Metals Limited (formerly Metallgesellschaft Ltd) v Her Majesty's Commissioners of Inland Revenue and Another* [2007] UKHL 34.

[65] More common were re-arguments following a referral of a point to the ECJ, eg *Her Majesty's Revenue & Customs v Stringer* [2009] UKHL 31 and the *Marks & Spencer v Commissioners of Customs and Excise* [2009] UKHL 8.

The constraint imposed by the expectation that judges in the final court should confine their propositions of law to points that they have at least put to counsel has probably been reinforced for a while by the publicity surrounding the *Assange* case. In *Cukurova (No 1)*[66] the Board of the Privy Council hearing the case, having decided that the appellants should be given relief from forfeiture, could not agree on what the terms of that relief should be since they had not been addressed by counsel on the relevant authorities.[67] The Board re-listed the case to hear argument on these authorities. The issue also arose in the *Prest* case,[68] (on whether a millionaire businessman, who was being sued for divorce, could defeat his wife's property claims because almost all of his wealth was held by companies, which he owned and controlled, outside of the UK). There, Lord Sumption's lead judgment states that the case law on looking behind the corporate persona of companies at the true state of affairs in those companies is covered by only two principles, the concealment principle and the evasion principle.[69] Although Lord Neuberger expressly agrees with this analysis,[70] Lords Clarke and Mance[71] were not prepared to accept this (obiter) conclusion as being a definitive statement of the law, since it had not been put to counsel or argued by them. Baroness Hale,[72] Lord Walker[73] and Lord Wilson do not mention the expectation, but seem to have been more in the Clarke/Mance camp than the Sumption/Neuberger one, on this point.

However, the force of the expectation that the Court's reasoning should be confined to issues dealt with by counsel should not be exaggerated. Most of the Justices take the view that it is sufficient if they offer counsel the opportunity to address the court on the issue. As the exchange from *Assange* quoted above shows, even a brief judicial suggestion (which was immediately withdrawn in part) which the Justices do not indicate that they attach much importance to, will, it would seem, satisfy the Justices that they have complied with the convention.[74] Should counsel choose for whatever reason not to take up the judges' invitation, it seems clear that this would not necessarily have deterred many of the Law Lords or Justices in the last decade or so from determining the appeal on the point irrespective of the absence of argument by counsel, as indeed occurred in *Assange*.

---

[66] *Cukurova Finance International Ltd and Cukurova Holding AS (Appellants) v Alfa Telecom Turkey Ltd* [2013] UKPC 2.

[67] Ibid [126].

[68] *Prest v Petrodel Resources Ltd* [2013] UKSC 34.

[69] Ibid [28].

[70] Ibid [60].

[71] Ibid [103] and [102].

[72] Ibid [92].

[73] Ibid [106].

[74] *Assange v Swedish Prosecution Authority* (application to re-open appeal) [2012] 3 WLR 1, see judgment of the Court, para 3.

This might even have stretched to a case where they were departing from one of their own precedents,[75] however, there are recent counter-examples. Thus in *Edwards v Chesterfield*[76] Lord Dyson noted that 'at para 36 of Mr Botham's written case, Mr Reynold QC invited the court to depart from *Johnson v Unisys Ltd*,[77] but this suggestion was not developed in the written case or in the oral argument'. In the same case Lord Phillips[78] concluded that 'It may be that this area of the law merits fundamental review. That is not, however, the battleground on which this Court was invited to tread'. Counsel having chosen ultimately not to challenge *Johnson*, the Justices seem to have decided that discretion was the better part of valour. Again in *Jones v Kernott*[79] the Court of Appeal, having unusually given leave to appeal, in the hope of seeing the uncertainties caused by *Stack v Dowdon*[80] cleared up, must have been a little disappointed that counsel did not challenge *Stack v Dowden* more directly, or indeed, refer to the substantial academic criticism that had been directed at that case, in oral argument before the Supreme Court. The Justices drew on the research of their judicial assistants to rectify the latter omission but the majority showed little inclination to depart from *Stack v Dowden* in a more radical way.[81]

The expectation that the final court will restrict its propositions of law to those argued or put to counsel is one that has gone in parallel with another, though less binding, convention as we have seen, namely that: 'It is an unwritten, but firm rule of the House not to consider arguments which have not been considered by the courts below'.[82] As a result the rules of the House of Lords and the Supreme Court require that points which are being raised for the first time at the level of the final court must appear in the printed Case of the counsel seeking to raise the point. This provides the judges and the other side with fair notice of the point. Allowing the Appellant to raise such points in their Reply—which are not contained in their Case is something which has occurred very occasionally in the final court and never without rancour from the opposing counsel. Although this understanding appears more like a constraint on counsel's arguments (which it is) it is also a method by which counsel through concessions or through the arguments which they ran in the lower courts[83] can constrain the ground for decision in the final

---

[75] For a recent instance where the US Supreme Court did just this in a re-hearing at their own request to reconsider one of their own precedents, see *Citizens United v Federal Election Commission* 558 US 50; 130 S Ct 876.

[76] *Edwards v Chesterfield Royal Hospital NHS Foundation Trust* [2011] UKSC 58, para 1.

[77] *Johnson v Unisys Ltd* [2001] UKHL 13, [2003] 1 AC 518.

[78] [2011] UKSC 58, para 88.

[79] *Jones v Kernott* [2011] UKSC 53, [2012] 1 AC 776.

[80] *Stack v Dowden* [2007] 2 AC 432. A case on the property rights of cohabitees once the relationship has broken down, in which Lord Neuberger dissented and which attracted some considerable academic criticism.

[81] See chapter 5 of this volume for a fuller discussion of *Stack v Dowden*, at p 192 below.

[82] Blom-Cooper and Drewry in *Final Appeal* (above, n 13) at 247. In only 12 cases [between 1952 and 1968] was this rule expressly waived.

[83] See the quotation by David Pannick QC at n 22 above.

appeal court. However, even by the late 1970s Law Lords were indicating that the expectation was not a compelling argument. As Lord Cross put it,

> It is completely a matter of discretion … it rather depends on how good … [the Law Lords think … [the point is]. If they think there is not much in the point anyway, they probably say 'Oh, we couldn't listen to that it was not mentioned in the Case.' But if they think it is something that really goes to the root of the thing, if they think the whole thing would be rather a mess if they did not allow it to be argued, then they would probably allow it on terms as to costs.[84]

Certainly I was left in little doubt from my recent interviews that recent Law Lords or Justices regard the issue in exactly the same pragmatic way as Lord Cross. As one senior barrister told me,

> If [the point] was conceded in the court below then you might be in trouble. However, if it was a pure point of law even if conceded below and you could say I want to withdraw that concession … I've never found that a difficulty. After all they're a final court and I have found them, the House of Lords and the Law Lords sitting in the Privy Council the least technical of any court. Sometimes as a point of criticism your opponent will say this wasn't the way it was argued in the court below, but there it is. If it's a point where if you'd raised it in the court below there might have been some evidence then it would be different, but if it's on a pure point of law I've never known them to say that.

INITIATING THE DIALOGUE

Few counsel, even bencher Queen's Counsel[85] are on such good terms with the judges in the final court that they will feel the inclination to initiate a dialogue with them about cases in which they are involved even after the appeal is over, and even then it would almost invariably be at the level of light-hearted banter. However, the etiquette of the adversarial system ensures that there would never be any serious discussion between a final court judge and a counsel about a case that they were both about to take part in.[86] It follows that the start of the dialogue for most counsel and judges is at the petition for leave or permission to appeal stage. Whilst these are initiated by counsel they will know from experience or the shared knowledge of the elite legal community how they should be framed.[87] The initial petition is in writing and is governed by the Rules/Practice Directions of the final court. Its job is to establish to the satisfaction of the panel of three judges in the final court to whom it will go that it raises an arguable point of law of sufficient general public

---

[84] See also Lord Reid in *Kaye v Hosier and Dickinson* [1972] 1 All ER 121, 124.

[85] Senior barristers who have been elevated to the upper ranks of the members of one of the Inns of Court in the Temple area of London.

[86] See, eg *The Law Lords*, above, n 2, 30–31 and Justice Stephen Breyer of the US Supreme Court in his C-SPAN interview, B Lamb, S Swain and M Farkas (eds), *The Supreme Court* (New York, Public Affairs, 2010) 134.

[87] See, eg Atkin's Court Forms, 2nd edn, vol 5(1) Appeals (London, Lexis/Nexis, 2004).

importance to warrant being heard as an appeal. In the House of Lords it was rare for any other Law Lord than those sitting on the Appeal Committee to have a say in whether an appeal should be admitted. This led to the occasional instance of one Appeal Committee admitting an appeal on a point of law and a differently constituted Appeal Committee refusing to admit an appeal raising an identical issue of law.[88] Now in the Supreme Court all of the Justices are enabled to see all of the petitions for permission electronically should they wish. It is understood that in general it remains only the three Justices who are on the panel who will determine whether the appeal should be admitted. If the judges are unanimously in favour of admitting the appeal or of refusing to hear it, that is the end of the matter. But if they are divided then objections to the appeal will be invited from the respondent and in a few cases an oral hearing will be held.[89] Generally speaking the Justices prefer there to be two judges in favour of admitting an appeal for it to be let in, however, there have been cases where a single judge has felt so strongly that the appeal should be admitted that the other members of the panel have agreed. In the US Supreme Court the position is clearer cut. Certiorari (leave) petitions go to the whole court and four Justices from the nine must vote for the appeal to be heard before it is admitted. The greater difficulty for appeals to be accepted in the US Supreme Court is in part due to the fact that the US Supreme Court receives around 10,000 petitions a year, whilst the House of Lords/Supreme Court receives fewer than 300.[90] In reality these figures exaggerate the difference in potential caseloads between the two courts since around 80 per cent of the certiorari petitions are 'in forma pauperis' where the petitioner (often a prisoner) has no lawyer and no means. Very few of these are admitted.[91]

In one sense, of course, the fact that the final court now largely controls its own docket indicates the extent of the powers of curtailment that it can exercise

---

[88] In such instances one the Appeal Committees could be re-convened to achieve a consistent outcome. See B Dickson, 'The processing of appeals in the House of Lords' (2007) 123 *Law Quarterly Review* 571, 587.

[89] The frequency of such oral hearings has been declining over the years, probably on cost grounds. In the period 1952–68, 95% of petitions were heard orally. However, the great bulk of them were manifestly incompetent or palpably hopeless (L Blom-Cooper and G Drewry, *Final Appeal* (Oxford, Clarendon Press, 1972) at 130) so a change of practice direction in 1970 allowed many of these to be dealt with without a hearing. In 1996 oral hearings had fallen to 10 a year (4.8% of petitions), and from 2002–05 the average was 15 a year (5% of petitions). See B Dickson, 'The processing of appeals in the House of Lords' (2007) 123 *Law Quarterly Review* 571. In the three years of the Supreme Court until the end of March 2012 there were only seven oral hearings before permissions panels (1% of applications).

[90] See SCOTUS Blog, B Dickson, 'The processing of appeals in the House of Lords' (2007) 123 *Law Quarterly Review* 571 and the Annual Reports of the UK Supreme Court.

[91] Curiously, the US Justices spend only 20% of their time in disposing of certiorari petitions, and the UK Justices spend not a great deal less. Lord Goff's evidence to the Royal Commission on the Reform of the House of Lords (2000, Cm 4534) includes the statement that 'Consideration of petition for leave is burdensome, and occupies a significant part of our time'. See A Le Sueur, 'Panning for Gold: Choosing Cases for Top-Level Courts' ch 12 in A Le Sueur et al (eds), *Building the UK's New Supreme Court: National and Comparative Perspectives* (Oxford, Oxford University Press, 2004) 271, 290. Partly this is because in the US Supreme Court the clerks play a greater role than the judicial assistants in the UKSC in the disposal of such petitions

on the dialogue, and the rarity of oral hearings relating to leave or permission petitions further limits the dialogue with counsel. Most damaging of all for the dialogue is the Justices' continuing reluctance (inherited from the Law Lords) to provide much by way of reasons for refusing petitions for permission, thus inhibiting the ability of counsel to learn from experience.[92] For appellants an effective dialogue is to get the appeal in, whereas for a respondent it is the reverse, or occasionally, to limit the issues on which the appeal will be admitted. For those seeking to appear in an appeal as an intervener, efficacy in the dialogue with the presiding judge or committee is very simple. Can they persuade the committee to allow them to appear and may they address the court (as opposed to merely submitting written arguments)? It is thought that regular interveners such as the Government, JUSTICE or Liberty have become adept at crafting their petitions such that they have a very considerable degree of success.

Having secured leave or permission to appeal, counsel's next opportunity to engage in dialogue within the final court of appeal is in the framing of the facts and issues. The Rules of the House[93] and of the Supreme Court[94] require the appellant's counsel to submit a statement of the relevant facts and issues in the appeal to all the respondents in the appeal, with a view to reaching agreement on these if possible. If agreement cannot be reached the statement should indicate the items that are disputed. Such unresolved issues will be dealt with by a three Justice PTA (permission to appeal) committee or the presiding Justice, almost always in writing.[95] However, the first real opportunity for counsel to engage in dialogue with the panel assigned to hear the appeal is in the printed or written Cases. This historically derived from the skeleton arguments which accompanied the judgments in the lower courts. Gradually skeleton arguments became less skeletal as counsel seized the opportunity to focus the appeal through the framing of the issues they wished to be resolved in the hearing (the curtailing role of counsel) and to set the scene in as attractive a way as possible for their side (the

---

[92] Although the House of Lords agreed in 2003 (Le Sueur, ibid 285) to provide reasons such reasons were and remain sufficiently formulaic as not to provide much guidance to the parties or observers of the final court. Brice Dickson has argued forcefully ('The processing of appeals in the House of Lords' (2007) 123 *Law Quarterly Review* 571, 588) that the court should provide fuller reasons for rejecting (or even admitting) petitions for leave or permission. However, since 2012 the Supreme Court has gradually begun to provide fuller reasons for refusing to grant permission—though not in every case.

[93] House of Lords Practice Directions 11, 12, 13 and 30.

[94] Rules of the United Kingdom Supreme Court, r 22(1)(a). See also United Kingdom Supreme Court Practice Directions 5.1.3.

[95] Very occasionally parties who could not get the other side to agree with their proposed issues wrote to the presiding or senior Law Lord to request that their additional issues be heard. It is understood that appellants in the *Gentle* case, *R (Gentle and Clarke) v The Prime Minister* [2008] 1 AC 1356 asked that the issue as to whether the UK's participation in the war in Iraq was legal in terms of International Law, be added to those contained in the agreed statement of facts and issues, since the respondents would not agree to this, in part because the point had not been argued below. In the event the appellants were not permitted to argue the point before the House.

persuasive role of counsel) before the judges had read the judgments in the Court of Appeal.

> It's essentially exactly the same as oral advocacy, it is having an eye for the winning point, it's not an eye for the clever point, it's an eye for the winning point … you've got to find a way of making the judges want to come with you and I think a lot of it is, it's not just sort of cosmetics but it's finding a way of presenting your story in an attractive way; it's that simple. (Senior counsel)

The difficulty for counsel is that this phase of the dialogue is asynchronous. Counsel cannot see if his or her arguments have had an impact on the judges of the final court until the oral hearing begins and possibly not even then. Whilst today every Justice (and their judicial assistants) will read the Case in advance, this was not always the case. Counsel could not tell in advance what the position would be. Michael Beloff QC outlined one strategy to overcome the problem of the preparedness or otherwise of the bench.

> One wants to reserve something quite deliberately for oral advocacy—as it were to take a forensic punch, to start off with something that captures their imagination immediately. Whereas, I would regard written advocacy as just a way of setting out as fully and as perhaps neutrally as possible the basic information they will need to have in order to determine the point or points of law and to identify what the issues are and clearly to set out what one's case about them is. But … my oral would not reflect my written … they would be two quite different exercises.

THE COURTROOM DIALOGUE

As Resnik and Curtis illustrate in their powerful and seminal text on *Representing Justice*,[96] courtrooms are part of the state's apparatus of control. Yet, ironically the committee rooms of the House of Lords and the courtrooms in the Supreme Court lack much of the iconography of power and justice typically found in the lower courts. The judicial bench (actually a curved table) is on the same level as that of counsel, the judges do not wear wigs or gowns, and in 2011 Lord Phillips, President of the Supreme Court granted a dispensation that counsel need not wear a wig and gown if all of the counsel in an appeal so agree.[97] None of this is serendipitous. The proximity of the judges' and counsel's benches in the Supreme Court is designed to encourage a conversational style of advocacy, as was the lack of a fixed lectern for counsel. We can see this from the metaphors which were coined to describe the unique character of the exchanges which took place between counsel and Law Lords in the Appeal Committees and Appellate

---

[96] J Resnik and D Curtis, *Representing Justice* (New Haven, CT, Yale University Press, 2011).
[97] As late as 2009 counsel appearing before the Lords in the chamber of the House had to wear a full bottom wig and gown.

Committees of the House of Lords.[98] These ranged from 'an academic seminar'[99] or Oxbridge tutorial,[100] to 'an informed dialogue',[101] and 'a dialectic between Bench and Bar',[102] which resembles nothing so much as a 'conversation between gentlemen[103] on a subject of mutual interest'.[104]

In truth, while these descriptions were certainly true of the Court in the Bingham era and remain so of the Supreme Court of today, in earlier times, particularly the 1930s, 1940s and the 1980s there were times when the exchanges in the oral hearings were rather more robust that these adjectives might suggest. Lord Pannick QC,[105] hinted as much in his valedictory column on the House in *The Times*[106] when he referred to its unique atmosphere as a mixture of academic seminar, comfortable club and all-in wrestling match.[107] Whether the dialogue between Bench and Bar in the final court more resembles a refined conversation than a bear garden turns in part on where the balance is drawn between the judicial expectation that their time (and the public purse) should not be wasted and counsel's expectations that they (and their clients) should be a given a fair hearing. It also turned on the temper and temperament of the presiding Law Lord. Thus when counsel in an eighteenth-century Scots appeal announced, 'I will now, my Lords proceed to my seventh pownt (sic)' the Lord Chancellor (Thurlow) riposted, 'I'll be damned if you do … this House is adjourned till Monday next'.[108] Presiders in the nineteenth and early twentieth centuries seem not to have become

[98] The atmosphere was in part a product of the physical geography of the Committee Rooms in the Lords where the hearings took place, with its semi-circular table(s) for the Law Lords and a large central lectern for counsel towering over the seated Law Lords, who wore no wigs and gowns but only lounge suits.

[99] Coined by a senior Law Lord.

[100] B Markesinis, 'Five Days in the House of Lords' (1995) 3 *Torts Law Journal* 169–204.

[101] Senior counsel, Michael Beloff QC told me 'I do regard the Lords as having a much more conversational and relaxed atmosphere than other courts … it is very much a dialogue exercise … Sometimes they allow you to go for a little while, but when that happens you begin to wonder a little bit if something's gone wrong'.

[102] A Law Lord.

[103] The gendered nature of this remark is telling. In the period 2000–12 only 10% of the QCs to appear in the final court to conduct a dialogue with the judges, were female. Only one of the 17 QCs during that time to have appeared 10 or more times as a QC before the final court, was a woman. Occasions such as the *Assange* case [2012] UKSC 22 were therefore unusual in that the two opposing leaders, Dinah Rose QC and Clare Montgomery QC, were female. Of course, there was only one female judge on the final court in all of this period. The dialogues in the Court are overwhelmingly male.

[104] David Pannick QC in *The Times*, 1 October 2009, observed that in the new building counsel sit 'close enough to conduct a conversation designed to identify the right answers, or at least the best available answers, to difficult problems'.

[105] A veteran of 100 appearances in the House of Lords—the last of which was the final (and unscheduled) hearing in the Lords of a leave petition in the *JFS* case which took place on Friday 31 July, the day after the official end to judicial hearings in the court .

[106] *The Times*, 30 July 2009.

[107] The US Supreme Court in the last half century by contrast with the Bingham court, perhaps because of the severely curtailed periods of oral argument permitted there has been described as 'designed as the Agincourt of the mind': L Baker, *Brandeis and Frankfurter, A Dual Biography* (New York, Harper & Row, 1984) 132.

[108] Lord Campbell, *Lives of the Lord Chancellors*, 2nd series (London, John Murray, 1846) vol V, 664.

much more patient.[109] Thus DN Pritt QC recorded a case where Lord Buckmaster endeavoured to 'smash' an appeal which Pritt was arguing. The case was a complex one but Buckmaster,

> began at once, with all the advantages of his quickness of thought, with a long series of interruptions … The warfare went on for a day or two, and then Lord Buckmaster said: 'Mr Pritt, their Lordships … would like to know how long this nonsense is going to continue'. [Pritt] replied: 'About ten days, if interruptions continue on their present scale, and a few days less if they diminish'.

After further interruptions Pritt could endure it no longer and, slamming a book on the lectern before him, he shouted, 'Your Lordships are going to hear this case!' They did. Pritt won. On other days the Law Lords were quite capable of sustaining the argument of an appeal with only the occasional assistance of counsel. Lord Guest experienced Lords Dunedin, Thankerton and Blanesburgh when he was a counsel and described the interruptions as 'constant, counsel was *only* allowed to say a few words before another judge would interrupt him'. Lord Radcliffe agreed with him,

> A good presiding judge counts a lot here … There have been fine lawyers, for instance, such as Lord Blanesburgh and Lord Atkin, themselves the nicest of men, who seemed positively to prefer that a case should go on forever to the possibility of an argument of which they disapproved remaining on its legs: whereas Lord Simonds, whom many think of (wrongly) as an obstinate and prejudiced judge, was a model in his conduct of a hearing, concise, courteously patient and resignedly fair.

Indeed Viscount Simonds and Lord Reid between them did much to re-set the tone of the Appellate Committee from the 1950s until the 1970s as presiding Law Lords. They and their colleagues had become more tolerant and polite, with the average appeal taking three to four days. Most of the Law Lords I interviewed in the 1970s confirmed this change in atmosphere and that counsel were getting more opportunity for developing their argument. In their eyes, Lord Reid dominated the House 35 years ago because of his forensic skills, his length of service as a Law Lord and his ability to give a lead to his colleagues.[110] Lord Reid was in his element in the hearings, his interventions were legendary—courteous but devastating, for there was no malice in them—becoming part of the enduring folklore at the Bar.[111] Lord Pearce gave a graphic account of the master craftsman's modus operandi,

---

[109] In 1825, 86 appeals were heard by the House in 89 days, in 1908, 84 appeals took only 83 days to hear.

[110] *The Law Lords*, above, n 2, at 72. As Lord Wilberforce in a tribute at his death observed, '[H]e has guided us with the influence of an equal in status, of a superior in wisdom, common sense, and where appropriate, imagination'. TB Smith, 'Reid, James Scott Cumberland, Baron Reid (1890–1975)' *Oxford Dictionary of National Biography* (Oxford, Oxford University Press, 2004).

[111] Lord Rodger, 'The form and language of judicial opinions' (2002) 118 *LQR* 226, 242.

Scott Reid when he talks, always gets the argument one stage further ... He says, 'Well, does what you are arguing really amount to this?', then he puts something clearly and fairly and then counsel is doubtful for a moment, and Scott says, 'Well, I think you have got to put it as high as that, haven't you, in order to make your point that so-and-so and so-and-so?', and then counsel thinks again, and then he says, perhaps, 'No, I don't think I have got to put it quite like that'. Then Scott Reid says, 'I think you have to, don't you, because if you admit so-and-so', and then perhaps it is agreed either ... It is more often that Scott's right, but often counsel can get out of that one. Scott is not demolishing him, you understand, at all. He just wants to see where all this is leading, and then we have got to another stage in the argument. It is now agreed that if this is the right way of looking at the case, then one has got really to accept proposition A, or to amend it, or to accept proposition B. Well then, you are one forward, you see, then you go on. Well, none of that can ever be got into any brief, because if you start rewriting a brief in the alternative, with about 100 different alternatives, you get nowhere. It doesn't convince.[112]

The practically unlimited scope for oral arguments at that time (although cases lasted three to four days on average, they could last for weeks)[113] entailed that the Law Lords in Reid's era relied far more on oral arguments than on counsel's submissions in the printed Case.[114] At that time some Law Lords did not even read the printed Case, or if they did so, only skimmed it casually in advance of the oral argument, including such heavyweights as Lords Denning, Radcliffe, Reid and Devlin. As Lord Devlin put it, 'I never used to read the printed Case. I would have done if I hadn't known it was going to be said all over again in oral argument'. Lord Wilberforce, it would seem, was not in this camp. Patrick Neill QC records[115] how, when informing their lordships on day one of a hearing in an Australian appeal to the Privy Council that the case had settled overnight, he was met by Lord Wilberforce's retort that, 'Their Lordships are *not at all pleased* to hear this news. We have spent hours, some of us days, preparing for this interesting appeal'. Those Law Lords who did read in advance were sometimes regarded as something of a mixed blessing by their colleagues. Lord MacDermott, for example told me he'd 'known some who've read their written material closely beforehand who have tended to push others into a line of thought too early'.

The point was made repeatedly to me in my original interviews that the advantage of a predominantly oral approach lay in the flexibility it gave to the arguments. Counsel were expected to respond to the thoughts expressed by the Court and to adjust their arguments accordingly. As Mark Littman QC observed,

---

[112] Interview with the author.

[113] Between 1952 and 1968 25% of civil England and Wales appeals to the Lords lasted more than five days and 10% of them took seven days or more. L Blom-Cooper and G Drewry, *Final Appeal* (Oxford, Clarendon Press, 1972) at 235. As late as 1989 in the Tin Council case, *JH Rayner Ltd v Department of Trade and Industry & Others.* [1990] 2 AC 418, the oral argument lasted for 26 days.

[114] In contrast to the US Supreme Court, who relied predominantly on the written briefs because of the 30 minute limit on oral hearings there.

[115] Address at the memorial service for Lord Wilberforce at St Margaret's Westminster, on 15 May 2003.

The House is a clinical environment. It's as though you had a sort of mortician's slab in the middle and five searchlights trained on it. Lord Reid once told me that the difference between advocacy in the Lords and any other court was that you couldn't so easily get away with prepared positions. In the House of Lords it's absolutely essential that the advocate should be able to think on his feet.[116]

Frequently, a case would change course in mid-stream as a result of a point thrown up in the debate.[117] At any rate, the Law Lords and counsel interviewed in the 1970s were strongly in favour of retaining the predominantly oral approach of the Lords—some even complained that counsel were putting too much effort into printed Cases.[118]

Curiously, within 10 years much had been transformed through the aegis of one man, Lord Diplock. As Lord Wilberforce wryly observed after Diplock's death,[119]

I think that as a general point you cannot really estimate a judge's influence without knowing from behind the scenes what influence he had on his colleagues ... Lord Diplock possessed the quality of persuading his colleagues to the extreme ... it almost got to the stage of a mesmeric quality ... Lord Diplock was a very persuasive man. He was a man who got his way in almost everything.

Counsel found Diplock even more problematic than his colleagues. It was not unusual for him to have made his mind up before the appeal began and indeed it is alleged that he sometimes even wrote the judgment before the appeal began. The truth is that in the Appellate Committee Diplock was a bully 'who really didn't have much time for advocacy', particularly if he thought it was off the point. His 'consciousness of his own ability made him dismissive of ideas at which his own fast brain had not arrived first', and he would 'mine the advocate's path with Socratic questions the answers to which would in due course, as he knew, destroy the case'.[120] Once[121] he announced to counsel at the outset of the appeal that there was no point in argument since the House had only given leave to sort out the poor reasoning in the Court of Appeal's judgments, but the result of the case was not going to change. Counsel were effectively told to have a polite discussion, but not to argue the case.

---

[116] Interview with author.

[117] In the key public law case of *Anisminic v The Foreign Compensation Commission* [1969] 2 AC 147, the appellants' counsel were so pessimistic of success (having lost in the lower courts) that they informed the Judicial Office before the appeal began that they estimated that the hearing would last two only days at the most. Following key interventions by Lord Reid, the appeal took on a different complexion, the hearing lasted for 12 days and the appellants won the case. (Patrick Neill QC my informant.)

[118] *The Law Lords*, above, n 2, at 38.

[119] In G Sturgess and P Chubb, *Judging the World* (Sydney, Butterworths, 1988) at 275.

[120] S Sedley and G Le Quesne, Diplock (William John) Kenneth, Baron Diplock (1907–85) *Oxford Dictionary of National Biography* (Oxford, Oxford University Press, 2006).

[121] *Antaios Compania Naviera SA v Salen Rederierna AB (The Antaios)* [1985] AC 191.

As Lord Hope told me,

[When] Lord Diplock [presided] … the attitude was a good deal more brisk then. He didn't allow arguments to develop that he thought had nothing in them and he would sit on you at the very start of an appeal and really cut you short. It was very difficult to get through and his colleagues on the whole did seem to be pretty compliant and didn't really feel that they could speak up if he was saying there wasn't anything in the case, and then you found he wrote the judgment.

Lord Diplock, unlike the heavyweights of Reid's era, believed in reading the printed Case and having read the Case he saw no reason why counsel should be allowed to say it all again in the oral hearing, just to suit his 'less industrious' colleagues, even if they were only seeking to avoid making their minds up too early. In consequence, when Diplock was in the chair, the length of the oral arguments came down. So too did the length of the printed Cases following a stiffly worded injunction from Lord Diplock on behalf of the House in 1982 on the matter.[122]

After Lord Diplock, the Lords reverted to type with Lord Fraser in the chair. He was so courteous that he once allowed oral argument to go for nine days over the meaning of two words in a statute, namely, 'ordinarily resident'.[123] Yet, Fraser's contemporaries Lords Brandon and Templeman (the latter being generally known to counsel under the soubriquet of 'Sid Vicious')[124] had nothing to learn from Diplock in terms of aggressive behaviour on the bench. Generally when they sat together they would constantly snipe at one another, a blessed relief to counsel who when assailed by Brandon could be sure that Templeman would weigh in on his side, and vice versa. If either was rebuffed he would sulk. Lord Templeman raised a point in one oral argument that hadn't been argued in the court below and counsel said he'd like time to look at the authorities. When Lord Templeman observed that new authorities had to be lodged well in advance of the hearing, counsel retorted quite fairly that it was a new point so he didn't have the authorities to hand. Eventually counsel asked the presiding Law Lord if he might bring the authorities the following day. When this request was granted Lord Templeman put the cap on his pen and folded his arms in disgusted petulance. As a presider he was not much better. In one case the appellant had not been on his feet two minutes when Templeman handed both counsel a typed note from the Law Lords indicating that they saw no merit in the respondent's argument and did the appellant want to add anything?

If the reputation of the House at that time was not damaged by the behaviour of some of its judicial members, it probably was by the debacle of the *Lonrho* contempt hearing, where their failure to bring in the Lord Chancellor at an early stage when faced with what looked like a crude attempt by one of the parties to

---

[122] See *MV Yorke Motors v Edwards* [1982] 1 All ER 1024, 1025j.

[123] *R v Barnett London Borough Council, ex parte Shah* [1983] 2 AC 309.

[124] See M Beloff QC, 'The End of the Twentieth Century' in L Blom-Cooper, B Dickson and G Drewry, *The Judicial House of Lords 1876–2009* (Oxford, Oxford University Press, 2009) ch 15.

influence the Court, proved very costly.[125] Nor was the sight of the House shortly thereafter spending 26 days of argument on the *Tin Council* case[126] guaranteed to restore its reputation. After that case the Judicial Office began to ask for clearer estimates from counsel as to the possible duration of appeals.

As the 1990s wore on and Lord Browne-Wilkinson took over the chair the atmosphere began to change and the oral hearings grew more relaxed again.[127] Occasionally, even humour would creep in, something Lord Diplock would not have tolerated. Unfortunately, tensions returned in the aftermath of the *Pinochet* affair, when Lord Hoffmann failed to recuse himself from the appeal over the attempted extradition of General Pinochet from England to Spain.[128] It took the appointment of Lord Bingham to finally establish the conversational style of the Lords of the 2000s. A grateful counsel commented,

> The atmosphere that Lord Bingham … imposed through sheer force of personality rather than by actually saying anything [was] an atmosphere in which you had a very informed dialogue with the bench without there being any of the sort of acrimony that one used to have.

Lord Bingham was a strong believer in the value of oral advocacy but unlike Lord Diplock would never let his impatience with poor advocacy show in the court-room. However, in one respect Lord Bingham did go along with Lord Diplock, namely in seeking to keep the work of the court moving on. It was during his time that counsel's estimates as to the amount of time they would need came under real scrutiny, and if the parties wanted more than two days of the House a good case had to be made out. With time limits for hearings in place, Bingham took on the role of ensuring that counsel for either side did not overrun, either causing problems for the House or for their opponent. Lord Bingham had a way of saying '*Yes*' which would quicken and multiply if counsel failed to take the hint. Lord Phillips when he took over as presiding Law Lord and subsequently as President of the Supreme Court was more relaxed on this issue than Lord Bingham. In consequence there has been no tendency for our Supreme Court to move towards the much truncated oral arguments which prevail in the US Supreme Court.[129] Lord Neuberger, however, is in his own words, 'a bit more of a speed merchant' and is likely to press counsel to avoid unnecessarily drawn out arguments.

---

[125] *Re Lonrho Plc (Contempt Proceedings)* [1990] 2 AC 154. In all, the proceedings accounted for 13 judicial sitting days and costs in excess of £1,000,000, without much by tangible result except embarrassment for the Law Lords. For further details of the case see chapter 3 of this volume below.

[126] *JH Rayner Ltd v Department of Trade and Industry and Others* [1990] 2 AC 418.

[127] See F Gibb, 'The law lord who took the rap over Pinochet', *The Times*, 19 October 1999 (cited in P Darbyshire, *Sitting in Judgment* (Oxford, Hart Publishing, 2011) at 379).

[128] For further details of this case see chapter 3 of this volume, below.

[129] Today this is half an hour for each side, although in exceptional cases eg the appeal where the Obama health care provisions were being challenged the oral arguments were conducted over three days, see *National Federation of Independent Business et al v Sebelius, Secretary of Health and Human Services, et al* 567 USSC (2012).

HOW HAS THE DIALOGUE BETWEEN COUNSEL
AND THE COURT CHANGED?

Clearly the last 40 years have witnessed significant changes to the dialogue between counsel and the judges in the final court. Following the introduction of time constraints to oral advocacy, the average length of oral hearings has dropped to two days from an average of three to four days 40 years ago.[130] Despite the efforts of Lord Diplock the size of the printed Cases and skeleton arguments has probably increased by a greater margin in the same period. Finally, in a small way some of the judges have begun to use their judicial assistants as sounding boards where previously they would have relied on counsel's arguments.

These changes in the forms of advocacy have in turn had a further consequence. In Lord Reid's era where the bench was cold or lukewarm at best the appellant was thought to have a significant advantage in the opportunity to set the legal and factual framework for the appeal. Anyone who has read the judgments of Lord Denning or Lord Atkin will know the importance of the way the facts are presented. As Lord Atkin's daughter recalled,[131]

> When he gave us the facts of a case and asked us what we thought about it, his way of presenting the problem was such that there was never any suggestion in our minds that the other side would have a leg to stand on.

Hardly surprising then that almost every counsel that I interviewed first time around considered that the appellant had an advantage from speaking first.[132] The Law Lords were evenly divided between those who thought it was an advantage, those who thought it was not, and those who said it depended on the case. Interestingly, the minority who paid more attention to the written materials were the ones who considered it was an advantage to speak first, almost as though they had developed a practice of reading the Case to neutralise the advantage they perceived the appellant to gain from going first.[133] Now, all of the Justices[134] read the Cases and skeleton arguments in advance with some discussing the appeals in advance with their judicial assistants. The resulting 'hot bench' means that nowadays few counsel or judges consider that it is an advantage to be the appellant, and those that do, attribute this to the fact that the appellant has a right of reply which is denied the respondent.

Today's shorter oral hearings, hot benches and changed case type have also reduced the very limited potential which used to exist for counsel to tailor their arguments to the individual traits of the judges sitting on a particular panel. Whilst it remains the case now as it was then that a proportion of all appeals turn

---

[130] See nn 72 and 79 in chapter 3 of this volume, below.
[131] *The Law Lords*, above, n 2, at 53.
[132] Ibid, at 57.
[133] Ibid, at 58.
[134] It may be that Lord Rodger was a partial exception to this near universal practice.

on which judges actually sit on the case,[135] counsel's difficulty is that what appeals to one judge may not appeal to the others.[136] As David Pannick observed, the old advocate's ploy of dangling an attractive fly before a chosen Law Lord is,

> unrealistic nowadays. It perhaps was an appropriate analogy at a time when ... the Law Lords had done far less preparation and where perhaps the subject matter of the cases that came before them was far more esoteric, whereas nowadays the diet of the Appellate Committee, certainly in the cases that I'm dealing in, tends to be Human Rights Act, public law issues where any sort of attempt to dangle is likely to lead to your finger being bitten off.[137]

That is not to say that counsel should not be sensitive to their audience—including what they have said in earlier cases. Moreover, there may be occasions when a focus on a specialist or a dominant judge may be justified in the hope that (s)he will play a disproportionate part in the disposal of the appeal, but it remains a high-risk strategy.[138]

Being sensitive to one's audience also means dealing with the points that are troubling the judges when they arise. Whilst the judges in the final court can use the dialogue to constrain counsel's arguments as we have seen, they also use the dialogue to clarify what counsel are arguing, to test counsel's arguments, and to put their own theories of the case to counsel. The most common form of judicial intervention today seeks clarification as to the page in the bundle or electronic bundle that is being referred to by counsel, but questions seeking to know what the limits of counsel's argument are, are also very common. Testing counsel's propositions was a particular forte of Lord Reid's as we have seen,

> Of course you have got to be reasonable, but broadly speaking I would think that the job of the man on the Bench is always to be rather against the man who is on his feet. In other words you are trying to test him out, you see, and to find any weak points in his argument.[139]

By and large, counsel welcome these interventions. They show where the judges' doubts lie. Equally vital for the success of the dialogue is the judicial intervention that raises points of law that the judges consider to be important to the case, which have not appeared in counsel's arguments. As we know, counsel consider that if the judges in the final court are going to allow such points to determine

---

[135] There is no consensus as to what proportion of cases comes into this category. Nowadays around 25% of all appeals involve a dissent so perhaps the figure can be set at least at 25%.

[136] Thirty years ago counsel were not even told in advance which Law Lords would sit on their appeal. Even though counsel can now learn the make-up of the panel some weeks in advance it has not really changed the perceptions of counsel that seeking to target arguments at one or two judges in a panel is a tricky and potentially dangerous tactic.

[137] The problem has been exacerbated by the fact that the Supreme Court now sits in larger panels than five much more often than was the case in the House of Lords.

[138] The bench's counterpart to this—where a Justice feeds a line of questioning ostensibly to counsel but actually in the hope that it will impact on his companions is more commonplace. See chapter 3 of this volume below and the *The Law Lords*, above, n 2, ch 4.

[139] Extract from Lord Reid's interview with the author, 1973.

their decision—as they did in the *Assange* case—then they should at least be put to counsel. These are the judicial counterpart to the restrictive powers of counsel, but if counsel declines to run with the point for whatever reason, it can cause difficulties for those judges who believe in adhering to the principles of the adversarial system.

That said, in terms of the efficacy of the dialogue (and often for the efficacy of advocacy) in general the least helpful thing that counsel can do is to decline to engage in the dialogue. This as Lord Bingham observed, is almost a golden rule of appellate advocacy and reinforces the point that it is about dialogue rather than sequential monologues:[140]

> Enter fully and readily into dialogue with any member of the tribunal who raises any point or question. When a judge asks a question or challenges any point in your argument—or makes a point in your favour—you have his or her attention. Any discussion of this kind involves an engagement, if not a meeting, of minds. It is your best opportunity to persuade. If you evade the question or duck the discussion you may find yourself addressing a tribunal of the deaf and mute.

One of the leading counsel of today agreed,

> What you have to remember ... with the House of Lords is ... they are going to have a certain conception as to how things should work and if they ask you a question you should really treat it as both evidence to indicate what they're thinking but also an opportunity to try to respond to that way of thinking or to show how your conceptual framework can accommodate whatever concern [they were raising]... The most important element in the course of oral advocacy is to answer the tribunal's points convincingly. A fluent and compelling response to an adverse judicial intervention is the holy grail of oral advocacy.

Even in American appeal courts where oral advocacy is much more limited, the judiciary expect counsel to engage with their questions,

> Attempted evasion in an oral argument is a cardinal sin. No answer to an embarrassing point is better than an evasive one ... Lack of candour in meeting a difficult point ... goes far to destroying the effectiveness of a lawyer's argument, not merely as to the point ... but often as to other points on which he should have the better of it. For if a lawyer loses the confidence of the court, he is apt to end up almost anywhere.[141]

Chief Justice Roberts of the current US Supreme Court also emphasised the importance of the oral dialogue.[142]

> You have to appreciate that [the Justices] are going to ask hard questions. They're going to ask questions that don't put your case in the best possible light, and you need to

---

[140] 'The Role of an Advocate in a Common Law System', Lecture delivered at Gray's Inn on 6 October 2008.

[141] Justice JM Harlan II, 'The Role of Oral Argument' ch 12 in DM O'Brien (ed), *Judges on Judging* (Washington DC, CQ Press, 2009).

[142] In his C-SPAN interview on 19 June 2009. See B Lamb, S Swain and M Farkas (eds), *The Supreme Court* (New York, Public Affairs, 2010).

appreciate that … They like you to be part of the process that is helping them come to the right result. They understand you've got a client to represent and they expect you to do that. But if you can convince them that you're on their side and helping them reach the right decision, as opposed to something that they have to push against to get you to give an answer, I think that's very helpful, not only to the Court but also to your client.

HAVE THE QUALITIES OF GOOD APPELLATE ADVOCACY CHANGED?

If the dialogue between counsel and judges of the final court has changed significantly in the last 40 years, what impact has this had, if any, on what counts as good advocacy in the final court? To answer this we need first to look at what constitutes persuasive advocacy in that court, next to look at the qualities of robustness, courage and timekeeping and finally to examine the rise in written advocacy.

Persuasive Advocacy

The object of appellate advocacy, oral or written, is persuasion. It is, however, an art rather than a science[143]—this means that different counsel when faced with the challenge of arguing a final appeal will adopt different routes. David Pannick QC and Jonathan Sumption QC were repeatedly identified by the Law Lords I interviewed as at the top of the profession but their styles were quite different. As one leading counsel put it,

> The function of the advocate is to comfort the tribunal by conveying to them the sense that his argument is credible. Putting it pejoratively, it is a con trick—in the sense that you need to win the confidence of the tribunal. There are many different ways of doing that—through sheer intellectual superiority, through pedestrian diligence, through force of personality, through eloquence, sometimes even with humour—but the most important element in the course of oral advocacy is to answer the tribunal's points convincingly.

Whatever the differences in approach taken by those who appear in the tournament of champions which is the final appeal court their ultimate goal is the same—to win (or lose)[144] in a way that assists their clients' interests. Moreover, each has in their own way to gain the trust[145] and confidence of the court. Here the leading performers undoubtedly have an advantage through the trust placed in them by the members of the final court,

---

[143] See Lord Judge LCJ, 'Developments in Crown Court Advocacy', Kalisher Lecture delivered on 6 October 2009.

[144] Leading counsel are well aware—as are their clients—that they cannot win every case. Where the case is likely to be lost their job is to minimise the damage to their clients' interests.

[145] On the importance of trust in professionals see Onora O'Neill's Reith Lectures, *A Question of Trust* (Cambridge, Cambridge University Press, 2002).

There are certain advocates who are given a lot of leeway because they are highly respected who I think actually get a slightly unfair advantage. [Its a question of] alighting on the right points and putting them across and picking out the way the court's going. (A Law Lord).

One senior counsel added,

However clever the Lords are they're not computers, they're human beings and you've got to make them want to decide in your favour, and that's what advocacy means, it's working out a way of making them feel comfortable coming with you.[146]

As we have seen, with hot benches, appellants have lost much of their ability to set the legal and factual framework for the appeal, and with it part of their influence on the dialogue with the court. However, there remains plenty scope for different styles of oral advocacy. The very best speak with an authority that makes them seductively dangerous to the court. A seeming simplicity can be equally beguiling, as Lord Walker told me, 'sometimes the most effective advocacy is quite brief and has at any rate a superficial appearance of simplicity although no doubt there's an awful lot of art that goes into that'. Equally dangerous are the advocates who appear so dispassionate in their presentation as to be more concerned with assisting the court to come to the right answer than in winning the case. As one Law Lord observed, 'I think the really good debater is the one that makes you feel he's joining with you in seeking the right answer, whatever his point is'. Rather less common today is the seductive power of deliberately underselling one's case in the hope that the Law Lords will re-state it in a more powerful way. Lord Halsbury LC explained why he considered a little-known barrister was the best advocate that he had ever heard. 'Well, he had the great gift of always making it appear that he had a first class case being hopelessly ruined by a third class advocate'.[147]

Most respondents this time round were of the opinion that good appellate advocacy remains what it always was: being well prepared, succinct, resilient, addressing the questions from the bench and only putting your good points. Dealing with your opponents' good points is a trickier art. As counsel put it,

One of the skills of advocacy is, to traduce would be too strong a word, but not fairly to represent the argument that they are rejecting … you will use the arts of advocacy to belittle, so far as you can, the argument that you are addressing and if there are strong points in it you may be advised to try to attack them by stealth rather than full on.

Jonathan Crow QC added,

In this context, one thing that I have learned … is that you can still win a case even if you cannot necessarily refute all of your opponent's arguments. Indeed, you can sometimes gain considerable credibility with the tribunal if you acknowledge that your opponent has got a good point on X to which you do not have a direct answer, so long as you can also persuade the tribunal that you have a better point on Y to which your opponent has no answer.

---

[146] Trust is primarily garnered through demonstrating excellence in advocacy skills including diligence. Curiously, trust is not dictated by whether one is on close personal terms with any of the Law Lords or not.

[147] See *The Law Lords*, above, n 2, at 60ff.

Robustness and Resilience

One area where oral appellate advocacy has undoubtedly changed in the last 40 years is in the degree of robustness required of counsel. In the Diplock era one route to success was to batter the Law Lords into submission. Gordon Pollock QC's astonishing success in the *Lonrho* case,[148] where after two and a half days of dogged persistence he forced the whole panel of resistant Law Lords to recuse itself, has already entered the annals of the House.[149] The only way to deal with Lord Diplock was to take him on. As one Law Lord said to me, 'hit the ball back to him as hard as possible in the hope of stunning his hand. It was the only way to stop him walking all over you'. Robustness and resilience are closely related virtues and the latter was also needed in earlier times. If Lord Reid was devastating in his ripostes he lacked the 'dripping sarcasm'[150] of Lord Diplock or the sheer combativeness of Lords Bridge, Brandon and Templeman. On one such occasion where the senior had taken a terrific hammering from all three of them and his junior was then asked by Lord Bridge if he wished to add anything, the junior replied, 'Not without a helmet'. The Law Lords had the grace to laugh.[151] Resilience under fire to this degree was fortunately not an essential quality in the Lords in its final decade. Lord Bingham was determined that the court should eschew the excesses of the Diplock era and even Law Lords who might have been tempted to stray were held in check by respect for Lord Bingham's authority. This is not to say that some resilience[152] is no longer necessary. In both the UK and US Supreme Courts the bench continues to emphasise the significance of the Socratic dialogue, as we have seen.

Courage

Good appellate advocacy has always required courage whether you are DN Pritt, Gordon Pollock or Dinah Rose. Robust resilience may no longer be required, but other forms of courage are needed. A recurring theme in American writings on

---

[148] *Re Lonrho Plc (Contempt Proceedings)* [1990] 2 AC 154.

[149] Michael Beloff QC, 'The End of the Twentieth Century' in L Blom-Cooper, B Dickson and G Drewry, *The Judicial House of Lords 1876–2009* (Oxford, Oxford University Press, 2009) at 235 describes Pollock as trading blows with Lord Ackner over the relevance of the fact that Ackner's father had been Tiny Rowland's dentist.

[150] Lord Rodger, 'Appreciation: The Hon Lord Davidson (1929–2009)' 2009 SLT (News) 157, 158.

[151] Certainly in the case of Lords Brandon and Templeman several of my respondents indicated that these particular Law Lords respected counsel who stood up to them. On one occasion when Templeman had goaded counsel into a less than polite riposte, which drew from the presiding Law Lord an insistence upon an apology, Lord Templeman himself demurred indicating that he had provoked the response that he deserved.

[152] 'Counsel, it's a good thing you've got a lot of fall-back arguments', Chief Justice Roberts told one struggling attorney recently, 'because you fall back very quickly'. M Doyle, McClatchy Newspapers, www.mcclatchydc.com/2007/05/16/16193.

appellate advocacy is the importance of 'going for the jugular', ie getting to the heart of the case by selecting and arguing its one or two controlling points. This is the best way, it is said to 'capture the issue' and to 'stick that capture' into the minds of the judges. Unsurprisingly, counsel and the judges in the UK's final court agreed with this, both in the original interviews and those of today,

> Good advocacy is what it always was, which is to identify the points that the court thinks are good. (Law Lord)

> I personally prefer the counsel who puts his best point and doesn't necessarily throw all his points at you. A good advocate uses discretion in his presentation. (Lord MacDermott)

However, as Sir Patrick Hastings KG observed, 'The ability to pick out the one real point of a case is not by itself enough; it is the courage required to seize upon that point to the exclusion of all others that is of real importance'. Great advocates of the past are said to have had this daring, eg Sir Walter Monckton QC and Lord Wilberforce when at the Bar and faced with eight points to choose from, are said to have picked the best one and abandoned the other seven to press it. Jonathan Sumption (whilst a QC) was cited to me by a Justice as a very good example of somebody who decides what the case is about and decides what points he wants to run and runs them. Such role models are easier to admire than to copy, since it requires the judgement to select the best argument and the courage to stick with that choice. An excellent example of this occurred in an appeal where the respondent, feeling that he could not successfully defend the reasoning with which his clients had been successful in the Court of Appeal, sought leave at the outset of the appeal to run the case on an argument that had been abandoned in the court below. His opponent addressed the Committee for about an hour with a plenitude of authorities indicting why this should not be permitted. However, in reply the respondent spoke for only two minutes saying,

> It's a very short point and it's going to come up again so if you don't let me argue it on this appeal and you find against me on the first point, it will leave an unanswered question hanging that will make the case a pointless appeal.

He then promptly sat down, much to the surprise of all in the Committee Room. The Law Lords, nonplussed by the turn of events, eyed each other, concluded that nothing more need be said and let the respondent run the point.[153] Nonetheless, more risk averse counsel will be attracted by David Pannick QC's observation that,

---

[153] A similar story from an appeal court in the United States describes how the appellant 'took such a battering from the court that it was obvious to everyone the judgment below would be affirmed. Counsel for the respondent arose, bowed, and said, "If the Court please, I must apologize for an error in my brief. At page 32, second line from the bottom, the citation should be to 112 Federal Second and not to 112 Federal. Unless there are any questions, I will submit the respondent's case on the brief", and sat down. I have it on excellent authority that it was one of the most effective arguments ever heard by that court'. FB Wiener, 'Oral Advocacy' (1948) 62 *Harvard Law Review* 56, 59–60, quoted in A Scalia and B Garner, *Making Your Case: The Art of Persuading Judges* (St Paul MN, Thompson/West Publishing, 2008).

I don't think that it can be good tactics *only* to go for the point that you think is your best point. It seems to me the right approach is to pursue all the good points, there may be more than one of them even if the second or third is not as good as the first.[154]

Another senior counsel had his own take on the 'good points' thesis,

> As a client once said to me: 'Anyone can prepare their good points. What matters is how you deal with the bad ones'. There is much in this. Some advocates lose considerable credibility with the tribunal by banging on about a point that is not going to win them the case. Others lose credibility by giving up a tricky point too easily. This is a difficult judgement call because, on the one hand, you do not want to collapse with the first signs of judicial opposition but, on the other hand, you do not want to ruin your case by flogging away at a point they are not going to find in your favour. So one has to avoid both being pusillanimous and being stubborn—and the path between the two is a judgement that one often has to make literally on one's feet in the course of oral argument.

Lord Bingham on the other hand identified another form of courageous appellate advocacy to which he was attracted, namely the counsel who says,[155]

> My Lords, I have six propositions. They are the following. If any of these propositions is unsound, I must fail. But I submit that they are sound, and I shall now seek to make them good.

The attraction of this approach is in the clear road map which it provides to the court and the opportunity it affords to test the building blocks of counsel's argument for their consistency with principle and as to their consequences.

Timing

The reduction in the length of time allowed for advocacy, especially in complex cases, has entailed that counsel must acquire the timing skills of a *Today* presenter on Radio 4 to bring their argument to a close on time. Counsel have to give accurate estimates as to how long they will need for their argument without knowing how interventionist the judges will be during the case.[156] Moreover, some opponents will leave their discussions as to the length of time needed for reply until the robing room. This can lead to what in other circumstances might be seen as gamesmanship, especially if the presiding judge allows one of the counsel to significantly overrun. Not the least of Lord Bingham's skills in the chair was his

---

[154] The dangers of only running your best argument were graphically illustrated in the Obama Healthcare case, *National Federation of Independent Business et al v Sebelius, Secretary of Health and Human Services, et al* 567 US (2012). The point that ultimately won over Chief Justice Roberts (the swing voter) was the third string argument of the Government's counsel, which the latter had little faith in. See DC Weiss, 'Solicitor General's Third Backup Argument is Winner in Health Law Case', 29 June 2012, American Bar Association Journal on-line.

[155] Lord Bingham, 'The Role of an Advocate in a Common Law System', Lecture delivered at Gray's Inn on 6 October 2008.

[156] See DN Pritt QC on this point in *The Law Lords*, above, n 2, at 68.

ability to manage timing issues in a fair and seemingly effortless fashion. As one experienced counsel remarked,

> Lord Bingham liked to be told in advance, usually in a letter, that I had spoken to the other counsel and that we had agreed a timetable … If you overran by over half-an-hour then certainly in Lord Bingham's case he would intervene very forcefully and tell you that you had to finish in the next five or ten minutes and he actually made out a timetable of his own if you had overrun.

One noticeable feature of the modern day leaders in the final court is the speed of their delivery. It is markedly faster than that of their counterparts 20 to 30 years ago. As one observer noted,

> One of most extraordinary things about [leading counsel] is that they do it all at an enormous speed so quickly so that the slower members of the class as it were are still trying to work out what [counsel's] last point is or his last point but three is.

Finally, the reduction in time for oral argument is an added impetus to counsel to stick to the key points in the case. As David Pannick QC put it,

> You need to work hard to prepare the Case because you know that you are not going to be able to take time developing the background and responding to the thoughts that judges may have as to background. You've got … to get to the heart of the case and that requires very different skills. It means that you have to be much more aggressive in focusing on the issues in the Case.

Written Advocacy

Above all however the last 40 years have seen the rise in importance of written advocacy. Whilst not identical to oral advocacy in its characteristics there are nonetheless many more similarities than differences between the two art forms. Each of them is about persuasion—which, as Lord Bingham has noted, requires communication and communication requires the advocate to engage with the mind of the audience.[157] The views of counsel were remarkably consistent on this—pointing to the symbiotic relationship between the Case and the oral argument,

> In terms of what wins cases in the Supreme Court, oral advocacy on its own is not enough. Written advocacy matters every bit as much. If you have not at least started to win them round with your printed Case, you are very unlikely to finish the job on your feet. By 'written advocacy' I do not just mean persuasive writing. It is far more complex than that. The real skill in presenting a written argument is to identify the winning point [from amongst those available to you]. Any lawyer can think of legal arguments, but you

---

[157] Lord Bingham, 'The Role of an Advocate in a Common Law System', Lecture delivered at Gray's Inn on 6 October 2008. Lord Bingham's recipe for the good printed Case is a neutral and fully referenced statement of the facts, clarity of purpose, appropriate simplicity, sparing citation of authority, brevity and clarity of expression.

do not win appeals by smothering the Court with mere arguments. What you need to do is to identify the point that matters. (Jonathan Crow QC)

If you know that the Law Lords are going to spend a substantial amount of time preparing, then it's in your interests to argue the Case more fully perhaps than you would otherwise do and also deal not just with the bare assertions, the strengths of your case but also try to anticipate the points against you and deal with them. On the oral side the consequence of the printed Case is that they will not accept in my experience you simply going through your printed Case because they have read the printed Case. You're expected to focus your oral argument on meeting the points made by your opponent in their printed Case. Obviously some elaboration of your side of the case is necessary; they won't sit and listen to the printed Case being read out. (David Pannick QC)

You might say, 'The steps in the argument go A, B, C. You've seen our written Case on A, we say our argument's very powerful, I'm not going to take up time developing that. B is more debatable and perhaps you'd take a little bit of time on that, but then you say the main point we say is C and I'm going to take my time on that' and so the written materials give you a certain degree of freedom then to concentrate on your oral advocacy on the pressure points and that means that you can be more reactive in the oral advocacy. (Mr Justice Sales)

What you're doing is taking the whole thing as read but saying the real key point is paragraph 15, this is why it matters, these are the cases that support it and then you go to the authorities and read them the passages and wrap it all up, so you just dwell on one or two key points under each section of the argument. Actually, you don't parrot each point as you go through, you just home in on what you think is the winning point under each heading. (Senior counsel)

However, the printed Case lacks a crucial element which is present in oral advocacy, namely flexibility. Almost invariably a case will develop in an unexpected direction whether due to the line of questioning which emanates from the panel or the answers provided by counsel. When writing the Case counsel can never cater for all the possible avenues along which the oral hearing may progress. As David Pannick QC put it,

I don't think you can anticipate all the avenues not least because no case ever proceeds in a way that you can predict … it always goes off on byways that are unexpected. It may end up at a conclusion that you realised was very likely but it always travels along a route that is unexpected and that is inevitable. But the drafting of the written Case does require particular skills,[158] because although it is longer than it ever was, it is still necessary to seek to be concise in the analysis of each particular point. Further, it is necessary to try to identify your arguments to anticipate as best you are able the arguments against you which is much more difficult if you are the Appellant than if you are the respondent. If you are the Respondent you know what the printed arguments are against you and

---

[158] Including, not overstating the case. As Lord Walker observed in *Davies v Commissioner of HM Revenue & Customs* [2012] UKSC 47, para 65: 'The stronger appeal is that of Mr Davies and Mr James, but it is by no means as strong as is claimed by the exaggerated opening of their printed case'.

then you've got to deal with the arguments in the Court of Appeal below which are not necessarily the same arguments as your opponent is going to run, and that's difficult. There may also be cases that you're aware of that haven't been cited in the court below which either help you or hinder you and you've got to deal with those as well.

DOES ADVOCACY MATTER IN THE FINAL COURT?

If the nature of the dialogue between judges in the final court and counsel has changed in the last 40 years and with it the qualities required of a good advocate, what impact, if any, have these developments had on the efficacy of advocacy in the Court? Clearly advocacy can have an impact in a range of ways. As will be seen from the first four parts of this chapter It may affect (1) the speed and efficacy of the decision-making process in the court, (2) the stress and enjoyment experienced by the decision-makers, (3) the cost of the decision-making process , and (4) the decision-makers' trust in and the reputation of, counsel. Whilst these are matters of some consequence, from the perspective of the client the most significant issue is whether advocacy makes a difference to (5) the outcome of the case, or at the very least to (6) the quality of reasoning and therefore the appropriate development of the law.

Slightly to my surprise a number of the counsel whom I interviewed this time round were sceptical as to how often in the final court advocacy had a determinative effect on the eventual outcome of appeals. David Perry QC when asked if advocacy made a difference in the Lords replied,

> That's a very good question because in the vast majority of cases I think the answer to that is probably, No. I'd be very surprised if five Law Lords or sometimes seven or sometimes nine didn't, when they go away and analyse all the materials come to their own conclusions and see that if they had been beguiled by what an advocate had said, if they didn't recognise that fact.

Michael Beloff QC was more optimistic,

> Yes, advocacy does matter; after all the very questions put (and discussion between the Law Lords) shows that they frequently start off with a completely open mind (in sense of being undecided) and we would all give up if we thought we were merely there to make up numbers. Who would pay us if that were so? The reason why the route of ECJ and USASC has not been taken is because the Judges here believe in the value of oral advocacy.

Mr Justice Sales:

> Yes. It's one of these difficult questions as to when advocacy matters anywhere in courts and it's always a little bit difficult to generalise but I think that it does matter in the Lords. Often in the Lords you are getting cases which are difficult, there isn't an obvious answer, that's how they tend to get up that far and so that's a factor which points in favour of advocacy making more of a difference. On the other hand you've got very strong-minded, very clever [judges] who are likely to have some quite strong views themselves,

so that pulls in the other direction. So where does that balance out? I'd say perhaps in about 30 per cent of cases it makes a significant difference, very roughly.

Another experienced counsel drew a distinction between oral and written advocacy,

Not to the outcome, No … Having seen the Supreme Courts of other countries and seen the ECJ and the European Court of Human Rights as well, where in all of those jurisdictions the system is much more based on paper anyway but given the calibre and the intellect of the judges that we're talking about I'd be surprised if they're likely to be swayed all that much by the oral hearing; because they're not likely to hear much that they haven't already read about and thought about to some extent at least.

However, he did think that the printed Case could make a difference,

Yes, absolutely, I think written advocacy certainly does, so the quality of the printed Cases is undoubtedly important … I think that's your most important opportunity in effect to set out what you think the Law Lords' judgments in due course should look like.

Perhaps the most telling answer came from Jonathan Sumption QC (as he then was),

I think that advocacy matters much more in perceiving what are likely to be regarded as the meritorious points, what is likely to be regarded as the direction the Lords will want to move in than in actually the analysis of case law or statutes … I don't think it ever makes the difference between success and failure but I think it makes a difference to the reasoning of a decision, which can be in the public interest … I have found myself quite often reformulating the way that the issue is argued, not fundamentally, it's not jettisoning the grounds below, but trying to suggest a completely different approach to the problem. I think that's part of the function of counsel and I think it's an exercise which can make a considerable difference to the quality of the reasoning. Most judges start from the answer and work backwards. The House of Lords do that even more often than other courts. I think that it is quite unusual to shift the majority of the House from an opinion that they have initially formed. It happens but it's not that common, what you can shift is the reasoning.

These relatively modest assessments by counsel of what advocacy can achieve in the final court might, if they were the whole story, make clients wonder why they pay out sometimes in excess of £20,000 a day for the QC of their choice. True, if resources are not an issue, people going into a litigation with a lot at stake will always opt for the most formidable counsel they can get, almost as an insurance policy to get the benefit of any marginal edge that the best advocates can bring. Nonetheless it is an expensive insurance policy. Fortunately, the Law Lords and Justices were in general rather more positive as to the impact of good advocacy. All of them told me that they had changed their mind during the oral argument, and not that infrequently, in some cases.[159] This was true 40 years ago and remains true today. Thus Lord Dyson assured me,

---

[159] One Justice commented, 'we recently had an absolute feast of advocacy in the *JFS* case, [2009] UKSC 15 and I have no hesitation in saying that my mind was changed more than once in the course of the hearing by absolutely superb advocacy'.

Quite often ... I spend a lot of time reading the written Cases beforehand, and reach a provisional view, and quite often in the course of the argument my view changes ... it can swing backwards and forwards and at the end will have been influenced by the oral argument.

Another Law Lord stressed the importance of the oral argument for bringing about changes of mind,

It can be [due to] points made by counsel. There have been some very good replies one can think of, or indeed responses, but very often it's because the case is one where there are differing competing values and thinking about the case you gradually convince yourself that this is a case where contrary to your previous impression, the other value is the dominant one ... I think a lot of the course of an oral hearing is spent thinking your own thoughts, stimulated by the oral argument you're hearing ... and trying to digest it and to relate it to the overall picture. That's why I think the oral argument adds so much to the impressions one has got from reading the Cases.

Even in the US Supreme Court where oral advocacy has been reduced to 30 minutes a side, it is thought that 'the best attorneys can still capture a swing vote in a close case and carry the day'.[160] This was confirmed recently by Chief Justice Roberts[161] and Justice Stephen Breyer of the US Supreme Court,[162]

If you say how often, when I hear the oral argument, do I think differently about the case? ... Thirty per cent could be in the ballpark. If you say how often do I come in thinking this side wins, now I think the other side wins?, I'd say it's a much smaller number. But 5 per cent maybe, 10 per cent, somewhere in there. I do change my mind.

A UK Justice voiced a similar view to me,

The ability to marshal arguments in a persuasive way ... and the presentation of the case in a way that illustrates your mastery of it can make an enormous difference to the way in which we receive arguments. Now ultimately whether it will make a pivotal difference to the outcome of the case, that's a different question.

Lord Clarke in our interview, agreed,

Oh I think it does, it definitely does. Whether it really makes any difference to the ultimate result or not I think we'd like to say the answer to that is no, but I can't help thinking it probably does.

---

[160] The quote comes from a former clerk in the Supreme Court, Edward Lazarus, *Closed Chambers* (New York, Penguin Books, 1999) at 35. Further support for the continued importance of oral advocacy in the US Supreme Court can be found in the C-SPAN interviews with the Justices contained in B Lamb, S Swain and M Farkas (eds), *The Supreme Court* (New York, Public Affairs, 2010).

[161] See his C-SPAN interview published in Brian Lamb, Susan Swain and Mark Farkas (eds), *The Supreme Court* (New York, Public Affairs, 2010) at 21–22.

[162] Ibid, 132. Although Justices Scalia and Alito in their C-SPAN interviews indicated that it was not common for them to change their minds, particularly as to the outcome, as a result of the oral argument, ibid, 61 and 158.

Lord Dyson was less sure,

> All I can say is that a good advocate can make a difference, does make a difference sometimes ... Certainly as far as the reasoning is concerned, it is very important. I don't think one should under-estimate the importance of the reasoning, because it obviously influences the development of the law. However, as regards outcome I would like to think that it would only be in a very rare case that an advocate has actually lost a case here through bad advocacy.

On the other hand, Lord Wilson shrewdly observed that there is a difference between written and oral advocacy. As to the former he considered that

> the standard of the written argument in Case and skeleton is now exceedingly high, and those definitely do win and lose cases which might have gone the other way, in the case of more capable or less capable hands, as the case may be,[163]

but as to oral advocacy he noted that because it depended in part on performance on a particular day as opposed to days of constant refining, it could disappoint in comparison with the written Case.

In part it depends on the extent to which Justices retain a relatively open mind after reading the printed materials in the case.[164] Some, like Lord Diplock in the House of Lords or Justice Clarence Thomas of the US Supreme Court, make up their minds largely on the written materials and get relatively little from the oral arguments. Others, like Lord Hutton,[165] Lord Rodger or Lord Hope tried not to reach any firm conclusions before hearing the oral argument. As the last observed,[166]

> I try not to form preconceived views and I don't actually usually do so. I tend to keep an open mind before I go into a hearing ... I find advocacy, good advocacy from some of the people we see immensely helpful and it helps you to think into a case. If you are writing a judgment it's much easier to write it after you've heard the oral argument than it could possibly be if you've just read about it ... The oral presentation can alter your view quite dramatically as the hearing goes on ... [it also] helps you both to probe more deeply into what the case is really about and to begin to test the argument with the contributions from people on either side of you.

Lord Neuberger similarly observed,[167]

> I think pre-reading and keeping your mind open are not mutually exclusive. On the contrary, you often find having had a quick look that the answer you think is very clear , when you read the submissions in the written Case of the party you think is wrong, you begin to see that there is more in it than you thought.

---

[163] Interview with the author, May 2012.

[164] Lord Lloyd told me, 'The great merit of the old system where you knew very little about the case till you heard the oral argument was that you could change your mind any number of times as the thing went on'. Interview with the author, January 2009.

[165] 'I think probably it's a mistake to form too definite a view before the hearing'.

[166] Interview with the author, October 2008.

[167] Interview with the author, February 2013.

Lord Bingham was characteristically balanced and concise as to whether advocacy matters, 'In some cases certainly, but not all', before going on to observe of oral advocacy,

> Sometimes undoubtedly. There are some cases where I think the truth is that by the time everybody has read two judgments below and two quite lengthy Cases they've formed a view one way or the other and they don't change it. But, I think there are quite a lot of cases in which people read one Case and they think that's very persuasive and then they read the other and they think that's very persuasive and so they do genuinely go into court with open minds looking to counsel to try and get an answer. Not only does it vary, as you would expect, from case to case but it varies from individual to individual because I think some people reach much firmer opinions early on than others do.

Case Studies in Effective Advocacy

Both counsel and the judges pointed to a wide range of cases in which the exercise of appellate advocacy skills by counsel had influenced the outcome or the reasoning within appeals.[168] From the 1970s came the *Johanna Oldendorff*,[169] one of the earliest exercises of the 1966 Practice Statement freedom to depart from an earlier precedent of the House. The respondents were sure that they would win but Robert MacCrindle QC persuaded the House 5:0 to reverse a longstanding decision of the House. Equally, Kemp Davidson QC achieved a major success in *McGhee v National Coal Board*,[170] such that for 'many years there was a feeling that Kemp had won too well—that he had pulled the wool over their Lordships' eyes', until the result was vindicated in *Fairchild v Glenhaven Funeral Services*.[171]

Gordon Pollock QC scored a range of unlikely victories in the Lords. Most famous was probably the *Lonhro plc*[172] case, where he persuaded a resistant panel of five Law Lords in a contempt of court hearing to recuse themselves after a day and a half of trench warfare. Equally notable was when he turned Lord Diplock for what was perhaps the one and only time in the Lords, in a shipping case where the ship's master had the odd habit of preferring to navigate from charts that were at least 10 to 15 years old, leading to damage to an oil pipeline costing US$25,000,000 to repair.[173]

---

[168] Including the occasions when counsel sees the structure of their argument—and sometimes part of its content—re-appear in the Law Lords' judgments. See *The Law Lords*, above, n 2, at 63.

[169] *The Johanna Oldendorff; EL Oldendorff & Co GmbH v Tradax Export SA* [1973] 3 All ER 148.

[170] *McGhee v National Coal Board* 1973 SC (HL) 37.

[171] *Fairchild v Glenhaven Funeral Services Ltd* [2002] UKHL 22.

[172] *Re Lonrho Plc (Contempt Proceedings)* [1990] 2 AC 154. Pollock also prevailed in a 3:2 appeal, *Alfred McAlpine Construction Ltd v Panatown Ltd* [2001] 1 AC 518, despite severe hostility at one stage from Lord Goff.

[173] *Grand Champion Tankers Ltd v Norpipe A/S (The Marion)* [1984] AC 563.

The Pinochet litigation also threw up a notable piece of advocacy. One reason why *Pinochet (No 3)*[174] produced a much narrower ruling against General Pinochet than *Pinochet (No 1)*[175] was the fact that the senior counsel who had led in *Pinochet (No 1)* was unavailable for some of *Pinochet (No 3)* and in his absence Clare Montgomery QC ran an argument which her leader had not run in *Pinochet (No 1)*. It was that argument that prevailed in the later case. As Jonathan Sumption QC told me,

> I regard that as a good example of a case in which advocacy made a considerable differ-
> ence, not to the initial starting point of the tribunal, nor to the tribunal's propensity to
> carry a starting point through to the finish, but to the particular reasoning, which can
> have a very considerable effect in the particular case as well as on the developments of
> law. That's a striking example of something that in my experience happens really quite
> frequently and the Lords are in the business of formulating general rules for long-term
> application and very often their initial instincts about which way the case should go are
> very sensitive to the particular circumstances of the case. You offer them a way of doing
> what they want to do in the particular case which produces a more acceptable result in
> the long term and you've probably got the wind behind you.

Sumption himself is thought to have won over a majority in the final court on a number of occasions. One of these was in the second *Shayler*[176] case where he per-suaded the House contrary to its initial stance that injunctions, once broken must be contempt of court otherwise it would lead to complete chaos in circumstances where the Law Lords took a different view of the merits. Not to be outdone, David Pannick QC is believed to have won one appeal in the last few years in his reply alone and to have assisted Lord Hoffmann in the remarkable turn-around in the *Prolife* case[177] (whether the BBC could censor the party election broadcast of the Prolife Alliance party). Counsel in my interviews were generally sceptical that appeals could be won on reply, but the judges were less so and in addition to Pannick's success, counsel for the appellant is understood to have won the much debated *Doherty*[178] case with an argument raised in reply.

Other recent cases are thought to have been influenced by advocacy[179] but the most spectacular of these was undoubtedly the *Chagos Islands* case.[180] This was an appeal where the Government's position was morally indefensible. Between

---

[174] *R v Bow Street Metropolitan Stipendiary Magistrate, ex parte Pinochet Ugarte (No 3)* [2000] 1 AC 147.

[175] *R v Bow Street Metropolitan Stipendiary Magistrate, ex parte Pinochet Ugarte (No 1)* [2000] 1 AC 61.

[176] *Attorney General v Punch Ltd and Another* [2002] UKHL 50.

[177] *R v British Broadcasting Corporation, ex parte Prolife Alliance* [2003] UKHL 23. After several switches of mind during the hearing the original divide at the end of oral arguments was 4:1 to Prolife. It is believed that Lord Hoffmann won round a majority to his persuasion since the final result was 4:1 to the BBC.

[178] *Doherty and Others v Birmingham City Council* [2008] UKHL 57.

[179] Eg *R (on the application of Mullen) v Secretary of State for the Home Department* [2004] UKHL 18, Belmarsh (*A and others v Secretary of State for the Home Department* [2004] UKHL 56), *Huang v Secretary of State for the Home Department, Kashmiri v Secretary of State for the Home Department* [2007] UKHL 11 and *R v Governing Body of the Jewish Free School* [2009] UKSC 15.

[180] *Bancoult v Secretary of State for Foreign and Commonwealth Affairs* [2008] UKHL 61.

1965 and 1973 the British Government had ruthlessly (and deceitfully) expelled the indigenous inhabitants from the Chagos Islands to secure the principal island, Diego Garcia, as a military base for the United States of America. Under challenge, the Foreign Secretary announced in 2000 that the islanders would be permitted to return home to the Islands, except Diego Garcia. However, the Government secretly reversed its policy in 2004, covertly passing orders removing the islanders' right of abode in the Islands. The validity of the orders was challenged by Bancoult, who was successful before the Divisional Court and the Court of Appeal. The Secretary of State brought in new senior counsel and squeaked home in the Lords by a 3:2 margin, to the astonishment of many observers. The key was the advocacy adopted in the printed Case, where Jonathan Crow QC conceded all of the Government's bad behaviour in earlier times but, by re-defining the merits, successfully argued that the refusal to permit the re-settlement of islanders in 2004, whilst unpopular, was a rational policy for the Government to adopt.

Factors Which Make a Difference

Even if advocacy does make a difference, what determines in which cases it is more likely to do so? There have been a number of empirical studies in various jurisdictions which have sought to look at this. None has aspired to the level of a double-blind trial on the lines of those used in medical research, in part because whatever the difficulties of using a 'mystery shopper' methodology to assess the quality of legal advice,[181] these are multiplied several fold when applied to courts and tribunals,[182] far less the final court of appeal. Typically the research has looked at the experience of the advocates (as a proxy for expertise) or at the impact of party status, eg what is the Government's win-loss record as compared with other litigants. As for experience, there is research in the US and the UK which argues that more experienced advocates do better than less experienced ones, in the final court of appeal.[183] However, given that experience is not the same as expertise and that not every counsel who appears regularly before the final court of appeal in the

---

[181] See A Paterson and A Sherr, 'Quality Legal Services: the Dog that did not bark' ch 10 in F Regan et al (eds), *The Transformation of Legal Aid* (Oxford, Oxford University Press, 1999); R Moorhead et al, *Quality and Cost* (London, HMSO, 2001).

[182] Nonetheless, in a startling break-through Hazel Genn and Cheryl Thomas have persuaded 230 industrial tribunals throughout the UK to consider the same standardised case as part of their research into tribunal decision-making. See H Genn and C Thomas, 'Tribunal Decision-Making: An Empirical Study': www.nuffieldfoundation.org/tribunal-decision-making.

[183] S Haynie and K Sill, 'Experienced Advocates and Litigation Outcomes: Repeat Players in the South African Supreme Court of Appeal' (2007) 60 *Political Research Quarterly* 443; J Szmer, S Johnson and T Sarwer, 'Does the lawyer matter? Influencing outcomes on the Supreme Court of Canada?' (2007) 41 *Law and Society Review* 279; A McAtee and K McGuire, 'Lawyers, Justices and Issue Salience: When and How do Legal Arguments Affect the US Supreme Court?' (2007) 41 *Law and Society Review* 259; C Hanretty, 'Haves and Have-Nots before the Law Lords' Working Paper, published 30 November 2011, available at: chrishanretty.co.uk/blog/wp-content/uploads/2011/11/article.pdf.

UK is perceived by the Law Lords and Justices as equally effective, it seems likely that experience is only one operative factor. Thus other researchers have suggested that (1) the quality of counsel's arguments as assessed by one or more Justices,[184] (2) counsel's win/loss record in past cases before the court[185] or (3) whether the case involves issues which are new to the Justices[186] can be better predictors of success in the final court, than mere experience in the court. Whilst these represent an improvement on looking at experience alone, they remain inexact proxies for expertise. For example, the 27 judges of the final court of appeal in the UK that I have interviewed over the past six years evinced a fair degree of consensus as to who were the best advocates to appear before them, with Jonathan Sumption and David Pannick repeatedly mentioned as being at the top of the tree. However, this does not mean that their win/loss record in the final court was significantly better than a range of others—in part because well-resourced corporate clients with challenging if not hopeless cases are likely to try to give themselves an edge by instructing the 'best' counsel in order to improve their chances of an acceptable outcome.[187] Further, type of case or party status (eg being instructed by the Crown or central government in criminal or immigration appeals) can distort success rates.[188]

Evidence that party status can have relevance to outcomes in the final court comes from Hanretty's recent study of House of Lords cases.[189] Thus he found that the Government was considerably more likely to win in the Lords than its opponent (65 per cent of the time), between 1969 and 2003. This, however, may have been due to a number of factors, eg the Government relying on better counsel—Treasury juniors—or the type of case, eg appeals in criminal or tax cases (where the Crown or the Government is usually the respondent and usually wins). Whatever the case, Hanretty's findings seem not to hold true for the later

---

[184] T Johnson, Paul Wahlbeck and James Spriggs, 'The Influence of Oral Arguments on the US Supreme Court' (2006) 100 *The American Political Science Review* 99 examined cases where counsel's arguments had been assessed by Justice Blackmun in his contemporary notes. Counsel rated with the better arguments by the Justice, were more likely to win their case.

[185] Stacia Haynie and Kaitlyn Sill, 'Experienced Advocates and Litigation Outcomes' (2007) 60 *Political Research Quarterly* 443 found that advocates before the South African Supreme Court with better win/loss records than their opponents did better than those who were merely more experienced in appearing before the court.

[186] Andrea McAtee and Kevin McGuire, 'Lawyers, Justices and Issue Salience: When and How do Legal Arguments Affect the US Supreme Court?' (2007) 41 *Law and Society Review* 259. One UK Justice told me that he was more likely to be shifted off his initial take on a case by advocacy if the case related to a subject area with which he was unfamiliar.

[187] Between 2000 and 2012 Lord Pannick QC appeared in around 33 full hearings, winning about half. Jonathan Sumption QC in the same period had around half as many appearances but won more than three quarters of them. The difference is down to them being instructed often in different types of case.

[188] One of the best win/loss record in modern times before the final court is that of David Perry QC, who has been the counsel of choice of the Crown in their cases for more than a decade. Between 2000 and 2012 he appeared in 33 cases in the final court and was successful in 21 of these.

[189] C Hanretty, 'Haves and Have-Nots before the Law Lords' Working Paper, published 30 November 2011, available at chrishanretty.co.uk/blog/wp-content/uploads/2011/11/article.pdf.

part of Bingham's era in the House of Lords or for the Supreme Court era. In the 207 cases disposed of in the Supreme Court between September 2009 and March 2013, central government bodies won 47 cases out of a total of 87 cases in which they were involved, thereby winning only marginally more than they lost, although the Crown Prosecution Service and HM Revenue & Customs lost only a handful of cases between them. This suggests that in criminal and tax matters, the advantage continues to lie with the Government. Indeed this is also true in human rights cases where the Government won 15 and lost nine cases, which will doubtless come as a surprise to the Home Office. However, in public law cases the Government has been encountering a losing streak, having won only 11 and lost 17 in the Supreme Court.[190]

While the judges in the final court whom I interviewed were generally agreed as to the best counsel to appear before them, they were also of the view that a few of those appearing before them—sometimes on more than two or three occasions, lacked the skills to perform well in the unique atmosphere of the final court of appeal in the UK. This has not changed over time, in part because in the last 40 years the change in caseload for the final appeal court (see Table 2.1 above) has significantly increased the number and variety of counsel who appear before the final appeal court. Thus, while the caseload of the court rose by 11 per cent between 1990–92 and 2009–12, the number of senior counsel appearing before the court in these periods rose from 195 to 273—an increase of 40 per cent. Between 2000 and 2012, 602 QCs appeared on 1,322 occasions in the final court making an average number of appearances of just over two per QC. However, we can gauge how well distributed appearances are and how difficult it is to build up a degree of experience before the final court from the fact that of the 602 QCs to appear in this period, only 17 had appeared on 10 or more occasions as QC in the final court. Curiously, there has been a minor concentration effect amongst these frequent attendees. Thus, whilst 96 per cent of senior counsel appearing before the court in 1990–92 did so on three or fewer occasions, in the first three years of the Supreme Court the comparative figure was 88 per cent of senior counsel had done so on three or fewer occasions. In other words, only four per cent of senior counsel appearing before the court in 1990–92 did so on four or more occasions, but three times as many—12 per cent of senior counsel appearing before the Supreme Court in its first three years did so on four or more occasions.[191] Indeed the 17 QCs to appear most often in the final court between 2000 and 2012 had an average of 16 appearances each. Most of these counsel are likely to command the respect and trust of the Court and to have the opportunity of particularly

---

[190] In a total of 87 appearances over 207 cases heard between September 2009 and March 2013, the Crown or central Government departments acted as respondent 60 times out of 87 (69%). For further details on the success rate of Government in the final court see chapter 7 of this volume below.

[191] The significance of the concentration effect is that in terms of shared understandings between counsel and the Court, if the group having the dialogue is broader and the shared understandings are weaker then the constraining effect of counsel's arguments based on such shared understanding should be less powerful than in the past.

influencing it. The dialogue between the Court and them has the potential to be particularly significant.

The concentration effect in counsel appearing before the US Supreme Court, however, has been far more marked. There, Rehnquist CJ asserted in 1986 that there was almost no expert Supreme Court Bar and certainly if we exclude the distorting effect of the Solicitor General (who appeared in cases involving the Government) the facts seem to bear this out. Thus, attorneys who had argued five or more cases before the Court were responsible for only 5.7 per cent of the successful petitions for leave to appeal (certiorari) to the Court in 1980. However, market forces were soon to alter this. By October Term 2000 the figure had jumped to 25 per cent and in October term 2008 the experienced Bar was responsible for 56 per cent of successful certiorari petitions.[192]

Interesting though the empirical research from other jurisdictions may be, there are reasons to be wary of drawing conclusions from them which might apply in the UK. There are many contextual differences. Not only is the caseload different between the courts, but so too is control of the docket, the length of oral arguments and the role of the court. Nonetheless, in pointing as the research does to (1) the calibre and characteristics of those engaged in the debate, (2) the context and characteristics of the debates, and (3) the nature of the cases being argued—including their intrinsic merits, as factors likely to impact on the efficacy of advocacy and of the dialogue with the final court, the research is surely on the right lines.[193]

The Primary Opponents

The first factor is the calibre of the debaters. As illustrated above, counsel with excellent appellate advocacy skills are perceived by the judges in the final court as having an impact on the quality of decision-making in the final court and sometimes on the outcome of the appeal. Equally important are the characteristics of the primary opponents in these debates—who are, of course, the Law Lords. As Lord Kilbrandon told me in the original interviews:[194] 'if you really want to know ... the debate is really much more between counsel and the Bench than it is between opposing counsel'. Indeed, one of my original counsel described the dialogue between Bar and Bench as 'like a football game: you only play as well as the opponents let you—and by opponents I mean the tribunal'.[195] The quality of their intellect can be taken for granted although some have been exceptionally fleet of thought in the oral arguments, eg Reid, Diplock, Bingham and Hoffmann

---

[192] Richard J Lazarus, 'Advocacy Matters Before and Within the Supreme Court' (2008) 96 *Georgetown Law Journal* 1487 and RJ Lazarus, 'The Power of Persuasion Before and Within the Supreme Court' [2012] *University of Illinois Law Review* 231, 250.

[193] Although they will be analysed independently, in reality, like oral and written advocacy, the three factors interact with each other.

[194] *The Law Lords*, above, n 2, at 50.

[195] *The Law Lords*, above, n 2, at 51.

as compared with some of their colleagues. When in the chair they were able to give a lead to their colleagues[196] and a steer to counsel which tended to have a significant effect on the course and length of the dialogue. Some presiders over the years, however, have been more silent or less directive, eg Lords Wilberforce, Radcliffe, Fraser, Keith, Nicholls and Phillips, leaving counsel more influence on the direction of the dialogue. In truth, UK counsel find silence from the bench particularly disconcerting whether it is the House of Lords,[197] or the Supreme Court, eg Lord Walker,[198] or in the Strasbourg or Luxembourg Courts, since they are unable to gauge what is troubling the bench and consequently whether to alter course or not. The opposite challenge is little more palatable. As we have seen the combativeness of certain Law Lords over the years, eg Lords Diplock, Brandon, Bridge and Templeman required a degree of robustness in counsel if the latter was to contribute effectively to the nature, duration and outcome of the dialogue.

The open-mindedness of the judges in the final court also impacts on the efficacy of the oral arguments. Although David Robertson[199] endeavoured valiantly to explain decisions in the Lords from the ideological preferences of the Law Lords taking part, most commentators on the final court today have not found that a fruitful line of analysis to pursue. The easy identification of the swing voters on the US Supreme Court over the years because of their centrist ideological position, eg Justices Powell, O'Connor and Kennedy, has no crossover to the final court of the UK.[200] Moreover, even where the judges are not silent it is not always easy even for experienced observers to tell from which direction their interventions are coming. Some make their positions pretty transparent in their interventions,[201] eg Lords Hoffmann, Steyn, Hobhouse and Carswell. Others, eg Lord Rodger, were thought occasionally to adopt the role of the devil's advocate.

Hot benches not only influence both the length and content of the dialogue, as we have seen, they may also impact on the open-mindedness of the bench, as Lord Bingham noted earlier. Similarly, one senior counsel noted,

> Whether or not oral advocacy can change somebody's mind if it's already been made up, I think, probably depends upon the individual. Some Law Lords come into the

---

[196] In *The Law Lords*, above, n 2 (ch 4) I established that the Law Lords use their powers of intervention in the dialogue for the purposes of curtailment and focus, testing counsel's and their own propositions, clarification and to persuade their colleagues. These were still the primary purposes of Law Lords' interventions in 2009.

[197] *The Law Lords*, above, n 2, at 70ff.

[198] Lord Walker, whilst a much less regular intervener than most of his colleagues, was positively garrulous when compared with Justice Thomas on the US Supreme Court, who has not asked a question during the oral hearings in that Court since 22 February 2006. (He did make a joke about Yale Law School in a hearing on 7 January 2013, but this was not framed as a question).

[199] D Robertson, *Judicial Discretion in the House of Lords* (Oxford, Clarendon Press, 1998).

[200] That is not to say that watchers of the House could not over the years predict with some considerable accuracy the likely position that would be taken by some Law Lords in certain types of case before the oral argument had begun.

[201] As one experienced counsel put it, 'I'd like to play poker against some of them more than I would against others because some of them simply don't have poker faces, they let you know exactly what they are thinking'.

hearing knowing what they think the answer is and they cannot be shaken. I think they've all read in advance and some of them are more sure of their own judgements than others.

In fact, Lord Diplock's reluctance to shift from his initial position gained from doing his homework thoroughly, affected his tolerance as presiding Law Lord to hear arguments and material which he felt was covered in the written material. Lord Bingham favoured greater open-mindedness at the start of hearings and he was not alone. As one of today's leading counsel commented,

> You don't suddenly stand up in court with an adverse tribunal and persuade them round … when people ask the question 'does oral advocacy matter in the Lords?', what they have in mind is a relatively … harsh concept of an adverse tribunal whom you then persuade. I think that that is probably not a situation that arises very often, partly because I don't think a majority come into court with their minds made up and partly because if you are in one of the rare situations where five or at least three have made their minds up I think it's very rare that one could actually persuade them to change their minds. I think that what happens in oral advocacy and why it does matter is that you come into a tribunal where maybe one is firmly of one view, maybe another is firmly of a different view and you've got three swing votes and they haven't made their minds up, and you then do try and talk them through.

Similarly Lord Hope told me,

> I tend to keep an open mind before I go into a hearing and you sometimes say casually to yourself well this looks a fairly straightforward case one way or the other but by the time you get into the oral argument it may not seem nearly as straightforward as you thought it was.

The Calibre of the Secondary Opposition

The calibre of opposing counsel and the quality of their arguments inevitably has some impact on the development of the dialogue between Bench and Bar and on efficacy of the advocacy of the initial counsel. This is true whether the opponent's advocacy is good or bad. The good opponent presents a constant threat to the success of one's advocacy. As one counsel put it: 'There are some barristers that one is concerned about who can turn any case round, others that you're less concerned about. So even with a strong case if I was going against [one of the greats] I'd be nervous'. However, even being a brilliant counsel is not enough. As another experienced counsel recalled,

> I was involved in a case against a senior counsel and I sat there for a day listening to a brilliant tutorial given by him with hardly any interruptions from the committee. This was on topic one. Then he came to deal with topic two; not his field. I could tell that the appeal was slipping away on topic one, because when your opponent starts quoting classic works of economic philosophy off the top of his head, and the Committee sit there absorbing it all, you know that all is lost. But when it came to topic two, it was quite interesting. There were some interventions, but then there came a point when

the interventions stopped, as if to signal that the argument was not going anywhere. Sure enough, his arguments on topic one were accepted, and his arguments on topic two rejected.

What happens if the opponent is a weak advocate or has an off day? Can bad advocacy lose a case that should be won? Some judges and counsel considered that it could. Rabinder Singh QC considered that an appeal could be lost in the printed Case and others similarly noted that a bad printed Case could lose a case or at least ensure that counsel was starting several steps behind when they come to the hearing. Often the judges will make up for any deficiencies in the argument put by counsel, but judges are human too and confronted with an incoherent, convoluted and obscurely expressed Case, may not strive as hard as they might to find the killer point in dense materials, especially if there are attractively packaged points put up by the good advocate on the other side. However, one counsel commented,

> I think it's easier to lose a case at the oral hearing because that's when they test the propositions and if the arguments don't stand up to scrutiny in the forum of debate, as the House of Lords is, then that's when it becomes clear that the argument is a bad one … The printed Case may have been expressed in such an obscure way that they're not really sure about whether your argument is a good one or a bad one, but that becomes clear at the hearing.

Counsel do not improve their prospects by being rude to the Law Lords or ignoring Bingham's golden rule of advocacy by failing to answer the judges' questions, as happened in one major appeal in the last seven years. Such advocacy loses the trust (and the ear) of the tribunal. As Gordon Pollock QC told me,

> [T]ake Donald Nicholls, he disliked counsel who didn't answer his questions properly and whenever you appeared in front of him you had to be very, very careful if he asked you a question that you answered it … and you didn't try and give him an answer that skated round the problem. You either met it head on or basically in my view he shut off and he didn't take you seriously from then on … [H]e focused on usually the one point that might sink you … If he thought you were treating him properly on a proper intellectual basis then he would go along with you. If he thought that you were just flim-flamming, away it went … Lord Oliver was exactly the same.

Another experienced counsel reiterated the dangers of failing to engage in the dialogue with the judges,

> [I]f they ask you a question you should really treat it as both evidence to indicate what they're thinking but also an opportunity to try to respond to that way of thinking or to show how your conceptual framework can accommodate whatever concern [they were raising]. So I always attached huge importance to answering the questions directly as soon as they were asked. I always thought that it was bad news to say 'I'll come back to that later' unless your answer involved some major argumentation and then a conclusion and you didn't want to go at it half baked. In which case you'd have to say 'my submission will be this, there's going to be some argument and I'll come to that in due course and I won't forget'. For the most part I thought you were best advised to try and

answer straight away and to treat your answer as not just … well it would depend on your judgement. Sometimes it would be 'Yes or No' but usually to treat your answer as an opportunity to, if you like, put your conceptual picture of the case … turn it in the direction of that Law Lord and then take a minute or two to give a little bit of hinterland to your answer to the question, to explain why your answer fitted particularly well with other legal concepts so that they were getting a bit of a sketch picture of how the case looked like if you looked at it from that perspective.

Equally, if counsel's arguments lack conviction this may undermine their efficacy in the dialogue. Whilst counsel are divided as to whether it is necessary to believe in the arguments that they put before the Lords, some were of the opinion that if you could not convince yourself as to the merits of your arguments your voice and body language would be unlikely to convince the House.

Other Factors

The second factor to influence the quality of the dialogue and counsel's role in it lies in the context and characteristics of the debates themselves. The physical geography of the courtroom, counsel's proximity to the bench, the conversational style encouraged by today's judges,[202] the shift to shorter oral and more written advocacy all contribute to an atmosphere which has an impact on the successful use of the technical skills of advocacy.

The third, and by no means the least factor which affects the success of advocacy skills is the intrinsic merits of the appeal itself. Taking first the moral merits, the majority of counsel and Law Lords/Justices today believe that even at the level of the final appeal court, the perceived equities of an appeal are relevant and may significantly influence its outcome. Lord Bingham told me, 'I think they matter enormously. [If] it seems grossly unfair that a certain result is achieved, people are going to be much more receptive to any alternative solution'. A number of examples were cited in which an advocate's skill in boosting the justness of his side of the case had paid dividends.[203] Even more important for the outcome of the case is the perceived legal merits of the respective sides. In a significant proportion of the appeals the balance of the respective legal arguments is such that even good advocacy is unlikely to secure a result and bad advocacy will be rectified by the Law Lords.

More often the three factors will combine to influence the efficacy of counsel's arguments. In assessing the factors one counsel told me,

One would be the basic strength of your case … partly, again, it would be a function of your opposition and thirdly the Law Lords have track records. You get a sense of their general disposition towards particular sorts of argument and if you put those three together I'd say … [advocacy makes a difference in] something like 50 or 60 per cent of the time.

---

[202] The absence of a fixed lectern in the new Supreme Court courtrooms is understood to stem from a desire to enhance the 'conversational' atmosphere in hearings there.
[203] Eg *EB (Kosovo) v Secretary of State for the Home Department* [2008] UKHL 41 and *Société Générale London Branch v Geys* [2012] UKSC 63.

CONCLUSION

We return now to the question of the significance of the dialogues which take place between counsel and judges for understanding judicial decision-making in the final court of appeal in the UK. We have seen how the dialogue has changed over 40 years. Time limits on oral advocacy, a greater emphasis on written advocacy and a weakening of the ability of counsel to impose constraints on decision-making in the Court, have altered the nature of advocacy and the dialogue between Bar and Bench. The dialectic may remain with the tribunal rather than the other side, but the form of the dialectic has changed. Nonetheless we have seen that counsel's advocacy continues to matter before the final appeal court, though tempered by other factors including the calibre of the opponents and the merits of the case. However, there is another issue. Focusing on the efficacy of counsel's advocacy overemphasises the perspective of counsel and underplays the perspective of the judges in the final appeal court. If counsel is concerned to achieve an acceptable outcome for his/her client, the judges in the final appeal court wish to reach an appropriate outcome to the case—something which may be quite different. Taken in this light, counsel who is playing for rules may accept that an outcome in the final appeal court which provides a more satisfactory statement of legal principle for the wider interests of his/her client than the status quo, is an outcome not to be undervalued.[204] The judges, on the other hand, are likely to consider the dialogue with counsel to be an effective one if counsel are assisting them in reaching a decision which is the best that can be achieved. From this perspective counsel whose clarity of thought and expression enables the judges to reach a decision with a minimum of mental gymnastics and anxiety has participated in a more effective dialogue with the judges (even when they have lost the appeal) than the counsel who wins his case despite the fog of confusion and obfuscation caused by the poverty of his or her advocacy. This is the process that Jonathan Sumption (as a QC) was adverting to when told me,

> I think that advocacy ... makes a difference to the reasoning of a decision, which can be in the public interest ... I have found myself quite often reformulating the way that the issue is argued, not fundamentally, it's not jettisoning the grounds below, but trying to suggest a completely different approach to the problem. I think that's part of the function of counsel and I think it's an exercise which can make a considerable difference to the quality of the reasoning.

This puts a different slant on assessing the role of advocacy in the dialogue with the judges—it is not just about persuasive advocacy to win the case but whether

---

[204] Examples of cases where the House of Lords produced more acceptable statements of the law for the appellant than pertained in the status quo include, eg *Three Rivers District Council v Bank of England (No 3)* [2003] 2 AC 1 on the scope of legal professional privilege or *Pinochet (No 3) (R v Bow Street Metropolitan Stipendiary Magistrate, ex parte Pinochet Ugarte (No 3)* [2000] 1 AC 147) as compared with *Pinochet (No 1) (R v Bow Street Metropolitan Stipendiary Magistrate, ex parte Pinochet Ugarte (No 1)* [2000] 1 AC 61) in terms of the requirements of International Law.

the input from counsel in the adversarial setting assists in the attainment of the final decision. From this perspective efficacy in the written Case may consist in producing phrases and a structure which are taken up by one or more of the judges. Furthermore, oral advocacy invites greater participation from both sides, by responding to the judges' interventions in ways that clarify counsel's arguments, thus underlining the strengths and weaknesses of those arguments. And by providing a sounding board for the judges' ideas, counsel play an important role in a dialogue in which they are acting as partners in the decision-making process with the Law Lords and Justices.

It should be clear from this chapter that in a variety of ways the dialogue between counsel and the judges in the final court can play a very significant role in determining the outcome or the reasoning in the case. Despite this, students of judicial decision-making have long had to labour under a handicap that does not exist in the US Supreme Court, the European Court of Justice or the Australian High Court, namely, the lack of detailed transcripts of the oral argument in the final court. Tape recordings were not made of oral argument in the House of Lords and although oral arguments before the Supreme Court are broadcast live by Sky television, it is not possible to record the broadcasts and thus impractical to produce extended transcripts of the dialogue. True, the law reporters do produce synopses of the oral argument for inclusion in the official Law Reports but it is rare for the judicial interventions and counsel's answers thereto to appear in these synopses. This has the unfortunate side-effect of perpetuating the notion amongst academic scholars that the real work of the judges in the final court lies in the production of their judgments. This concentration on the end product, to the exclusion of the process by which it was arrived at, is intellectually dangerous and academically unsound.

What of the future? Some have argued[205] that on grounds of cost alone the way forward for the UK Supreme Court should be to impose even greater constraints on the length of oral arguments, as presently exists in the US and Canadian Supreme Courts, the European Court of Justice and the European Court of Human Rights. The loss in input from counsel could, they say, be rectified in part through the greater availability of judicial assistants which now exists in the Supreme Court.[206] However, few of the Law Lords, Justices and counsel that I interviewed this time round favoured such a move, which would have greater consequences for the dialogue between Bench and Bar than is often appreciated

---

[205] See eg, R Gordon, 'The Relationship between the Bar and the House of Lords' in A Le Sueur (ed), *Building the UK's New Supreme Court* (Oxford, Oxford University Press, 2004) ch 14. Lord Bingham raised the possibility unenthusiastically in his lecture on 'A New Supreme Court for the United Kingdom' delivered at The Constitution Unit on 1 May 2002. Penny Darbyshire in her ethnographic tour de force, *Sitting in Judgment* (Oxford, Hart Publishing, 2011) at 380 and 404 argues for changes which would reduce the length of oral advocacy such as time limiting parties at each stage of an appeal and banning recitation.

[206] The number of judicial assistants has doubled from the four that existed in the final year of Lord Bingham.

and with it the quality of decision-making in the final court of appeal. Currently, ideas derived from the debates in the lower courts are developed in the printed Cases, refined during the oral exchanges between counsel and the Justices, tested in the Justices' exchanges with their judicial assistants, distilled in the draft written judgment of one or more of the Justices and polished through the circulation of opinions between the Justices. The dramatic curtailment of oral advocacy in the final court would reduce costs but only at the expense of the efficacy and impact of oral advocacy,[207] and the loss of a nuanced refining process for ideas. Written advocacy and the input of largely inexperienced judicial assistants are unlikely to produce better judgments at the end of the day. Written advocacy lacks the flexibility of its oral counterpart and the Justices' use of judicial assistants as sounding boards is only a partial substitute for the rigorous testing of propositions which occurs in the forensic arena of the final court. The complex of parallel and interactive dialogues which are the hallmarks of current appeals would be replaced by fewer and less fruitful dialogues. This, in turn, might presage the demise of the shared responsibility between Bench and Bar for the development of the law in the final court identified by Wetter.[208] It would also see judicial advocacy in the dialogue between Justices replacing counsel's advocacy in terms of significance in the decision-making process of Supreme Court. It is to that judicial dialogue that we now turn.

---

[207] It is widely recognised that the general quality of oral advocacy in jurisdictions which severely limit the length of oral hearing is lower than that in jurisdictions such as the United Kingdom and Australia where oral advocacy in the final court is relatively untrammelled. See D Terris, C Romano and L Swigart, *The International Judge* (Oxford, Oxford University Press, 2007) at 85. Nevertheless, there is an argument that greater case management by the Supreme Court at the Permissions phase could be used to regulate more precisely the length of hearing that is appropriate for a given appeal— see Darbyshire, above, n 205, 381.

[208] G Wetter, *Styles of Appellate Judicial Decisons* (Leyden, AW Sythoff, 1960) at 72.

3

Dialogues with Colleagues—The Stages for Discourse

INTRODUCTION

I N THE LAST chapter we saw that scholars of the highest courts in the
United Kingdom and United States have tended to neglect the significance of the
dialogue between the judges and counsel for the form and content of the judgments that emerge from these courts. It would seem unlikely that scholars would
make the same mistake in relation to the dialogue between the judges themselves. Yet,
that is precisely what will be argued in the discussion of these dialogues in the next
three chapters, although curiously, media commentators in the US have produced
several revealing works focusing on judicial interactions in the Supreme Court.[1]

In part, the comparative neglect stems from the fact that these inter-judicial
dialogues were and are the most complex and subtle of all the judicial dialogues.
Clearly they are enduring in nature—some Law Lords and now Justices have
known each other since the date of their entry to the Bar. Whilst such links do not
necessarily lead them to think alike on key legal and policy matters, they do make
it easier to drop into each other's rooms to discuss the issues of the day. These dialogues aid decision-making in a myriad of ways—from suggesting lines of travel
to be put to counsel, to testing the possible consequences of one outcome rather
than another. In this chapter we will look at when and where these dialogues take
place during the different stages of the decision-making process.

THE PREPARATORY STAGES

Laying the Groundwork

The earliest and most premeditated dialogues are amongst the least common,
since they relate to the efforts of strategic minded judges who are seeking to

---

[1] E Lazarus, *Closed Chambers: The Rise, Fall and Future of the Modern Supreme Court* (New York,
Penguin Books, 1999); J Rosen, *The Supreme Court: The Personalities and Rivalries that Defined
America* (New York, Times Books, Henry Holt and Company, 2006); A Ward and D Weiden, *Sorcerers'
Apprentices: 100 Years of Law Clerks at the United States Supreme Court* (New York, New York University
Press, 2006); T Peppers, *Courtiers of the Marble Palace* (Stanford CA, Stanford University Press, 2006);
JC Greenburg, *Supreme Conflict* (New York, The Penguin Press, 2007); J Toobin, *The Nine: Inside the
Secret World of the Supreme Court* (New York, Anchor Books, 2008).

get cases brought to the Court at a later juncture. This can either be through dissenting judgments made with an eye to the future (eg Lord Atkin in *Liversidge v Anderson*[2] or Lord Bingham in *Smith v Chief Constable of Sussex*[3]), or who use their existing cases to encourage litigants and counsel to bring them appeals on topics which they want to debate. Amongst the clearest examples of the latter, recently, have been the barely disguised efforts in a range of cases by the Justices to signal their dislike of the wording of the 'neither more nor less' test in *Ullah*[4] to describe the final court's relationship with Strasbourg. These remarks were aimed both at potential litigants and at their colleagues, present and future.

Involvement in Permission to Appeal Decisions

As in the US Supreme Court, the UK Supreme Court largely controls the cases which it hears. It was not always thus.[5] Now, however, an early judicial dialogue in these courts relates to the sifting of would-be appeals to sort the wheat from the chaff. It is not simply choosing the appropriate cases to admit but equally importantly (especially in the case of the minority faction on the US Supreme Court),[6] ensuring that certain cases do not progress onto the docket.[7] In the US each of the Justices in the Supreme Court—in theory—assesses all 10,000 petitions for leave (known as certiorari petitions) that they get per year. In practice, all but one participates in the certiorari pooling arrangements which share the burden of assessment amongst the Justices' clerks—and it requires four of the nine Justices to vote to admit, for the case to come in.

In the UK the House of Lords left the determination of leave to appeal petitions to panels of three Law Lords sitting on Appeal Committees, as we saw in the last chapter. In the decade to 2009 the average number of leave to appeal petitions was the rather more modest figure of about 220 a year, with an average of 240 between 2003 and 2005.[8] The task of selecting the panels for these committees was one for the Principal Clerk to the Judicial Office. In the 1970s and 1980s he tended to take whoever was available when Appeal Committees were required,

---

[2] *Liversidge v Anderson* [1942] AC 206.

[3] *Smith v Chief Constable of Sussex Police* [2008] UKHL 55. A case concerning whether the police could ever be liable for failing to protect an individual whose life and health had been subject to multiple and repeated threats which had been reported to the police on an equally repeated basis. Lord Bingham felt strongly that in such extreme cases the police could be held liable without imposing an unreasonable burden on them.

[4] *R (Ullah) v Special Adjudicator* [2004] UKHL 26. See chapter 6 of this volume below at 229ff.

[5] See eg chapter 6 of this volume below on the dialogue with the Court of Appeal.

[6] Currently those appointed by a Democrat President.

[7] This is a far more important task than merely excluding the run-of-the-mill appeal cases that do not warrant to the attentions of the Supreme Court. It extends to excluding premature appeal cases where the lower court jurisprudence is not yet ripe or cases where a Justice fears that consideration by the Court might lead to the loss of an important precedent. As such, it is a form of 'playing for rules' which we discussed in the last chapter at n 2.

[8] See S Shah and T Poole, 'The Impact of the Human Rights Act on the House of Lords' [2009] *Public Law* 347 and B Dickson, 'The Processing of appeals in the House of Lords' (2007) 123 *LQR* 571.

rarely troubling the senior Law Lords or trying to tailor the panel to the types of appeal being considered.[9] Over the years the senior Law Lords came to take a more prominent role. Indeed, as Brice Dickson showed in his invaluable article on 'The Processing of Appeals in the House of Lords',[10] by 2003–05 the senior Law Lords were carrying out most of the work, demonstrating the significance which Lord Bingham attached to this function (as well as his own work ethic).[11] The composition had also changed in other ways. In the final years of the House, the Clerk to the Judicial Office (Brendan Keith) used to read the petitions and then allocate them to what he considered to be an appropriate trio of Law Lords taking account of their specialisms.[12] Thus Lady Hale would be on the Family law petitions, Lord Walker on the Tax ones, Lords Scott and Neuberger on the Landlord and Tenant cases, Lords Bingham, Rodger, Carswell or Brown would do the Criminal petitions and Lords Bingham and Hope and Lady Hale got most of the Human Rights cases. This change entailed that specialists could now have a significant impact on the dialogues over the cases to be admitted to the docket. Shah and Poole showed that in Lord Bingham's time the proportion of Human Rights petitions which were successful in getting leave averaged 50 per cent as compared with the standard 33 per cent for other types of petitions.[13] It seems probable that the 'A' team for Human Rights cases (and Lord Bingham in particular) was responsible for this. In a similar vein, Lord Hope has stated publicly that Lady Hale helped to transform the regularity with which Family cases came to the House after her appointment to the final court.[14]

Some Law Lords were put out by the use of a 'horses for courses' methodology, for it meant that those not on the relevant 'A' team usually had less input into the selection of specialist cases than the specialists. Moreover, there was growing disquiet that the nine Law Lords who were not on a particular Appeal Committee effectively had no say in whether the six or so petitions which it dealt with should be admitted or not. Thirdly, there was no mechanism to prevent two different Appeal Committees going in different directions on closely related points.

These deficiencies in the judicial dialogue over the handling of leave to appeal petitions have been addressed in part with the transition to the Supreme Court. Now each of the Justices has the opportunity (time permitting) to comment on every permission to appeal (PTA) petition—running at 204 a year in the first three years of the new Court (rather less than the average in the House in the

---

[9] See Paterson, *The Law Lords* (London, Macmillan, 1982) at 87.

[10] See above, n 9.

[11] Lord Bingham sat in 266 petitions and Lord Hoffmann in 254 during this period. Dickson, above, n 9, 579.

[12] Although very experienced, Brendan Keith was not a lawyer and he did not always know all of the areas that individual Law Lords had experience in. This was why he would run the panel compositions past the senior Law Lords for approval. They were rarely changed.

[13] S Shah and T Poole, above, n 8. As against this the HR appeals that were admitted—in greater numbers—were less successful than other appeals, with a success rate of only 33% as compared with a 50% success rate for other appeals.

[14] At the Wood Lecture at Glasgow University in 2011.

previous decade)—and to email or pass comments to a member of the relevant three-Justice PTA committee which is dealing with the case. However, the practice of using specialists for specialist petitions persists and it is understood that it is still relatively rare for the Justices to intervene concerning a PTA petition which is being handled by another panel.[15] The role of the senior Justices remains paramount, for the practice of the Registrar (Louise Di Mambro) is to operate with four PTA committees chaired by the four most senior Justices (currently Lord Neuberger, Lady Hale, Lord Mance and Lord Kerr).[16] The more junior Justices are then allocated according to specialism, availability and conflicts.[17]

Today, the Court of Appeal rarely grants leave to appeal to the final court but where it does it is a very clear signal in their dialogue with the Court that they feel an issue needs to be cleared up, eg where they gave leave in *Jones v Kaney*[18] in order that problems stemming from *Stack v Dowden*[19] might be resolved. That this dialogue does not always work was demonstrated both in the case of *YL*[20] and in *Jones v Kaney*, since in the latter the Justices declined to consider the soundness of *Stack v Dowden*, whatever the Court of Appeal and scholars may have thought of the case. Indeed, counsel at the hearing in the Supreme Court, in a surprisingly low key approach, neither suggested that *Stack v Dowden* should be reconsidered nor even cited the critical articles of academics to the Justices—suggesting that it is not just the *judicial* dialogue with the Court of Appeal that is somewhat patchy in nature. On the other hand, in the old days in the House of Lords there were odd occasions when the senior Law Lords were aware that a key appeal was being heard in the Court of Appeal and a phone call would be made between the courts to intimate that their lordships would like to hear the case and would the Court of Appeal be sure to grant leave?

If the dialogue with the Court of Appeal over leave is losing its salience, a new dialogue—that with the judicial assistants is filling the breach. Indeed the primary stated function of the judicial assistants to date (although it may be changing) has been to divide up the PTAs between them and to provide a neutral memorandum of the key points in the case, which is circulated to all the Justices, although only those on the relevant panel are expected to read them. As in the House of

---

[15] It is not clear that any of Justices views the details of all the petitions arriving at the Court. Lady Hale, as a Family law specialist, keeps an eye on all family petitions and doubtless other specialists similarly watch out for petitions in their specialism.

[16] Occasionally, the President and Deputy President have been on the same PTA committee.

[17] Justices recently promoted from the Court of Appeal or the Court of Session cannot sit on appeals from cases where they involved in the lower court—although many years ago Lord Chancellors presiding in appeals to the House of Lords did just this. Nor may Lord Mance sit in a case from the Court of Appeal in which his wife Dame Mary Arden was present.

[18] *Jones v Kaney* [2011] UKSC 13.

[19] *Stack v Dowden* [2007] UKHL 17. A decision on the property rights of separating cohabitees which had given rise to critical comments, especially from academics.

[20] *YL v Birmingham City Council* [2007] UKHL 27. A long anticipated—and swiftly reversed by Parliament—3:2 case which held, a little surprisingly, that residents funded by public money to stay in private care homes are not protected by the Human Rights Act.

Lords the practice is for the judicial assistants who drafted the memoranda for a particular panel to attend the discussion of the petition at that panel. Once the Justices have made their decision, the judicial assistants will be asked for their views. Indeed, in the case of certain Justices they will discuss the petitions with their judicial assistants before the PTA committee meets.[21]

Being Chosen: The Selection of the Hearing Panel

The Justices, and the senior ones in particular, may be gaining increasing control over the appeals that get into the Court, but there is little point in securing an appeal on the docket if you cannot ensure your presence on the panel to actually decide the case. In the 1970s and 1980s no particular effort was made by the Permanent Secretary of the Lord Chancellor's Department to ensure that any of the Law Lords on the Appeal Committee also sat on the Appellate Committee to hear the case.[22] He did seek to have a specialist on the Appellate Committee wherever he could but the difficulties of synchronising hearings with the Privy Council (since hearings lasted longer in those days) and other logistic problems could defeat his best intentions.[23] There was no question of the Law Lords of the time asking to sit on particular cases, although they would occasionally ask not to sit on a case, because they wished to recuse themselves. Usually this was initiated by the Law Lords themselves, but not always.[24] Following the *Pinochet*[25] debacle where Lord Hoffmann failed unaccountably to reveal that he had a connection with one of the intervening parties (Amnesty International) the House became

---

[21] For a discussion of the role and influence of the judicial assistant in the Supreme Court today, see chapter 6 of this volume below.

[22] See Paterson, *The Law Lords*, above, n 9, at 87.

[23] Ibid.

[24] In the extraordinary *Lonrho* case, *R v Secretary of State for Trade and Industry ex parte Lonrho plc* [1990] 1 AC 154, the company was challenging the Government for publishing the Inspectors' report into the acquisition of Harrods by the Al Fayed brothers (who had defeated Lonrho's attempt to acquire Harrods). Two years before in an earlier appeal by Lonrho, propaganda material had been sent to their lordships which favoured Lonrho. The presiding and senior Law Lord, Lord Keith, gave a verbal warning to Lonrho about this behaviour. Just before the second Lonrho case more propaganda (a special edition of *The Observer* newspaper—whose chairman, 'Tiny' Rowland was also the chairman of Lonrho) was sent to the Lords of Appeal including those sitting in the case. Lord Keith was furious at the repetition of 'the offence'. After the appeal had been heard the Appellate Committee sat to consider a contempt of court charge which they had initiated against Lonrho. Against the advice of the Lord Chancellor and the judgement of the then Principal Clerk, James Vallance White, the Committee refused to change its composition. As we saw in the last chapter, Gordon Pollock QC fought a running battle with the Committee for two and a half days before they admitted defeat and accepted that natural justice—not being judges in your own cause—required them to recuse themselves: *Re Lonrho Plc (Contempt Proceedings)* [1990] 2 AC 154.

[25] *In re Pinochet* [1999] UKHL 1.

a lot stronger on recusal as evidenced in *Jackson*[26] and *Belmarsh.*[27] US Supreme Court Justices do not have to ask to sit on cases since that court sits *en banc* but they can have recusal issues.[28]

By the time of the arrival of Lord Bingham as senior Law Lord in 2000 the composition of the Appellate Committees was, in practice, largely in the hands of the Principal Clerk to the Judicial Office, who oversaw the drawing up of the proposed panels for the appeals listed for each term. Although, by convention, the final say lay with the two most senior Law Lords, since the proposals of the Principal Clerk would be put to them in a meeting once a term (dubbed the 'horses for courses' meeting), in practice neither of the Law Lords made many changes to the Clerk's proposals. The two most senior Law Lords tended not to sit together in appeals—splitting the task of presiding in the House and the Privy Council between themselves, except when the occasional seven or nine judge Committee was scheduled.[29] In such cases, however, especially in nine-judge cases, Lord Bingham took the view that the Committee should consist of the more senior Law Lords—rather to the dismay of the most junior Law Lords. In the case of the normal five-judge panel, the Clerk—as with leave petitions—took account of a number of factors including availability, conflicts of interest, workload, who had sat on the Appeal Committee,[30] and the needs of the Privy Council. However, the most significant factor was specialisation and here again the Clerk (Brendan Keith) worked with his notion of 'A' teams.[31]

---

[26] *Jackson & Others v Her Majesty's Attorney General* [2005] UKHL 56. In this case neither Lord Hoffmann nor Lord Scott took part because they had spoken in the debate on the Hunting Bill, the legality of which was being challenged in the case.

[27] *A v Secretary of State for the Home Department* [2004] UKHL 56. Lord Steyn reluctantly accepted that he had to recuse himself from participating in that case because he had, a year earlier, spoken out on the topic of indefinite detention without trial—albeit in Guantanamo Bay.

[28] Where Justices in the US or the UK Supreme Courts have an interest in a case they are duty bound to 'recuse' themselves from sitting in that case. The obligation, and the decision whether to fulfill it lies on the Justice. The criterion is whether an independent, fully informed, reasonable non-lawyer would think that the Justice might be biased because of their interest. In the US Justice Kagan had served as Solicitor General and was therefore involved in many of the Obama Government cases being argued before the Supreme Court, when she was appointed to the Court. Where she had had an involvement in any such case, she recused herself. There have been controversial cases where some US Justices have declined to recuse themselves. Justice Scalia went duck hunting with Vice President Dick Cheney but then declined to recuse himself from a later case involving Dick Cheney's business interests. Again, Justices Kagan and Thomas declined to recuse themselves from the *Obamacare* case. Justice Kagan stated that she had not been involved with the healthcare law while Solicitor General. In Justice Thomas's case the problem was his wife who was a very high-profile supporter of opposition to the healthcare law. On recusal generally, see G Hammond, *Judicial Recusal, Principles, Process and Problems* (Oxford, Hart Publishing, 2009).

[29] Between 2000 and 2009 the House of Lords sat with an enlarged panel of seven or nine Law Lords on 13 occasions.

[30] An attempt was made to include at least one of the Appeal Committee on the Appellate Committee.

[31] Information derived from interviews with Mr Keith and from B Dickson, 'The Processing of appeals in the House of Lords' (2007) 123 *LQR* 571, 590, Darbyshire, *Sitting in Judgment* (Oxford, Hart Publishing, 2011) 370 and R Cooke, 'The Law Lords: An endangered Heritage' (2003) 119 *LQR* 49.

How did all this affect Law Lords who wanted to sit on particular cases? Could they approach the Clerk? Any such dialogues were unheard of in 2000, when the work allocations were accepted without question. However, towards the end of the House it was not unknown for some Law Lords, but by no means all, having heard that a particular appeal was on its way to the House, to ask the Principal Clerk if they could sit on that appeal since it raised a point of law in which they had a special interest. Where possible their name might well be included in the draft list of appeals and panels considered at the 'horses for courses' meeting. Even latterly such requests were not the norm. Of course, the perversity of life ensured that if you did manage to get onto a key appeal, eg the *Chagos Island* case,[32] other events might occur to force you to have to decline to sit—which might even affect the eventual outcome of the case.

Have things changed in the Supreme Court? 'Not much' appears to be the answer. The panels to hear appeals are largely selected by the Registrar, in practice, using the same criteria as in the last years of the House. Now, as then, the selector's preference for specialists at the PTA and full hearing stages has produced a situation of greater consistency between the PTA panel and hearing panel than existed 20 years ago. Thus in only seven of the 113 successful PTA petitions (six per cent) dealt with up to the end of 2011 were none of the members of the PTA on the hearing panel. Indeed of the 339 Justices to sit on these 113 PTA petitions, 230 (68 per cent) made it onto the eventual appeals panel.[33] Of course, the 'horses for courses' meeting still places the ultimate authority in the hands of the President and Deputy President. That said, Lord Phillips was and Lord Neuberger is no more likely to tinker with the proposed panels than Lord Bingham, although Lord Hope was known occasionally to make some alterations.[34]

There have been two small changes from the House. With seven- and nine-Justice cases far more common than in the House,[35] Lord Phillips, heeding the protests of the junior Justices, no longer chose the composition of the larger courts mainly on seniority. Secondly, it was agreed by the Justices that they would not ask the Registrar to consider their names for selection when interesting cases were coming up. Nonetheless, it appears that some still do ask, and are occasionally

---

[32] *Bancoult, R (On the application of) v Secretary of State for the Foreign and Commonwealth Office* [2008] UKHL 61.

[33] The high percentage is also partly explained by the frequency with which the Supreme Court has been sitting in larger panels than five.

[34] It was not unknown for Lord Hope to step down from larger panel cases to give his place to a more junior Justice.

[35] From 2000–09 the House sat on 13 occasions with enlarged panels. In contrast, between October 2009 and August 2013 the Supreme Court sat on 57 occasions with an enlarged panel. The discrepancy is largely down to (1) the House not having the accommodation to hear many enlarged panel cases and (2) Lord Phillips and most of his colleagues feeling the force of the criticism that in 3:2 cases the result might well have been different if a differently composed panel had sat. Large panels might still lead to close calls but would be less vulnerable to the 'who sat matters' argument. The Supreme Court website sets out the criteria for sitting with an enlarged panel. Essentially these are where the Court is being asked to depart from one of its own precedents, or where the public, constitutional or human rights importance of the case demands it.

successful,[36] and that those appointed after 2009 have not been told of the 'ruling', although more than one told me that they would never consider doing so, at least whilst they remained comparatively junior in the pecking order. In short, on the Supreme Court as in the House under Lord Bingham, the senior Justices have the most say in which appeals are admitted and in whether they get to participate in the hearing.

Doing the Homework: Reading of the Preliminary Materials

Having got on the panel to hear the case, the next question is how much of the printed materials to read in advance. In the old days many of the heavyweight Law Lords—Reid, Radcliffe, Denning and Devlin—read them very sparingly if at all, knowing it would all come out in the oral hearing.[37] This limited meaningful exchanges between the Law Lords about a case prior to the start of the hearing, although Lord Diplock—who read assiduously in advance—would constantly seek to share his views of the case with his less prepared colleagues (either in their chambers or in the Library) in an endeavour to close down avenues of debate in the oral hearing. In the modern era with printed Cases having doubled in size, and oral argumentation halved, the divide between 'clean sheeters' and 'swotters' disappeared. It was replaced by a slightly different divide between what Lord Neuberger calls Impressionists and Pre-Raphaelites: those like him who prefer just a vague idea of the case in advance, and those who want to be right on top of the detail.[38]

> Some read their material very carefully and read all of it. Others tend to concentrate on a few documents, particularly the written Cases and the decision below, and sometimes the contract or the statute. (Lord Neuberger)[39]

This should have facilitated a fruitful dialogue between the Law Lords prior to the hearing eg over the lines of argument that they would most like to hear from counsel. However, when Lord Bingham was parachuted into the House of Lords in 2000 as senior Law Lord he found that a tradition had grown up of not discussing cases prior to the hearing, contrary to the practice in the Court of Appeal.[40]

---

[36] Darbyshire (above, n 31, 372) refers to one Justice who protested to Lord Phillips that he was not on the seven-judge panel for *Radmacher (formerly Granatino) v Granatino* [2010] UKSC 42—the landmark ante-nuptial contracts case—leading the panel to be expanded to nine to accommodate him, and the quote that 'the President is infinitely malleable on size and constitution of panels'.

[37] See A Paterson, *The Law Lords*, above, n 9.

[38] See M Engel, 'British Institutions: The Supreme Court', *Financial Times*, 19 April 2013. Practice Direction 6.6.7 of the Supreme Court indicates that counsel may assume that the Justices will have read the Cases and the judgment being appealed from, but not necessarily any of the other papers. The more computer literate Justices have the advantage that instead of lugging 18-inch thick bundles of papers home at the weekend, they can use a small pen-drive to plug into a laptop on the train or in the study.

[39] Interview with the author, 2013.

[40] There were a few exceptional cases where the members of the Appellate Committee would meet before the hearing if there was some problem that had to be dealt with.

The tradition was a reaction to the perceived dangers of forceful presiders such as Lord Diplock pushing the court in a preferred direction too early. Lord Bingham came to see the value of this tradition for keeping minds open for as long as possible and did nothing to encourage early discussion of cases. A fellow Law Lord commented,[41]

> [What took me by surprise when I was promoted from the Court of Appeal was that] there was almost nothing said before or during the case amongst us to indicate where our preliminary views might be and what we thought it would be most useful to be listening to and what areas of the case we want to explore and so forth. Tom felt very strongly the advantage of letting this happen and keeping as open a mind as long as possible. There are undoubtedly advantages because if you get a very strong member of the court who everybody admires and who expresses his view at an early stage, it's rather difficult not to have your own view coloured by it.

Lord Mance expressed a very similar view,[42]

> I'm not sure that it would be particularly helpful to have any detailed discussion beforehand with expressions of provisional views … [indeed] it might be rather dangerous. I think there are strong characters in the House of Lords and I don't think you want people setting too firm a mark on cases before they've heard the argument and so at the moment I find the present approach understandable and quite sensible, though there may be different views.

Lord Bingham was assisted by the physical geography of the House of Lords where meeting space was at a premium. By default and custom therefore the Law Lords assembled in the Lords' Library just before the beginning of a hearing, but any discussion at that stage was inhibited by the negative reactions of other peers to the silence of the room being thus interrupted. This did not stop more strategic Law Lords such as Hoffmann and Millett from seeking to elicit their colleagues' views at this early stage. Interestingly, the practice of other appellate courts varies. In the US Supreme Court the Justices read the case papers in depth prior to the oral hearing but by tradition do not discuss the appeal with their colleagues (as opposed to their law clerks) at this stage. In the Australian High Court and the Court of Appeal of England and Wales on the other hand, the judges meet beforehand to discuss the key points in the case with a view to offering a steer to counsel (and thereby saving time). Lord Phillips, who succeeded Lord Bingham as senior Law Lord, saw the merits of the Court of Appeal's approach.[43] Accordingly, when

---

[41] Interview with the author, 2008.
[42] Interview with the author, 2008.
[43] 'In an ideal world I think there would be an advantage in our meeting well beforehand having read at least each side's Case, and the statement of facts and issues in order to see which issues we found most difficult and where we thought the problems were going to arise. Then one could inform counsel that we would particularly like help on this or on that. Having discussed the difficult areas the Law Lord in the chair would know that he could push the counsel along quickly through areas where we didn't really feel we needed help. At the moment if you don't know what your colleagues are interested in, there's a reluctance to say, 'Oh you needn't bother with that, get on to the next one', because you don't know whether he does need to bother with that'. (Interview with the author, 2009).

the move to the Supreme Court—with its abundance of meeting rooms—was complete, with the help of a few like-minded colleagues he introduced a short, 15-minute meeting prior to the start of each hearing. It is unclear how successful the innovation has been. While it may have achieved efficiency gains in certain appeals,[44] not all of the Justices are convinced. Some feel that it encourages the expression of preliminary views on the merits of a case at a stage when it is pointless or even unhelpful. As one observed,[45]

> In the Court of Appeal, there is a sort of macho practice of meeting sometimes just a couple of minutes before the hearing and expressing a very, very superficial and quick view. It is rather hard sometimes to change your mind in those circumstances. On the other hand, some presiders in the Court of Appeal encourage a very full discussion which does allow you to express doubts.

Lord Neuberger can see both sides of the argument,[46]

> There is a slight tendency if somebody has expressed a strong view for them to feel that somehow they are going to lose face if they change their minds and some people do express themselves, I do it myself, more strongly often than I really feel. It is probably going into advocate mode almost and it is a problem with pre-hearing discussions a little bit but not much.

However, he sees other merits in the pre-hearing meeting and his enthusiasm may win round the doubters,

> It is a fifteen minute meeting but that is the sort of thing I welcome … if on the morning of the hearing when you read the papers you realise—this happened quite recently in two cases—that one party is saying, look this is an academic point or this wasn't argued below. I would think it essential that I say to the four colleagues, look, it seems to me that we should deal with this as a preliminary point. I don't think there is much in it but if there is we ought to deal with it … The other thing you might do is if there were five points on the case you might sound out everybody to see whether they thought point three was rubbish. Or whether we should decide point five if we decide point four in favour and so on … It is procedural things and occasionally, particularly when I am (a) not sure I have quite understood the case (b) I am slightly confused about something, or (c) I really have a completely open mind, I am quite interested to see what colleagues think provisionally.

Lord Carnwath seems to be on his side of this argument.[47]

> It can give a feel for where people are going … I don't think we ever close off options which are realistic, but quite often we will realise that we all think that certain issues are simply non-runners and it is about one or two issues and so one wants to try and make sure that the debate is directed towards those.

---

[44] Lord Clarke told me, 'Some of these cases on the face of them have endless points and one reason to meet is just to try and focus on what people regard as the key issues, so that the oral argument can be directed to the key issues'.

[45] Interview with the author, 2009.

[46] Interview with the author, 2013.

[47] Interview with the author, 2013.

THE ORAL HEARING

Judicial Dialogues in the Courtroom

The view that prior discussion can encourage too early decision-making in a case, directs us to consideration of the process—and timing—by which appellate judges make up their minds in a case. Chief Justice Roberts of the United States Supreme Court provided a revealing account of the process in a television interview. When asked whether he changed his mind in the oral hearing he replied, 'All the time. Partly because you don't make up your mind before you go into the courtroom. It's a continuous process of narrowing down your decision window'. Roberts went on to explain that when he starts to read the briefs he has little idea how he thinks the case should come out and that as he reads his views are tempered by the competing arguments, leaning first one way and then the other. Although he may acquire a predisposition for one side or the other from reading the briefs, Roberts delays getting to the point of decision for long enough for his mind to be swayed in the oral hearing either by the dialogue with counsel or with his colleagues.[48] Lord Neuberger made a similar point,[49]

> I think pre-reading and keeping your mind open are not mutually exclusive. On the contrary, you often find having had a quick look that the answer you think is very clear, when you read the submissions in the written Case of the party you think is wrong, you begin to see that there is more in it than you thought.

Of course, as some psychologists would argue, appellate judges are as likely as other human beings to make fast, intuitive judgements based on their first impressions. Not all of them, however, will thereafter test their intuitive judgement against the slow deliberative thought which underlies our more reflective judgements.[50] Lord Diplock, for example, made up his mind on the basis of the written materials and had no time for oral argument and Lord Atkin was sometimes not much better.[51] Lord Hoffmann, in contrast, usually reached a firm conclusion based on the written matter but could be moved off it by oral argument. Lords Reid, Radcliffe, Devlin, Hope and Bingham, on the other hand, would leave it until the oral argument stage before reaching preliminary conclusions. Such differences in the approach to appellate judicial decision-making are likely to influence what the appellate judges use the dialogues in the courtroom interaction for. From

---

[48] See his C-SPAN interview published in Brian Lamb, Susan Swain and Mark Farkas (eds), *The Supreme Court* (New York, Public Affairs, 2010) at 21–22.

[49] Interview with the author, 2013.

[50] See Daniel Kahneman, *Thinking, fast and slow* (London, Allen Lane, 2011). For an application of Kahneman's ideas to judges see C Guthrie, J J Rachlinski and A J Wistrich, 'Blinking on the Bench: How Judges Decide Cases' (2007) 93 *Cornell Law Review* 1 (in the top 10 most frequently cited law review article on Google in 2007–11). Rachel Cahill-O'Callaghan would argue that the intuitive value judgements of the judges will pre-dispose them in a particular direction even if value trading occurs later, 'The influence of personal values on legal judgments' *Journal of Law and Society* (forthcoming).

[51] See Allan Hutchinson, *Laughing at the Gods* (New York, Cambridge University Press, 2011) at 136.

the last chapter (and also the *The Law Lords*)[52] we know that the Law Lords and Justices have used the dialogues in the hearings for a range of purposes: to curtail prolix counsel, to test counsel's arguments, to sound counsel out as to the judge's own line of thought, or simply to clarify matters. Some are transparent in their objective, like Lord Bingham. Others, of whom Lord Rodger was thought to be one, appeared to take the stance of the devil's advocate. However, it has long been recognised that a proportion of judicial interventions, whilst ostensibly aimed at counsel, are in reality intended for their judicial colleagues.

This dialogue with colleagues is inter-related with the dialogue with counsel, but is one which occurs proportionately rather more frequently in the US Supreme Court than in the UK Supreme Court. Indeed it has been argued in relation to the US Supreme Court that the primary purposes of their very truncated oral hearings[53] are (1) to enable the Justices to learn for the first time what their colleagues think about the case (since tradition prevents them from engaging with each other beforehand),[54] and (2) to debate with their fellow Justices. Inevitably, the two activities often overlap. Of the former Justice Breyer noted,[55] '[Oral argument] does matter. Law clerks think it doesn't ... [but] I see what my colleagues are thinking very often. I listen to their questions'. Of the latter, Chief Justice Roberts is reported to have observed,[56] 'Quite often the judges are debating among themselves and just using the lawyers as a backboard. One of the real challenges for lawyers is to get involved in that debate'. Similarly Justice Kennedy has said,[57]

> One of the reasons you ask a question is to advise your colleagues what you're thinking or what your concerns are. A good attorney can realise that he or she is engaging in the conversation that the Court is having with itself.

Roberts, too has adverted to the fact that some of his devil's advocacy is designed to influence his colleagues,[58]

> If I think that the lawyer has a good answer to a question that appears to be concerning one of my colleagues, I might ask an aggressive question that looks like I'm hostile. But I know he or she is going to come up with a good answer that might help respond to that other justice's concern.

---

[52] *The Law Lords*, above, n 9, at 72–82.

[53] Normally one hour for each appeal nowadays.

[54] See the C-SPAN interview with Roberts CJ (at 18) and JP Steven, *Five Chiefs: A Supreme Court Memoir* (New York, Little, Brown and Co, 2011) at 118–19.

[55] See his C-SPAN interview published in Brian Lamb, Susan Swain and Mark Farkas (eds), *The Supreme Court* (New York, Public Affairs, 2010) at 132.

[56] See Adam Liptak, 'Nice Argument, Counsellor, But I'd Rather Hear Mine', *New York Times*, 5 April 2011.

[57] See his C-SPAN interview published in Brian Lamb, Susan Swain and Mark Farkas (eds) *The Supreme Court* (New York, Public Affairs, 2010) at 74. One recent commentator on the Court in describing the oral arguments said, 'As usual ... the lawyer was largely a spectator as the justices talked to one another'. Jeffrey Toobin, *The Nine: Inside the Secret World of the Supreme Court* (New York, Doubleday, 2007) at 195.

[58] See his C-SPAN interview published in Brian Lamb, Susan Swain and Mark Farkas (eds), *The Supreme Court* (New York, Public Affairs, 2010) at 19.

Justice Breyer is thought to do the same. According to Jeffrey Toobin, 'Breyer planned his questions with care not because he was especially interested in the answers but because his questions were a way of making his case to his colleagues'.[59] As another seasoned court watcher observed,[60]

> During oral arguments the justices are definitely having a conversation among them-selves and not just asking questions of the advocate at the lectern. They're telegraphing their own interest in the case. They're trying to make arguments to each other … oral arguments give the individual justices a chance to actually make their case … before they all go into the private conference.

Interestingly, Lord Radcliffe wrote of the House of Lords in remarkably similar terms,

> [I]f properly conducted, the legal debate is uniquely effective in enabling a committee of judges to arrive at a matured committee decision. The presence and, under control, the participation of counsel serve as a valuable catalyst. They enable members of the court to advance conflicting views for consideration without direct confrontation with each other or too early commitment to one point of view; and the mere maintenance of the debate is a great help to making progress towards an ultimate conclusion.[61]

After the era of Lords Reid and Radcliffe, Lord Diplock achieved an ascendancy in the House of Lords. Towards the end of his time as senior Law Lord and in the following decade the oral hearings could be somewhat lively if not rather aggressive affairs with inputs from Lords Templeman, Brandon and Bridge which amounted to little less than point-scoring against each other, with counsel some-times little more than a cipher in the middle.[62] Several counsel who experienced this, commented on the benefits for counsel of these explicit judicial dialogues.[63] Even when things settled down in subsequent years the Law Lords and counsel still recognised the value of inter-judicial dialogue in the hearings. Thus a later Law Lord remarked,[64]

> [T]o some very limited extent I think nowadays you are supposed to be trying to put a point of view across to your colleagues … where you feel you have a point worth making and you're troubled that one or more of your colleagues haven't got it … you try and make sure that they have got it via some interjection of your own.

Similarly a counsel of the Bingham era described the judicial dialogue as follows,[65]

---

[59] J Toobin, *The Nine: Inside the Secret World of the Supreme Court* (New York, Doubleday, 2007) at 129.

[60] Jane Biskupic in Brian Lamb, Susan Swain and Mark Farkas (eds), *The Supreme Court* (New York, Public Affairs, 2010) at 209.

[61] From his review of *Final Appeal* (1973) 36 *Modern Law Review* 419.

[62] See Paterson, 'Does Advocacy Make a Difference in the Lords?' ch 12 in J Lee (ed), *From House of Lords to Supreme Court* (Oxford, Hart Publishing, 2011) 258.

[63] Interviews with the author, 2009.

[64] Interview with the author, 2008.

[65] Interview with the author.

You could always tell when [Lord Hutton] was trying to influence his colleagues because he'd start off by saying 'Mr ** this particular concern has been raised', he wouldn't identify who raised it, but 'surely Mr ** the way that this can be analysed is …', or 'would you say that this could be analysed in this way?', and 'I suppose an answer to that …?' And I always used to think, 'Lord Hutton please ask me more of these questions', that's if he was on my side … How that would go down with the person who had been testing my propositions and showing that they were pretty threadbare, I don't know.

Another counsel added,

Lots of the questions you get asked by the Lords are actually ways of scoring points off their colleagues whose position they know to be in some respect different … What they do is they ask the kind of questions which they expect will provoke what they regard as the conclusive argument against a particular position that's been expressed outside the court by one of their colleagues.

Again, a third counsel recalled,

I can think of occasions where Lord X would be putting questions to the counsel and then he would look round to see whether his point had gone home with his colleagues.

These comments show that the dialogue between the Law Lords in hearings could be deliberate and proactive: a pre-meditated form of judicial advocacy. Indeed, Lord Hoffmann, as we will see below, sought to influence his colleagues from an early stage. However, the dialogue could equally be reactive, for example, where a fellow Law Lord made an argument which a colleague thought was a bad one,[66]

Lord X of all people made a point … that I thought was a bad point and I didn't think counsel answered it very well so I put a question to counsel which contained what I thought was the clearly right answer to the point being made.

This dialogue continues in the UK Supreme Court with Justices overtly engaging with their colleagues in the oral hearings, although to a somewhat lesser extent than in the United States, as is evidenced by the live Sky transmissions of the UK arguments and the transcripts of the US Supreme Court arguments.[67] Thus, Lord Clarke, when I interviewed him in 2009, considered that most of the Justices aimed some of their remarks in the hearing at their colleagues. He himself might do so where counsel was making an argument with which he strongly agreed and he wanted to make sure that the argument was put as clearly as possible in order to win round a colleague. Lord Kerr, in interview also referred to this aspect of the dialogue,

---

[66] Interview with the author.

[67] For all its transparency the UK Supreme Court does not produce transcripts of its hearings, although video copies of the Sky broadcasts can be obtained on cause shown. The US Supreme Court on the other hand produces free transcripts of the oral arguments within a week, but has steadfastly set its face against television broadcasting of the hearings. Interestingly the two most recent appointees to the Court, Justices Sotomayer and Kagan initially favoured such broadcasts but no longer do so.

[A] question will be asked and then another member of the panel will come in with either an explanation or an enhancement to that question or a reference to another aspect of the case that might shed light on another question that has been asked but it is nominally conducted via counsel. You would say, 'Well Lord Pannick you've been asked this question by ... Lord Clarke, now perhaps you would want to say such and such in response' but that is essentially a dialogue between the two members. [It] doesn't happen very often but that can happen on occasion and I think that's entirely a healthy thing, there should be as open a dialogue and as free an exchange of ideas as is possible.

Interestingly, a colleague who had on occasion experienced counsel responding to challenges from Lord Kerr with a concession, recounted how he had interjected with the formulaic 'I suppose the answer to Lord Kerr would be as follows' and been met by Lord Kerr with 'and the answer to that would be this'. The colleague was not just engaging in dialogue with Lord Kerr. His aim was to suggest to all of his fellow Justices on the panel that counsel was conceding a particular argument too easily. Lord Hope, by contrast, generally appeared to engage much more in the dialogue with counsel than with his colleagues in the hearings, intervening primarily to clarify his own thinking. However on occasion even he could be stirred into engaging with his colleagues,[68]

I think sometimes people do ask questions as a means of bouncing ideas off counsel to provoke ... responses elsewhere or vice versa, [for example] if somebody's asked a question which seems to indicate one view and you're provoked into putting a question which is putting the other point of view. Yes, I am conscious of doing that and I think all of us do, but this is beneficial, I think. Because it opens up the discussion and it frees it from the rather formal argument which no doubt counsel are expecting to present and gets it into the area which we really find important and interesting and which we want to test out.

Lord Dyson thought that the dialogue was more likely to arise where a colleague had made a point with which he did not agree, '[I]think that does go on to some extent. If somebody has made a point which you think is plainly wrong, counsel may get in first but if he doesn't then I think one would say something'.[69]

From the foregoing we can see that the Law Lords and Justices have engaged in dialogues with their colleagues in the hearings, to varying degrees. While no Law Lord or Justice in living memory has stopped asking questions of counsel altogether, as Clarence Thomas of the US Supreme Court has since 22 February 2006, there have been several Law Lords, eg Lords Keith, Nicholls, Carswell and Walker, who interrogated counsel sparingly and when they did so largely did so to clarify a point that was troubling *them*. Even they, however, would be listening hard to the questions being asked by their colleagues since it helped them to understand how these individuals were thinking. If the more silent Law Lords tended not to engage in a *responsive* dialogue with their colleagues in the hearings, most of the Law

---

[68] Interview with the author, 2008.
[69] Interview with the author, 2009.

Lords and Justices would engage with both counsel and their colleagues. Indeed, it is not unusual today for debates between the Justices to take the form of a direct dialogue between them designed to correct a point, in a sentence or two.[70]

Clearly such differences in when and how to engage with one's colleagues are partly down to the idiosyncrasies of the different Justices. However, we may hypothesise that those who make up their mind early will use the interaction to try to influence colleagues more than others. This was certainly true of Lords Atkin, Diplock, Hoffmann, Steyn and of Scott.[71] As Lord Hoffmann told me,

> [The oral hearing] is the stage at which you make your view known both for benefit of counsel and for the benefit of your colleagues. It's an opportunity not just for counsel to exercise advocacy on the bench but for the judges to exercise advocacy on each other. I've changed my mind in the course of oral argument, well I wouldn't say often but on several occasions.

We explored in the last chapter the efficacy of the judicial dialogue with counsel. Lord Hoffmann's final comment, of course, raises the interesting question of the efficacy of the inter-judicial dialogues in the oral hearings, a topic to which we will return in the next chapter. All of the Law Lords and Justices whom I interviewed conceded that they had changed their minds during the oral arguments—though it was often unclear whether this was due more to the dialogue with counsel than that with their colleagues. As with the dialogue with counsel the judicial dialogue might only effect a change in a Law Lord's reasoning; at other times it would affect the outcome of the case. However, judicial advocacy at this stage in the proceedings was not always successful and could be counter-productive. As one counsel told me,

> [T]here are some Law Lords of recent experience … the purpose of whose interventions is to persuade their colleagues that the view they have already formed is the correct one, that is much less helpful to the course of the argument and it is that which I perceive irritates the other Law Lords.

Conclaves Off-stage: Dialogue Outside the Courtroom

In the House of Lords 30 or 40 years ago oral hearings in the typical case would last four days on average[72] (although the *Tin Mines case* weighed in at a staggering 26 days).[73] Throughout the lengthy process there were constant exchanges

---

[70] In the House, the Law Lords would address remarks to each other during a hearing but with the exception of a humorous aside to a neighbour it was done through notes. Lord Bingham's notebooks contain a sprinkling of these (postcards with the House of Lords' crest on them) but their import is either about counsel's argument, sitting longer or some tangential issue or quirk that had struck the writer.

[71] Lord Scott appeared to use his interventions for a similar purpose but since his take on cases was frequently slightly different from that of some of his colleagues, the interventions did not always have their intended effect.

[72] In the early 1970s. Between 1952 and 1968 25% of English appeals to the Lords lasted more than five days and 10% of them took seven days or more. L Blom-Cooper and G Drewry, *Final Appeal* (Oxford, Clarendon Press, 1972) at 235.

[73] *JH Rayner Ltd v Department of Trade and Industry & Others* [1990] 2 AC 418.

between the Law Lords. They would chat in the library or the lift before the start of an appeal, at lunch in Peers' Dining Room and at the end of the day's hearing leaning against the wall in the corridor. In direct contrast to the drawn out arguments from counsel, these debates were highly compressed—almost in shorthand,[74] 'But if you say that, then it leads to [such and such] consequences' or somebody says 'No, because in that case ...'.[75]

By Lord Bingham's era the opportunities for dialogue with colleagues had declined considerably, in part because hearings were much shorter. Some Law Lords, eg Lord Rodger or Lady Hale, seemed almost to vie with each other to see who could assemble in the Library at the latest possible moment before the hearing began, and in any case discussion of cases before the oral hearing was not really encouraged, as we have seen.[76] Moreover, lunch had shifted to Strangers— the House of Commons cafeteria—where there was less privacy and not all of the Law Lords attended.[77] As one Law Lord told me,

> We do chat as the case is going along and so I think that usually if it is a case that runs over an adjournment ... I would have got a feel which way they're going just by chatting to them before that moment arrives ... there's usually a group in Strangers [for lunch] but it's as you're walking along the corridor ... It doesn't take long just to say surely the point in this case is X or that's complete rubbish or something ... It's very shorthand.

Darbyshire also reports that lunchtime conversations tended to be along the lines of 'X is being long winded' or 'Y is making a good point look bad'.[78] Collective discussions at the end of day in mid-hearing were not the norm in Lord Bingham's time, although ones and twos would often drop in on colleagues' offices, especially in the Law Lord's office next to the Secretaries' room. It seems that in the Bingham era much more of the dialogue between the Law Lords about cases was in writing than had been the case in time of Lord Reid.

Today oral hearings in the UK Supreme Court last just over half as long as 40 years ago.[79] This is a considerable reduction but still in excess of the normal hearing in the Court of Appeal and much more than the one hour typically permitted in the US Supreme Court. Nevertheless, there are possibly even more

---

[74]   *The Law Lords*, above, n 9, at 91.

[75]   As one of them put it, 'You break off say at four o'clock, then starts the argument. Three people arguing, then up drifts a fourth, and you really thrash the thing out. Then somebody raises a point which you think you can demolish ... [Since] you want to convince them that the other point is right, [y]ou look at a Law Report when you come in, in the morning beforehand, and casually remark as you gather in the library for a quarter of an hour, that it seems to you that the case of so-and-so really has got the right principle much more. Then the argument starts again'. *The Law Lords*, above, n 9, at 91.

[76]   See the text at n 42 above. This is contrary to the practice in the Court of Appeal, the European Court of Justice, the European Court of Human Rights and now the UK Supreme Court.

[77]   Lady Hale preferred to have a working lunch in her office and Lord Scott preferred a light lunch in his office.

[78]   P Darbyshire, *Sitting in Judgment* (Oxford, Hart Publishing, 2011) ch 15.

[79]   Cases determined by the Supreme Court between October 2009 and July 2012 lasted 2.18 days on average.

opportunities for the Justices than Bingham's Law Lords to engage informally in dialogue with their colleagues and their judicial assistants about the case should they so wish. A pre-hearing meeting has been introduced, as we have seen, and there is a private dining room where the Justices often lunch together. However, since not all of them are sitting in the same case the scope for talking shop can be limited. If anything, moreover, discussions in colleagues' rooms have become more fragmented, now that the Justices are located on two floors. What has really changed from the House has been the amount of email traffic between the Justices. Since the middle of 2013 all of the Justices have been comfortable with the use of email to circulate drafts and comments even if only a minority (Lady Hale, Lord Kerr and Lord Neuberger) took a laptop into the hearings and accessed the bundles electronically.

THE FIRST CONFERENCE

Irrespective of the dialogues which may take place between the Law Lords or Justices at earlier stages in the proceedings there is one, and usually only one occasion when the whole panel gather together to discuss the disposition of the case, in a sustained fashion. This is the first conference,[80] which takes place at the end of the oral hearing. Forty years ago, with the completion of counsel's submissions, an usher would call out 'Clear the Bar' and counsel, solicitors, parties and spectators were swept hurriedly from the room. If it was close to the lunch recess the Law Lords' deliberations would take place in the Conference Room, after the adjournment. Alternatively, in a handful of complex or high-profile cases, frequently those with an enlarged panel, the conference would take place in the Conference Room in the next day or two, or very rarely, during the following week. In the great majority of cases in the House of Lords, however, the conference took place in the Committee Room more or less immediately when the bar was cleared—which in most cases was just after 4 pm. This had an effect on the duration of the conference, some said because of the uncomfortable nature of the seating, but more likely because one or more of the panel had to leave for another engagement at around 5 pm. Thus in general the conference lasted for no more than three quarters of an hour (although they could range from 10 minutes,[81] where the case was clear and the panel unanimous, to half a day, if the case was complex, the Law Lords were divided and the conference had been postponed from the end of the hearing).[82]

---

[80] The conference has no official title and did not in the House of Lords either. In this work I refer to it as 'the first conference' since that is what it is.

[81] Apparently Viscount Simonds kept the first conference to not much more than 15 minutes and discouraged other formal gatherings to consider the case.

[82] The politically charged case of *Heaton's Transport* had a conference of a whole day and *Ross-Smith v Ross-Smith* took half a day. In *Etridge v Royal Bank of Scotland* [2001] UKHL 44 the seriatim presentations started at 3.25 pm and lasted until after 6 pm—before any general discussion. It seems that conferences which were postponed until later in the week took longer because more of the Law Lords had had a chance to prepare for the discussion.

In the US Supreme Court the duration of the conference discussion of individual cases has also varied, but in their case it has been not simply the complexity or otherwise of the appeal, but also the approach taken to the conference by particular Chief Justices which made the difference.[83] Some Chief Justices have allowed their colleagues to talk for as long as they wished—entailing that a scheduled one-day conference often became two days. Others have seen little point in prolonged discussion, taking the view that by the conference stage the majority of the Justices had already made up their minds.

Sharing of Preliminary Conclusions and Discussion

Unfortunately for historians, as in most appellate courts, these formal conclaves of the judges are not held in public nor are they video or tape-recorded, and there are no witnesses.[84] Our understanding of the form and content of these conferences comes from interviews with the judges, extra-judicial writings and the emergence of the judges' private notes in their papers after their death. Nevertheless the accounts that have appeared in the US and the UK are consistent enough to instil confidence in the picture that emerges. In the US Supreme Court the Chief Justice speaks first at the conference giving him an advantage—that some have seized with greater enthusiasm than others—in setting the parameters of the discussion. Thereafter each Justice speaks in order of seniority of appointment with the later, more junior Justices speaking with greater brevity to avoid repetition. In the House of Lords and the Privy Council, the tradition has been to work in inverse order of seniority, probably out of a desire to forestall any tendencies of more junior Law Lords to be overly deferential to more senior and more trenchant colleagues. As a further hedge against deference, as in the Privy Council and the US Supreme Court, the conference at this stage is generally akin to a series of seriatim speeches or monologues rather than a discussion, for it was and remains unusual[85] for the presenters to be interrupted, with no one speaking twice until all have spoken once. As Lord Hope put it,[86]

---

[83] This too varies—conferences under Rehnquist CJ were shorter than those under Roberts CJ. The latter preferring time for an exchange of views in the hope of consensus building, the former considering that there was little point.

[84] In the House of Lords—but not the UK Supreme Court a clerk was present at the conferences that took place after the hearings—but no minutes were taken by them. In the Court of Appeal and the US Supreme Court no witnesses at all are permitted in the room. Darbyshire (*Sitting in Judgment*, above, n 78) was given unprecedented access to judging in action, including the deliberations of an Appeal Committee meeting in the House of Lords, but was not afforded the opportunity to witness a first conference in the House of Lords. (She did witness conclaves in the Court of Appeal).

[85] In one case where it occurred in 2002 the junior Law Lord was followed by two others before speaking again. The two others were then allowed to comment on this before the fourth and fifth Law Lords got to speak at all!

[86] Interview with the author, 2008.

The understanding is that you're listened to without interruption and that's quite important, particularly for the people starting off because the first person is expected to set out in some kind of order the points which are important and deal with them in a sort of logical manner, discarding the points which are not important and saying so, building up the ones which are important in coming to a view.

Lord Bingham, when he was presiding Law Lord, strengthened the position of the junior Law Lord still further,[87]

I warned those who became the junior members during my time, '[A]t the end of the hearing you'll be called on to give your view first and people will expect quite a detailed piece from you, 10 minutes, quarter of an hour perhaps'. This sounds rather patronising but I think it's rather a good feature of the system that those who are newest and … most junior do have this rather important role because otherwise they may wonder why they're there at all [laughs]. So I've encouraged them to address the subject quite fully and that means that everybody else tends to be a good deal briefer because they'll say 'Well I agree with him on this and I'll agree with her on that' or 'I agree completely with what X has said and I'll therefore give my own reasons very briefly'.

A scrutiny of 90 judicial notebooks from this era[88] confirmed the accuracy of Lord Bingham's account. In general the most junior Law Lord did speak for the longest—especially if it was Lord Rodger or Lord Millett and subsequent Law Lords would often preface their remarks with 'I agree' or 'totally agree' or 'I agree with Lord Rodger' or 'I agree with Lord X on the jurisdiction point but not on the Article 6 point' or again 'I agree with Lord Rodger and Millet LJ in the Court of Appeal, although I'm not saying Lord Y (another Law Lord in case) is wrong!' or 'I've nothing to add on point 1'. This is an interesting combination of monologues in which each engages with the last. Even where the case was a specialist one, eg a Scots or a patent appeal, the notebooks show that all of the Law Lords would speak, although not always as long as the specialist Law Lords. Indeed the evidence suggests that individual Law Lords would sometimes deliver substantial extempore speeches in the conference even if they then did not write an opinion in the case.

If the case was a complex one, where the Law Lords were divided, they might depart from the usual pattern by having a discussion as part of the presentations. Lord Carswell explained,

[I]n a case that's difficult … there's quite a lot of cross-talk even during it. People don't get on their high horse and say well I want to finish what I'm going to say, because the others don't chip in too easily. But sometimes quite a lot of discussion would go on, particularly by the time you get to the end of the last one, if it's not clear where everybody stands then there can be quite a while banging it backwards and forwards.

---

[87] Interview with the author, 2009.
[88] See chapter 1 of this volume, above at n 13.

More normally the discussion was confined to commenting on whether the speaker agreed with one or more of the earlier speakers, as Lord Hoffmann remarked,[89]

> Well, as you go round each person who speaks will comment or may comment on what the previous people have said so to that extent there is a discussion. It's not common for someone who's already spoken then to come back and say 'No, hang on a second you've got that entirely wrong, what I meant was such and such' but it happens occasionally. I mean there's no inhibition about it because … the discussion at the end is seldom an isolated thing. It's seamless from the discussion which took place while counsel was present.[90]

Once all the Law Lords had spoken, if they were divided or it was a case of any complexity, and time permitted, a general discussion would then ensue which could be quite protracted (particularly if the first conference was not taking place at 4 pm). The presiding Law Lord has a particular role here as Lord Hope observed,

> [O]nce everybody has said their piece it may then be possible to go back and say, 'Look that's fine, we actually have a fair amount of agreement but there is this point where we really haven't got anything very clear'. It may be possible to [then] have a discussion on the point. [You want] either to emphasise a good point or possibly to open up where there's disagreement to see whether that disagreement is going to remain, or whether it's something that can be resolved round the table there, or whether further thought is needed. Of course it's all provisional anyway, because it has to be written about later.

Lord Hope added,

> [I]f I'm chairman … I might well go back to number one: 'You weren't very sure of your position, you've now heard from us and you were uncertain about so and so, is that how you still feel and … are there things you'd like us to think about again while we are reflecting on the discussion'. So it's really a means of trying to develop some kind of position at the end of the hearing, because one of the things one has to realise is that getting the same group together again with all the papers in front of them is not going to be terribly easy.

Lord Hope's last comment is a telling one and emphasises the significance of the inter-judicial dialogues at this stage. Since the almost invariable norm in the last 30 years has been for panels to change from one appeal to the next in the House of Lords (and the Supreme Court) it is logistically difficult to re-convene a meeting of the original panel to reduce differences and to ensure that there is a majority ratio in the case. Such re-convened meetings were therefore relatively unusual in the House of Lords, occurring no more than two or three times a year.[91] Amongst

---

[89] Interview with the author, 2008.

[90] An observation which illustrates the inter-connectedness of the various dialogues.

[91] That was true in the 1970s (*The Law Lords*, above, n 9, at 89), the mid-1990s (D Robertson, *Judicial Discretion in the House of Lords* (Oxford, Clarenden Press, 1998)) at 15, and when I interviewed them in the last five years.

the most famous in the final few years was *Kay*[92] (the second of a trilogy of cases in the Lords which were akin to trench warfare, over whether the law on eviction was covered by the Human Rights Act) where Lord Hope and his majority colleagues sought unavailingly to produce a clearer agreed paragraph 110 to form the ratio of the decision, and *Norris*[93] (a controversial extradition case to the United States) where a single judgment was considered desirable.

It was expected by some that with the advent of the Supreme Court, matters would change. As pressure grew for more single, composite or plurality judgments, so it was expected that more meetings would occur. Lord Phillips as President hoped that there would be greater deliberations at all stages and another Justice suggested that the model of debate between law commissioners when debating proposals for law reform was one that could be adopted. Indeed the Justices agreed to have a meeting day at regular intervals to discuss not simply policy issues for the court but also follow-up meetings for important cases. However, in reality these meetings have been restricted to policy issues and only occur once every two months. Moreover, the Registrar has not been asked to schedule slots for follow-up meetings of panels. Such follow-up conferences as have occurred in the Supreme Court have been on Mondays, when fewer cases are scheduled, have remained relatively uncommon and are reserved for complex cases or those where the panel is divided on a point of principle. In *Pinnock*,[94] the requirement of several meetings was to enable a single judgment to be produced.[95] Nevertheless there seem to have been a increase in the number of second case conferences since Lord Bingham's era. Between February and October 2012 there were around four cases (out of a total of 40 heard in that period) with reconvened conferences.[96] For the most part the first conference under the Supreme Court has stayed much as it was in the House of Lords, with the exception that, unlike Appellate Committees of the House, the Justices do not deliberate in the courtroom but always in one of their meeting rooms.[97] In the summer of 2011 the Justices decided at one of their meeting days to seek to shift the balance at the conference between seriatim presentations and the general discussion. As Lord Dyson recalled,[98]

we have been discussing this, and I think we seem to be moving towards having rather shorter presentations, no more than five minutes, followed by discussion and I think that is probably better actually than having set piece presentations and then we all go away.

---

[92] *Kay v London Borough of Lambeth* [2006] UKHL 10.

[93] *Norris v Government of the United States of America* [2008] UKHL 16.

[94] *Manchester City Council v Pinnock* [2010] UKSC 45, [2011] 2 AC 104.

[95] *Norris* was written in several parts by different Law Lords, whilst *Pinnock* was drafted by Lord Neuberger who then accepted multiple suggestions from his colleagues.

[96] Including *Oracle America Inc (formerly Sun Microsystems Inc) v M-Tech Data Ltd and Another* [2012] UKSC 27; *R v Waya* [2012] UKSC 51; *Flood v Times Newspapers Ltd* [2012] UKSC 11.

[97] Meeting rooms were a problem in the House of Lords—which is why the tradition grew up of 'Clearing the Bar' and leaving the Law Lords to deliberate *in situ*. In the UK Supreme Court there are plenty meeting rooms so it is the Justices who clear the room, leaving it to counsel, agents and spectators.

[98] Interview with the author, 2011.

Lord Neuberger's account[99] was very similar,

> I think it is slightly less formal, with more interruptions, though not many. Yet it was unthinkable in the old days that anybody would interrupt any one of us five when we were giving our views. If one was searching for something, somebody might help you. If you made an obvious mistake somebody might correct it but otherwise you'd just listen. Now, particularly when the fourth or fifth person is speaking and there is a momentum going, it will break into a discussion. The other change is that there is much more likely to be discussion following the exchange of views.

However, the decision did not immediately lead to any dramatic change in format or atmosphere and some Justices appointed after that date seem unaware of the decision. In seven- and nine-Justice cases there has been an understandable desire on everyone's part to avoid spending hours on seriatim presentations, but no guidelines have been produced for newer Justices and presiding Justices have never, to date, intervened to curb the presentations of their colleagues.

The change has, however, the potential to alter the dynamic of the first conference and perhaps to reduce the protections against deference that Lord Bingham had so carefully reinforced. David Robertson who interviewed all of the Law Lords in the mid-1990s, argued that the format of a conference in which first reactions to a case had to be produced 'face to face, rapidly, and orally in an atmosphere that very much resembles a committee charged with solving a problem rapidly' afforded opportunities for personal styles, human interactions, latent predispositions and specialist expertise to play a significant if not decisive role.[100] In his view it should not be surprising if the resulting decisions tended to reflect the strong views of only one or two Law Lords.[101] Even allowing for the force of the personalities who were in the Court in Robertson's time such as Lords Diplock, Bridge, Brandon and Templeman, Robertson's account seems to underplay the strength of character of the typical judge who reaches the final court. Nevertheless, whether as a reaction to Lord Bingham's well-intentioned challenge to the most junior Law Lords or as evidence that Robertson has a point, it seems to have been the case that whilst *most* of the contributions to the first conference were confidently stated, some have come with varying degrees of tentativeness. As we have seen, some Law Lords made up their minds at an early stage in proceedings, sometimes even before the hearing. These Law Lords tended to be very confident in the first conference. Others were more often tentative about the outcome, or claimed to be so, particularly the most junior Law Lords. As Lord Bingham recalled, 'there were some cases where … people [said] "Well my provisional view is this, but I would

---

[99] Interview with the author, 2013. Lord Neuberger was able to contrast the difference between the House of Lords where he began as a Law Lord before going to be the Master of the Rolls in the Court of Appeal and then returning to the final court of appeal in 2012 as President of the Supreme Court.

[100] D Robertson, *Judicial Discretion in the House of Lords* (Oxford, Clarendon Press, 1998) at 16.

[101] Robertson goes on to show that in particular types of case certain Law Lords or combinations of Law Lords tended to emerge on the winning side with a frequency that could not have been down to chance. He attributes this to a combination of legal realism and deference.

like time to think about it and look at the authorities again and I might change my mind'".[102] Lord Hope made a similar observation,

> [S]ometimes people are quite tentative because number one hasn't really been able to gauge how everybody else feels and doesn't want to commit himself too hard to a particular position, and may end up by saying 'well that's my view for the moment but I would like to hear from others before I commit myself', and that's perfectly in order of course.[103]

As Lord Hope hints, the tentativeness of the junior judges who were new to the Court was probably due to a range of factors: (1) simply being in two minds on the topic; (2) having to go first when they didn't know which way the case is going and preferring not to look foolish if they ended up on their own; (3) being inexperienced or unfamiliar with new colleagues and therefore less able to predict how they would come out in the case; or (4) not being a specialist in the relevant area and therefore being cautious before committing to a definitive view of case law that some colleagues will be much more familiar with.[104]

Taking these in turn: Every Law Lord and Justice will encounter cases in which they are unsure or find it difficult to decide which side to come down on. It is clear from subsequent vote switches and from judicial notebooks that this is the case. Secondly, several of the Law Lords and Justices that I interviewed confessed to feeling a little nervous or on their mettle at having to speak first in their early months on the Court. This phenomenon exists also in the US Supreme Court despite the fact that there the junior Justice speaks last in the conference. Justice Souter, for example, found his first year on the Court 'a crushing burden' and was said to have a tendency to say in conferences that he found decisions 'very difficult' or that his vote was merely tentative.[105] Thirdly, most Law Lords could tell in most cases 40 years ago which way the bulk of their colleagues were likely to vote[106] because of the longer hearings and the greater opportunities for dialogue during those days. In the Bingham era, however, when hearings were half as long as hearings were 40 years ago and the scope for dialogue with colleagues during and before those hearings had been reduced, even Lord Bingham commented[107] that at the outset of conferences,

> There would be quite a significant minority of cases in which I simply wouldn't know how people were going to go and wouldn't know what the balance was going to be. I might know that he looked as if he was going that way and she looked as if she was going that way but I wouldn't *know*. They wouldn't know probably what I thought, and I wouldn't know whether I was going to be in the majority or the minority.

---

[102] Interview with the author, 2009.
[103] Interview with the author, 2008.
[104] This is true of Scots appeals or patent appeals or criminal appeals for Chancery judges.
[105] See JC Greenburg, *Supreme Conflict* (New York, The Penguin Press, 2007) at 129.
[106] See A Paterson, *The Law Lords*, above, n 9, at 92.
[107] Interview with the author, 2009.

Finally, we should not be surprised when non-specialists are cautious in disagreeing with those who are experts in a field. Lord Bingham shrewdly summed up the alleged tentativeness of the junior Law Lords as follows,[108]

> Well, I think they tended to *say* that. I think they tended to say that, as I would have said if I had been in their position. I think if you express a totally concluded view and then everybody goes the other way you want to be in a position to say 'Well OK, you know, it's not something I'd want to dissent on'. I'm not sure they usually *were* tentative but I think they tended to *say* so and people quite often say 'Well this isn't my field and there are various people here much more experienced and who know much more about it than I do' but that didn't usually prevent them disagreeing with the people who knew more about it.

Whilst Lord Bingham's thesis was that junior Law Lords might exaggerate their tentativeness as a form of damage limitation to their credibility there were other ways to achieve the same goal. Thus, one of the advantages of postponing the first conference to a later day is that it affords the Law Lords and Justices time for reflection and to prepare their presentations.[109] Several Law Lords and Justices[110] that I spoke to indicated that in any event they had made a practice of taking time before the last day of a hearing and during lunchtime[111] to prepare notes for their presentation at the conference. Others used preparation for another purpose. For a minority of Law Lords, including Lord Hoffmann, the first conference was perceived as the best opportunity for judicial advocacy, namely to win round any colleagues who might be wavering. For those judges preparation was an offensive tactic not a defensive one. Others still chose not to prepare, simply speaking off the cuff, drawing on their experience in the Court of Appeal or other appeal courts in producing extempore judgments as an everyday occurrence. Curiously, although the contrast between non-preparers and those who prepare very thoroughly can be quite marked, sometimes the 'off the cuff' judges can turn out to be right.

Lord Bingham had clear views on inhibiting deference at the first conference and, as we have seen, put them into practice. Lord Phillips seems to have run the first conference in a relaxed fashion allowing his colleagues, like counsel in the hearings, to have their head. Lord Neuberger is reverting more to the Bingham model. In the face of colleagues who vary from diffidence in manner (though not in content) to the super-confident ones with a punchy delivery style, from the sketchy and short to the well thought out, even didactic ones, Lord Neuberger's hope (like Bingham's before him) is to reduce the overlap between the seriatim presentations. As he put it,

---

[108]   Interview with the author, 2009.
[109]   For this reason a minority of Justices would like the first conference to be postponed in every case.
[110]   Often the most junior but not always. Research into his judicial notebooks indicates that Lord Reid as presiding Law Lord always had three pages of notes for his extempore 'judgment' at the first conference, while his more modern counterpart, Lord Bingham rarely did so.
[111]   And, one suspects, during the appellant's reply argument at the end of the hearing.

It's my duty to lead by example so I will tend to say, 'I agree with Justices a, b and c, and on the difference between b and c I agree with b, and the only other point I'd make is this ...'.

Whilst Lord Neuberger's approach reduces repetition it could also have the unintended consequence of partly negating the influence of more senior Justices who, whether for tactical or other reasons, prepare their presentations thoroughly in advance.[112]

The Allocation of the Lead Judgment

Once the discussion phase of the conference is over the third and most fluid phase ensues. Forty years ago where the Law Lords were all agreed for substantially the same reasons, the presiding law Lord might say: 'Well, look here, there is no point in having five speeches in this case. Who's going to do this?' Taking account of their respective workloads, expertise and interest in the case, the Law Lords would then decide who was to write the lead opinion, including the detailed statement of the facts, or who was to deal with a particular aspect of the case. This did not prevent other Law Lords writing if they so wished. Although the presiding Law Lord might take the lead in suggesting such assignments, in the normal course of events these opinion assignments were not made solely by him but were the product of collective agreement. Nevertheless in very exceptional cases (eg *DPP v Smith*,[113] *Heaton's Transport v TGWU*[114] and *Rookes v Barnard*[115]) a presiding judge might decide that for policy reasons, only one opinion of the court should be produced and that it should appear under his name.[116] The Law Lords were, of course, quite familiar with the technique of producing a single judgment of the court, because they all sat in the Privy Council. But for most of them, that was an excellent reason for not introducing more single judgments in the Lords. Either it really was the work of one man with the others leaving him to it, or it was a 'fudge'. Although a few felt that the compromises required by such a format were beneficial, rather more considered that it was a cause of weakness in the Privy Council that multiple amendments from different quarters had to be included in judgments in order to keep the majority in the court onside.

---

[112] Especially where they are less adept at thinking on their feet.

[113] *DPP v Smith* [1961] AC 290.

[114] *Heaton's Transport (St Helens) Ltd v Transport and General Workers Union* [1973] AC 15. Unfortunately, a scrutiny of the Minute Book provides no explanation as to how this sleight of hand had been achieved. Bingham quizzed Lord Wilberforce about it many years later but he could cast no light on the matter other than to say 'How dreadfully irregular'.

[115] *Rookes v Barnard* [1964] AC 1129. Lord Devlin's 'codification' of the law of exemplary damages was actually the product of various suggestions from others on top of his basic framework. See *The Law Lords*, above, n 9, at 99.

[116] Even then he required the acquiescence of his colleagues. In *DPP v Smith*, Lord Kilmuir LC insisted that there should be only one judgment. Although it appears under his name it was apparently drafted by the Lord Chief Justice, Lord Parker.

When Lord Diplock became senior Law Lord he was strongly in favour of single judgments of the court, often penned by himself.[117] Curiously, Lord Bingham, no fan of Lord Diplock's penchant for single judgments, seized on the precedent set in *Heaton's* (in which he had been a counsel) to persuade the Principal Clerk that the Appellate Committee in the case of *R v Forbes*[118] could have a single report of the Committee (as opposed to a single judgment in the name of one Law Lord). In the ensuing eight years the House repeated the ploy 23 times out of 510 appeals[119] in cases where Lord Bingham and his colleagues felt that the need for certainty in the criminal law required the statement of the law with a single voice.

Usually, however, Lord Bingham was very happy for as many Law Lords as wished, to write. He considered that he, as senior Law Lord, should write in many of the significant cases in which he presided[120] and announced to his colleagues that this was a case where he anticipated that they might all wish to write (which was his way of saying that he was writing anyway but they might write if they wished). His successor, Lord Phillips, preferred the more direct formula 'I think this is one that I ought to write', although the outcome was the same. In the majority of cases, where the Appellate Committee was unanimous on the outcome, it might be obvious who was the Law Lord best placed to write the major opinion (through specialism[121] or particular interest) if the presider was not to write. Failing that, the presider would ask for volunteers, indeed occasionally a Law Lord may have agreed with the presider that he or she would write in the case (or not write in the case), even before the hearing (although this was not very common).[122] Where the Court was sharply divided it would be clear that all or most of the Law Lords would write but sometimes the Law Lords would leave the conference without discussing who might write. Different presiders adopted different practices, making it difficult to generalise on the process.

However, Lord Bingham did try to sort out which Law Lord was going to be responsible for setting out the facts of the case in their speech. If he was writing, then he would generally do it,[123]

> I always tried to decide who was going to write the facts because it seemed to me almost mischievous for everybody to have a go ... so that I did try to achieve a position where we went out of the committee room knowing who was going to do the facts and encouraging everybody else to leave them alone, but one wasn't always successful in that ...

---

[117] Which is not quite the same as an opinion of the Court. On single judgments see text below at n 138.

[118] *R v Forbes* [2001] 1 AC 473, Lord Bingham.

[119] See James Lee, 'A Defence of Concurring Speeches' [2009] *Public Law* 305, 311.

[120] Lord Bingham gave a speech in 73% of cases in which he presided in the Lords. Whilst Lady Hale and Lords Hope, Millett and Neuberger wrote in a higher percentage of cases in which they sat in the Lords, they were rarely, if ever, the presiding Law Lord in these cases.

[121] Almost always a Scots judge will be allocated to write the major opinion in a pure Scots law case.

[122] This was the pattern in the Court of Appeal, which may help to explain the Law Lord who told Penny Darbyshire that the fact that it was rarely sorted out in advance of the hearing who was going write led to unnecessary duplication of effort.

[123] Interview with the author, 2009.

some go away and write opinions as if they were starting from scratch and it's very difficult to stop them doing that and some people are worse at it than others.

Interestingly, Lord Bingham would sometimes assign the facts to a Law Lord who was dissenting on a part of the case, and would allocate who was to write the facts even when he himself was in the minority, unless he thought the majority side was really misguided,

> I think if I was in the minority I might still want to do the facts myself [laughs] not with a view to putting a slant on them … but because … other things being equal its quite good to get the facts at the beginning of five opinions … [rather] than later on. Sometimes, [however] I would feel that it was up to the majority to organise how they were going to organise their opinions. [Thus] in cases where one just flatly disagreed with what the majority were agreeing … one would rather say 'Well, how you're going to construct your house is a matter for you and not me'.[124]

Lord Bingham's suggestion that it helps the reader if the facts of the case appear in the first judgment to appear in the Law Reports was one that has been taken up in the Supreme Court. Since the Court was no longer bound by parliamentary rules about speeches being published in the order of seniority, the Court decided that there should be a lead judgment in each case, taken from the majority side, chosen by the presiding Justice and containing the facts of the case. This would be the first opinion to be printed in the Law Reports. The move to the Supreme Court also saw a push for more single judgments of the Court or joint or composite judgments of two or more Justices.[125] As in Lord Bingham's era, the presiding Justices took it on themselves to do a disproportionate number of lead and single judgments. (See Table 3.1 below). Thus Lord Phillips wrote the lead or single judgment in 23 of the 73 (32 per cent) cases in which he presided in the Supreme Court and Lord Hope wrote the lead or single judgment in 46 of the 139 (33 per cent) cases in which he has sat in the Supreme Court which were published before the end of July 2013. Where the presiding Justice chooses not to allocate the lead or single judgment to themselves, the pattern is very similar to the House of Lords under Lord Bingham. Workload and willingness to volunteer play a significant role. Indeed, one presiding Justice is said to have joked that the seriatim presentations at the first conference were like 'auditions' to see who should get the lead opinion to write. Specialists will be called on to write the lead, as Lord Neuberger was in *Pinnock*, and Lords Hope, Reed and Rodger were and are in Scots cases or Lord Walker was in tax and company law cases.[126] Lord Neuberger has taken a slightly different approach from his predecessors, as a presider. He sees the virtue of the President giving the lead in

---

[124] He told me he had cases like *Qazi v London Borough of Harrow* [2003] UKHL 43, *Kay v London Borough of Lambeth* [2006] UKHL 10 and *YL* [2007] UKHL 27 in mind.

[125] See below at n 138.

[126] Curiously, there are also occasions where the obvious specialist is not chosen to do the lead judgment eg *Re B (A Child)* [2009] UKSC 5.

the more important cases but feels less under an imperative to do so. In a changing Court he is aware of some of the complexities involved in the allocation decision. As he put it,[127]

> There can be competition for who is to write the lead judgment and in making the choice I have to take into account issues of fairness as well as 'horses for courses'. We had one case where a more senior Justice and a more junior Justice were both very keen to write the judgment. The senior one was visibly upset when I gave it to the junior one, and I was wrong. I should have given it to the senior one, so in the next (and more important) case in which we were in, where I had decided that I should write the lead, instead I gave it to the senior one.

Nevertheless despite the innovations of the Supreme Court, whilst it will very largely be clear who will start out as being responsible for the lead judgment there have been many cases, especially in the early years, where it was not clear by the end of the first conference, who else would be writing and who would not.

Since the drive for a majoritarian judgment now resembles the situation in the US Supreme Court, it is interesting to note that there the assignment process takes place a few days after the conference. Either the Chief Justice if he is in the majority, or the senior Associate Justice in the majority if he is not, will assign the Justice who will be charged with writing the majority opinion for the Court. The choice can be subject to tactical factors, however, there is also a strong convention that each Justice should be given a more or less equal number of majority judgments to write during the year (now around eight a year), and a spread of weighty and run-of-the-mill cases. This convention applies whoever is making the assignment.

Implications for the Future

With single majority judgments in the UK Supreme Court running at 55 per cent of all judgments in the first half of 2013 and the competition between Justices to write the lead judgment sometimes becoming quite fierce, it begins to look as though the UK Supreme Court President may have to adopt a formal convention, as in the US Court that each Justice (with the possible exception of the President and the Deputy President)[128] should write very much the same number of lead or sole judgments. Otherwise as the pressure grows for fewer substantial judgments in cases, so too may the potential for misunderstandings and hurt feelings

---

[127] Interview with the author, 2013.
[128] As we have seen, Lords Phillips and Hope considered that they should shoulder the burden of writing a disproportionate share of the lead and sole judgments in cases in which they presided. Lord Neuberger has not followed this model so far.

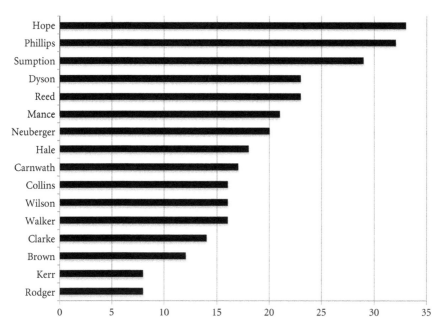

Table 3.1: Lead and single judgments in the UK Supreme Court as a percentage of total cases sat in during 2009–13 (July).

amongst Justices who feel that they are not getting to chance to write the lead or sole judgment frequently enough. (See Table 3.1).[129]

Given that the first conference is, for the great majority of cases, also the last conference, how should we assess its contribution to the decision-making process? This begs the question as to what the function of the first conference has been and might be in the future. As we have seen, over the years the first conference has had a range of purposes: to bring out everyone's views; to elicit whether there is a majority or even a unanimous view on the outcome and the key issues in the case; to endeavour, if necessary, to build such a majority position; to identify the parameters of disagreement; and to ascertain who will be responsible for writing the majority or lead judgment, including the facts. As for eliciting the individual views on the key issues and whether a majority position exists, the traditional format of the first conference was highly successful at flushing out the position of even the those most adept at keeping their cards close to their chest. Whilst any Law Lord or Justice can reserve their position at the first conference for further reflection, that is a rare eventuality and even then they would explain where their

---

[129] It should be stressed that, as we will see in chapter 4 of this volume, this table is not a fair indication of the workload of individual Justices or their propensity to write. Assenting or dissenting judgments do not show up in this table, nor do judgments written in the Privy Council.

reasoning had got to and which way their view was tending to go. A complete failure to contribute to the first conference is almost unheard off. Even in the highly exceptional situation where one of the judges is unable to attend the conference they will provide a written note to contribute to the debate. Moreover, whilst the junior judge is the one who is most often to be found expressing some hesitation, as we have seen, most Law Lords and Justices have cases in which they are unsure of the outcome. However, whilst some Law Lords were more disposed to sit on the fence than others, even the most indecisive Law Lord could not with credibility plead for more time for reflection on a regular basis. As for the conference's ability to make progress towards a majority or unanimous position this, in part, turned on the willingness of the presiding Law Lord or Justice to nudge his or her colleagues in that direction as Lord Hope's dicta indicate. Scott Reid was particularly adept at this.

Equally, some presiding judges have been more adept at allocating the lead judgment and the facts than others. This can be attributed in part to their ability to play the role of task leader and in part to notions of teamwork and collegiality to which we will turn in the next chapter. What is interesting about the first conference from the perspective of the social psychology of group decision-making is that the format of the conference as it evolved under Lord Bingham was well placed to counter potentially unhelpful features of small group decision-making. Thus it has been known for 30 years that group discussion is likely to shift judgments towards extremes.[130] This polarisation effect can be towards greater risk or greater caution, depending on the average position of the group members at the pre-deliberation stage. The effect is attributed by social psychologists to group dynamics based on pressure to conform, self-perception or reputation on the one hand and limited 'argument pools' on the other. Moreover group polarisation is enhanced if members have a sense of shared identity. However, the traditional first conference format was not a typical small group activity since there were clear understandings about how it was to operate which formalised (even ritualised) exchanges between members of the group. By giving additional prominence to the contribution of the junior Law Lord and by emphasising seriatim presentations over group discussion, Lord Bingham's format helped to neutralise the polarisation effect whether derived from group dynamics or the argument pool. Curiously the recent reforms to the conference in the Supreme Court to enhance discussion, debate and dialogue may have enhanced the potential for polarisation in group decision-making in that Court.

---

[130] See R Tindale, T Kameda and V Hinsz, 'Group Decision-Making' in MA Hogg and J Cooper (eds), *Sage Handbook of Social Psychology* (London, Sage Publications Inc, 2003) ch 18, and C Sunstein, 'Deliberative Trouble? Why Groups go to Extremes' (2000) 110 *Yale Law Journal* 71. 'In everyday life the exchange of opinion with others checks our partiality and widens our perspective; we are made to see things from their standpoint and the limits of our vision are brought home to us … Discussion is a way of combining information and enlarging the range of arguments': John Rawls, *The Theory of Justice* (Place, Publisher, 1971) 358–59.

Lord Neuberger, although instinctively in favour of further discussion if it would be likely to lead to a clearer *ratio* or to better articulate the differences between members of the panel, now has reservations. He experimented with holding more meetings after the draft judgments had been exchanged than was the case in the House of Lords, to see if this would bridge the differences of view through more discussion.[131]

> However, having tried this, I feel these meetings sometimes don't achieve anything because by the time of the exchange of drafts people are often going into advocacy mode, to defend their position. If anything they get more entrenched as a result.

One of his colleagues who shared Lord Neuberger's attraction to second conferences was more optimistic,

> I do think there is a tendency to assume that the views expressed by the individuals in the seriatim presentations [at the first conference] is going to be their final position … My view is that we ought almost always to have a further conference in a case where we disagree, after we have produced drafts. Then when we disagree the understanding should be that the draft judgment is really designed to be a note to each other of the way the author thinks that the case should go and why, so that we can discuss it.

It is too early to assess the impact of these changes on the Supreme Court. However, what is clear is that the relative lack of collective discussion before, during and at the end of the hearing in the House of Lords in the Bingham era meant that the principal dialogue between Law Lords in most cases took place in the shape of the general circulation of their opinions and individual comments (written or oral). It is to that stage of the decision-making process that we now turn.

THE DRAFTING STAGE

Order of Production and Circulation

Once the first conference is over, the curious process of drafting begins. Forty years ago this might have involved relatively little dialogue between the Law Lords, but in the UK Supreme Court the drafting stage is the key stage of the decision-making process and the dialogue between the Justices is central to this. In the US Supreme Court there is a convention that the first judgment to be put in general circulation is the majority one. There was no such convention in the House of Lords or in the UK Supreme Court in the early days. In any event whether there is such an understanding or not, it has never meant that the lead judgment is necessarily the first to be produced, since on both sides of the Atlantic there have always been some Law Lords and Justices to whom writing seems to come more easily and naturally than others—and others again who will sometimes labour

---

[131] Interview with the author, 2013.

over a multiplicity of drafts before being in any way satisfied. However, in the US Supreme Court these additional judgments might be exchanged informally with allies, they would only be formally circulated to everyone after the majority judgment appeared.[132] In the House of Lords, and the UK Supreme Court until very recently, there was no convention as to the order in which judgments should be circulated, unless the case was one where it had been agreed that there would be only one judgment. This enabled those judges who produced their draft judgment swiftly—be it through habit (Lords Bingham and Hope), desire to act when the case is fresh in their minds (Lord Dyson), or as a deliberate ploy to influence their colleagues[133] (Lords Diplock, Steyn and Hoffmann)—to circulate this within a short period of the end of the hearing.[134] Where the early writer was the majority or lead opinion writer it caused few, if any problems. However, where the lead writer took rather longer to produce his or her opinion, the first opinions to be circulated could sometimes cause complications since they lacked the definitive version of the facts, and might destabilise the majority on the court (as they were sometimes designed to do). The lack of a fixed rule on who wrote first did not seem to trouble Lord Lloyd, who observed,[135]

> I suppose if somebody has volunteered to do [the lead], then they will be doing the facts, we would all do our views on the law and we would certainly circulate that before seeing the facts and then if the facts turned out as it were to be different, you re-circulate them. Quite often there's a lot of re-circulation goes on.

Eventually, in 2012 the Justices in the Supreme Court resolved that in general the lead judgment should be the first to be circulated, and that the others should hold back their judgments or writing at all until the lead judgment was circulated. However, it is already clear that this 'resolution' is not being adhered to in every case or by every Justice.

Just as there have always been early circulators there have often been those at the other extreme. Very occasionally, judges who do not normally experience difficulties in composition encounter cases where the opinion will not write. In an extreme situation judges may even end up writing an opinion the other way, since they are unable to produce one which they find intellectually acceptable, that supports their original view. But such cases are rare.[136] Equally, there were

---

[132] This remains the case even though today the great majority of first drafts of US Supreme Court judgments are produced by law clerks.

[133] One Law Lord told me: 'The only way that people persuade others is by what they write and there are undoubtedly those who recognise this, because it is a fact that if you write well and early, that maximises your chance of influencing the others'.

[134] A few even wrote their opinions in advance of the hearing based on the written materials in the appeal—a habit acquired in some cases in the Court of Appeal.

[135] Interview with the author, 2009.

[136] Chief Justice Roberts' late switch in the *Obamacare* case (*National Federation of Independent Business et al v Sebelius, Secretary of State of Health and Human Services* 567 US 2012) in the summer of 2012, which moved the majority to supporting the Healthcare legislation, is a particularly striking recent example of this phenomenon.

cases in the past where one of the Law Lords was simply unable to make up his mind and stick to it, or where a Law Lord developed extreme levels of indecision. More commonly, Law Lords would delay writing through conscious choice, either because they were finishing off judgments from earlier cases, or because the court was divided and they wished to see what one writer from each camp would produce.[137] Finally, a Law Lord may have delayed writing because he planned not to write unless his colleague's judgment contained something unexpected with which he could not agree. While several judges told me that a cogently argued piece might swing votes even if produced as the last of the panel, there are probably more instances where Law Lords have delayed in producing their judgment only to find that the rest of the panel have moved on and were reluctant to re-open what they regarded as past history.[138]

Multiple Judgments and the Pursuit of Unity

What kinds of consideration lead a Law lord or Justice to write if they are not the one who has been assigned the lead or majority judgment? In the House of Lords 40 years ago there was no hard and fast answer to this question.

> If you feel that something ought to be said and somebody else is going to give the leading judgment, well then you say it. I think, so as not to complicate the thing too much, one concurs if you are in substantial agreement with what the other man says and may add something if you want to. But it's … a matter of judgement as you go along, there is nothing like a rule. (Lord Reid)

Lord Pearson added,

> I think unless it has been pretty definitely arranged that only one of us should write …
> I would think it otherwise better that two or three should write.

The Law Lords were more likely to write if the House was divided or overruling a unanimous lower court decision. However, even then, most of the Law Lords were agreed that unnecessary multiplication of opinions was to be avoided. This meant that sometimes opinions which had been circulated would be withdrawn or severely pruned, but this could be a delicate process. Like other authors, the Law Lords were reluctant to see their efforts consigned to oblivion. There was no expectation that the most junior Law Lords should be the ones to fall upon their sword. Indeed such a requirement would be doubly unfair in a scenario where the

---

[137] Forty years ago the Law Lords were evenly split as to the wisdom of waiting in this way in evenly divided cases. One half, including Lords Cross and Radcliffe, would sometimes wait in such circumstances but Lords Denning, Gardiner, Guest, Hailsham, Pearce and Reid said that they had never done it. Characteristically Lord Reid said 'I don't think it is a good way to wait and see how the cat jumps'. (Paterson, *The Law Lords*, above, n 9, at 96).

[138] This happened in *Stack v Dowden* where Lord Neuberger's dissent was circulated much later than the other judgments.

junior Law Lord had been the first to circulate, dealing with the whole case—why should he have been expected to withdraw his judgment at a later stage because some of his seniors have chosen in the end to write (with the benefit of the sight of the earlier judgments)?

The academic critics of the period were not sympathetic, with one caustically referring to 'the second or third speech in the House of Lords which concurs in the result reached by its precursors after the same review of all the authorities with as little reference to principle'.[139] The learned authors of *Final Appeal*, who came out in favour of single opinions of the court (allocated on a rota basis) were equally unconvinced,[140]

> Not infrequently [assenting judgments] serve only to fudge the areas of real agreement, and sometimes in the interstices of an apparent assent there lurk all the signs of a partial dissent … As such, they are insidious to … clarity and certainty in the law.

The Law Lords and counsel of that era whom I interviewed in the first study were very conscious of the criticism—they had thought more about this topic than any other which I discussed with them. Opinion, both at the Bar and in the House, was divided, as it has been off and on for more than 40 years. A clear majority of counsel were against multiple judgments but less sure when a single judgment was called for. Roughly a third of those interviewed at the Bar favoured the then status quo. A significant majority of the Law Lords favoured the retention of multiple judgments over a single opinion in every case.[141] In this they are likely to have been influenced by the views of the senior Law Lord, Lord Reid. He was strongly in favour of multiple judgments, taking the view that the limited experiments with single judgments of the court had not been a success and that one of them *DDP v Smith*,[142] had been a *'disaster'* which might have been mitigated had there been more than one judgment. In his view,[143]

> it is often not possible to reach a final solution of a difficult problem all at once. It is better to put up with some uncertainty—confusion if you like—for a time, than to reach a final solution prematurely.

However, in the late 1970s Lord Diplock, although he was not to become senior Law Lord until 1982, began to exert more and more influence on the court. Lord Wilberforce, the senior Law Lord of the time, later confessed that Lord Diplock had 'mesmerised' his colleagues. Suffice it to say that Lord Diplock was strongly in favour of having only one judgment in the Court, as we saw earlier, and such was his dominance of his colleagues that by the time of his death in 1985 he had

---

[139] Rupert Cross cited in *The Law Lords*, above, n 9, at 97.

[140] L Blom Cooper and G Drewry, *Final Appeal*, above, n 72, at 93.

[141] See Table 7.2 *The Law Lords*, above, n 9, at 186.

[142] *DDP v Smith* [1961] AC 290.

[143] See Lord Reid, 'The Judge as Law Maker' (1972–73) 12 *Journal of the Society of Public Teachers of Law* 22, 29; *The Law Lords*, above, n 9.

driven the proportion of single judgments in the House of Lords to 68 per cent.[144] FA Mann QC, who as instructing solicitor had taken many appeals to the Lords in that era, was no fan of the single opinion. Lord Reid feared that the wording of single judgments would be read as though they had a statutory authority, and in Mann's view that is precisely what had happened in practice under Lord Diplock, pointing to,

> numerous decisions which include sentences that have acquired, but do not necessarily deserve, almost statutory authority. Their authors may have intended nothing of the kind, but since there is no qualification or differentiation to be found, they are liable to be misunderstood.[145]

David Robertson, writing of the period soon after Lord Diplock, similarly noted that,[146]

> [T]he Lords have moved to the expectation that there will only usually be one major speech ... [which] many leading counsel find distinctly unhelpful ... it can also cause problems for their Lordships themselves, who sometimes find that they are deemed to support interpretative positions that they later have to withdraw.

Indeed, as will be seen in Table 3.2, under the aegis of Lord Keith as senior Law Lord, the percentage of cases with a single majority judgment reached a staggering 70 per cent in 1993—a height which even Lord Diplock had not quite achieved and which has never been achieved since.

However, as the 1990s wore on the number of single-opinion decisions of the House began to drop significantly, possibly through the influence of Lord Browne-Wilkinson. Lord Bingham was much more in sympathy with Lord Reid's approach to multiple judgments than Lord Diplock's. Thus in his first essay on the Rule of Law,[147] having affirmed his agreement with Lord Reid he added,

> A single lapidary judgment buttressed by four brief concurrences can give rise to continuing problems of interpretation which would have been at least reduced if the other members had summarised, however briefly, their reasons for agreeing. And a well-constituted committee of five or more can bring to bear a diversity of professional and jurisdictional experience which is valuable in shaping the law.

Lord Hoffmann agreed with him,

> Diplock gave a bad name to insisting upon single judgments and so therefore as presiding judge I think that ... one should not try to persuade one's colleagues to assent to a single judgment whether by oneself or by another colleague except in cases where you think it's really important.

---

[144] Between 1974 and 1983 he delivered the sole judgment in about 25% of cases in which he sat in the Lords. A Bradney, 'The Changing face of the House of Lords' [1985] *Juridical Review* 178, 187–89.

[145] FA Mann, 'The single speech' (1991) 107 *LQR* 518, 520.

[146] D Robertson, *Judicial Discretion in the House of Lords* (Oxford, Clarendon Press, 1998) at 77–78.

[147] Lord Bingham, 'The Rule of Law' (2007) 66 *CLJ* 67.

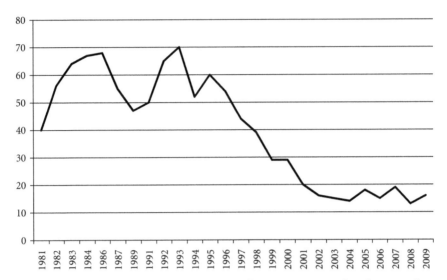

Table 3.2: Single judgments in the House of Lords as a percentage of total cases sat in during 1981–2009.

Lord Bingham did articulate some caveats—first, that however many judgments there were, there must be a clear majority ratio, and secondly that there might be a case for single judgments where the special need for certainty in criminal law required it. Thus, as we saw above, he re-invented the concept of a single Report of the Appellate Committee in the case of *R v Forbes*[148] and the House repeated it on 23 occasions in 500 or so appeals[149] between 2001 and 2008. Lord Bingham's commitment to multiple judgments (and that of most of his colleagues)[150] is amply evidenced by the fact that in the period that he was senior Law Lord (2001–08) there was not a single year when the proportion of cases with a single judgment in the House rose above 20 per cent. It is further reinforced by Table 3.3, which shows the willingness of the Law Lords to write a judgment in the cases in which they sat between 2000 and 2009.[151]

---

[148] *R v Forbes* [2001] 1 AC 473.

[149] See James Lee, 'A Defence of Concurring Speeches' [2009] *Public Law* 305, 311. The format was not restricted to Criminal cases. For a civil example see *Henderson v Novia Scotia Ltd* [2006] UKHL 21. Sometimes the report is given no author, or sometimes a single author, even if more than one Law Lord contributed.

[150] In their interviews Lords Brown, Carswell, Hoffmann, Hope, Hutton, Mance, Millett, Scott and Steyn articulated broad agreement with Lord Bingham's stance in this debate.

[151] Lord Reid of Drem managed to write a judgment in 79% of the cases in which he sat between 1952 and 1968: Blom-Cooper and Drewry, *Final Appeal*, above, n 72, 156, a truly astonishing strike rate over a 16-year period.

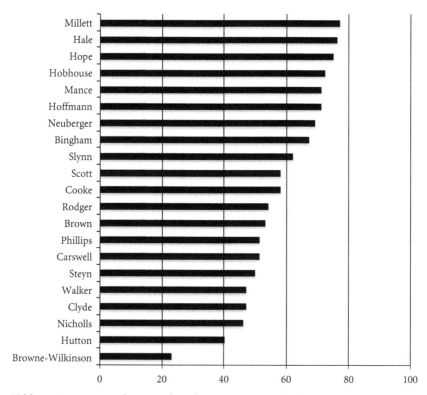

Table 3.3: Percentage of House of Lords cases sat in, in which Law Lords wrote an opinion during 2000–09.

Nevertheless by the time of my second set of interviews beginning in 2008 it was clear that the old debate had once more been ignited. The impetus came primarily from the Court of Appeal as we will see below, with Lord Justice Carnwath's impassioned *cri de coeur* for a single majority judgment in the House of Lords,[152]

> Was it necessary for the opinions of the House to have come to us in the form of six substantive speeches, which we have had to subject to laborious comparative analysis to arrive at a conclusion? Could not a single majority speech have provided clear and straightforward guidance, which we could then have applied directly to the case before us?

If Lord Justice Carnwath was the most vocal, many of his colleagues, including the then Master of the Rolls, Lord Clarke, agreed with him. In the QMUL Supreme

---

[152] See *Doherty v Birmingham City Council* [2006] EWCA Civ 1739, at para 62.

Court Seminars[153] in 2008 there was an extensive debate between Law Lords, Lord Justices and others on the topic. Those for the status quo argued that multiple judgments support judicial independence, and enrich our legal system. On the other hand, they argued, single judgments give a spurious certainty to the law, were often drab and lacking in colour and their proliferation was likely to lead to frustration among judges from an inability to write or the need to make uncongenial compromises. Further, single judgments might lead to collectively less attention to points of detail and an increase in the power and influence of the senior members of the court.[154] In reply a Lord Justice pointed to the fact that leading supreme courts around the world had chosen not to follow the House of Lords' model of seriatim opinions, adding that there was a substantial value in a coherent and certain statement of the law and, if there were to be concurring judgments, that they should make clear what it is they are agreeing with and not agreeing with. The judge ended by stressing the value of 'internal engagement' between the Law Lords for the pursuit of coherence and the proper development of the law. In the discussion that followed it was observed that Strasbourg and the US Supreme Court both had majority judgments of the court coupled with concurring and dissenting judgments. Several Law Lords pointed to the value of more discussion between members of the Court which might reduce the need for long, repetitious concurring judgments.

By the time the Supreme Court opened in 2009, the groundswell of support for the single majority opinion with such other concurring and dissenting judgments as were necessary was growing more discernible. Lady Hale was a strong proponent of this approach,[155] and had a measure of support from Lords Neuberger,[156] Saville and Walker who similarly wished to see a reduction in concurring opinions. Lord Phillips, in his early days as senior Law Lord, saw merit in a flexible approach,[157]

> I think there are horses for courses. I think if it's an area of law that is developing … it is much better that if people are coming at it from slightly different viewpoints they should express their view rather than trying to get some kind of compromise single judgment by laying down inflexible principles. Having delivered it, it would then be set in concrete and very difficult to move on from, that's one situation. Quite a different situation is if you've got an issue of criminal law: what does this particular criminal statute mean? There I think to have a variety of different views is very unfortunate. Even if you don't

---

[153] Andrew Le Sueur, A report on six seminars about the UK Supreme Court (London, Queen Mary, University of London, 2008).

[154] Here again the spectre of the unhelpful dominance of Lord Diplock over his colleagues was being adverted to.

[155] In *OBG Ltd v Allan* [2007] UKHL 21 and several speeches referred to in Darbyshire, above, n 78, 388–89. But see *Woodland v Essex County Council* [2013] UKSC 66 at [28].

[156] Interview with the author, and Lord Neuberger, 'Open Justice Unbound?' Judicial Studies Board Annual Lecture 2011. It is striking that two of the most prolific Law Lords (see Table 3.2 above) are amongst those favouring a single majority judgment.

[157] Interview with the author, 2008.

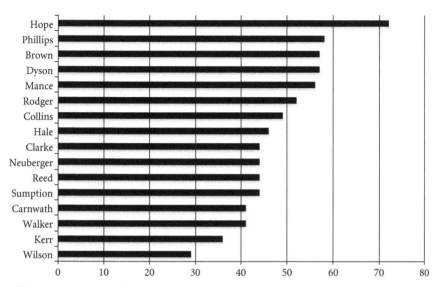

Table 3.4: Percentage of UK Supreme Court cases sat in, in which Justices wrote a judgment during 2009–13 (July).

all agree, you need to have something that the country can apply. If Parliament doesn't like what you say they can legislate.

The retirement of Lords Bingham, Carswell, Hoffmann and Scott left the two Scots Law Lords (Lords Hope and Rodger),[158] together with Lords Brown and Mance as the main protagonists of the status quo. The tipping factor has been the appointments to the Supreme Court since 2009 (mainly from the Court of Appeal). Lord Collins did not share the prevailing view in the Court of Appeal,[159]

> I am on the whole of the Francis Mann school which says that if you have the practice of a single judgment, that inevitably leads to a certain intellectual laziness and a tendency to go along with the majority.

However in the course of my interviews it emerged that Lords Clarke, Kerr, Dyson and Carnwath were all more clearly in favour of a single majority judgment with supporting concurrences where appropriate. The extent of the swing in opinion can be gauged in part from Table 3.4.

In the first full year of the Supreme Court the proportion of single judgments more than doubled that of the last year of the House, although the divisions of 2011 (it was a bumper year for dissents) reversed that trend, only for a significantly

---

[158] See J-Y Gilg, 'Supreme Craftsmanship' interview with Lord Hope, *Solicitors Journal*, 8 December 2009.
[159] Interview with the author, 2011.

Table 3.5: Percentage of single judgments in the House of Lords and the Supreme Court during 1981–2013 (July).

increased proportion of single judgments to re-emerge in 2012–13 as can be seen in Table 3.5.

When we contrast Table 3.4 with Table 3.3, we can see that this swing has had a corresponding impact on the proportion of cases in which Justices sat, for which they wrote an opinion, which has dropped significantly except in the case of Lord Hope. Thus a comparison of the two tables shows us that most of the Law Lords in the Bingham era wrote an opinion in over 50 per cent of cases they sat in, whilst over two thirds of the Justices wrote in *less* than 50 per cent of the cases in which they sat. This reduction in the proportion of cases sat in, in which Justices write a judgment as compared with the Law Lords, tells only part of the story. Curiously, the writing habits of most of the Law Lords who became Justices did not change greatly.[160] Yet when we look at the length of what the judges wrote, there has been a dramatic shift. Whilst the length of their opinions and judgments varied depending on whether they were dissenting or writing the lead or sole opinion[161]

---

[160] Only Lord Rodger and Lady Hale saw the percentage of cases in which they wrote fall substantially between the two courts—although probably for different reasons.

[161] Most Law Lords in the Bingham era wrote significantly longer lead and single opinions (33 paragraphs on average) than dissenting opinions (24 paragraphs on average), although some Law Lords, notably Bingham and Millett (with Hope, Mance and Rodger not far behind) wrote similarly long leads and dissents. In the Supreme Court the picture was the same. The average lead and single

or merely a concurrence,[162] the average length of opinions per case in the House of Lords was 68 paragraphs. In the Supreme Court the average number of paragraphs per case had risen to 89 by March 2013. In short, whilst fewer judges are writing judgments in the Supreme Court as compared with the House of Lords, those that do write are writing more.

Along with a significant number of judgments of the court and a larger number of single majority judgments since 2009, there has been a parallel growth in judgments by one Justice with which one or more colleagues will join or agree. From 12.5 per cent (2) of cases in 2009, this rose to 26 per cent (14) in 2010, 45 per cent (27) in 2011, 79 per cent (48) in 2012 and 96 per cent (54) (up to end of July 2013).[163] Much slower has been the rise in the composite judgment where two or more Justices have jointly written the judgment. This phenomenon has become commonplace in the Court of Appeal[164] but occurred rarely in the House of Lords.[165] Up until the end of July 2013 there had only been about 10 overtly composite judgments in the Supreme Court,[166] but many more in which unnamed Justices have contributed whole passages to the lead majority judgment.

What about substantive concurring judgments (to the lead judgment) which last for more than a paragraph or two? These were commonplace in the House. They have remained relatively common in the Supreme Court with 62 per cent of cases under Lord Phillips' presidency containing one or more concurrence judg-

---

opinion was 48 paragraphs long and the average dissenting opinion was 30 paragraphs long. Only Lord Brown wrote similarly long leads and dissents but Lords Mance, Phillips and Sumption were not far behind. This is of relevance because in the Supreme Court the form of 'team-working' that they have now espoused means that lead and single judgments will be ones to which other Justices have contributed, and therefore are likely to be longer than multiple assenting judgments or dissents (unless the latter is a consolidated one). Certainly, on average, sole leading judgments are longer than multiple leading judgments in the Supreme Court.

[162] The average length of a substantial concurrence in the House was 7 paragraphs; in the Supreme Court it was 12 paragraphs.

[163] From October 2009 to end March 2013 52% of cases in the Supreme Court (107 out of 207 cases) featured such judgments.

[164] See R Munday, '"All for One and One for All": the Rise to Prominence of the Composite Judgment within the Civil Division of the Court of Appeal' (2002) 61 *CLJ* 321.

[165] See *Home Office v Harman* [1983] 1 AC 280 (a joint dissenting opinion by Lords Simon and Scarman), *Cullen v Chief Constable of the Royal Ulster Constabulary* [2003] UKHL 39 (a joint dissent by Lords Bingham and Steyn), *Norris v Government of the United States of America* [2008] UKHL 16 (a composite report of the Court, which in fact was written in several parts by different Law Lords and then amalgamated), and *R (Aweys) v Birmingham City Council* [2009] UKHL 36 (Lady Hale and Lord Neuberger).

[166] In the Supreme Court see *Principal Reporter v K* [2010] UKSC 56 (Lord Hope and Lady Hale), *Lucasfilm and Others v Ainsworth and Another* [2011] UKSC 39 (Lords Walker and Collins), *Jones v Kernott* [2011] UKSC 53 (Lord Walker and Lady Hale), *R v Gnango* [2011] UKSC 59 (Lords Phillips and Judge), *R v Waya* [2012] UKSC 51 (Lord Walker and Sir Anthony Hughes) (Lords Phillips and Reed in a composite dissent), *Al-Siri v Secretary of State for the Home Dept* [2012] UKSC 54 (Lady Hale and Lord Dyson), *O'Brien v Ministry of Justice (Formerly the Department for Constitutional Affairs)* [2013] UKSC 6 (Lord Hope and Lady Hale) and R v Hughes [2013] UKSC 56 (Lords Hughes and Toulson). Although not labelled as such, *Geys v Société Générale London Branch* [2012] UKSC 63 is akin to a composite judgment in that Lord Hope, Lady Hale and Lord Wilson share out the treatment of the four main points in the appeal between them.

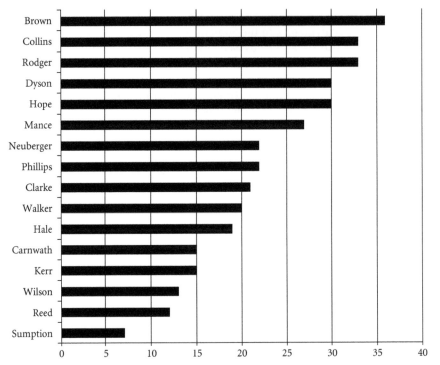

Table 3.6: Substantial judgments and concurrences in the UK Supreme Court as a percentage of total cases sat in during 2009–13 (July)[1].

[1] Excludes leading judgments and dissenting judgments.

ments to go along with the lead judgment. From Table 3.6 we can see that there are variations between the Justices.

Not surprisingly, those supportive of multiple judgments (eg Lords Hope, Brown, Rodger and Mance) tend to be the greatest concurrence writers and those favouring single majority judgments are (with the exception of Lord Dyson) generally more restrained in writing concurrences. The same holds true for those who write the only concurring judgment in a case (solo concurrences) although Lady Hale was a partial exception. In her case (as in the case of Lord Hope) the Justice is seeking to put a particular point of view on the record which it is unreasonable to expect to be included in the majority judgment.

There is therefore now a prevailing view amongst the Justices that concurrences should be curbed unless they are going to add something to the lead judgment. As one Justice put it,[167]

[167] Interview with the author.

If I wanted some comments added I would tend to go to the person that I was agreeing with and say, 'Can you see your way to adding these observations?' If he says, 'No' I would then think very carefully whether the comments were important enough to warrant a separate judgment, and the answer would probably be not. But I can think of lots of cases where I have simply agreed without additional comment on the footing that the additional comments I would have made have been incorporated in the judgment I am agreeing with.

Whilst academe may generally support this view, there have been two substantial attempts to defend concurring opinions in the last 10 years. The first, by Roderick Munday,[168] asserts that concurrences (1) remind us that litigation is not just about outcomes, but the reasoning by which it is achieved, (2) sharpen the focus of the lead opinion writer and (3) demonstrate to the parties that it is not only the lead judgment writer who has engaged with the case. James Lee in his seminal article, 'A Defence of Concurring Speeches'[169] argues that concurring judgments can enhance the value of the decision through a variety of approaches (1) buttressing the lead judgment from dissenters, (2) mediating between differing lead judgments (3) agreeing the outcome but disagreeing as to the reasons[170] (4) summarising the essence of the other judgments (5) providing greater accessibility of the decision to the public and (5) adding a dramatic touch.[171]

Lee also points to the existence of 'dissenting' concurrences which provide a 'misleading patina of harmony'[172] as to the result but not the reasons, which resemble something very similar, namely, the 'tactical assent' designed to encourage the majority to adopt a somewhat different principle than they originally intended. One instance of this appears to have been Lady Hale's speech in *AL (Serbia) v Secretary of State for Home Department*.[173] Such 'concurrences' provide a way for the writer to seek to influence his or her colleagues without having the judgment dismissed as a dissent. In keeping with her use of the solo concurrence, Lady Hale, has come out in support of short and to the point concurring judgments for similar reasons to James Lee. Whether multiple concurrences, or even idiosyncratic or subversive concurrences or dissents will survive the critique they received from the incoming President of the Supreme Court, Lord Neuberger, in his Bailii lecture[174] will remain to be seen. There his call for fewer and shorter concurrences and dissents—although accompanied by an avowal of any intention to move to a compulsory single judgment—is only likely to reinforce the trend to more single majority judgments in the Supreme Court. Already under Lord Neuberger's presidency we can see that the concurrence rate is declining further.

---

[168] R Munday, 'Judicial Configurations' (2002) 61 *CLJ* 612.

[169] J Lee, 'A Defence of Concurring Speeches' [2009] *Public Law* 305.

[170] Sometimes known as a 'tactical assent' or a 'dissenting concurrence'. Some judges are thought to engage in such judgments in an endeavour to reduce the weight of the lead judgment.

[171] See Lord Rodger in *Secretary of State for the Home Department v AF (No 3)* [2009] UKHL 28 at [98].

[172] Lee, above, n 169, 318.

[173] *AL (Serbia) v Secretary of State for Home Department* [2008] UKHL 42.

[174] Lord Neuberger, 'No Judgment—No Justice', delivered on 20 November 2012 (see Bailii website).

It may be that the Supreme Court is heading in the direction of the House of Lords in the decade from 1979 onwards under the influence of Lord Diplock, as illustrated in Table 3.2. Whether this is route worth re-inventing is a more difficult question. Lord Neuberger and Lady Hale[175] are aware that there are dangers associated with too great a trend to single or single majority judgments but that trend continues, as Table 3.5 illustrates.

On the other hand where there are multiple 'lead' or substantive judgments attributable to either the lead judgment writer ultimately failing to convince his or her colleagues[176] or because there never actually was 'a' lead judgment in the first place, it can be unhelpful for lower courts or the legal profession who are seeking to elucidate what the judgment stands for. The *Jewish Free School* case[177] is held up as the exemplar of this type of case which supporters of fewer judgments deplored but it was followed in other high-profile cases.[178] As against that, in *R v Waya*, a case that like *Jewish Free School* split the Court into several different positions, through much judicial dialogue the original multiple judgments were reduced to one majority judgment (in which five Justices agree) and one dissenting judgment (in which two Justices agree). Further there are signs that in later cases in 2013 the efforts of the Court to avoid cases in which every Justice writes, was bearing fruit.

Dissenting Opinions

On paper, dissenting opinions might appear to be evidence of a failure of judicial dialogue in a case, since they indicate that such judicial dialogue as has taken place throughout the case has not yielded a consensus amongst the judges. Reality is more complex than that, 'failures' of judicial dialogue can exist in unanimous cases where the court defers to a specialist member or though pressure of time has not engaged with each other in fruitful dialogue. In other cases such as *Waya*, dissents are very hard fought statements that have shifted the majority to tighter ground which will be more defensible in the future, without quite winning round a majority of the Court. In these cases the dissent has played a major and successful part in the judicial dialogue. In such cases there is little to be said for withdrawing the dissenting judgment at that stage and much to be said for retaining it as delimiting where the judicial dialogue has got to. As one Justice put it,[179]

---

[175] See Baroness Hale, 'Judgment writing in the Supreme Court' First anniversary seminar 30th September 2010.
[176] In several of these cases the lead judgments actually changed hands (see next chapter, below).
[177] *R (on the application of E) v Jewish Free School Governing Body* [2009] UKSC 15.
[178] See chapter 4 n 91, below.
[179] Interview with the author.

You may initially dissent in the hope that you won't be dissenting. You produce a draft judgment which is designed to persuade your colleagues to change their minds. Well, if you have done that, it is quite hard to withdraw your judgment and say, 'I agree', and it becomes impossible if, at least one of your colleagues says he agrees with you.

In any event it is far-fetched to posit that dialogue, given enough time, will always lead to consensus.

Moreover as we saw in the last section, some concurring judgments look suspiciously like dissents.[180] These 'tactical assents' seem designed to encourage subsequent readers of the case to see the lead judgment as ameliorated to a certain extent by the thoughts of the assenting Justice.[181] Since such assents are perceived by their critics as having similar drawbacks to dissents—eg the loss of unanimity, a potential to undermine certainty and confidence in the law[182] (especially in criminal or statutory interpretation cases), and a waste of judicial resources[183] with little practical impact[184]—it is not surprising that some commentators who seek to curb the former also wish to curb the latter.[185] Moreover, many of the arguments for concurrences also apply to dissents eg allowing all members of the panel to participate in the decision, sharpening the reasoning of the majority, identifying the limits to the majority decision, demonstrating that judges other than the lead judgment writer have applied their minds

---

[180] Which may explain Lord Neuberger's comment that 'dissenting judgments, *properly identified as such*, can be of immense value', in his Bailii lecture, above, n 174, at 10.

[181] One observer of the final court described to me instances of what he called the subversive assent in which rather than dissent, which intellectually the judge would obviously prefer to do, the judge would tactically assent but introduce into the concurrence qualifications upon the reasoning of the others which were designed to mitigate or possibly even undermine the logic of the majority.

[182] Blom-Cooper and Drewry described dissent as 'the most apparently poignant judicial tragedy in a legal system founded upon the dramatic conventions of certainty and unanimity' in *Final Appeal* (Oxford, Oxford University Press, 1972) at 83 and Judge Learned Hand at about the same time claimed that dissent 'cancels the impact of monolithic solidarity on which the authority of a bench of judges so largely depends'. *The Bill of Rights* (Cambridge MA, Harvard University Press, 1968) at 72. Somewhat later, in 2000 John Alder entitled an article on the topic as 'Dissents in Courts of Last Resort: Tragic Choices?' (2000) 20 *Oxford Journal of Legal Studies* 221.

[183] Studies in North America have established that cases with dissents or concurrences lead to longer majority or lead judgments. See D Songer, J Szmer and S Johnson, 'Explaining Dissent on the Supreme Court of Canada' (2011) 44 *Canadian Journal of Political Science* 389 and L Epstein, W Landes and R Posner, 'Why (and When) Judges Dissent: A Theoretical and Empirical Analysis', Chicago University Law and Economics Working Paper No 510, January 2010. However, this finding would not hold good for the House of Lords in the early Bingham years when there was little engagement between the opinions of the Law Lords.

[184] There is considerable scope for research into how often dissents in the final court lead at a later date to changes in the law. However, even at the time they are given they will often delimit the parameters of the majority judgment.

[185] See Lord Neuberger, 'No Judgment—No Justice', 1st Annual Bailii lecture, 20 November 2012. Both James Lee and Roderick Munday discuss the arguments for dissenting judgments alongside their defence of concurring judgments. (See nn 169 and 168 above).

to the case,[186] comforting the losing party,[187] engaging in a dialogue with the future which later judges may pick up,[188] promoting freedom of expression, as well as providing a safety valve for the minority voice.[189] Nevertheless, most of those who favour single majority judgments have regarded the right to dissent as a key element of judicial independence (including Baroness Hale)[190] and a freedom which should not be given up lightly.[191] Usually, therefore, as with the ABA Judicial Code of Ethics in an earlier form,[192] the most that supporters of single judgments will do is call for dissents to be used sparingly and confined to differences of opinion on matters of fundamental principle.

In truth the difference between a tactical assent and a dissent may be very little, depending on how 'dissents' are defined. Traditionally a dissent is an opinion or a vote that goes against the outcome supported by the majority of the judges deciding a case.[193] However, in practice some observers treat judgments which lead to the same outcome as the majority but by a radically different route in terms of legal reasoning, as more akin to a dissent.[194] Thus Lord Hoffmann's judgment in *Belmarsh* is frequently classed as a concurrence, but since it departs completely from the basis of the majority reasoning in many respects—at least from the perspective of posterity—it is more akin to a dissent.

---

[186] Lord Neuberger whilst he was still in the Lords told me, 'I actually quite like dissenting occasionally [since] it just confirms to yourself that you are not just going along with everybody. I think dissenting for its own sake is ghastly but never dissenting I think is a bad thing'.

[187] As one Law Lord observed, 'I don't see why the losing party shouldn't at least have the comfort of recognising that the merits of his case were perceived'. Lord Mance similarly noted, 'A dissent is a matter of intellectual honesty ... I think it can be a consolation to the parties that their argument's been understood [and] accepted by at least some members of the court'. (Interviews with the author, 2008).

[188] Chief Justice Hughes, in an aphorism so celebrated that it is regularly attributed to other Chief Justices, asserted that 'a dissent in a court of last resort is an appeal to the brooding spirit of the law, to the intelligence of a future day': CE Hughes, *The Supreme Court of the United States* (New York, Columbia University Press, 1928) at 68.

[189] As Lord Ackner put it, 'One dissents where one's sense of outrage at the majority decision outweighs one's natural indolence'. Quoted in A Paterson, *Lawyers and the Public Good: Democracy in Action?* (Cambridge, Cambridge University Press, 2012) at 173.

[190] See Lee, above, n 169, 305.

[191] In fairness, Lord Neuberger expressly states that he would not seek to curb dissents by his colleagues, rather, he hopes that they will exercise self-restraint with regard to dissents and concurrences.

[192] Taft CJ introduced the words 'Except in case of conscientious difference of opinion on fundamental principle dissenting opinions should be discouraged in courts of last resort' to the ABA Code of Judicial Ethics in 1923 but they were dropped in 1972. See J Alder, 'Dissents in Courts of Last Resort: Tragic Choices?' (2000) 20 *Oxford Journal of Legal Studies* 221, 244.

[193] For a detailed exposition of what should count as a dissent or a concurrence for empirical purposes see A Lynch, 'Dissent: Towards a Methodology for Measuring Judicial Disagreement in the High Court of Australia' (2002) 24 *Sydney Law Review* 470.

[194] See Justice Michael Kirby, 'Judicial dissent—common law and civil law traditions' (2007) 123 *LQR* 379.

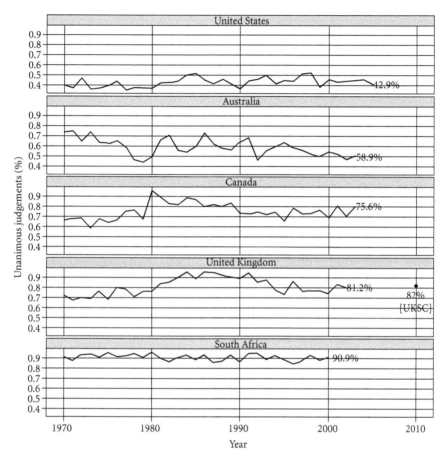

Table 3.7: Comparative dissent rates in the US Supreme Court, the Australian High Court, the Canadian Supreme Court, the House of Lords and UK Supreme Court and the South African Constitutional Court[2].

[2] This data is taken from the blog of Chris Hanretty to whom grateful thanks are due for permission to reproduce this table. http://ukscblog.com/dissenting-opinons-in-the-uksc

As for the frequency of dissents, as Hanretty has argued[195] the House of Lords was somewhat less prone to dissenting judgments (based on outcomes or on reasoning) than its counterparts in the United States and Australia. (See Table 3.7)

However, until its last decade the House's dissent rate was comparable with that of the Canadian Supreme Court and higher than the South African Court. As can be seen from Tables 3.8 and 3.9, since the middle of the last century dissent has

[195] C Hanretty, 'The Decisions and Ideal Points of British Law Lords' (2013) 43 *British Journal of Political Science* 703.

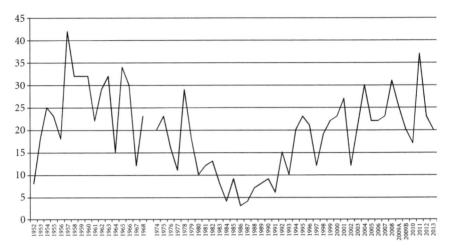

Table 3.8: Percentage of House of Lords or UK Supreme Court cases containing at least one dissent during 1952–2013 (July).

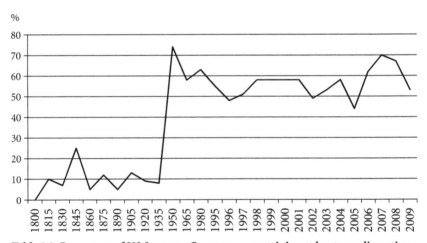

Table 3.9: Percentage of US Supreme Court cases containing at least one dissenting opinion 1800–2009.

been approximately one and a half (160 per cent) times less common in the House of Lords than in the US Supreme Court.

The three graphs in Tables 3.7, 3.8 and 3.9 illustrate that over time the dissent rates in courts of last resort in the principal common law countries vary quite considerably. How might we account for this? There is no single explanation but some parameters can be suggested,

1) *Legal tradition.*[196] Courts associated with the French civilian legal tradition generally speaking do not permit the publication of concurring or dissenting judgments in their highest courts. This includes much of Europe, parts of Asia and certain international courts such as the European Court of Justice. Most other courts of last resort that adhere to, or are influenced by the common law tradition—in the US, the UK, Canada, Australia, other parts of the Commonwealth—usually allow both concurring and dissenting judgments.[197] Certain European countries of a Germanic civilian tradition (Germany, Switzerland etc), the Scandinavian countries and some other international courts eg the European Court of Human Rights and the International Court of Justice, also permit the publication of such judgments. Comparative scholars attribute these differences in part to the collegiate culture of the career judiciary in the civilian tradition, which emphasises the value of certainty, clarity and collective decision-making, and in part to a greater emphasis on the importance of judicial independence in an individualistic sense in common law countries.[198]

2) *Leadership attributes.* Studies of the US Supreme Court, Australia and Canada suggest that the level of dissenting and concurring judgments in the highest courts is often influenced by the views of the chief judge in the court. As we have seen this seems to hold true also for the concurring judgments in the House of Lords and the UKSC. It seems to have a measure of credibility also for dissents. Dissents were frowned on in the Lords in the late 1940s[199] but in Lord Reid's era his robust laissez faire infected half his colleagues who saw no reason for not dissenting if you wanted to. The other half saw the virtue of self restraint—especially where they were on their own (see Tables 3.8 and 3.10).

Under Lord Diplock the antipathy to concurrences fed through to dissents which, as Table 3.8 shows, dropped to their lowest levels since the 1940s. Under Lord Bingham dissents (and concurrences) rose again through his more relaxed approach to multiple and dissenting judgments. It remains to be seen whether Lord Neuberger, in articulating a desire for fewer concurring *and* dissenting judgments, will precipitate another decade like the 1980's

---

[196] On this see Michael Kirby, 'Judicial Dissent- common law and civil law traditions' (2007) 123 *LQR* 379 and John Alder 'Dissents in Courts of Last Resort: Tragic Choices?' (2000) 20 *Oxford Journal of Legal Studies* 221.

[197] Although there are curious anomalies eg Court of Appeal Criminal Division which has never allowed separate concurrences or dissents (without the permission of the presiding judge), and the Privy Council which only formally allowed dissents and concurrences in 1966.

[198] See J Alder, 'Dissents in Courts of Last Resort: Tragic Choices?' (2000) 20 *Oxford Journal of Legal Studies* 221, M Kirby, 'Judicial dissent—common law and civil law traditions' (2007) 123 *LQR* 379. Interestingly, Robin White and Iris Boussiakou, in research conducted at Leicester University, found that having a background in a common law tradition tended to increase the likelihood of a judge filing a separate concurring or dissenting opinion in the ECtHR. See R White and I Boussiakou 'Separate opinions in the European Court of Human Rights' (2009) 9 *Human Rights Law Review* 37.

[199] See *The Law Lords*, above, n 9, 103.

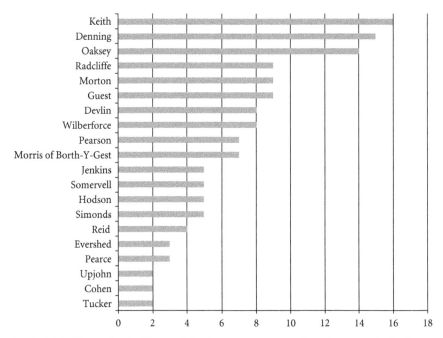

Table 3.10: Dissents in the House of Lords as a percentage of total cases sat in during 1952–68.

when Lord Diplock's call for more sole judgments and fewer and shorter concurrences produced a spectacular decline in both concurrences and dissents

3) *Norms of collegiality and team-working in the court.* This factor can be linked to the previous one. Where the culture of the court inhibits separate dissents and concurrences, as in the era of Lord Diplock, or places a higher value on team or collective working,[200] as appears to be the case in today's UK Supreme Court, then this is likely to have an impact on dissent rates (as we shall see further in the next chapter).

4) *Place in the legal hierarchy.* Greater pressure and greater workload tend to lead to the judges on appellate courts working more closely together as a team, and a desire for clearer guidance from the top court, as in the case of the Court of Appeal of England and Wales in the last 15 years.

5) *Panel size.* Comparative studies appear to suggest that the larger the panel in which the judges of a final appeal court sit, the greater potential for differences of opinion leading to concurring judgments or dissents. This may

---

[200] See D Songer, J Szmer and S Johnson, 'Explaining Dissent on the Supreme Court of Canada' (2011) 44 *Canadian Journal of Political Science* 389, 393 et seq and L Epstein, W Landes and R Posner, 'Why (and When) Judges Dissent: A Theoretical and Empirical Analysis', Chicago University Law and Economics Working Paper No 510, January 2010.

partly explain why the US Supreme Court (nine Justices) and the Canadian Supreme Court (seven Justices) which sat in greater numbers than the House of Lords had higher dissent rates than the House. Again, of the 166 Grand Chamber decisions of the ECtHR (17 judges) published between 1999 and 2007, 96 (58 per cent) contained at least one dissent. As Table 3.8 shows, there has been a small but noticeable rise from the dissent rate which prevailed in the House of Lords (22 per cent of cases) to that prevailing in the UK Supreme Court (24 per cent). Again this may reflect the fact that Supreme Court has sat in panels of seven and nine to a much greater extent that the House of Lords, as we saw earlier.

At the level of the individual judges there are also interesting variations, as a comparison of the dissent rates for the judges in the House of Lords and in the UK Supreme Court reveals (see Tables 3.10, 3.11 and 3.12). Indeed, this is true even as between the same individual in the two courts. In terms of overall levels, none of the modern Law Lords and Justices, despite Lord Neuberger's call for fewer dissents, has attained the levels of dissent over a sustained period achieved by Lord Keith[201] (16 per cent) and Lord Denning[202] (15 per cent). However, the propensity to dissent is clearly one that has varied widely in Law Lords and Justices since 2000. Some, like Lord Kerr and Lord Scott, have shown themselves to be unshrinking dissenters both in terms of dissenting on their own and with others. Lord Kerr told me (even before he had dissented for the first time in the Supreme Court) that 'if you feel that the decision is wrong or that the reasoning supporting the decision is wrong, you shouldn't shirk from writing a dissent'.[203] Lord Wilson, on the other hand, is of a different persuasion,[204]

> I think you have got to dissent only when you feel quite strongly about the decision, and are almost surprised at the decision. I would swallow hard and accept a majority decision unless there was a sort of propulsion ... of objection. I can't live with it, I am sorry I can't live with it—then I think you dissent. Otherwise, and I may have the balance wrong in this regard, otherwise I would tend to go along with it.

The difference between individual judges seems (as with attitudes to concurring judgments) to turn substantially on the weight which they give to the arguments that multiple judgments (whether assenting or dissenting) (1) delimit or confine the reach of the majority judgment, (2) detract from the authority of the opinion of the majority and thereby reduce the certainty and coherence of the law, (3) serve a useful purpose by offering a dialogue with the future, and (4) demonstrate judicial independence. Sometimes, as we have seen, there are enough judges who are convinced by the first two arguments that the court moves towards a single majority judgment with fewer concurring and dissenting judgments. Sometimes

---

[201] This is Lord Keith, the father of the later Lord Keith. The first Lord Keith sat from 1954–63.

[202] 1957–62.

[203] See also Lord Kerr, 'Dissenting judgments—self indulgence or self sacrifice?', The Birkenhead Lecture, 8 October 2012 (see UK Supreme Court website).

[204] Interview with the author, 2012.

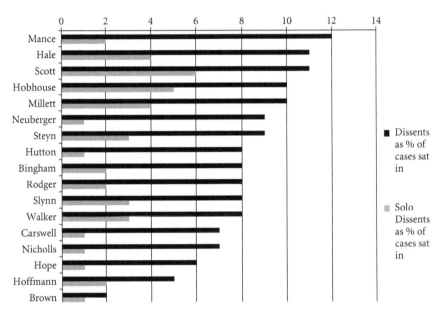

Table 3.11: Dissents and solo dissents in the House of Lords as a percentage of total cases sat in during 2000–09.

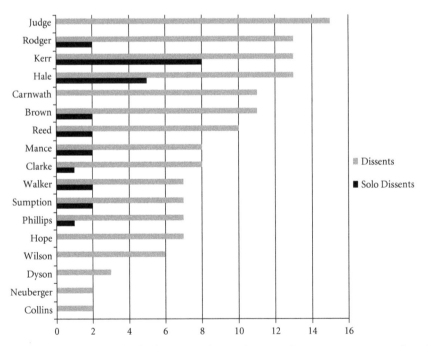

Table 3.12: Dissents and solo dissents in the UK Supreme Court as a percentage of total cases sat in during 2009–13 (July).

(as under Lords Reid and Bingham) the balance of opinion amongst the judges has been the other way.[205] However, just as many of the judges in the last 40 years have considered that single judgments are strongly to be desired in certain types of case, so too in this period there has been a significant minority of Law Lords and Justices who have not thought it worthwhile to dissent on their own unless it was on a point of principle.[206] In the last decade alone the Law Lords and Justices have been twice as likely to dissent with a colleague as to dissent on their own (see Tables 3.11 and 3.12).

Thus, Lord Mance, who when in the House of Lords was frequently involved in 'close call' cases[207] on the minority side, rarely dissented on his own.[208] Again, Lord Hoffmann dissented less than half as often as Lord Mance[209] but when he did, like so many of his colleagues, he tended to do it in company with one or more colleagues.

In such cases where two or more judges are dissenting together, other factors come into play, around the internal decision-making processes and dialogues in the court (which are the focus of the next chapter). Suffice it to say, the picture presented in this chapter of the judgment writing process in the UK's final court has been a slightly static one. We have touched on the order in which judgments are produced and the implications this may have for the final product but there may be far more interchange between the judges once judgments are being circulated than the foregoing account might suggest. Indeed, unlike the position in the Privy Council where, although there was a single judgment of the court, more often than not it was written by one of the judges and the others took little part in the drafting, whenever the Court is striving for a single judgment there will be much toing and froing between the Law Lords and Justices. The exchanges are mainly in writing—memoranda are generally addressed to all members of the panel, although sometimes there will be a bilateral exchange between the opinion writer and one of the other judges—often orally or by way of an email. Generally speaking, the greater the desire for a single judgment, the greater the pressure on the judgment writer to compromise on the argumentation in order to prevent a concurrence or even a dissent. Alternatively when the court is deeply divided—it

---

[205] Lord Kerr in 'Dissenting judgments' (above, n 203) said, 'In my firm opinion … the existence of contrary views and their enunciation in dissenting judgments do *not* inevitably detract from the authority of the opinion of the majority'.

[206] 'Sole dissents in the House of Lords are nothing, they are not encouraged, they are in a sense completely pointless' (Lord Lloyd in interview with the author).

[207] One where there were at least two dissents. For a fuller definition see chapter 1 of this volume above.

[208] *Dubitante* opinions by Lord Mance can be found eg in *Caldarelli* [2008] UKHL 51, para 40: 'I must confess to having found the answer to the present issue not easy. But it is an issue on which certainty under United Kingdom domestic law is probably more important than anything else, and this is now offered by the speeches of my noble and learned friends…' and in *Doherty v Birmingham City Council* [2008] UKHL 57, paras 162 and 164.

[209] 'I think you dissent if you are really cross about the way in which the majority has decided it. If you look for example at the dissents which Tom Bingham and I wrote in *Chester v Afshar* [2004] UKHL 41 … you can see a sort of tone of impatience from both of us'.

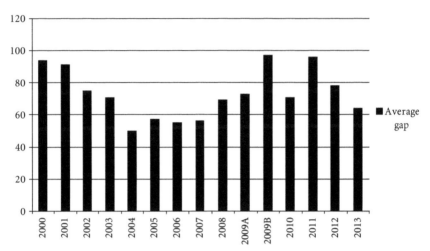

Table 3.13: Average gap (in days) between hearing and judgment in the House of Lords and the UK Supreme Court during 2000–13.[3]

[3] '2009A' refers to January–July 2009 during which the judgments were delivered in the House of Lords, with '2009B' referring to judgments delivered October 2009 onwards in the Supreme Court.

is a close call in other words—here too there may be scope for dialogue between the opposing camps—with oral and written lobbying. Both types of situation will tend to take time, resulting in delays in producing the final judgment.

Circulation Time

To ask how long the drafting and circulation period lasts is to ask how long the judges give themselves for dialogue before reaching closure. Forty years ago in the Lords the average figure was six weeks.[210] By the millennium, however, the circulation of opinions amongst the Law Lords had become a drawn-out process typically exceeding three months and sometimes taking more than eight months.[211] Lord Bingham's arrival in the final decade of the House seems to have had a significant galvanising effect since the average gap from hearing to handing down of the judgment dropped to less than two months, with very few taking more than five months (see Table 3.13 above). However, when Lord Phillips took over as senior Law Lord and then first President of the Supreme Court the average time taken to produce began once more to rise. He was more relaxed than Lord Bingham as

[210] Between 1952 and 1968 it was said to be six weeks: L Blom Cooper and G Drewry, *Final Appeal* (Oxford, Clarendon Press, 1972) at 236.
[211] In 2000 the average delay between hearing and judgment was 95 days with two cases taking a year and a further two taking more than 250 days.

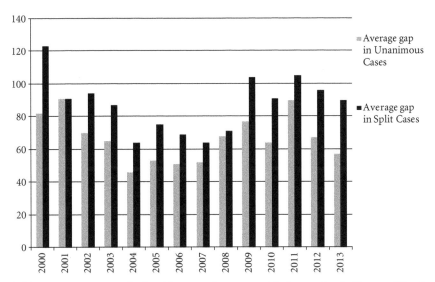

Table 3.14: Average gap (in days) between hearing and judgment in the House of Lords and the UK Supreme Court during 2000–13 (July), differentiating between split cases and others.

to when judgments were produced (as Table 3.13 reveals), taking the view that judgments should take as long as is required to get them right. It is noticeable that under Lord Neuberger (who is more like Lord Bingham in this respect), the average time between hearing and final judgment has come down again.

The second point of note, as already hinted, is that where there is a divided court—the average length of time between the first conference and the handing down of the judgment increases substantially (see Table 3.14).

This indicates that, as we will see in chapters four and five below, where there are collective efforts to enhance the dialogue between the judges on the panel, possibly involving several case conferences, or a sharp split in the panel with the possibility of minds and votes changing, the process of producing the final judgment(s) will generally (and unsurprisingly) take longer. It also suggests that some unanimous cases which takes considerably longer than the norm to emerge in judgment form, may be ones which at the time of the first conference were close calls or at least split, and that efforts were made in the circulation process to move the members of the panel in one direction or the other.

CONCLUSION

There are many opportunities for dialogue between the Law Lords and Justices at different stages of the decision-making process. Whilst some dialogues are predominantly oral—especially at the stage of the hearing and the first conference—increasingly the dialogues, whether in the shape of emails and circulating judgments and memoranda commenting thereon, are in writing. To sum up, although the types of dialogue between the Law Lords themselves have remained fundamentally the same over the last 40 years, there had been several changes. Taken together, these sometimes subtle alterations in the Law Lords' and Justices' practices meant that by the middle of 2013 the character of these exchanges was different. From a decision-making process 40 years ago which used to be largely oral, it had become one that was significantly more in writing. In the next chapter we will examine the efficacy of these dialogues and the impact of the move to less oral decision-making.

4

Dialogues with Colleagues—Efficacy in Judicial Dialogues

INTRODUCTION

WHEN AND WHY are some dialogues more effective than others? The last chapter looked at the types of dialogue that occur between Law Lords and Justices and the junctures in the judicial decision-making process at which they occur. In this chapter we will look at some of the factors which influence the frequency and efficacy of these dialogues. This, of course, merely begs the question as to what constitutes an effective dialogue between the judges in our final court. For the purposes of this chapter, at least, efficacy in dialogue will be taken to mean an exchange that influences or enhances the reasoning or outcome favoured by one or more of the judges in the panel deciding a particular case.[1] This will usually involve an engagement (oral or written) between the arguments of two or more of the judges—but the engagement may never be reflected in the published judgments.

What then are the principal factors which influence the frequency, efficacy and impact of dialogues in the decision-making process? The two main ones appear to be (a) the context in which the dialogue takes place; and (b) the composition of the panel determining the appeal. The former includes the differing stages of the decision-making process and the opportunities for interchange presented in particular cases (covered in the last chapter), and issues of timing. The latter includes (1) the view taken by panel members on group orientation or on single majority judgments, (2) the leadership skills, confidence and workload of the panel members, and (3) the links between panel members in terms of office location, friendship or voting record.

CONTEXT

Stages

Taking first the differing stages of the decision-making process, as we saw in the last chapter, dialogues between the judges before the hearing commences have

---

[1] Of course, it is possible that an intervention by a judge will be counter-productive and produce the opposite effect on his/her colleagues to what is intended. These will be treated as ineffective dialogues in this book.

generally been of a limited nature and significance in the final court, although this has changed a bit under Lord Neuberger. Even during the hearing the exchanges between the judges, whether couched as questions to counsel or to colleagues in the hearing or during the breaks, have again been of a limited nature and therefore of limited impact. Certainly they assist other members of the panel to learn how some of their colleagues view the issues in the case,[2] and occasionally such exchanges can sway the opinions of some of the panel members. More often it is at the first conference that judges have their most sustained opportunity[3] to influence their colleagues by their presentations. However, it is mainly in those cases where the first conference reveals a split between the panel members as to reasoning or outcome that the first conference features any extended discussion as opposed to seriatim monologues.[4] It is difficult to put a figure on the percentage of first conferences in which this occurs. The proportion of cases in the final court since 1952 in which there have been one or more dissents has averaged around 22 per cent and solo dissents have been consistently at around 11 per cent.[5] These figures potentially exaggerate the degree of debate at the first conference because (a) not all dissents provoke a debate, especially if the 'dissenter' is the junior and expressing tentative views;[6] (b) some dissents only become manifest at a later stage; and (c) sometimes the discussion has to be truncated for other reasons. On the other hand, these figures probably also understate the level of disagreement in the first hearing since in a significant minority of cases the judges are divided as to their reasoning but not as to the preferred outcome, or initially divided as to the proposed outcome but subsequently come together. It would seem therefore that extended discussions at the first conference are confined to no more than 25 per cent of all cases.[7] Since, until 2012 or so, reconvened conferences occurred on only a few times a year, it follows that in general it was at the stage of the circulation of the judgments that the greatest opportunities existed for telling exchanges to occur, should the judges choose to use them. In the House of Lords[8] 40 years ago, it was rare for a Law Lord to comment in writing on the draft judgments of his colleagues. Either the Law Lord would comment orally to his colleague on the opinion or he would simply adjust his speech to take account of the points made in the circulated opinion,

---

[2] In the US Supreme Court that is sometimes said to be the principal advantage of the truncated hearings held in that court.

[3] An opportunity which has changed relatively little in the last 40 years.

[4] Information obtained from various interviews with Law Lords over the years.

[5] See Table 3.8 of this volume, above.

[6] As we will see, because junior judges speak first at the first conference they will regularly express their view guardedly or tentatively until the position of the rest of the panel is clearer.

[7] This figure is compatible with the estimates which I received in interviews with the judges.

[8] As far as I could discern the draft judgment of the Judicial Committee of the Privy Council at that time was circulated with a slip attached, and the draft and slip are returned to the opinion writer with a variety of comments from his colleagues written on them. The comments range from 'Approved', 'I agree', 'No comment' to 'I dissent and am writing a dissent' and 'I don't agree but won't write anything'.

At the stage where the opinions are circulated one's colleagues are very polite. If there is an obvious omission you draw attention to it, but you would seldom re-argue the merits. (A Law Lord)

Generally, you'd leave it alone unless it was a case where you'd agreed that only one judgment would be delivered or if you were going to follow a particular man you might go to him and say, 'Look I'm really almost in entire agreement with you so I just propose to say, "I agree" but I'm a bit stuck about this [phrase] …'. You might do that. (Lord Devlin)

You would more frequently [comment] when the judgment was agreeing with yours, but if it was dissenting from you altogether, there would not be much point in doing it … But in cases where the judgment is concurring with yours, you might say, 'Well, do you think we want to put it quite as you put it?' But then you would probably go and do that orally. You go and see the man. You would not circulate a formal statement saying 'I cannot agree with paragraph 4b' in terms. You go round to the man and say, 'Oh, that was a wonderful piece of work you did', whether you thought it was or not, 'But don't you think perhaps this sentence might be modified, doesn't it go too far?' (Lord Cross)

You would not, I think, *write* comments. You would make them orally in the Library. It is most important to emphasise the informality of this: but it is not the less effective for that. This must be an extreme difference from a court in which there are recognisable political or ideological differences between groups of judges. (Lord Kilbrandon)

Nor did the presiding judge have any particular role in this area. Lord Guest commented,

It's not his duty to vet the speeches of the other judges; they're their own responsibility. Very, very seldom does the presiding judge make any comment to a member of the House upon his written judgment, unless there's something which he plainly wants to ask about or which he thinks is plainly wrong.

Lord Reid (who presided from 1962–75) concurred,

I very, very seldom criticise anybody else's opinion when we get them in draft. They are always circulated and we readjust our own in light of what anybody else says, but I very seldom have suggested to anybody that it would be better to leave something out, and if I do it's more from the point of view that it wouldn't be tactful, than anything else.

Lord Lloyd, describing the practice in the House in 2000 or so, remarked that if he had a point to make about a colleague's judgment he would go and chat with him or, occasionally, *write* a short, personal memo.[9] The subtle movement from an almost entirely oral form of dialogue to a mixed oral and written one was even clearer in the final years of the judicial era of the House of Lords when my second set of interviews took place,

Its unusual [to write], unless I actually want somebody to make amendments [to their judgment] in which case I'll draft something. But I would not normally [write], I would go and speak to them. (Lord Hoffmann)

[9] He could not remember ever writing a memo to all his colleagues, it was always a one-to-one thing.

I would talk to them and say 'Can I give you a draft of what I think is the paragraph that I might want to put it in', something like that, it varies enormously, it's very informal. I might talk to Lord Rodger and say 'I find a bit of difficulty in paragraph 17'. In one case the presider wrote and one of the others had a fairly strong view about what he had said, and I think probably gave him a memo, but certainly gave him a draft of his own views. The first chap looked at the second chap's views and said 'I see a lot of force in that. I'm going to take out a whole section and not go into it at all. I think you've got that section right and it brings us more or less into the same camp' … And it did and the result was that we all agreed on the result with two rather different strands of argument. (Lord Carswell)

Sometimes you read a long judgment and I might write many corrections on it and then I put it in his cubby-hole and he'd take it away and sometimes there'd be typos but sometimes there'd be a thought, 'would it not perhaps …', so you occasionally go into their room. Which way you do it just depends on what's most convenient at the moment of the day. (A Law Lord)

A different Law Lord observed that whether he made an effort to persuade a colleague at this stage depended on the colleague and his relationship with them,

Lord Steyn particularly was somebody who was almost un-persuadable to change a word in his judgment at all and Lord Hobhouse was the same and there was no point in asking because they wouldn't listen to you. Whereas there are others here who would say, 'Yes that's perfectly all right, I'm quite happy to do that' and would go along with it. So it depends on the personalities of the judges, some are very willing to be adapted, as it were, to construct something, but others are not.

Lord Carswell drew a comparison with the Privy Council,

The Privy Council's rather different because there we do try to have a single view and therefore we try to accommodate the views of people who have a slightly different slant and that can involve a bit of re-writing, taking in suggestions, people saying 'I think you might deal with Section 42 rather differently, could I make a suggestion about it' and generally if you're writing it, you'll say 'Well of course, I'd be very happy to look at that' but sometimes, very rarely, you'd go back and say 'Well I don't agree with that, and I just can't do it' but usually you would say 'Yes I'm quite happy to incorporate that'.

Thus, by 2009 it was not uncommon for Law Lords to write memoranda (sometimes via email) either to the author of a draft judgment or to all of the panel in relation to the draft judgments that were circulating. This more formal approach might even be used to correct an error by a colleague—a process that might more tactfully have been done orally. Intriguingly, by then some Law Lords found it easier to engage with their colleagues in writing rather than dropping in on them. Thus, instead of debating the draft judgment in person they would write and circulate their own draft out of diffidence from engaging more directly with more senior colleagues. As one said to me,

I'm pretty diffident at the moment about that kind of process though I do go and say 'What do you think?', but I haven't been trying advocacy to talk people round very much. If they've got a view that's fine and I've got a case at the moment in which I'm in a minority of one … and I feel really that my position is obviously right but the other four don't. It's slightly frustrating not to be able to go to them, to go to each one and say look 'For God's sake, how can you possibly think this having read my judgment?'.

The trend towards commenting on drafts in writing (whether by email or circulated memoranda) has accelerated in the Supreme Court. Geography (in the guise of the location of the Justices' rooms) plays a role (as we will see later in the chapter) but otherwise it is becoming the norm for Justices to email the lead judgment writer to raise either particular points on an individual basis, or to email all of the panel with suggestions as to how the judgment might be amended. Similarly, where Justices are considering dissenting or putting in a concurring judgment they will often liaise with a like-minded colleague by a lateral email or in a conversation if their room is nearby. One Justice described a typical exchange as follows,

> Well, what happened in that case, and I think this is reasonably typical, is that I wrote the judgment, and I circulated it … [B]y and large [comments] will come as memoranda. Occasionally you will have an oral exchange. For instance, in that case although I'm the author of it Lord Collins is responsible for the first paragraph. I just launched into a narrative of the background to the case and as he very sensibly pointed out to me, 'I think it's important because this is an important case and we are reaffirming a principle just to flag up in the first paragraph the significance of the case', and he came along and he and I had a chat about it and I then sat down and drafted it as a result of that … whereas Lady Hale and Lord Hope both sent a memorandum making suggestions and I reworked the judgment and put in a couple of paragraphs as a result of their memoranda but that was shared with everyone.
>
> When I produced the second draft of the judgment as a result of my discussion with Lord Collins I sent it to everyone and I said 'Lord Collins has helpfully made a suggestion to me and I have now put in a different first paragraph' … There was a suggestion made to me which I didn't think I should follow and we had a frank exchange and I pointed out that if a reference was included well then it would blunt the message that I hoped that we would convey. We then discussed it and eventually it was agreed that I shouldn't include that particular reference … That particular exchange of emails came from my colleague to me but copied to all the others, likewise my reply.

Another Justice observed,

> Because it is a small place and we are all meeting pretty regularly at lunchtime and dropping into each other's rooms, things can be done in a fairly informal way according to the personalities involved in a particular case. When judgments are circulating, you can either send a memo round to everybody saying this is what I think of this or you can go next door … I suppose I wouldn't circulate something generally if it was likely to cause embarrassment. For example, if I thought someone had made some howler about the law I would mention that privately.

Time and Timing

Part of context relates to issues of time and timing. Generally speaking these should not be issues which significantly affect the efficacy of the judicial dialogues, since most judges in the final court assert that they are prepared to take whatever time it takes to get the decision right. In practice, it does not always work like that. On occasions, pressures of time intrude. This has been exacerbated by the steady decline in the length of oral hearings over the last 40 years, in part because presiding Law Lords and Justices are taking a tougher line on adherence to time estimates. This not only reduces the time for dialogue with counsel but also with fellow judges during and around the hearing stage. As we saw at the end of the last chapter,[10] under Lord Bingham the gap between the hearing and the judgment being handed down was considerably reduced. Although Lord Phillips was more relaxed in relation to this, under Lord Neuberger the pressure to get judgments out seems to be increasing. Ironically, this is at a time when some of the Justices would like to have more deliberation between themselves. One of the curiosities of appellate decision-making is how little time is spent in collective deliberation.[11] In the UK final court the first conference typically lasts less than an hour (in part because it usually begins when the hearing ends at 4 pm) and in the great majority of cases is also the only conference of any significance during the case. Some Justices find this unsatisfactory and would like there to be more conferences—or for the first conference to be delayed by a day or so, in order to enable the Justices to be better prepared and to have more time to deliberate than a 4 pm start affords. As one put it,

> I think we would reach better decisions if we had an open mind for a bit longer but the system of post-hearing conferences discourages that. A better system would be to have a routine principle under which, wherever we didn't agree as to the result or the reasons for the result, we then had a further conference to discuss draft judgments because I think it would then be clear that the draft judgments were very much drafts.

Lord Carnwath's account[12] of the first conference suggest that there are slight moves in that direction,

> We are going through a transition between the very formulaic approach and a feeling that really we shouldn't be forcing ourselves to take a position immediately. So sometimes the debate is acknowledged to be a preliminary canter.

---

[10] See Table 3.13, above.

[11] R Posner, *How Judges Think* (Cambridge MA, Harvard University Press, 2008) at 2: '[The real secret is that] they do not deliberate (by which I mean deliberate *collectively*) very much'. The academic debate over the need for more collective deliberation in the United States Supreme Court, to assist in collective judgments and to overcome the need for proliferating dissents has been ongoing for many decades. Professor Henry M. Hart was a long-time advocate of such a process. See Hart, 'The Time Chart of the Justices', 73 *Harvard Law Review* 84, 98–100 (1959). Judge Thurmond Arnold rejected the view that 'reason would replace the conflicting views now present on the Court if the Court had more time for "the maturing of collective thought."' . . . There is no such process as this, and there never has been; men of positive views are only hardened by those views by such conferences.' Arnold, 'Professor Hart's Theology', 73 *Harvard Law Review* 1298, 1312 (1960). He went on to opine in addition that 'I have no doubt that that longer periods of argument and deliberation, and more time to dissent, would only result in the proliferation of opinions.' *Id* at 1313.

[12] Interview with the author, 2013.

That was rarely the case in the House of Lords. In one celebrated case in Lord Bingham's time—let us call it *A v B*—the panel was split 3:2 at the first conference with Bingham in the minority. Unfortunately for the minority, the discussion at the conference had to be truncated because some of the Law Lords had a function to attend and this prevented them from arguing round the swing voter on the panel who was wavering. By the time the judgments were being circulated the opportunity had been lost.

Interestingly, in the United States, time was also a factor in *Bush v Gore*:[13] the case which decided the 2000 Presidential election. Although the court was initially split in accordance with the party of whichever president had appointed each Justice, Justices Souter and Breyer later expressed the view that with a bit more time, they might have won round Justice Kennedy—then the swing voter on the Court—to join with them. They did persuade him about the poverty of the reasoning of the lower court—insufficient guidance on equal protection matters—but failed in the short time available to sway him on the issue of whether the recount should be halted.[14]

Timing can also be important in relation to the circulation of drafts. Although Lord Rodger regularly wrote his draft judgments some time after his colleagues,[15] with devastating effect on occasion[16]—and indeed a minority of Law Lords over the years have considered that the best course of action in a case where opinions are divided is to wait for representatives of each camp to circulate a draft judgment before writing their own—there have also been occasions, as in *Stack v Dowden*,[17] (the property rights of separating cohabitees case) where the tactic has been spectacularly unsuccessful. Having seen his initial majority disappear following the emergence of Lady Hale's draft judgment, Lord Neuberger in his very first case in the Lords spent much of the Easter vacation in writing a trenchant dissent in response to his colleagues' circulated judgments. As he later recalled ruefully, it did no good. People had made up their minds and moved on long before his draft appeared. Again, in a case involving Lords Hoffmann and Goff, a delay by Lord Goff in writing what was meant to be the lead judgment cost him his majority. As Lord Hoffmann recalled,

> We had a case in the late nineties[18] about the construction of a notice under the Landlord and Tenant Act in which we divided 3:2. Robert Goff, Charles Jauncey and I were for holding it invalid and Johan Steyn and James Clyde were for holding it valid. Robert, who was going to write the leading judgment, took about four months to produce it and

---

[13] *Bush v Gore* 531 US 38 (1985).
[14] JC Greenburg, *Supreme Conflict* (New York, The Penguin Press, 2007) at 176 (Kennedy denied that time had made a difference).
[15] See T Nesterchuk, 'The View from Behind the Bench' chapter 11 in A Burrows, D Johnston and R Zimmermannl (eds), *Judge and Jurist: Essays in Memory of Lord Rodger of Earlsferry* (Oxford, Oxford University Press, 2013).
[16] See chapter 5 of this volume below.
[17] *Stack v Dowden* [2007] UKHL 17.
[18] *Mannai Investment Co Ltd v Eagle Star Assurance* [1997] UKHL 19; [1997] AC 749.

during that time I must have written about eight or nine drafts of a supporting judgment. I was not satisfied that I'd got it right in any of these drafts and I'd tried this way and that way and eventually it seemed to me the reason why I wasn't getting it right was because I was wrong. So I changed sides at that point and it went 3:2 the other way. I tell the story because I think if Robert had produced his judgment within a couple of weeks the case would have been decided differently.[19]

Similarly, in the *Lloyds Bank* case[20] it seems that Lord Mance got his dissent out before the lead judgment emerged—with the result that he was able to win over the majority to his side of the argument.

THE COMPOSITION OF THE PANEL

Approaches to Collective Decision-making: The Art of Persuasion

Since individual Law Lords and Justices vary widely in the centrality which they accord to collective decision-making in the court, it follows that the composition of each panel hearing appeals in the final court is likely to have a significant influence on how collectively or otherwise the panel works when deciding a complex problem. Just because the court of last resort in the United Kingdom sits in panels of five, seven or (occasionally) nine judges, does not mean that the court necessarily operates collectively—far less as a team—when engaged in decision-making. In the Privy Council over the last 40 years and more, it has been commonplace for the presider to decide who will be writing the opinion of the court.[21] Whether because of the greater pool from whom judges in the Judicial Committee of the Privy Council are drawn[22] or the less challenging nature of some PC cases, over the years the Law Lords and Justices have often been content to allow the opinion writer to get on with his/her task and not to engage greatly in the drafting process after the first conference. What therefore looks like as though it should have been the product of a collective decision-making process transpires in the end to be predominantly the work of a single judge, after that first conference. At the other end of the spectrum are the decisions such as *Pinnock*[23] in the Supreme

---

[19] Recounted in an interview with the author in 2008.

[20] *Lloyds TSB Foundation for Scotland v Lloyds Banking Group plc* [2013] UKSC 3 [2013] UKSC 3 at [33] and [48].

[21] Because the Privy Council was in constitutional theory offering advice to the Crown, the convention was that such advice should be univocal. This meant that neither concurrences nor dissents were permitted for many years. It is thought that at some stage judges did begin to write dissents but that these were never published. It is said that these dissents and other old judicial papers of the Privy Council were destroyed by fire caused by bombing during World War II. Dissents were allowed to be published in 1966 and after the creation of the Devolution jurisdiction from Scotland in 1990 both concurrences and dissents became commonplace.

[22] The range of judges who can sit in the Privy Council is considerably broader than those that can sit in the UK Supreme Court. This can mean that members of a particular panel are not familiar with each other or each other's forms of working.

[23] *Manchester City Council v Pinnock* [2010] UKSC 45, [2011] 2 AC 104.

Court where what appears to be the work of a single Justice, Lord Neuberger, was in fact the product of several meetings of the whole panel of nine Justices and multiple emails, with direct contributions from most of the Justices (in some cases quite substantial contributions) to the single judgment.[24] In the same way, Lord Bingham's innovation of reports of the whole committee often involved several Law Lords having an input to the report.

Form of judgment is therefore no guide as to how collective or otherwise was the process by which the final judgment was arrived at. In truth, decision-making in the House of Lords in the last 40 years and the Supreme Court since 2009 has been a delicate balance of individual and collective effort. As we have seen in the earlier chapters, interaction between the judges takes place at different stages of appeals. Sometimes the process most resembles five individuals in action;[25] sometimes it is genuinely collaborative;[26] mostly it is somewhere in between the two.[27] This can be true of any given case in the final court, and often at different stages of it. This suggests that Law Lords and Justices engaged in dialogues with differing levels of enthusiasm, and that only some of the judges availed themselves of such opportunities as existed to try to influence their colleagues. Such differences were in part due to differences in perception of that part of the judges' role which related to decision-making.

In short, there has long been a spectrum of individualism and collective orientation amongst the judges of the final court. In the House of Lords in its last 40 years there was a small minority of individualists who attached only peripheral importance to the attribute of group membership in deciding an appeal (at least outside the Committee Room) perhaps because they viewed group membership as inimical to judicial independence and considered it illegitimate or pointless to win their colleagues round. Lord Guest was one of these. I asked him in my original interviews if he thought it was legitimate to try to persuade his colleagues to adopt a particular view. He replied,

> No. I do not consider that one judge has any right to influence another judge's decision. I usually made up my mind at the end of the case and drafted out very roughly the opinion that I was going to express, and it's very rarely that I changed that opinion by listening to the views of my colleagues. I have done so, of course, on several occasions, but I'm not sure that it's a good thing to be influenced too much by one's colleagues in what I consider to be the wrong direction.

Rather more numerous were those who claimed to be happy if their contributions to the first conference or their draft judgments persuaded some of their colleagues to follow their lead, but disclaimed any more proactive endeavours. Interventions in the hearings by judges of this persuasion were rarely aimed at their colleagues

---

[24] See Lord Neuberger, 'Open Justice unbound?' Judicial Studies Board Annual Lecture 2011, 16 March 2011, at 10. This account was confirmed in interview with the author in 2012.

[25] As in the first conference.

[26] As in the post-hearing meetings in *Manchester City Council v Pinnock* [2010] UKSC 45, [2011] 2 AC 104.

[27] See A Paterson, *The Law Lords* (London, Macmillan, 1982), at 243.

and while they might visit a colleague's room to discuss a case it was more with a view to elucidation rather than persuasion. Law Lords of this mien either (1) did not consider lobbying a seemly or legitimate activity, or (2) took the view that while there was nothing wrong in principle with seeking to influence one's colleagues, in practice they rarely did so or considered it to be a worthwhile exercise, since few of their colleagues changed their minds in discussion.[28] If true, this last observation is a telling one since the published judgments of the Law Lords and Justices over the years, and many of their interviews with journalists or scholars, are replete with admissions that the author's mind has changed in the course of the case. Possibly, these respondents—as Lord Wilberforce asserted of Lord Radcliffe[29]—were poorer at persuasion than some of their colleagues, or like Lord Denning were on a sufficiently different wavelength from the bulk of his companions as to render his overtures barren.

However, the bulk of the Law Lords in the Court's final 40 years seem to have taken the view that group membership was at least a relevant attribute in their decision-making role. Law Lords in my original sample who were of this persuasion included Lords Cross, Gardiner, Kilbrandon, MacDermott, Pearce, Pearson, Radcliffe, Reid and Salmon. There were, however, differences between them. Some appeared to restrict their discussions very much to a group context, for example at lunch, in the corridor, the Conference Room or the Library. Thus Lord Reid while observing that, 'We might often have a talk … if we're two or three on the one side, we might often have a talk amongst ourselves, that's not uncommon', was sceptical about the value of trying to win round dissenters.

> Well, of course you can't hope to convince your colleagues. Remember most of the cases that come up to us are cases of difficulty, and it is not sensible to suppose that five people are always going to agree; you know perfectly well that they are not.

Lord Radcliffe would argue for his point of view in the course of the hearing and the conference afterwards but rarely tried to influence his colleagues in discussion thereafter. It was not that he considered such behaviour to be illegitimate: it was simply that he preferred to rely on his circulated speech. Other Law Lords were prepared to try to persuade their colleagues individually as well as in a group. Lord Devlin replied, 'If I thought it an important point and if a man was doubtful I might have a go at persuading him'. Lords Cross, Gardiner and MacDermott were in agreement, though Lord Cross added that his efforts were more usually directed at those with whom he was concurring and that he saw little point in trying to win round a dissenting colleague.

Similarly, there was a difference between those collectively minded (group-oriented) Law Lords, whose primary aim was to engage with their colleagues for elucidation as to how they might together best resolve the problems posed by the current appeal, and those more tactically minded Law Lords (tacticians), who

---

[28]   Lords Hailsham and Denning were in this camp.
[29]   See n 113 below.

were seeking to promote their own point of view as providing the best solution to the appeal. The latter recognised that to win the appeal took, in most cases, only three votes[30] and acted accordingly. As far as I could ascertain, at least three of the 19 Law Lords in my original sample fell into this category, which included Lords Diplock and Wilberforce. As Lord Wilberforce later wrote about Lord Diplock,[31]

> You cannot really estimate a judge's influence without knowing from behind the scenes what influence he had on his colleagues. There are many brilliant judges who have not got the ability to persuade their colleagues, or to bring them into line with a particular approach to the law. Lord Diplock possessed the quality of persuading his colleagues to the extreme. It almost got to the stage of a mesmeric quality. He had this sort of intellectual superiority, coupled with enormous hard work. He had always done his homework far better than anybody else, which enabled him to persuade his colleagues to follow his point of view. He would work on persuading people to his point of view during the conduct of the case, in the lunch intervals, in the corridors, in their rooms. I do not know anybody else who had this ability, and the desire to exercise it so strongly as he did ... Lord Diplock was a very persuasive man. He was a man who got his way in almost everything.

Another of the tacticians explained to me how in a difficult case he would frequently 'go into a colleague's room, particularly a sympathetic one, one you hope to enlist for your point of view, to try to share ideas with them'. Lord Simon, however, observed that there were limits that there was no point in trying to exceed.

> If I can influence or control the majority, it is not worthwhile arguing [the dissenters] round. It merely tires them and tires me. I think it was Disraeli who said, 'A majority is the best repartee'.

It also emerged from my interviews in the 1970s that certain celebrated Law Lords of the past had been in this camp, notably Lord Atkin and Viscount Simonds. The latter in particular disliked being in a minority and would use his best endeavours to win round anyone whom he considered to be persuadable. As one Law Lord told me,

> Gavin minded very much if anybody whose opinion he respected didn't agree with his. He felt it personally ... He wasn't the only Law Lord who did that, but he did feel it very much.

In later years a number of Law Lords also shared this view, eg Lords Dilhorne, Millett and Hoffmann. As Lord Hoffmann told me, 'I don't think of it as a collective [process], I think of it as a situation in which you want two other votes ... that's what you've got to do'.

The group-oriented Law Lords intervened in the hearings primarily to clarify points in counsel's argument that were troubling them or to test the limits of

---

[30] The overwhelming majority of cases in the House of Lords involved a panel of five. Space considerations made sittings of seven or even nine Law Lords relatively scarce.

[31] See G Sturgess and P Chubb, *Judging the World* (Sydney, Butterworth, 1988) at 275.

counsel's propositions, and in the first conference spoke primarily to state their views on the main points in the appeal. The 'tactician' Law Lords, in contrast, used interventions in oral argument and at the first conference to push their own line of thought. Thus Lord Hoffmann in his exchanges with counsel was often making points to his colleagues,[32]

> That is the stage at which you make your view known both for the benefit of counsel and for the benefit of your colleagues. It's an opportunity not just for counsel to exercise advocacy on the bench *but for the judges to exercise advocacy on each other* (emphasis added).

Lord Hoffmann extended his judicial advocacy into the first conference,[33] but thereafter his efforts switched to writing, hoping to have an impact by a very early circulation of his opinion. This tactic could irk a few of his colleagues and amuse others if it emerged more or less with the end of the hearing. Over the years two Law Lords are thought to have written a draft judgment before or during the oral hearing, based on the papers, on a regular basis. One was Lord Diplock and the other Lord Hoffmann.[34]

Curiously, for some tactician Law Lords that was as far as the lobbying went. If the circulated judgment couldn't persuade the rest of the panel, then face to face lobbying in their rooms was generally not seen as a worthwhile option. Any further engagement would be in the shape of written memoranda. Lord Hoffmann was generally in this camp along with such famous non-tactician Law Lords as Reid, Radcliffe and Bingham. However, other collectively minded Law Lords, eg Lords Brown, Hope, Mance, Millett, Neuberger, Phillips, Scott and Steyn, continued to engage with each other both orally and in writing at the circulation stage. While some of these were tacticians others were simply group-oriented Law Lords striving to solve the appeal collectively—especially if a majority *ratio* was not emerging from the circulating drafts.

What of the Supreme Court? Very little has changed. Some Justices (notably Lord Rodger) continued largely to plough their own furrow, others (like Lord Hope) behaved more collectively or tactically, with the bulk somewhere in between, eg Lords Brown, Clarke, Collins, Dyson, Kerr, Neuberger, Phillips, Sumption and Wilson. Lady Hale, too, saw herself as a 'mid-spectrum' judge,[35]

---

[32] Lord Scott appears to have used his interventions for a similar purpose but since his take on cases was frequently slightly different from that of some of his colleagues, the interventions did not always have their intended effect.

[33] Aided by the convention that it is not the practice to interrupt a Law Lord's statement of his/her views at the conference unless the presentation contains a factual error or a misunderstanding of what an earlier (and more junior) Law Lord had said.

[34] They were not unique in writing early, and some Law Lords and Justices have had a habit of writing quickly after the end of the hearing, producing and circulating a draft judgment the following week or two, eg Lords Bingham, Hope and Dyson. However, in their cases the primary motivation was to write while the case was fresh in their minds rather than having to work it all up again several weeks after the hearing.

[35] Interview with the author, 2008.

I think there probably is a spectrum of people who take an extremely individualistic attitude to things and people who take a more consensus-seeking attitude, which is rather different from an authoritative, a directive thing. I don't think anybody tries to be directive and some place more weight on trying to get as many people to sign up to a particular identifiable point of view than others do … [I'm probably] in the middle [but] … towards consensus seeking if possible … Also recognising that there are issues on which I am quite likely to take a different line from my colleagues for a variety of reasons, and it's one of the reasons I'm here.

As with the Law Lords in the Bingham era and 40 years ago, the Justices tend to range on a spectrum with respect to each phase of the decision-making process. Few are complete individualists and few are out and out tacticians. Most are in the middle. However, some are more prepared to seek to influence their colleagues at different stages, as Lords Bingham and Hoffmann were.

Engagement of Judgments

A second aspect of collective decision-making is engaging with the reasoning of one's fellow judges, in one's own judgment. For most of the 50 years before the demise of the House of Lords in 2009, until the last few years, whatever was said between the Law Lords out of the public gaze, it was relatively uncommon for them to engage[36] with each other's published judgments. The exceptions to this rule—eg Lord Atkin's reference to the reasoning of the majority Law Lords in *Liversidge v Anderson*[37] smacking of the logic of Humpty Dumpty, and on matters affecting the liberty of the subject of being 'more executive-minded than the executive', or Lord Simonds accusing Lord Denning of 'heresy' in *Scruttons Ltd v Midland Silicones*[38]—stand out not simply for their directness but for their infrequency. More recent exchanges between Law Lords have generally been somewhat milder, although undoubtedly deeply felt.[39] Lord Hope's remarkable

---

[36] By 'engagement' I mean critical engagement with the reasoning. I do not include 'For the reasons given by Lord *X*, I would uphold the appeal'. Nor do I include 'Whilst respecting the views of Lords *A* and *B* and the lines of reasoning which they employ, I prefer the view of Lord *D* as being more realistic'.

[37] *Liversidge v Anderson* [1942] AC 206.

[38] *Scruttons Ltd v Midland Silicones* [1962] AC 446.

[39] The robust disagreements between Lords Brandon, Bridge and Templeman generally did not make it to the printed judgments. However, in the *Spycatcher* case, *Attorney General v Guardian Newspapers Ltd (No 1)* [1987] UKHL 13 there was a furious row between Templeman (in the majority) and Bridge (in the minority—but in the Chair) as to the correct form of words to be used in the motion to the whole House of Lords to adopt the report of the Appellate Committee (on 30 July 1987) for reasons which would be given later. Lord Templeman got his own back, as is clear from Lord Bridge's judgment. Since he was leaving the country for much of the vacation he considered that it would not be possible to provide the reasons for maintaining the injunctions against publication of extracts from the book, until after his return in September. Lord Templeman seems to have persuaded his colleagues that this would not do and that the judgments should be published much sooner than that (on 13 August). This forced Lord Bridge with ill-disguised fury to produce his dissenting judgment without having seen the majority's reasoning.

attack on Lord Hoffmann for the way in which the latter presided over the *Pitcairn Islands* appeal[40] began with a coded reference in his dissent in the case, to the fact that the issues in that appeal were in his view considerably more complex than Lord Hoffmann's judgment of the Council acknowledged.[41] This veiled critique of Lord Hoffmann's cursory treatment of the case, became a full-blown criticism based on Lord Hope's contemporaneous diary records, contained in the Foreword to *Justice, Legality and the Rule of Law*.[42]

> To the great misfortune of counsel who had put such an effort into preparation, our Board in the Privy Council was presided over by Lord Hoffmann ... who was determined to cut to the bone the scope of any argument ... it was a devastating start to the proceedings, which resulted in the whole affair being over in under two days after the thinnest of arguments. He has just produced a draft judgment which is just as terse. The novelty and difficulty of the issues is not apparent from what he has written.

Yet to observers familiar with the long-standing, frequently robust and regularly *ad hominem* public exchanges between US Supreme Court justices the abstinence of the Law Lords was striking. For the most part the published judgments in the House in its last 40 years resembled ships passing in the night. Only in the final few years of the House did direct references (in disagreement) become more common. These exceptions were almost always in the 11 per cent of cases in which the House was sharply divided (cases where the majority prevailed by a single vote), and in the great majority of them for many years it was the norm for there to be little or no reference in any of the Law Lords' judgments to the reasoning contained in the other speeches.[43]

This lack of engagement partly helps to explain those, happily not too frequently occurring, cases like *Boys v Chaplin* where there is no majority *ratio*. With the exception of those cases—primarily in criminal law—which he considered merited a single voice,[44] Lord Bingham did not greatly favour single majority judgments as we have seen—but he was equally opposed to cases where there was no majority

---

[40] *Christian and others v The Queen* [2006] UKPC 47.

[41] [2006] UKPC 47 at [46].

[42] See Dawn Oliver (ed), *Justice, Legality and the Rule of Law: Lessons from the Pitcairn Prosecutions* (Oxford, Oxford University Press, 2009) at vi.

[43] See eg *Mannai Investment Co Ltd v Eagle Star Assurance* [1997] UKHL 19; [1997] AC 749, *Agnew and Others v Länsförsäkringsbolagens AB* [2000] UKHL 7, *R v Secretary of State for Employment, Ex parte Seymour Smith and Another* [2000] UKHL 12, *Berezovsky v Michaels and Others; Glouchkov v Michaels and Others* [2000] UKHL 25, *In re Burke* [2000] UKHL 35, *R v Secretary of State for Health and Others, Ex parte Imperial Tobacco Limited and Others* [2000] UKHL 60, *R v Secretary of State for the Environment, Transport and the Regions and Another, Ex parte Spath Holme Limited* [2000] UKHL 61. However, exceptional split cases where there is engagement included *Arthur JS Hall and Co v Simons* [2000] UKHL 38 (a 4:3 case) and *R v Leeds Crown Court, Ex parte Wardle* [2001] UKHL 12, a 3:2 criminal procedure case, where a clearly irked Lord Nicholls in a 19-line dissent described his majority colleagues' reasoning as 'frankly, absurd', 'nothing short of a nonsense' and 'irrational'.

[44] This arose in only 23 out of 510 appeals heard between 2003 and 2009 see James Lee, 'A Defence of Concurring Speeches' [2009] *Public Law* 305. Usually, these were penned by Lord Bingham but he entertained suggestions from his colleagues and in some cases the single judgment was, in reality, a composite divided amongst the Law Lords hearing the appeal.

ratio. His colleagues agreed and it was in his era as senior Law Lord that the lack of engagement began to change,[45] a move accelerated by the appointments of Lords Mance and Neuberger to the House. A good example of engagement designed to ensure that there was a clear majority *ratio* arose in a 'confusing' Scots appeal in 2008.[46] The lead judgment emanated from Lord Hope but the other four Law Lords circulated judgments of their own agreeing the outcome but for different reasons. Eventually, Lord Hoffmann (who was presiding) called a meeting to discuss how best to achieve a clear majority *ratio.* After discussion, Lord Hoffmann persuaded Lord Hope to make a few changes to his draft in return for withdrawing his own judgment and Lord Mance also agreed to withdraw the bulk of his judgment, thus producing three votes for the reasoning contained in Lord Hope's judgment.[47]

Similarly, in the *Kay* case[48] Lord Hope, who presided, held several meetings to try to achieve consensus amongst the majority group,

> In *Kay* the best we could do was for everybody on the majority side of which I was the leader, to agree a paragraph (para 110), which in retrospect was extremely difficult to understand because it was an amalgamation of all our views. [Agreement] can be very, very difficult to achieve. I was prepared to give ground a bit in order to try to accommodate views, but it wasn't terribly successful.[49]

Today in the UK Supreme Court engagement with the published judgment of one's colleagues is an everyday event where there is more than a single majority judgment. It has occurred in every case where there is a significant disagreement in the court,[50] in almost all of the cases where there are any dissents at all and in many of the cases where there are multiple concurrences. The key issue about the judicial dialogue of engagement in published judgments, however, is that not only does it demonstrate that the judges are working together more collectively in the final court, but also that the dialogues with the parties, academics and the lawyers and judges of the present and future, are more effective. This is because the engagement reveals in a way that was all too frequently missing in the House

---

[45] Thus of a random sample of 34 cases decided in the House in 2000 only six (18%) contained examples of Law Lord engagement, and only one of them was sustained in nature (Lord Millett's dissent in *R v Smith* [2000] UKHL 49). The comparative figure for cases decided in 2005 was 43%, with several sustained in nature—especially *A v Secretary of State for the Home Department* [2005] UKHL 7. By 2008 the proportion of cases with engagement was 65% and substantial engagement was to be found in most of the 3:2 decisions. In *Mucelli v Government of Albania* [2009] UKHL 2 Lord Rodger (in dissent) explicitly engages with the reasoning of Lord Neuberger for the majority. For another 3:2 case with mutual engagement see *Somerville v Scottish Ministers* [2007] UKHL 44.

[46] *Common Services Agency v Scottish Information Commissioner* [2008] UKHL 47. The description was that of Lady Hale.

[47] My account of this case is derived from interviews with Lords Hoffmann and Hope.

[48] *Kay v London Borough of Lambeth* [2006] UKHL 10.

[49] Interview with the author, October 2008.

[50] Between 2009 and July 2012 there were 23 cases where there were two or more dissenting judgments. In every one of these cases there was engagement between the Justices indicating in clear terms which bits of the majority (and sometimes the minority) judgment(s) were not accepted and why.

of Lords, precisely which issues the Justices are in agreement about and those where they disagree, and why.

Beginning with the earliest, and still one of the most testing, cases considered by the new court,[51] the *Jewish Free School*[52] case on whether a school selection criterion giving preference to orthodox Jews was discrimination within the terms of section 1 of the Race Relations Act 1976, produced nine judgments and a 5:4 split on the issue of direct discrimination. The engagement between the Justices' judgments is frequent and sustained. Every one of the nine judgments makes a reference to the reasoning of one or more of the other Justices. Shortly thereafter, in *Martin*,[53] the only Scots case in which Lords Hope and Rodger were unable to present a united front in all their years of sitting in the final court together,[54] the 3:2 split produced an unusually blunt critique of the majority Justices by the dissenting Lord Rodger. Lord Hope and Lord Brown's reasoning on a key point he described as being based on no more than bare assertion, whilst Lord Walker's he described as resting on something which 'does not really look much like a rule of Scots criminal law reasoning'. He concludes his attack as follows,[55]

> Until now, judges, lawyers and law students have had to try to work out what Parliament meant by a rule of Scots criminal law that is 'special to a reserved matter'. That is, on any view, a difficult enough problem. Now, however, they must also try to work out what the Supreme Court means by these words. It is a new and intriguing mystery.

Lady Hale, as might be predicted given her perception that she has a slightly different role from her male colleagues, has engaged with them quite sharply on several occasions. In *Radmacher*[56] she not only famously observed that there was 'a gender dimension to the issue [of ante-nuptial agreements] which some may think ill-suited to decision by a court consisting of eight men and one woman',[57] but added also that she considered that the majority's approach to the financial relief provision in the statute was 'an impermissible gloss upon the courts' statutory duties'.[58] The majority did not respond to this, but in *R (McDonald) v Royal Borough of Kensington and Chelsea*,[59] they most certainly did. This case notoriously hinged around whether a local authority could withdraw care assistance at night for a former ballerina (Ms McDonald) and save money by providing incontinence pads instead, even though she was not incontinent. The four

---

[51] Lord Phillips in an interview described that case as the hardest he had ever had to decide, and in his judgment he hints as much by stating that '[the court] has not welcomed being required to resolve this dispute' and indicating (para 33) that he changed his mind and his vote on the key issue of direct discrimination after the oral hearing.

[52] *R (on the application of E) v Governing Body of Jewish Free School and Admissions Appeal Panel of Jewish Free School and Others* [2009] UKSC 15.

[53] *Martin v HM Advocate* [2010] UKSC 10.

[54] Lords Hope and Rodger sat together in 36 Scots appeals and disagreed publicly only in *Martin*.

[55] Ibid, at para 149.

[56] *Radmacher (formerly Granatino) v Granatino* [2010] UKSC 42.

[57] Ibid, at para 137.

[58] Ibid, at para 138.

[59] *R (McDonald) v Royal Borough of Kensington and Chelsea* [2011] UKSC 33.

majority (male) Justices considered that the local authority could do so. Lady Hale considered that they could not do so in the way that they had and attacked the logic of the decision of the majority for being sufficiently broad as to permit the local authority, if it so chose, to withdraw care assistance during the day also, and leave Ms McDonald to lie in her faeces. Lord Brown responded to this by suggesting that Lady Hale's logic would require the local authority to provide a carer irrespective of cost (something she denied). Lord Walker regretted the fact that Lady Hale's judgment made so many references to defecation,[60] before going on to 'deplore' Lady Hale's suggestion as to where the logic of the majority's reasoning might lead to. Lord Dyson endorsed Lord Walker's remarks although Lord Kerr made no reference to the exchange between Lady Hale and Lord Walker. Lady Hale responded by observing that it could be that the 'physical differences between men and women lead them to have different views of what dignity means in this context. So it is not surprising that women take a different view'. The media and the commentators[61] were rather more sympathetic to Lady Hale's position in the case and media speculation persisted for several months over an alleged breakdown in relations between Lady Hale and some of her male colleagues.[62]

However, sharp exchanges on the Court have not been confined to dissents by Lady Hale. In *In re Lehman Bros International (Europe)*[63] the engagement between the minority pair (Lords Hope and Walker) and the majority was exacerbated by the fact that the majority had switched, not only depriving Lord Walker of his lead judgment but leaving the law—in his opinion—in serious disarray. As he drily remarked, 'The majority's decision makes investment banking more of a lottery than even its fiercest critics have supposed'.[64] Surprisingly, some of the sharper exchanges were triggered by judgments of the President of the Supreme Court, Lord Phillips. Generally speaking Lord Phillips did not engage with his colleagues' judgments—especially if he was giving the lead judgment—but that did not inhibit some of his colleagues.[65] Thus in *Lumba*[66] Lord Dyson criticised Lord Phillips for challenging the correctness of a case stating that

---

[60] There are, in fact, four such references.

[61] Eg RH George, 'In Defence of Dissent: *R (McDonald) v Royal Borough of Kensington and Chelsea*', 2011 *Family Law* 1097.

[62] Lady Hale was unrepentant. She returned to the attack in a critical speech to the InterLaw Diversity Forum on 13 October 2011, observing that 'some key rulings by the Supreme Court might … have been significantly different had the court included more women': www.dailymail.co.uk/news/article-2049514/UKs-highest-female-judge-blasts-Garrick-Club-holding-women-back.html.

[63] *In re Lehman Bros International (Europe)* [2012] UKSC 6.

[64] Ibid, at para 85.

[65] Lord Collins told me that he was opposed to referring to his colleagues' judgments in his own, and it is clear that he very rarely did so, but in this he was in a minority of one (until Lord Sumption joined the Court). Lord Clarke shared Lord Collins' view as to the undesirability of engagement becoming an *ad hominem* exchange: 'I don't see any harm in it as long as you put it neutrally or fairly neutrally, as long as it's not a polemic' he told me.

[66] *Walumba Lumba v Secretary of State for the Home Dept* [2011] UKSC 12.

in my view it is not appropriate to depart from a decision which has been followed repeatedly for almost 30 years unless it is obviously wrong (which I do not believe to be the case), still less to do so without the benefit of adversarial argument.[67]

Again, Lord Wilson in the *Atomic Veterans* case[68] (about whether service personnel who witnessed atomic weapon testing in the Pacific had a right of action against the government) opens his lead judgment with a salvo aimed at Lord Phillips and the other dissenters. Closer examination of the judgments reveals that Lord Phillips' judgment (which contains the most detailed account of the facts and which makes no reference to any of the other judgments) was probably the first to be written and also the original lead judgment in the case. Thereafter, Lord Wilson appears to have written a characteristically powerful dissent asserting that the lead judgment's approach to the relevant statutory provisions was[69]

> misconceived and would throw the practical application of the subsections into disarray. I also consider that any exercise of the discretion under section 33 so as to permit any of the nine actions to proceed would be aberrant in circumstances in which they have no real prospect of success.

His companions were equally forthright. As Lord Walker observed,[70]

> Like Lord Wilson and Lord Mance, I most respectfully disagree with much of Lord Phillips's reasoning ... I consider that the practical result of Lord Phillips's analysis would be a situation that Parliament cannot have intended.

Nevertheless it would appear to be Lord Wilson's critique which won over one or more votes—since it was his judgment that then became the lead judgment in the case. If the *Atomic Veterans* case was challenging, the *Assange* case was even more striking.[71] This appeal by the Wikileaks founder Julian Assange was ultimately rejected by 5:2 but of the five reasons put forward by Lord Phillips in his leading judgment justifying this outcome, all but the fifth were explicitly rejected, not just by the minority Justices, but by most of his colleagues, most pointedly by Lord Dyson.[72]

However, it would be wrong to leave the impression that the inevitable tensions created by having to solve one intractable problem after another have spilled into acrimonious exchanges on the UK Supreme Court on a regular basis. They are a long way from the acerbic exchanges which have been a regular feature of the US Supreme Court since Scalia became a member in 1986.[73] UK Justices still rarely

---

[67] At para 25. Lord Dyson was a frequent engager with his colleagues. His point-by-point rebuttal of Lord Kerr's dissenting opinion in *Ambrose v Harris* [2011] UKSC 43 was another clear example. *Al Rawi* [2011] UKSC 34 is even more marked. Originally conceived as a dissenting judgment, Lord Dyson sets out his disagreement with not only the arguments of the original lead judgment by Lord Clarke but with the Justices who agree with Lord Clarke and finds the energy to spend even more time explaining why he cannot accept the arguments of Jonathan Crow QC, counsel for the appellant.

[68] *Ministry of Defence v AB and Others* [2012] UKSC 9 at para 1.

[69] [2012] UKSC 9 at para [1].

[70] [2012] UKSC 9 at para [67].

[71] *Assange v Swedish Prosecution Authority* [2012] UKSC 22. For further details on the case see chapter 2 of this volume above.

[72] Ibid, paras 155–59 under the heading 'Lord Phillips' other reasons'.

[73] See, eg, *Lawrence v. Texas*, 539 US 558, 602 (2003) (Scalia, J., dissenting) in which he excoriates both the majority, the legal profession, and the American law school community for, in his view,

make outright *ad hominem* (or *ad feminam*) critiques of other Justices in their judgments. As one observed,

> I think that there is good cause on appropriate occasions to refer to a line of reasoning with which you agree and if you like to give it a greater emphasis, or on occasion a line of reasoning with which you disagree and explain why you disagree with it, but one needs to be reasonably judicious about using that [approach].

Team-working

The second significant change in the judicial dialogues in the Supreme Court has been the establishment of team-working practices under Lords Phillips and Neuberger to a far greater extent than was ever the case in the House of Lords.[74] This did not happen overnight—it evolved over the first three years of the Court. However, most of today's Justices now perceive themselves as part of a team—in a way that the Law Lords never did.[75] Both Lord Phillips and Lord Hope have described the Court as a 'team' in media interviews and Lords Neuberger, Sumption and Reed each told me that they saw themselves as part of a team in our interviews. Lord Reed added,

> It is a curious team because the value of the team depends on everybody using their own individual intelligence and their own experience and so forth and bringing all that to the party, but our working method is very collaborative.

Lord Reed's observations are a timely warning not to take the 'team' metaphor too far. The Justices do not go on team-building exercises; there is no manager,[76] no opposing team, no team strips, no team mascot and no league table of supreme courts. However, there are other team-related characteristics which will be examined in this chapter, eg team selection, team-work, team leaders, team-players and team spirit. This aspect of collective decision-making in appellate courts has attracted considerable commentary in the United States, where it appears under the soubriquet of 'Collegiality'. Indeed, Collegiality as a model of judicial decision-making is making some explanatory headway in the panoply of theories of judicial behaviour

---

'sign[ing] on to the so-called homosexual agenda, by which I mean the agenda promoted by some homosexual activists directed as eliminating the moral opprobrium that has traditionally attached to homosexual conduct.'

[74] See B Dickson, 'The Processing of Appeals in the House of Lords' (2007) 123 *LQR* 571, 595, description of the way the House reached decisions in 2005: 'It remains undeniable that far from being a group activity, the preparation of judgments is for each judge to consider individually. In this context the principle of collegiality does not presuppose active collaboration so much as mutual respect and collective responsibility'.

[75] This is not entirely true. There were occasions in the Bingham era when Law Lords would work together. Thus in one case the three junior Law Lords were concerned at the line of argument being taken in the draft opinions of the two seniors. They met twice to discuss a common line in response. Again in *Kay* (above, n 48), as we saw earlier, the majority met several times to agree on a common paragraph.

[76] Though there have been 'coaching sessions' since 2009, see T Nesterchuk, 'The View from Behind the Bench' chapter 11 in A Burrows, D Johnston and R Zimmermann (eds), *Judge and Jurist: Essays in Memory of Lord Rodger of Earlsferry* (Oxford, Oxford University Press, 2013).

which have emerged from Northern America in recent times.[77] Initially, it emerged as a riposte by the Federal judiciary to the political scientists who attributed the outcome of most federal appeal cases in the USA to judicial attitudes and values. The term does not refer to how well the Court's members get on with each other, but to how much they work together as a team pursuing a common enterprise (the pursuit of the 'right answer in law' in the case) and how much they function as individuals. The English Court of Appeal is a highly collegial court in this sense.[78] Its members regularly sit on the same panel for several weeks, they meet before cases to discuss points on which they wish to hear argument, to allocate who will write and to express preliminary views on the case. There may be subsequent meetings when the opinion has been circulated, especially if it is a composite judgment. The sheer pressure of business coupled with the need to play to the specialist strengths within each panel only emphasise their inter-dependence and the necessity for team-playing. However, curiously, although the great majority of Law Lords were promoted from the Court of Appeal, the House of Lords relatively rarely operated in such a collegial fashion. It was not—at least in Lord Bingham's era—that the members of the Court did not get on with each other. It was more that the ever changing panels of the appellate and appeal committees, the lack of pre-meetings and the scarcity of re-convened conferences (after the first conference), and Lord Bingham's support for multiple judgments in most cases, entailed that the Law Lords were rarely required to work together as they had done in the Court of Appeal.[79] True, Lord Bingham did re-introduce the concept of a Report of the Appellate Committee which sometimes involved team-working by the members of the Appellate Committee—but these were relatively unusual[80] and not all were composite judgments. There were also three or four examples of two Law Lords writing a joint judgment, but again these were very exceptional occasions.

For its principal proponent, Chief Justice Edwards, 'Collegiality' is not just working together in a group or team, it's where judges have a common interest in getting the law right or reaching the best answer available.[81] 'Collegiality is a process that helps create the conditions for principled agreement by allowing all points of view to be aired and considered'.[82] Deliberations are 'a complex conversation, both in conference and during the drafting of opinions', rather than the simple exchange of values and attitudes, 'which are characterised more accurately

---

[77] See HT Edwards, 'The Effects of Collegiality on Judicial Decision-Making' (2003) 151 *University of Pennsylvania Law Review* 1639.

[78] See, Darbyshire, *Sitting in Judgment* (Oxford, Hart Publishing, 2011) ch 14.

[79] This held true even in the early days of the Supreme Court. As Lord Dyson told me: 'As regards whether there is less teamwork here than at the Court of Appeal, I think that probably is fair. But I think there is a certain amount of teamwork'.

[80] 23 out of 239 cases heard by Lord Bingham in the House of Lords.

[81] HT Edwards, 'The Effects of Collegiality on Judicial Decision-Making' (2003) 151 *University of Pennsylvania Law Review* 1639. Edwards is unaware of the Dworkinian debates as to whether there is always 'one right answer' or 'a better answer' and accordingly switches between these objectives as though they were inter-changeable.

[82] Ibid at 1656.

as a process of dialogue, persuasion, and revision'. Whilst there is undoubtedly a reasonable measure of truth in Edwards' general argument as to the importance of understanding the difference that collective decision-making—or multiple dialogues as I would put it—can make to the outcome of cases, I doubt the utility of focusing on the concept of 'Collegiality': first, because the technical meaning ascribed to it by Edwards and others is sufficiently different from the ordinary language meaning of the concept (which contains overtones of comradeship or friendship), to cause confusion in the mind of the reader; and secondly, because Edwards uses the concept as an 'ideal type' both in the Weberian sense of an abstract descriptive model and in the sense of a moral ideal. For Edwards 'Collegiality' is an imperative which it is the duty of all appeal judges to strive towards. In practice, as we have seen, the Law Lords and Justices vary in their commitment to collective decision-making and for many the obligation of 'Collegiality' in Edwards' sense is not one that they endorsed.

Nevertheless one of the most striking developments in the Supreme Court, which has accelerated under the Presidency of Lord Neuberger, is the frequency of team-working in the Court. As we saw in the last chapter the majority of Justices now favour having more single majority judgments and fewer concurrences. As a result the level of single majority judgments has risen substantially since Bingham's time. (See Table 4.1).

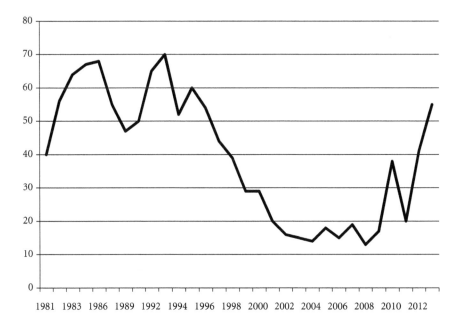

Table 4.1: Percentage of single judgments in the House of Lords and UK Supreme Court during 1981–2013 (July)*.

* Same as Table 3.5.

This can only be achieved by the Justices working together (rather than as individuals). There are more formal meetings than in the past. Thus there is a bi-monthly policy discussion, although it does not discuss individual cases. There is a short pre-meeting before each case and a few more second conferences than in the past.[83] Moreover, joint judgments written by two Justices are becoming more common than in the House,[84] and plurality opinions[85]—which were not possible in the House—are becoming commonplace.[86] There have been other indicators of collective working. For example the two Scots Justices seem very largely to have worked as a team in Scots appeals both in the final years of the House and now in the Supreme Court to the extent of sharing the burden of writing the lead judgment or dealing with particular aspects of the case and rarely showing a disunited front in the face of legal nationalism.[87] There is also evidence of small ad hoc examples of team-working emerging. Justices with offices on the second floor, perhaps because of their slightly isolated location, have generally talked to each other about cases in which they are involved on a regular basis, throughout the years of the Supreme Court. Again, in the *Axa* case[88] in 2011 three of the Justices would meet in the afternoons after the hearing to discuss where the case had got to. As one recalled, 'We wouldn't necessarily have the same ideas but it was very useful having somebody to … just speaking out loud forces you to form your ideas in articulate language'.

In fact the most clear cut example of team-working in the early years of the Supreme Court was the relationship of Lords Brown and Rodger. Fast friends from towards the end of the Bingham era in the House of Lords, they shared a judicial assistant and in 2009–10 began the practice of 'coaching sessions'[89] in which they debated the cases in which they were sitting together with their then shared judicial assistant Adil Mohamedbhai. Working together certainly seems to have brought their thinking closer. The two judges voted together in 92 per cent of the cases that they sat with each other in the House of Lords and the Supreme Court (the overall norm for the two courts at that time was around 86 per cent). Indeed, they voted together a very impressive 97 per cent of the time in the 29 cases (23 times in the majority and five times in dissent[90]) in which they sat

[83] Of which *Pinnock* (above, n 23) and *Waya* (below, n 92) were amongst the most celebrated.

[84] See chapter 3 n 166 of this volume, above.

[85] Where one or more Justices are listed as agreeing with the lead or main judgment, or principal dissenting judgment writer.

[86] There have been 107 plurality decisions in the Supreme Court between September 2009 and March 2013.

[87] See chapter 6 of this volume below. Lords Hope and Rodger only disagreed once on the outcome in a Scots case. Lords Hope and Reed never disagreed on the outcome of the 29 cases in which they sat together until Lord Hope retired at the end of June 2013.

[88] *Axa General Insurance Ltd and Others v Lord Advocate and Others (Scotland)* [2011] UKSC 46.

[89] The description was Lord Rodger's and it was Lord Rodger's habit to treat the judicial assistant as 'the coach'. See Tetyana Nesterchuk, 'The View from Behind the Bench: The Role of Judicial Assistants in the UK Supreme Court' chapter 11 in A Burrows, D Johnston and R Zimmermann (eds), *Judge and Jurist: Essays in Memory of Lord Rodger of Earlsferry* (Oxford, Oxford University Press, 2013).

[90] On two of them they were joined by Lord Walker—a mutual friend.

together in the Supreme Court in the last year of Lord Rodger's time there (June 2010–May 2011).

Finally, the pressure for fewer concurrences and more single majority judgments has resulted in a move in some cases to a single judgment representing the majority view and a single judgment representing the view of the minority. It will be recalled that in the *Jewish Free School* case in the early days of the Court, it produced nine judgments (perhaps because it only had a single conference). This pattern was repeated in the difficult, split cases in the following years with seven judgments in *Sainsbury's Supermarkets*, nine in *R v Smith*, seven in *Sienkiewitcz*, seven in *Jones v Kaney*, nine in *Lumba*, seven in *GC v Commissioner for Metropolitan Police*; eight in *Al Rawi*, six in *Gnango*, seven in the *MOD* case, and seven in *Assange*.[91] However in *Perry* (delivered in July 2012) despite the 7:2 split in the cross appeal there were only three judgments and in *Waya* (delivered in October 2012) which at one time appeared to be heading in the direction of nine judgments after an unsatisfactory first conference in which no majority view had emerged, there followed a re-hearing, another inconclusive first conference and several reconvened conferences from which a single judgment for the majority and another for the minority was eventually arrived at.[92] In the year following *Waya* there were several major cases[93] with multiple judgments—which Lords Reid and Bingham would see as a healthy sign. However, in two of the most significant cases in 2013, by team-working the majority side was able to produce a single majority judgment, namely the *Bank Mellat* cases[94] and *Smith v the Ministry of Defence*.[95]

If team-working, engagement and collective decision-making are partly the product of the individual views and personalities of the judges on the panel hearing the case, the efficacy of the dialogues that accompany them also turns on a range of other factors. These include leadership skills, the cordiality of relations between panel members, the propensity of panel members to vote together, and even, surprisingly, the location of the panel members' rooms.

---

[91] *R (Sainsbury's Supermarkets Ltd) v Wolverhampton City Council* [2010] UKSC 20; *R v Smith* [2000] UKHL 49; *Sienkiewitcz (Administratrix of the Estate of Enid Costello) v Greif (UK) Ltd* [2011] UKSC 10; *Jones v Kaney* [2011] UKSC 13; *Walumba Lumba v Secretary of State for the Home Department* [2011] UKSC 12; *R (GC) v Commissioner for Metropolitan Police* [2011] UKSC 21; *Al Rawi and Others v The Security Service and Others* [2011] UKSC 34; *R v Gnango* [2011] UKSC 59; *Ministry of Defence v AB and others* [2012] UKSC 9; *Assange v Swedish Prosecution Authority* [2012] UKSC 22.

[92] *Perry and Others v Serious Organised Crime Agency* [2012] UKSC 35. Lord Bingham would probably have retorted that *R v Waya* [2012] UKSC 51 was just the sort of criminal case in which he would have favoured a single judgment in any event.

[93] Eg *Prudential* [2013] UKSC 1, *VTB Capital* [2013] UKSC 5, *In the matter of B (a child)* [2013] UKSC 33, *Prest v Petrodel Resources ltd* [2013] UKSC.

[94] *Bank Mellat v Her Majesty's Treasury (Nos 1 & 2)* [2013] UKSC 38/39.

[95] [2013] UKSC 41. In *Geys v Société Générale London Branch* [2012] UKSC 63, every Justice gives a judgment but in reality three of them share the differing points in the appeal amongst them, so it is akin to a composite opinion.

Leadership in the House of Lords

More than 50 years ago David Danelski published a seminal paper[96] applying 'small group analysis'[97] to the decision-making process in the US Supreme Court. His argument was that effective decision-making on that court required two forms of leadership. 'Task leadership' which focused on persuading a majority on the court towards a particular outcome, and 'social leadership' which endeavoured to keep the court socially cohesive despite the inevitable conflicts which arose when important issues were at stake. The two forms of leadership required different skill sets. Task leaders 'exercise effective leadership concerning decisional outcomes', leadership which is affected by 'personality,[98] esteem within the Court, intelligence, technical competence, and persuasive ability'.[99] Social leaders, whilst institutionally very important, focus more on the emotional needs of the court, and in personality terms tend to be 'warm, receptive and responsive' and amongst the best liked members of the court. Danelski showed that although it was possible for a Justice to perform both roles—and particularly the Chief Justice—more often the roles were played, if at all, by different Justices. My study of the House 40 years ago suggested that leadership analysis could fruitfully be applied to the House of Lords and it appears just as true of the last decade also. In part this is because of the overlap between task leadership, group-orientation and team-working. In practice, therefore, those who have exercised task-leadership effectively in the final appeal court have almost all regarded collective decision-making as a central element in their decision-making role either through group-orientation or being a tactician or lobbyist. Thus it is clear that Lords Reid, Wilberforce, Diplock, Bingham and Dyson, for example, all exercised task leadership effectively, although not in the same way. This is apparent if we look at the different stages of a case.

Leadership at the Hearing Stage

As we saw in chapter two on the dialogue with counsel, Lord Reid was perceived by his contemporaries (and by his successors) as the greatest virtuoso in the dialogue with counsel to have graced the final court of the UK.[100] His task leadership extended far beyond the creation of an appropriate atmosphere for the intellectual debate—his fairness and patience impressed counsel almost as much as his

---

[96] 'The Influence of the Chief Justice in the Decisional Process' in Walter F Murphy and C Herman Pritchett (eds), *Courts, Judges and Politics: An Introduction to the Judicial Process* (New York, Random House, 1961) 497–508.

[97] Derived primarily from Robert F Bales, 'Task Roles and Social Roles in problem-Solving Groups' in Eleanor Maccoby et al, *Readings in Social Psychology* (New York, Rinehart & Winston, 1958) 437–47.

[98] In personality terms Danelski suggests that task leaders may be 'apt to be somewhat reserved'.

[99] Danelski, 'Conflict and its Resolution in the Supreme Court' (1967) 11 *Journal of Conflict Resolution* 71, 79.

[100] Alas, very few of his interventions have survived since there were no Sky broadcasts in his day and they were rarely included by the law reporters in their summaries of counsel's arguments in the official law reports.

legendary incisiveness in getting to the heart of the issue. He was also willing to provide leadership to his colleagues as to the direction that the hearing should take. Lord Bingham's leadership qualities as a presider were similarly admired by his colleagues. However, Lord Wilberforce was a relatively silent presider and Lord Diplock put little store in the oral hearing, as we have seen, and thought nothing of bullying counsel who failed to stand up to him. He did, like Bingham, seek to move the argument on, perhaps faster than Lord Phillips—but in a much less pleasant fashion.

Leadership at the First Conference

History does not record how Lord Diplock ran the first conference when he presided.[101] Clearly, given that he was a 'tactician' he will have used the conference to persuade wavering colleagues. In one respect, however, Lord Diplock must have envied his counterpart in the US Supreme Court. There the Chief Justice speaks first at the conference. This is a real opportunity for task leadership, although not all of them excelled at it. Justice Stevens[102] considered Warren Burger to have been poor at task leadership since (a) his introductory account of the issues in a case was sometimes incomplete or lacking in neutrality, (b) sometimes he would not wait until all eight colleagues had had their first say but would interrupt to add a point he had omitted or to repeat a point he had already made, and (c) he didn't always take accurate note of who had voted which way on multiple issue cases and as a result assigned the opinion to a Justice who was not in the majority. Rehnquist, it seems,[103] chose not to exercise task leadership very much in conference, since he considered that by that stage the Justices would have made up their minds. Chief Justice Roberts, on the other hand, is thought to offer effective task leadership at the first conference. Well prepared and fair he 'welcomed more discussion of the merits of the argued cases than his predecessor [Rehnquist]—including expansions of the reasoning behind his own votes—but he maintained the appropriate impartiality in giving each of us an opportunity to speak'.[104] However, he is also thought to take advantage of his ability to speak first, seeing it as a significant opportunity to re-frame the issues to fit his vision of the case. It is said that in his first year as Chief Justice he consciously pursued the objective of consensus-building in the Court through framing the issues in appeals in as narrow a way as possible, thereby achieving a substantial increase in unanimous decisions. Such tactics can reduce the value of decisions

---

[101] Regrettably, although a clerk from the Judicial Office was present throughout all first conferences in the House, nothing of the proceedings appears in the Minute Book.

[102] JP Stevens, 'Five Chiefs: A Supreme Court Memoir' (New York, Little, Brown Co, 2011) 154–56.

[103] Greenburg, above, n 14, at 15.

[104] Stevens, above, n 102, at 210.

from the final court of appeal and not surprisingly, the percentage of unanimous cases has fallen again.[105] (See Table 3.9 above).

Lord Bingham's approach in the House of Lords was quite different. He generously encouraged the junior Law Lord (who spoke first) to speak for longer than his colleagues, to give them a chance to make their mark. Of course, it made no difference to his influence when it came to his turn to speak. Several of his colleagues recalled how not infrequently when the Committee was divided[106] or occasionally even when it was not,[107] the sheer force of his intellect and the clarity of his thinking would win his colleagues round. Yet Bingham was not a tactician or a consensus builder or an individualist. He was in the middle as far as collective decision-making went. He did seek to persuade his colleagues at the first conference and with his circulated opinion but not in the way that Diplock did. 'He led by example and persuasion rather than necessarily setting out to do it' observed one colleague, but he didn't throw his weight about. It was said of Lord Reid that,

> When counsel had concluded their submissions, the time came for each of us, in conference, to outline his own provisional position. After Reid, speaking last, had given his opinion, one was left with the feeling, not so much that any other conclusion would be wrong in law, as it would be inadequate. The whole implications, often wider than the point in dispute, had been assembled and dealt with … Not only a judge, but a statesman was speaking.[108]

Lord Bingham's colleagues felt much the same about him.

Leadership and the Circulation of Judgments

Lord Diplock, as we saw earlier, thought nothing of writing his judgment before the oral hearing was over. Tom Bingham did not do that, but he was celebrated by his colleagues for writing as soon as the hearing was over—and very quickly—as he put it,

> Alan Rodger slightly teased me with having never grown out of writing a weekly essay [laughs] and there is actually truth in that. My regime over the last eight years … was

---

[105] In 2005, under the leadership of Chief Justice Roberts, 56% of decisions of the US Supreme Court were unanimous. The percentage of unanimous decisions fell to 30% in 2007 but rose to 46% in 2009. For a critical article on the downsides of pursuing a faux unanimity—it fails to provide clear guidance to the lower courts—see Adam Liptak, 'Justices are long on words but short on guidance', *New York Times*, 17 November 2010.

[106] 'It is not unknown to hear four views going one way, and then to hear Lord Bingham going the other way, after which the four eventually decide to come round to Lord Bingham's point of view': Lady Hale in 'A Supreme Judicial Leader' in M Andenas and D Fairgrieve (eds), *Tom Bingham and the Transformation of the Law* (Oxford, Oxford University Press, 2009) at 219.

[107] 'When four had given their views, [which were] varying a bit one way or the other, Tom Bingham would give his at the end and he got terrific attention, we really had respect for his views because of not just the intellectual quality but the quality of judgement that he always had'. (Lord Carswell interview with the author, 2008)

[108] A Paterson, 'Scottish Lords of Appeal 1876–1988' [1988] *Juridical Review* 235, 251.

a very, very clear routine. One would sit in court on Monday to Thursday, Thursday night we would go down to our house in the country where I have quite a considerable law library and I'd take all the papers and the cases with me and then Friday, Saturday, Sunday I would write my opinion and get it typed up on Monday and then circulate it.

Unlike Lord Hoffmann, who usually sought to exercise task leadership by circulating his judgment at a very early stage in an attempt to influence his colleagues, Lord Bingham produced his 30 manuscript pages a weekend, because that was how he liked to work—he wanted to get the thing off his desk before he was into another case. He was congenitally incapable of sitting on an opinion unless it was a truly exceptional case such as *Belmarsh*.[109] Although he recognised that it was sometimes a weakness he had a great reluctance to revisit an opinion which he had circulated some time before.[110] If he was writing what he thought was to be the leading opinion he would entertain his colleagues' requests for tweaks here or dropping a phrase there. But if he was not, he was reluctant to comment on others' opinions even where he thought they were misconceived—because he considered judicial independence involved independence from one's colleagues. As he explained,

> I think they have an expression in the Supreme Court in the United States, 'creeping around the hall' which is all the law clerks going off and lobbying the law clerks of other justices to try and build coalitions … Well, our law clerks don't do that at all but nor do the members mostly. Some do, but I myself absolutely never did. If people didn't agree with me, they didn't agree with me, but I wasn't going to indulge in 'robing room advocacy' to try and get them to change their minds.

Here, therefore, we can see the limits to Lord Bingham's willingness to exercise task leadership. His approach to collective decision-making was not that of a tactician such as Lord Diplock or Lord Hoffmann. Nor was he generally an intentional consensus builder.[111] If he didn't win his colleagues over at the first conference or with the circulated opinion, that was largely it. In this respect he was not very far apart from Lords Reid and Radcliffe, or indeed Lord Phillips. Occasionally, this had its downside. Lord Bingham lost the chance to prevail in the *A v B* case, which he felt strongly about, because of the truncated first conference, as we saw earlier, and because of his disinclination to counter the efforts of the majority Law Lords to persuade the swing voter to stay with them. Again the judgments in *Smith v Chief Constable of Sussex*[112] suggest that two of his colleagues might have been persuadable had he taken the opportunity to push his position beyond the first circulation. Lord Diplock, we know, would have had no such scruples. Nor, curiously, would Lord Wilberforce. The latter told me,

---

[109] *A and Others v Secretary of State for the Home Department* [2004] UKHL 56.
[110] One case in which he did was *R v Rahman* [2008] UKHL 45, but he didn't change his position and as a result ended up in a 3:2 minority on a sub-issue in the case.
[111] Except where there were judgments of the court.
[112] *Smith v Chief Constable of Sussex Police* [2008] UKHL 50 (30 July 2008).

One learns to one's surprise that some people who are thought of as wonderful judges are lacking in the art of persuading their colleagues to adopt their point of view. Whereas others who are not much on the record in print are extremely good at directing a decision in a particular way.

Lord Wilberforce undoubtedly had Lord Radcliffe in mind,[113] but his observation could equally well be applied to those tactician judges who were ineffective in their lobbying or attempts at task leadership. Successful task leaders have to persuade a majority of their colleagues on the panel to adopt their chosen outcome or their reasoning, either through their intellect, their competence, their charm or the clarity of their reasoning. Being good at persuading others, whether orally or in writing, in the long-term requires the judge to appear to be open to others' arguments. Law Lords who did not always manage to convey this impression such as Lord Atkin, Viscount Simonds and, it is said, Lord Steyn were at a disadvantage to those like Lord Wilberforce, who did. Similarly, a lobbyist who is too persistent or too entrenched in conference or too long-winded in his opinions is likely to alienate his colleagues. Lord Atkin frequently lobbied his colleagues. His daughter later recalled,

> He continued to use his powers of persuasion when he was sitting as a Lord of Appeal and would come home and say that he thought he had won his brothers over to his side or 'so and so is still not convinced but I think he may be tomorrow'.[114]

But it irked his colleagues that he was not open to persuasion in return. Lord Dunedin described him as 'obstinate if he has taken a view and quite unpersuadable',[115] and Lord Simon, whose overtures in *Liversidge v Anderson* had been rejected by Lord Atkin,[116] recorded in Atkin's obituary,

> I think he relied less than many members of [the House of Lords and Court of Appeal] do on the conference and discussion which takes place after the arguments are over. He was, therefore, a strong judge.[117]

Viscount Dilhorne also had a reputation of lobbying too eagerly and thus alienating some of his colleagues. Lord Hoffmann, although open to persuasion on occasion, did not often change his mind[118] as we will see shortly. However, his habit of circulating his judgment early—sometimes even before the end of

---

[113] He wrote of him, 'Lord Radcliffe, who was perhaps our most intellectually brilliant judge ... did not have [the power to persuade his colleagues] ... He did not want to exercise it and did not try to exercise it. See G Sturgess and P Chubb, *Judging the World* (Sydney, Butterworths, 1988) at 275.

[114] E Millar, 'Some memories of Lord Atkin' (1957) 23 *GLIM* 13, 14–15.

[115] RFV Heuston, *Lives of The Lord Chancellors 1885–1940* (Oxford, Clarendon Press, 1987) 481. Lord Dunedin himself was said to be 'eminently open to suggestion' by his colleagues. Sir Charles Mallet, *Lord Cave* (London, John Murray, 1931) 226.

[116] RFV Heuston, '*Liversidge v. Anderson* in Retrospect' (1970) 86 *LQR* 33, 46.

[117] *The Times*, 27 June 1944 (quoted in Heuston, ibid 46).

[118] Cases where he did include *Mannai Investment Co Ltd v Eagle Star Assurance* [1997] UKHL 19, [1997] AC 749; *Kleinwort Benson v Lincoln City Council* [1998] UKHL 38, [1999] 2 AC 349 and *Callery v Gray* [2002] UKHL 28.

the hearing—became so transparent an attempt to woo his colleagues as to be counter-productive. Lord Steyn, who similarly made up his mind at an early stage, would occasionally change it,[119] but was perceived as less open to persuasion by some of his colleagues, which reduced his effectiveness as a tactician.

One way to assess the efficacy or otherwise of Law Lords as task leaders or group decision-makers is to look at their records in 'close call' cases (cases in which two or more judges in the final court dissent from the majority outcome).[120] As Table 4.2 shows, the Law Lords in the last decade of the House had widely contrasting records in such cases.

There are three rough groupings. The first group, including Lords Brown, Hoffmann, Hope and Millett were twice as likely to be on the majority side of close calls as on the minority side. All of these were collectively minded judges who would talk to their colleagues throughout case including the circulation of

Voting Record in Close Call Cases in the House of Lords (2000–09)		
	In Majority	**In Minority**
Bingham	18	13
Brown	12	2
Carswell	14	9
Hale	12	12
Hobhouse	5	7
Hoffmann	20	10
Hope	27	14
Hutton	3	8
Mance	7	10
Millett	12	6
Neuberger	5	6
Nicholls	13	10
Rodger	10	12
Scott	16	11
Slynn	8	4
Steyn	15	12
Walker	17	10

Table 4.2: Voting Record in Close Call Cases in the House of Lords (2000–09).

[119] See eg *Director General of Fair Trading* [2001] UKHL 52, para 38.
[120] Definition derived from B Dickson, 'Close Calls in the House of Lords' ch 13 in J Lee (ed), *From House of Lords to Supreme Court* (Oxford, Hart Publishing, 2011). However, because Table 4.2 covers the year 2000 and because a wider definition of 'dissent' has been used than Professor Dickson did, the figures in this chapter are difficult to compare with those of Professor Dickson. He identified 52 close calls between 2001 and 2009. Our figure for 2000–09 is 79 close calls.

judgments stage. That might suggest that they were all successful task leaders. However it is possible that some of them preferred not to dissent if it served no purpose, for example, as we will see later, Lord Millett switched his vote to the majority at the draft circulation stage on six occasions in the Bingham era.

The second group, including Lords Bingham, Carswell, Scott, Steyn and Walker were rather more likely to be on the majority side than not. In the cases of Lords Bingham and Walker, neither of whom was a lobbyist or tactician, this is likely to reflect the respect in which they were held by their colleagues. Lords Steyn and Scott were both thought to be tacticians who tried to be task leaders, but not always with success. Lord Carswell, however, often considered that he was the swing voter in such cases.[121] The third group, including Lady Hale and Lords Hobhouse, Hutton, Mance, Nicholls and Rodger, contained those who were as likely to be in the minority as the majority. Although Lady Hale was by instinct a group-oriented Law Lord, she was not a lobbyist and believed that she had an individual role on the court.[122] The remainder were strong individualists.

Interestingly, when we look at the Law Lords' voting patterns in *all* cases where there is a dissent (see Table 4.3) it will be seen that the make-up of the three groups changes markedly. Now the majority of Law Lords are in the first group (Lords Bingham, Brown, Carswell, Hoffmann, Hope, Millett, Neuberger, Nicholls, Rodger, Slynn, Steyn and Walker). Only three are left in the individualists' camp: Lords Hobhouse, Hutton and Scott.

Dissents, Individualism and Collegiality

If group-oriented judges have an impact on the outcome of close calls, can we conclude that a judge with a dissent rate higher than the average (see Tables 3.10, 3.11 and 3.12) should by definition be classified as more of an individualist than a group-oriented judge? Interestingly, the evidence does not entirely support such a surmise. Of course, in times gone by (see Table 3.10) there were regular solo dissenters who were individualists by inclination such as Lord Keith (the father) and Lord Guest with overall dissent rates of 16 per cent and nine per cent respectively. Lord Denning, who dissented in 15 per cent of appeals while in the Lords, tried to be collegial but generally found his brethren reluctant to agree with him.[123] Lord Radcliffe also had a highish dissent rate (nine per cent) for all his intellectual brilliance, but as we have seen he lacked the power or the inclination to persuade his colleagues.[124] In truth, as both Table 4.3 and Table 3.11 show, there

---

[121] Interview with the author, 2008.
[122] On the other hand what looks like an occasional use of tactical assents (see chapter 3 of this volume above) is clearly a form of task leadership.
[123] See A Paterson, *The Law Lords* (London, Macmillan, 1982) 112.
[124] See G Sturgess and P Chubb, *Judging the World* (Sydney, Butterworths, 1988) 275, quoting Lord Wilberforce.

	Voting Record in Close Call Cases (2000–09)		Voting Record in All Divided Cases (2000–09)	
	In Majority	In Minority	In Majority	In Minority
Bingham	18	13	44	18
Brown	12	2	33	4
Carswell	14	9	30	11
Hale	12	12	28	19
Hobhouse	5	7	14	12
Hoffmann	20	10	43	15
Hope	27	14	58	18
Hutton	3	8	10	9
Mance	7	10	17	11
Millett	12	6	20	11
Neuberger	5	6	16	7
Nicholls	13	10	38	13
Rodger	10	12	33	17
Scott	16	11	32	25
Slynn	8	4	17	6
Steyn	15	12	33	17
Walker	17	20	34	16

Table 4.3: Voting Record in Close Call cases and in all divided cases in the House of Lords (2000–09).

is a difference between dissenting on your own and dissenting with others. The former is often an individualist act, the latter is not. Over the last 40 years a significant number of Law Lords have not thought it worthwhile to dissent on their own unless it was on a point of principle. In the last decade alone the Law Lords were twice as likely to dissent with a colleague rather than to dissent on their own. Dissenting with a colleague, however, is not simply to engage in a dialogue with the future, it may also be a dialogue with the present.[125] It may even induce one of the majority to swing over. Dissenting with others is therefore often a group-oriented or collegial response.

Even this analysis of dissents oversimplifies matters. This is because dissents have to be broken down further. Whilst 11 per cent of cases in the Lords in

---

[125] For example, it may be used to send a message to the Government that it may have won this case, but that it had only squeaked home by 3:2.

1952–68 and 2000–09 and 11.5 per cent in the Supreme Court from 2009–13 (March) were sole dissents, they were of two different types. Those where the dissenter was isolated from an early stage,[126] eg Lord Bingham in his later dissents,[127] and those where a Law Lord or Justice started out with one or more colleagues, like Lord Walker in the *Belmarsh*[128] case or Lord Neuberger in *Stack v Dowden*[129] only to find that when the dust had settled and vote switching was over, they were on their own as the sole dissenter. To treat the latter dissenters as individualists because they didn't withdraw their opinion and align themselves with the rest seems analytically dubious. Similarly the close call cases, which made up a further 11 per cent of cases in the Lords between 1952–68 and 2000–09, and 14 per cent of Supreme Court cases from 2009–13 (July), fell into three categories: those where the minority judges were formerly part of the majority but ended up in the minority through late vote changes; those where there was only ever one swing voter; and those where nobody was in any doubt about their position at any stage in the case. What this shows is that to categorise cases by their outcome (and judges by their final position in a case) is to underplay the dynamic process by which the outcome was achieved. Law Lords or Justices who started out thinking that they were writing the lead opinion occasionally found that due to vote switches they were now a dissenter.[130]

Task Leadership and the US Supreme Court

In the US Supreme Court the requirement for there to be a majority judgment commanding at least five votes for it to count as a firm precedent, has put a greater premium on task leadership, and in that court there is far more lobbying, bargaining and negotiation by the judges than has been the case in its UK counterpart. In such a context those who are more willing to compromise by removing or inserting passages in their lead/assigned judgment are more likely to have a greater influence on the outcome or the reasoning in the final majority judgment than those who are not. The philosopher Isaiah Berlin, drawing on the saying attributed to the Greek poet Archilochus 'the fox knows many things, but the hedgehog knows one big thing', distinguished between two types of thinking—moral single-mindedness

---

[126] Their dissent could be triggered by the consensus of the rest of the panel. See Edwards on dissent and collegiality (above, n 77).

[127] *Secretary of State for Defence v Al-Skeini & Others* [2007] UKHL 26 (13 June 2007); R (on the application of *Countryside Alliance and others*) *v Attorney General & Another* [2007] UKHL 52 (28 November 2007); *Chief Constable of Hertfordshire Police v Van Colle; Smith v Chief Constable of Sussex Police* [2008] UKHL 50 (30 July 2008).

[128] *A and Others v Secretary of State for the Home Department* [2004] UKHL 56.

[129] *Stack v Dowden* [2007] UKHL 17 (25 April 2007).

[130] This highlights the dangers of doing analyses on voting patterns or attitudinal- or value-based variables since in each case outcomes are being assessed irrespective of the process by which the outcome was arrived at.

and pluralism.[131] On the US Supreme Court, Justices Thomas and Scalia are classic hedgehogs[132]—neither is prepared to compromise their originalist principles and neither is prone to lobbying to attract votes to their position[133]—whereas Justices Breyer and Kennedy are more like pragmatic foxes—open to consequentialist arguments, less prone to over-arching theories and happy to reason from case to case. Breyer is said to have been the most active oral lobbyist in the Rehnquist court,[134] relying on charm and gentle persistence to cajole his colleagues. He was also aware of the dangers of hard-line liberal opinions driving the 'swing voting' moderates such as O'Connor, Souter and Kennedy towards the more conservative camp. In consequence he would liaise with his liberal colleagues to ensure that they delayed circulating their concurrences until he had completed his opinion and obtained the swing voter's agreement to it.[135] Chief Justice Rehnquist is said to have started out as a hedgehog, but he became increasingly pragmatic or result-oriented towards the end.[136] Chief Justice Roberts, in contrast, believes in consistent philosophies and is therefore viewed by some as a more principled decision-maker.[137]

If appearing to be open to persuasion and showing a willingness to compromise in order to secure a worthwhile outcome enhance one's chances of being an effective task leader, it should not surprise us that lobbyists or would-be task leaders who, like Black and Frankfurter on the US Supreme Court, fought 'hard, long and loud in the conference room and out'[138] for their views, ran the risk of alienating their colleagues. Justice Jackson publicly accused Black of using bullying tactics in conference,[139] and Frankfurter's pontifical 'lectures' to his brethren led some of them to regard him as a 'puffed up professor'.[140] Again Justice Scalia's undoubted intellectual abilities have not been enough to make him a regular task leader on the court, not only because he is unwilling to compromise or to lobby, but also because he is unwilling to curb his barbed public attacks on colleagues who disagree with him[141]—including his closest personal friend on the court,

---

[131] Isaiah Berlin, 'The Hedgehog and the Fox' *Russian Thinkers* (London, Hogarth Press, 1978).

[132] See Greenburg, above, n 14, 181 and J Toobin, *The Nine: Inside the Secret World of the Supreme Court* (New York, Doubleday, 2007) 128–29.

[133] See Toobin, above, n 132, 55 and A Kushner, 'Behind the Black Robes' 27/9/07.

[134] See Toobin, above, n 132, at 128 and Greenburg, above, n 14, at 182–83.

[135] Toobin, above, n 132, 134–35.

[136] See Greenburg, above, n 14, 180; A Kushner, Behind the Black Robes 27/9/07: 'Don't worry about the analysis and the principles in the case. Just make sure that the result is a good one ... Those principles you announce will be ignored'.

[137] Greenburg above n 14, 231.

[138] H Black, 'Mr Justice Frankfurter' (1965) 78 *Harvard Law Review* 1521.

[139] *New York Times*, 11 June 1946, p 2. See also M F Berry, *Stability, Security and Continuity* (Connecticut, Greenwood Press,1978), p 29.

[140] J Lash, *From the Diaries of Felix Frankfurter* (New York, W Norton, 1975), 211 and 227; Berry, above, n 139, p 49.

[141] Scalia regularly criticises his colleagues personally in his opinions. In one dissent he attacked Souter by name 18 times. See T E Yarbrough, *David Hackett Souter* (New York, Oxford University Press, 2005) at 188. In another case he dismissed a Justice's opinion as 'facile' and in a key case on abortion—which he lost—he described O'Connor's opinion as one that 'cannot be taken seriously'. See J Toobin, *The Nine* (above, n 139) at 55.

Justice Ginsberg.[142] Justice Thomas could also drive O'Connor towards the liberals by the uncompromising conservative stances that he took, but unlike Scalia, Thomas took note of hurt caused by his strong language and he was prepared to withdraw offending words in a judgment if pressed by O'Connor.[143] This suggests that charm, charisma and diplomacy are undoubted assets for those who wish to be effective task leaders. It is said that one reason that George Bush chose John Roberts to replace Rehnquist as Chief Justice was his charm and his ability to get on with others, thereby maximising his ability to forge links with those in the middle of the court—the swing voters. Roberts 'wouldn't alienate other justices or push them away'.[144]

Social Leadership

Whilst effective task leaders will frequently have the social skills required not to alienate their colleagues, social leaders are even better equipped to address the emotional needs of the court, and are generally the most congenial and popular members of the court. Generally, as Danelski showed, they are not the court's primary task leaders as well, although there have been exceptions. Social leaders tend to be good-humoured, empathetic and able to diffuse conflict—if debates get too heated—by pouring oil on troubled waters. The importance of social leaders can be seen from the aftermath of the Pinochet saga. As is well known, when General Pinochet was in London for medical treatment, a Spanish magistrate sought to have him arrested for alleged crimes against the people of Chile. The case was expedited to the House of Lords but Lord Browne-Wilkinson, the senior Law Lord, was attending the re-constitution of the ECtHR so was unavailable to sit, requiring Lord Hoffmann, a heavyweight intellectual on the Court to step in unexpectedly. It was known to the Clerk to the Judicial Office and the presider in the case, Lord Slynn, that Lord Hoffmann's wife was an employee of Amnesty International (whom Slynn, unusually, had agreed to becoming an intervener in the case). The Clerk, at Slynn's request, spoke to Lord Hoffmann to see if an interest should be declared and the matter seems to have been left unresolved. However, neither the Clerk nor any of the other Law Lords were aware that Lord Hoffmann himself was a trustee in a charity which raised money for Amnesty International. With the House having voted 3:2 against General Pinochet (with Lord Hoffmann in the majority), it was then discovered that Lord Hoffmann had failed to declare any connection with Amnesty International. Another appellate committee of the House, chaired by the senior Law Lord then annulled the

---

[142]   Rehnquist CJ is reputed to have telephoned Scalia having read one of his draft opinions attacking O'Connor asking him to back off because he was driving the centrist Justice O'Connor into the arms of the liberals. 'Nino, you're pissing Sandra off again. Stop it!' Quoted in Toobin, *The Nine* at 129.

[143]   Greenburg, above, n 14 at 128–29.

[144]   Greenburg, above, n 14, at 206.

decision on the grounds that Lord Hoffmann was automatically disqualified by his interest with Amnesty International.[145] The aftermath was a breakdown in personal relations between Lord Hoffmann, Lord Browne-Wilkinson and Lord Slynn. Lord Hoffmann's stock was reduced on the Court for several years but neither Lord Browne-Wilkinson nor Lord Slynn seem fully to have got over the affair. Each seemed wounded by the unparalleled events and there was no social leader on the Court to help the healing process to begin. The strain manifested itself, in part, in delays between the hearing of cases and the handing down of judgments.[146] Lord Bingham was brought in as senior Law Lord by Lord Irvine to stabilise the rocky ship that the House had become. He proved an inspired choice. His humanity, sense of humour and intellectual brilliance enabled him to win round all sides and to place relations back once more on an even keel. However, Tom Bingham was not an instinctive social leader. So while he was the most respected member of the Court, the nearest to a social leader in the House of Lords in its final years was undoubtedly Lord Brown. Gregarious, warm, and naturally sociable he positively encouraged his colleagues to drop into his office which was strategically situated next to the Secretaries' office, the coffee machine and the biscuit tin (and occasional cakes on birthdays). In Bingham's era the only Law Lord to regularly have several Law Lords in his room was Lord Brown. Lord Brown was a longstanding friend of Lord Phillips and Lord Walker and several other former members of the Court of Appeal. Indeed, it is almost inevitable that some Law Lords and Justices have friendships with colleagues stretching back many years. This is true for the final courts on both sides of the Atlantic. Thus in the US Supreme Court well-known friendships included, eg Burton and Frankfurter,[147] Burton and Harlan,[148] Frankfurter and Harlan,[149] Warren and Black,[150] and more recently Souter and Brennan, and Scalia and Ginsberg. (There have also been long-standing antagonisms in the two courts, eg Frankfurter and Douglas,[151] Black and Jackson, [152] Brandon and Templeman).

Nonetheless, friendship or the lack of it is not a good indicator as to whether individuals will vote together.[153] Lord Phillips, as we shall see, frequently discussed cases with Lord Brown, but their agreement level on outcomes in the Supreme

---

[145] *In re Pinochet* [1999] UKHL 1.

[146] See Table 3.13 above.

[147] Berry, ibid. See n 139 above.

[148] Berry, ibid, 205.

[149] J Lumbard, 'J.H.', (1971) 85 *Harvard Law Review* (1971) 372, 375.

[150] Berry, above, n 139, 211, 213.

[151] J Lash, *From the Diaries of Felix Frankfurter* (New York, W Norton, 1975) 78, 230.

[152] E Gerhart, America's Advocate (Indianapolis IN, Bobbs-Merrill, 1958) 262 and Berry, above, n 139 29. B Woodward and S Armstrong, *The Brethren: Inside the Supreme Court* (New York, Simon & Schuster, 1979) (eg 179 and 187) suggests the relations between Douglas and Burger were strained for much of the time when they were both on the court. Antagonisms on the Bench can have advantageous side effects for counsel, since if one judge asks counsel a question the opposing judge may answer it for him.

[153] See the Voting Relationships section below in chapter 5 of this volume. Scalia and Ginsberg are lifelong friends but that does not make them more likely to vote together.

Court (83 per cent) was below the average (86 per cent) for the Court. Friends do not always see eye to eye on the contentious issues which have to be resolved by final appeal courts, and given that 76 per cent of cases are unanimous in the UK's top court, judges who do not get on personally will often vote together. Nevertheless, Edwards CJ when discussing Collegiality strongly emphasises the importance of cordial relations between the judges if there is to be effective dialogue, debate and negotiation between them. What friendship and cordial relations with colleagues does do, therefore, especially if accompanied by social leadership, is make it easier to drop in on each other's rooms[154] and to initiate conversations on tricky and divisive issues. In fact, in Lord Brown's case the colleagues came to him. When he was in the House of Lords Lord Brown had much the lowest dissent rate of all the Law Lords (two per cent—the average was eight per cent). In finely balanced cases (close calls) certain Law Lords (as we saw earlier), including Lords Brown, Hoffmann, Hope and Millett, were twice as likely to be on the winning side as on the minority side in the Bingham era. For some of them, this was because they were task leaders—but in Lord Brown's case it was perhaps more likely because he was at the heart of the debate amongst the panel and because of his skills as a social leader.

Leadership skills in the Supreme Court

The choice of Lord Phillips as the first President of the UK Supreme Court was widely seen as conscious decision to appoint a moderniser. As Master of the Rolls and Lord Chief Justice, he had acquired a reputation for innovation, including getting rid of wigs for civil judges and remodelling their gowns.[155] True to form he was the driving force behind the decision to introduce gowns for the Justices, though only for ceremonial occasions, and the decision to allow counsel to appear in the Court without wig or gown, provided all the counsel in the case, agree. Equally visibly, with the enthusiastic support of the Deputy President, Lord Hope,[156] he persuaded a majority of the Justices to agree to the oral hearings in the Court being televised.[157] Again he endorsed the use of Press releases summarising each decision of the Court and the practice, largely unknown in the House of Lords, of a member of the panel reading out a summary of the majority decision taken by the court. Finally, in terms of visibility, he was primarily responsible

---

[154] The judges told me that they were more likely to visit colleagues whom they were friends with or whom they knew well from the past, eg Lords Phillips and Clarke who had at one time been in the same chambers, or Lords Phillips and Brown, or Lords Hope and Rodger, or Lords Walker and Brown, or Lords Clarke and Dyson. From an earlier generation Viscount Simonds and Viscount Radcliffe were close friends.

[155] A move that did not endear him to all of his colleagues.

[156] Who, when Lord President of the Court of Session in Scotland had been responsible for allowing television cameras into the courts for the first time in the UK.

[157] A reform that is still being resisted in the US Supreme Court.

for the Court sitting with much greater frequency than in the House, in panels of seven or nine.[158] Nevertheless, largely because he was appointed President rather late in the transition process, much of the planning for the new Court and its procedures was the work of others, particularly Lord Hope, Lord Walker, Lady Hale and Lord Mance.

What about the ways in which the new Court conducted its core functions of sifting and deciding appeals? As for the former, Lord Phillips changed very little. Applications for permission to appeal were very largely dealt with in the same way as leave to appeal requests had been dealt with by appeal committees (as we saw in the previous chapter). A new procedure was introduced to allow all of the Justices to see the papers for all applications coming before the court if they so wished, but to begin with the technology did not make it as simple as had been hoped. After a year or so of the new Court, and following critical remarks at the first annual Supreme Court conference, the Justices started to give slightly fuller reasons for refusing applications for permission to appeal. This was discussed at one of the regular (now bi-monthly) meetings held by the Justices, an innovation introduced by Lord Phillips, which had not existed in the House of Lords. He also introduced a short pre-meeting for up to 15 minutes before the hearing of a new case, to get preliminary views from the Justices, particularly about points which they would like to hear counsel on, a practice that already existed in the Court of Appeal, but which Lord Bingham had resisted. Yet when it came to the hearings, Lord Phillips did not endeavour to steer counsel or take a particularly strong line on counsel who over-ran their agreed time limits, being rather more relaxed than such famous predecessors as Lords Reid or Bingham (and certainly Lord Diplock) and his immediate successor, Lord Neuberger. Lord Phillips was in favour of more time for collective deliberation after the hearing was over, a view shared by several other Justices, but he was not very successful in getting it to come about. Thus the first conference after the hearing was run by Lord Phillips just as it had been in the Lords and although some of his colleagues persuaded a majority of the Justices at one of the regular meetings in 2011 that the seriatim presentations at this conference should be reduced in order to leave more time for discussion, it is far from clear that very much actually changed. Lord Phillips told me that he could never recall intervening at that conference to ask a colleague to speed up their presentation.[159] Again Lord Phillips was of the view that it was better to get the final decision of the court right rather than to reach a quicker decision which felt rushed. As a result the average gap between hearing date and judgment date rose in Phillips' time as compared with that of Lord Bingham (See Tables 3.13 and 3.14 above). Lord

---

[158] Something that had not been easy in the Lords because of a lack of suitable accommodation. The Court sat in panels of seven and nine on 57 occasions between September 2009 and August 2013.

[159] My researches did not suggest that this occurred in the House of Lords. As we saw earlier, Lord Bingham even encouraged the junior Law Lord to speak for longer than his colleagues, although we have no record as to how Lord Diplock ran the first conference in his time.

Neuberger is more of the Bingham disposition on this issue and keeps a regular eye on the production of judgments. As a result, as can be seen from Tables 3.13 and 3.14, the gap between hearing and final judgment has fallen to around the levels of the Bingham era.

But what of task leadership? The picture with regard to Lord Phillips is not clear cut. He saw the President of the Court as the leader of the court,[160] with a duty to lead his 'team'.[161] He was keen to foster the notion that the members of the Court were a team and his encouragement of lunching together and additional meetings (before hearings, after hearings and independently of cases, on a bi-monthly basis) were all part of this. Whilst his form of leadership was fairly relaxed in relation to the make-up of the panel,[162] the conduct of the hearing and the first conference, and the delivery date for the judgment, he did think that as President he should do the lion's share of the lead judgments for cases in which he sat.[163] (Curiously, he sat in a rather smaller number of Supreme Court cases than the Deputy President, but that was not through design). By convention the presiding judge (in the main, either Lord Phillips or Lord Hope in the first three years of the Court), could choose who would write the lead judgment even if he was in the minority (as we saw in chapter three) and they tried to allocate those that they were not doing themselves fairly amongst the Justices. In practice, this was not a scientific or strictly observed ordinance, since, as can be seen from Table 4.4, there are quite substantial variations between the Justices in terms of lead or sole judgments written as a percentage of cases sat in.

Excluding the President and Deputy President, who preside far more than any of their colleagues, some of those who were frequent dissenters ended up with considerably fewer lead judgments to write overall as can be seen from Table 4.4 and Table 3.12.

Yet, Table 4.4 and 4.5 show that whilst Lord Sumption gave the lead/single judgment in 29 per cent of the cases he decided up until the end of July 2013, Lord Kerr only gave the lead/single judgment in eight per cent of the cases in which he sat.[164] The contrast with the US Supreme Court, where the convention is that each Justice gets more or less the same number of majority opinions to draft, is striking. Lord Phillips saw a place for more single judgments—although he was far from the Diplock camp—and would sometimes strive vigorously to achieve a single judgment of the court, even in cases with an enlarged panel. He favoured a

---

[160] U Brain television interview 18/7/12.

[161] Suzanna Ring and Alex Novarese, 'Reflections of a jurist: Lord Phillips'. Interview with Lord Phillips on 28 September 2012: Legalweek.com: 'If you ask what additional qualities you need, it's essentially leadership—being able to lead a team'. Until 2012 or so it was not entirely clear that the majority of the Supreme Court did regard themselves as a team.

[162] Lord Phillips might well initiate a suggestion as to which cases merited a hearing before a larger panel, and—unlike Lord Bingham—he did not expect the membership of the larger panels to be based on seniority, but he rarely changed the proposed membership of the panel which the Registrar put to him.

[163] See Table 3.1.

[164] Lord Kerr, however, was one of those who wrote extensively in the Privy Council as well as writing multiple leading judgments.

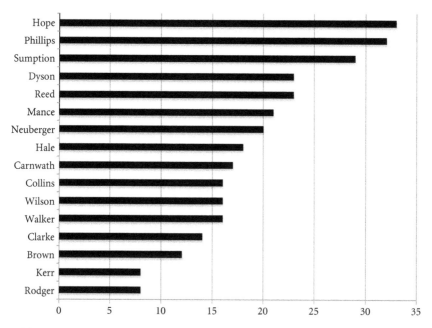

Table 4.4: Lead and single judgments in the UK Supreme Court as a percentage of total cases sat in during 2009–13 (July)*.

* Same as Table 3.1.

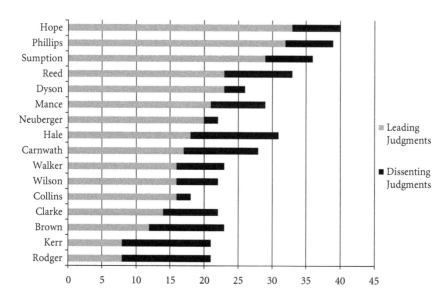

Table 4.5: Lead, single and dissenting judgments in the UK Supreme Court as a percentage of cases sat in during 2009–13 (July).

single judgment in the *Pinnock* case,[165] which put an end to a stream of disunited cases on the interface between Human Rights and private law which had begun in the House of Lords,[166] although the initiator of the suggestion that there be a single judgment in that case was Lord Rodger, who encouraged Lord Neuberger to propose this to Lord Phillips. Similarly Lord Phillips strove hard for a single judgment in *Waya*,[167] a tricky Proceeds of Crime case, even after it became clear that he was going to be a dissenter in the case. However, perhaps because he found them particularly difficult, there were cases where he was noticeably unable as President and presider to achieve fewer judgments, eg *Jewish Free School, Lumba* and *MOD*.[168]

There were 34 'close calls'[169] in the first four years of the Supreme Court. Lord Phillips presided in 15 of them and he was on the majority side in 11 of them. See Table 4.6. Since Lord Phillips was a collectively minded judge, this could indicate that in these cases he exercised a considerable degree of task leadership. Closer examination of the cases does not entirely support this hypothesis. True, he wrote the lead judgment in six of them (40 per cent) which is a very high strike rate[170]—yet in one of these (*Assange*) he gave five reasons for the decision, only one of which was supported by a majority of his colleagues. Moreover, Lord Phillips' support for a team or collective approach to decision-making was very rarely of a tactical or lobbying kind. Indeed, he tended to keep an open mind in difficult cases far later than most of his colleagues, leading him in several of the close calls either to reject the majority's reasoning (but not their result)[171] or, it is thought, to change his position—if not his vote—relatively late in proceedings.[172] If there were one or two other cases—not close calls—where he helped to win

---

[165] [2010] UKSC 45. For an account of how the Pinnock case fitted into the dialogue with Strasbourg at the time see chapter 6 of this volume n 118 below.

[166] See *Qazi v Harrow LBC* [2003] UKHL 43, *Kay v Lambeth LBC* [2006] UKHL 10, *Doherty v Birmingham City Council* [2008] UKHL 57.

[167] *R v Waya* [2012] UKSC 51.

[168] *R (on the application of E) v Governing Body of Jewish Free School and Admissions Appeal Panel of Jewish Free School and Others* [2009] UKSC 15, *Walumba Lumba* [2011] UKSC 12 and *Ministry of Defence v AB* [2012] UKSC 9. These were all cases where it is thought that he changed his mind (and his vote). Lord Phillips in media interviews several times indicated that he found certain cases in the Supreme Court so difficult that they woke him up at night, once describing the *JFS* case as the most difficult case which he ever had to decide.

[169] Cases in which there were at least two dissents. See fuller definition in chapter 1 of this volume above.

[170] *R (on the application of Smith) v Oxfordshire Assistant Deputy Coroner* [2010] UKSC 29; *R (Electoral Commission) v City of Westminster Magistrates Court and UKIP* [2010] UKSC 40; *Jones v Kaney* [2011] UKSC 13; *R (on the application of Adams) (Appellant) v Secretary of State for Justice* [2011] UKSC 18; *Assange v Swedish Prosecution Authority* [2012] UKSC 22; *Perry and others v Serious Organised Crime Agency* [2012] UKSC 35.

[171] *Stone Rolls Ltd (in liquidation) v Moore Stephens (a firm)* [2009] UKSC 39; *Al Rawi and Others v The Security Service and Others* [2011] UKSC 34; *Edwards v Chesterfield Royal Hospital NHS Foundation Trust* [2011] UKSC 58.

[172] *Jewish Free School* [2009] UKSC 15; *Edwards v Chesterfield Royal Hospital NHS Foundation Trust* [2011] UKSC 58; *Ministry of Defence v AB and others* [2012] UKSC 9.

Close Calls in UK Supreme Court 2009–13 (July)		
Close calls in Supreme Court	Times in majority	Times in minority
Brown	9	8
Carnwath	2	5
Clarke	9	7
Collins	7	1
Dyson	9	2
Hale	11	10
Hope	11	9
Kerr	14	7
Mance	9	6
Neuberger	5	1
Phillips	11	4
Reed	5	2
Rodger	3	7
Sumption	4	2
Walker	14	5
Wilson	8	4

Table 4.6: Close Calls in the UK Supreme Court during 2009–13 (July).

over support for his position[173] equally there were cases where he lost the majority or the lead judgment to others. Whilst his dissent rate was low (seven per cent) in part this was because, as President,[174] he saw little point in dissenting on his own. (See Table 3.12)

Lord Hope as Deputy President also provided considerable leadership to the Court. He played a major role in the transition team planning for the move to the new Court and its procedures (even although he did not favour its establishment). He presided in more Supreme Court cases than any other Justice (109) and gave the lead or single judgment in 46 cases (33 per cent of the cases he sat in), ahead of his nearest rivals (Lord Phillips 32%) and Lord Sumption (29%) (see Table 4.4) He, too was a collectively minded Justice but he was more of a tactician than Lord Phillips and he would negotiate changes in his own or others judgments with a

---

[173] Eg Lord Dyson in *R v Gnango* [2011] UKSC 59 and in *Flood v Times Newspapers Ltd* [2012] UKSC 11.

[174] Lord Phillips dissented on his own in three cases in the Lords but only once in the Supreme Court.

view to achieving a desired outcome. Yet in close calls he was less successful than he had been in the Lords (where he was twice as likely to be on the majority side as on the minority side).[175] In the Supreme Court[176] he was on the majority side in only 11 of the 20 close calls in which he took part. On the other hand, he gave the lead judgment in four of these (36%), he fought hard, and successfully, in *Martin* to keep his majority, and it seems clear also that he wrote what was to have been the lead judgment in the *Jewish Free School* case,[177] only to lose out by an apparent switch of votes by Lord Phillips. In other cases in the Supreme Court, it is thought that he more than once won over a majority to his position. However, like Lord Phillips his dissent rate was on the low side (seven per cent)—which was almost the same as when he was in the Lords—and he never (in the Supreme Court) dissented on his own.

Nonetheless there is evidence (in part from the close calls table)[178] that at least two other Justices played the role of task leader with considerable success. First was Lord Collins who was appointed to the Supreme Court in 2009 and was required to step down at the mandatory retirement age of 70. In the space of two years he took part in eight close calls and was in the majority in seven of them. Indeed in his 51 appearances in the court he only dissented on one occasion.[179] His colleagues in turn rarely dissented against him. His contribution as an intellectual leader of the Court probably accounts for the fact that his mean agreement rate with his colleagues was 90%—considerably higher than the average for the whole court of 86%—and equal with Lord Dyson as the highest on the Court at the time. As we will see geography possibly played a part since his neighbours on the second floor were amongst his highest levels of agreement, namely Lord Kerr (94%),[180] Lord Rodger (91%) and Lord Clarke 89%. However, there can be little doubt that the most successful task leader in the Supreme Court in its first three years was Lord Dyson. His overall agreement rate with his colleagues (90%) was equalled only by Lord Collins. Lord Dyson was the Justice with whom several

---

[175] See Table 4.2, above. This may be an indication that it is harder to be a tactician when the court sits much more often in larger panels.

[176] Up until the end of July 2013.

[177] Not only does he have the fullest statement of the facts, he also deals with the issue of costs (with which his colleagues all agree) which is unusual in a dissenting judgment.

[178] The Table suggests that others Justices were also possible task leaders including Lord Walker. His is an interesting case since he was a non-tactician and a principled analyst. Until February 2012 his record in close calls in the Supreme Court was about parity. Thereafter, until he retired in 2013 he was in eight further close calls and on the majority side in each of them. In only the important case of *Waya* did he give the lead judgment (although he gave the lead judgment in five other cases in that year).

[179] It is clear in *Secretary of State for Environment, Food and Rural Affairs v Meier* [2009] UKSC 11 he nearly dissented [at para 96] and he told me that he tried hard to dissent in *R (Coke-Wallis) v Institute of Chartered Accountants in England & Wales* 2011 but could find no intellectually satisfactory way of doing so. It may also be the case that he switched his vote in *In re Lehman Brothers International (Europe) (In Administration) and In the matter of the Insolvency Act 1986* [2012] UKSC 6 to go with Lord Dyson.

[180] It is also fair to note that Lord Kerr's real spurt of dissents was in the second half of 2011, by which time Lord Collins had already retired.

of his colleagues had their highest levels of agreement,[181] namely, Lords Walker (97%), Hope (95%), Clarke (94%) and Phillips (93%). Indeed the only Justices whose agreement rate with him falls below the Court average of 86%[182] are Lord Kerr and Lady Hale. His high agreement rate with his colleagues stemmed partly from the fact that in all nine close calls in which he sat whilst a full-time member of the Court he was on the majority side and indeed in the 18 cases in which he sat as a full-timer which had any dissent in them, it was not his, since he did not dissent once in 64 appearances on the Court, until he returned as Master of the Rolls in the *Bank Mellat* cases.[183] Indeed very few of his colleagues voted against him, either. It might be argued that such figures are compatible both with being a task leader and with being a follower of others' leads (who by indecision or changes of heart ended up on the majority side). The latter is not Lord Dyson. Lord Dyson wasted few opportunities to tell his colleagues (senior and junior) in his judgments precisely where he did and did not agree with them, as we saw in the engagement section at the start of this chapter.[184] Lord Phillips was several times on the receiving end of such forensic broadsides, however, there was no animus, and indeed Lord Dyson was won over by Lord Phillips' lead judgments in *R v Gnango* and in *Flood*.[185] Yet in four or possibly five other cases his attempts to write a clear and persuasive dissent were so successful that they became the lead judgment.[186] In his two years on the Court no other Justice succeeded in bringing over so many votes to his side after the first conference. In all Lord Dyson gave 14 lead or single judgments (21 per cent of his cases) ranking him (whilst he was a full-time member of the Court) as the most prolific lead writer after Lords Phillips and Hope.[187]

Social Leadership in the Supreme Court

What of social leadership? Although Lord Phillips would talk regularly with colleagues he had known for years, eg Lords Brown and Clarke, no more than Lord Bingham did he make a habit of visiting all of his other colleagues in their rooms. Having chaired the panel that appointed eight of his colleagues to the Court might have brought him closer to those whom he did not know well, but there is little evidence that it did. Being slightly reserved, the role of social leader seems not to have come naturally to him and when he did intervene in an effort to preserve the

---

[181] See Table 5.3 in chapter 5, below.
[182] See Table 5.3, below.
[183] *Bank Mellat v Her Majesty's Treasury (Nos 1 and 2)* [2013] UKSC 38/39.
[184] See text at n 36, above.
[185] *R v Gnango* [2011] UKSC 59 and *Flood v Times Newspapers Ltd* [2012] UKSC 11.
[186] *Jones v Kaney* [2011] UKSC 13; *R (on the application of GC) v The Commissioner of Police of the Metropolis* [2011] UKSC 21; *Al Rawi and Others v The Security Service* [2011] UKSC 34; *R v Maxwell* [2010] UKSC 48.
[187] For his ranking in July 2013 see Table 4.4 above.

Collegiality of the court in 2011 when feelings were running high between some of the Justices, his efforts were not crowned with immediate success. It might be expected that Lord Brown would continue to play the social leadership role that he had played in the House of Lords. In some ways he undoubtedly did, but as we shall see, the geography of the new Court is different from the House of Lords corridor, and it had a curious impact on social leadership in the court. There is no single strategically placed office in the new building so Lord Brown's room was no longer *the* focal centre of the court. His greater isolation (comparatively) from his colleagues was accompanied by a growing closeness with Lord Rodger which led them to work together on certain appeals, as we have seen. Lord Brown, rarely one to dissent on his own, now found a companion to dissent with. In the space of 12 months from June 2010 he and Lord Rodger dissented together on five occasions—and on two of them they were joined by Lord Walker—a mutual friend. Thus Lord Brown's dissent rate shot from two per cent in the House to 13 per cent in the Supreme Court, whilst Lord Rodger's rose from 8 per cent to 14 per cent making them at this time the lead dissenters on the Court (see Table 4.7).

This is easily the most striking illustration of paired voting so far on the Supreme Court. Lord Brown continued to play the role of social leader in his own corridor,[188] but neither he nor Lord Rodger was quite as at home in their new surroundings as in the old. Once Lord Brown had retired, however, several Justices remarked on the loss of fun that went with him. It was not clear who would replace him as the social leader in the Supreme Court. One of the strengths

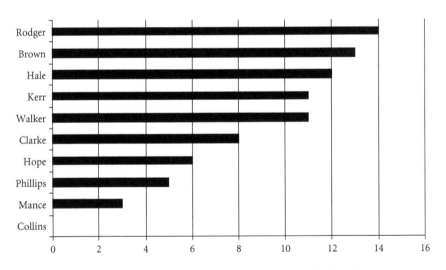

Table 4.7: **Dissents as a percentage of total cases sat in during 2009–11 (May).**

---

[188] On the second floor all the junior Justices seemed to share the social leadership role.

of Lord Neuberger as the new President was that he was perceived as being more naturally clubbable than his two predecessors and thus possibly more able to deal with the inevitable tensions which arise in a final court where most of the caseload is capable of being highly contested. Whether or not it is related to his outgoing nature and his efforts to visit his colleagues, his arrival seems to have coincided with a change of mood in the Court.

Geography

One of the curiosities of studying appellate judicial decision-making and the recent writings on the architecture of the courts[189] is the complete neglect of the topic of the office location of the judges. In reality geography does make a difference to appellate judicial decision-making, since judges—like other social beings—tend to interact more frequently with their neighbours than those who are situated at some distance from them, or on another floor. In the House of Lords the Law Lords' rooms were located off a long corridor on the second floor of the North side of the House of Lords.[190] Almost all of them were on the North side of the corridor while the Secretaries' office and the coffee machine were located at the East end of the corridor on the South side. Room allocation was largely based on seniority which entailed that in the main the more senior Law Lords were located adjacent to one another and closest to the Secretaries' office and the more junior Law Lords were to be found at the far end of the corridor,[191] near the Library.[192] The main exceptions were Lord Saville (located at the end of the corridor, because he was elsewhere[193] for much of the Bingham era), and Lord Brown who had the office on the South side of the corridor, next to the Secretaries' office and the coffee machine. The key location of this office and the fact that Lord Brown's door was always open entailed that any Law Lord who visited the Secretaries or the coffee machine was likely to engage with Lord Brown in conversation. Frequently several Law Lords were to be found in his office. As Lord Phillips (whose office was directly opposite Lord Brown's) observed,[194]

> I tend to drop in on Simon Brown in particular because he always sits with his door open and you walk past ... and if he's with me on a case when I come in in the morning I shall probably just exchange views with him, or even in advance, simply because of his geographical proximity, so we tend to know much more about the way we're looking

---

[189] J Resnik and D Curtis, *Representing Justice: Invention, Controversy and Rights in City States and Democratic Courtrooms* (New Haven CT, Yale University Press, 2011).

[190] Known as the 'Law Lords' Corridor'.

[191] Which can only have heightened the perception of isolation that they felt, having been used to the camaraderie of the Court of Appeal.

[192] Lords Hope and Rodger who were in the middle of the corridor, had adjacent rooms, which assisted them when working together on Scots appeals.

[193] Conducting the Bloody Sunday Inquiry.

[194] Interview with the author, 2008.

at things than I will with people down the corridor, simply because I don't walk past their door.

In the Supreme Court the geographic layout is quite different. The original plan to locate all 12 Justices on the top floor had to be abandoned on space grounds,[195] leading to a solution which placed four offices on the second floor (mainly on the North side) and eight on the third floor situated on three sides (the East, South and West sides) of a hollow square, with the tea room and open plan space for the law reporters and judicial assistants on the North side with the Secretaries on the West side. As before, the room allocation is largely by seniority, placing the President and Deputy President in adjacent rooms on the top floor and three of the most junior Justices on the second floor. As in the House, room location has a major influence on interactions.[196] The junior Justices on the second floor often keep their doors open and chat amongst themselves on almost a daily basis; however, their visits to their colleagues on the top floor are far less frequent.[197] Similarly the Justices on the West side of the top floor corridor (which included Lord Brown) tended (and tend still) to visit each other much more frequently than their colleagues on the lower floor or even the President and Deputy President.[198] As one remarked, 'if you have to go upstairs, you don't know whether they are there. I suppose you could ring. Whereas with [Lord Kerr] I just walk a few paces along the corridor'.[199] Lord Brown's office remained a focal centre for the Court but it had lost the strategic location which it had had in the House. The loss impacted, in part, on flows of information within the Court. This may seem strange, especially in the era of the internet and email, however, in the House even in 2009 there were three Law Lords who did not use email or the internet and even in the Supreme Court for a substantial period there were two Justices who preferred not to use the technology. For those that did it may be relevant to note that research suggests that the easy availability of email has had an impact on convivial chats

---

[195] Similarly, in the US Supreme Court the practice of housing all the Justices and their clerks, not to mention the retired Justices on the first floor has had to be abandoned. Now many of the clerks and one Justice have had to be re-located to the second floor. JP Stevens, *Five Chiefs* (New York, Little, Brown & Company, 2011) at 134.

[196] One junior Justice referred to the Justices on the two floors as the 'uppies' and the 'downies' and explained how when he had initially come to the Court he had been in the corridor with several of the senior Justices as neighbours, whom he visited regularly. When he re-located to the second floor he found that most of his interactions were with the other junior Justices who were his new neighbours.

[197] Another junior Justice told me that he would not have dreamt of visiting the most senior Justices in their rooms, indicating that the initiative for any discussion would have to come from them, given his position in the judicial pecking order. This form of distancing works both ways. In the Australian High Court or the US Supreme Court there have been Chief Justices who preferred to conduct business over a cup of tea in their room. On the other hand being requested to visit the President or Deputy President can appear like a summons to the headmaster's study.

[198] As we have seen, Lords Rodger and Brown worked closely with each other in 2010–11 although one was on the third floor and the other on the second. In fact, their offices were practically on top of each other and adjacent to the staircase linking the two floors.

[199] Curiously, it cannot be assumed that new arrivals will know where all of their more senior colleagues are situated. One junior Justice told me that it had taken him months to discover where a particular colleague was located.

in people's offices.[200] Further, the kind of discussion which occurs in a colleague's room would be hard to replicate electronically (or on the phone) since they are often simply occasions for the judges to mull over the issues which are troubling them in a case.[201] Certainly there were examples of more tactically minded Law Lords and Justices visiting a colleague in the hope of enlisting them to their cause. However, more often the chat with one's neighbours was an opportunity to think out loud with a sympathetic colleague, even if their take on the case was a rather different one. Nonetheless, the extent and nature of the judicial dialogues which occur in cases coming before the final court are affected by the room location of the panel members as well as their approach to collective decision-making.[202]

CONCLUSION

We have seen then that the frequency and effectiveness of the dialogues which take place between the judges in the final court are significantly influenced by the contexts in which the dialogues occur and the composition of the panel hearing the case. The former includes the differing stages in the decision-making process and issues of timing generally. In focusing on the latter, the prime focus is not on the judges' ideologies or even judicial philosophies. Rather it seems that the main influences on effective inter-judicial dialogues are where the judges stand on the individualism versus collective-mindedness spectrum, their use of leadership skills and the links between the judges (geographic or otherwise). In the next chapter we will look further at these links in terms of voting relationships and judicial philosophies, and also at the impact of group oriented judges on their colleagues in cases where the judges are strongly divided.

---

[200] See eg S Turkle, 'The flight from conversation' *New York Times*, 21 April 2012.

[201] As Lord Dyson put it me, 'Well, you can [use email to overcome geography] to some extent. I don't know, it is just much better to talk, I think'.

[202] As we will see in chapter 6, below, interestingly, the different geography of the House of Lords and the Supreme Court also impacted on the interaction between judicial assistants and the judges. In the House the judicial assistants were housed in a Hogwarts-like garret to which only the keenest Law Lord would ascend. Freed from the chronic shortage of space in the House, the move to Supreme Court allowed not only an expansion in the number of judicial assistants but a re-location to an open plan office (shared with the law reporters) situated between the Secretaries' room and the West corridor Justices. The strategic location 'cultivated and encouraged the daily interactions between judicial assistants and the Justices' and set the scene for the expansion in the former's role in the work of the Court. See T Nesterchuk, 'The View from Behind the Bench' ch 11 in A Burrows, D Johnston and R Zimmermann (eds), *Judge and Jurist: Essays in Memory of Lord Rodger of Earlsferry* (Oxford, Oxford University Press, 2013).

5

Inter-Judicial Dialogues in Practice

T HE FOCUS IN the last chapter was on efficacy in inter-judicial dialogues on the final court. In the next chapter we will examine two aspects of dialogues in practice. First, the voting patterns in the House of Lords and the Supreme Court, and secondly vote switches in the House of Lords and the Supreme Court.

VOTING RELATIONSHIPS

In the House of Lords during the Bingham era, as would be expected where the overall dissent rate was 23 per cent, the individual Law Lord's dissent rate was 8 percent and the average Law Lord sat on only half the cases heard in the House in any one year, the overall levels of agreement amongst the Law Lords were in the high 80 percentages. Table 5.1 shows the extent to which any one Law Lord agreed with any other.[1]

This ranged from 98 per cent (between Lords Bingham and Nicholls)[2] to 70 per cent (between Lords Carswell and Nicholls). Table 5.2 lists the top and bottom 10 pairings in terms of levels of agreement. From these we can see how infrequently, comparatively speaking, individual Law Lords sat together in the Appellate Committee, as compared with the US Supreme Court Justices.

The latter sit with each other in 60–70 cases a year. Yet Table 5.1 shows us that the most frequent pairing in the Lords in the whole period of 2000–09 was Lords Scott and Walker, on 85 occasions. The voting patterns seem to have little to do with friendship but do appear to have been influenced by group-orientation or tactician inclination, whether one had a very low or high dissent rate, possession and exercise of task leadership and social leadership skills and the respective intellectual and philosophical standpoints of the Law Lords.

---

[1] Provided they had sat together on at least 18 occasions. (This is to prevent the law of small numbers distorting the figure). 'Voting together' is confined to outcomes, not reasoning, and relates to cases not appeals.

[2] An impressive level of agreement between two of the Court's heavyweight intellectuals which spread over 50 cases in which they sat together.

	Brown	Carswell	Hale	Hobhouse	Hoffmann	Hope	Hutton	Mance	Millett	Neuberger	Nicholls	Phillips	Rodger	Scott	Slynn	Steyn	Walker
Bingham	87%	86%	83%	92%	87%	90%	90%	80%	86%	84%	98%	X	84%	81%	X	92%	90%
Brown		95%	88%	X	92%	94%	X	84%	X	93%	90%	93%	91%	87%	X	95%	90%
Carswell			84%	X	84%	90%	X	77%	X	89%	70%	78%	88%	87%	X	88%	83%
Hale				X	85%	91%	X	80%	X	79%	82%	83%	83%	88%	X	82%	82%
Hobhouse					83%	86%	93%	X	83%	X	88%	X	90%	91%	79%	80%	X
Hoffmann						83%	90%	87%	93%	83%	91%	X	93%	86%	93%	90%	92%
Hope							90%	82%	83%	81%	83%	X	92%	81%	90%	83%	87%
Hutton								X	76%	X	92%	X	97%	94%	97%	87%	X
Mance									X	83%	94%	X	87%	88%	X	X	80%
Millett										X	86%	X	X	93%	86%	71%	X
Neuberger											X	X	85%	88%	X	X	88%
Nicholls												X	96%	84%	78%	88%	85%
Phillips													78%	X	X	X	X
Rodger														83%	X	83%	93%
Scott															X	81%	75%
Slynn																88%	X
Steyn																	86%
Walker																	

Table 5.1: Overall levels of agreement amongst the Law Lords in the House of Lords 2000–09.

Top 10 (17) Highest Agreement		No. of Times Sat Together
Bingham + Nicholls	98%	50
Hutton + Rodger	97%	30
Hutton + Slynn	97%	31
Nicholls + Rodger	96%	55
Brown + Carswell	95%	63
Brown + Steyn	95%	22
Brown + Hope	94%	77
Mance + Nicholls	94%	18
Hutton + Scott	94%	33
Hobhouse + Hutton	93%	30
Hoffmann + Millett	93%	41
Brown + Neuberger	93%	28
Brown + Phillips	93%	29
Hoffmann + Rodger	93%	76
Millett + Scott	93%	29
Hoffmann + Slynn	93%	27
Rodger + Walker	93%	54

Top 10 Lowest Agreement		No of times Sat Together
Carswell + Nicholls	70%	20
Millett + Steyn	71%	45
Scott + Walker	75%	85
Hutton + Millett	76%	25
Carswell + Mance	77%	22
Carswell + Phillips	78%	18
Phillips + Rodger	78%	18
Nicholls + Slynn	78%	23
Hale + Neuberger	79%	29
Hobhouse + Slynn	79%	34

Table 5.2: Highest and lowest agreement rates among Law Lords in the House of Lords 2000–09.

In the UK Supreme Court the weighted average of the agreement rate for each Justice with their peers in the first four years was 86 per cent. Table 5.3 shows, the levels of agreement between pairs of Justices from 2009 until end March 2013.[3]

However, if we look at all voting pairs whose mean agreement rate is more than five per cent above or below the weighted average of 86 per cent (as contained in Table 5.4) some patterns do emerge. Whilst friendship and geography seem to have only a modest impact on voting pairs, Justices who are friends and/or have neighbouring offices are considerably more likely to be in the pairings voting together *most* often as in the pairings voting together *least* often. Since they are the Justices who most frequently visit each other's offices, and engage each other in spoken dialogue most often, the result is perhaps not too surprising, although it attests to the efficacy of oral dialogue.

Whilst it is certainly the case that individualist Justices or those with the highest dissent rates, eg Lord Kerr (13 per cent), Lady Hale (13 per cent), Lord Rodger (13 per cent) and Lord Brown (11 per cent) feature strongly in the column of those voting together least often, they do also appear in the pairings of those who vote together most often, eg Hale and Clarke, Kerr and Collins, Rodger and Collins, and Brown and Rodger. These latter pairings, however, are of Justices who thought alike, worked together or had offices near each other, again pointing to the impact of dialogue. Lord Collins—a group-oriented task leader, who only once dissented, scores above the Court weighted average for all his pairings and has the top equal individual weighted average. Lord Dyson, who was top equal individually with Lord Collins, was another group-oriented task leader who engaged extensively in oral and written dialogue with his colleagues. He, too, found it difficult to dissent, as we saw in chapter four, He features strongly in the pairings of those voting together most often, but he also has lower pairings with two of the most 'liberal' members of the Court. Interestingly, Lord Clarke with an average dissent rate of eight per cent had one of the higher average agreement rates with his peers (88 per cent) and still featured very strongly in the pairings voting together most often, perhaps because of his willingness to engage his colleagues in dialogue.[4] Inevitably, however, a significant feature of the pairings that voted most and least often together appears to be how closely aligned the legal and social philosophies of the Justices were.

---

[3] An 'x' in the Table indicates that the two Justices have sat together on less than 18 occasions in decisions handed down by the end of March 2013. This arbitrary figure was chosen to reduce distortions caused by Justices who had only sat together in a few cases.

[4] The same is true probably of Lord Brown, who despite a high-ish dissent rate (11%) has three pairings of 90% or more because of his success in dialogue as a social leader. It is noticeable, however, that he had nine pairings of 90% or more in the House of Lords attesting to his even greater success as a social leader in that Court.

	Clarke	Collins	Dyson	Hale	Hope	Kerr	Mance	Phillips	Reed	Rodger	Walker	Wilson
Brown	75%	x	93%	62%	89%	72%	78%	83%	x	90%	91%	x
Clarke		89%	94%	95%	88%	87%	88%	92%	89%	85%	86%	89%
Collins			x	89%	88%	94%	88%	89%	x	91%	89%	x
Dyson				79%	95%	79%	91%	93%	x	87%	97%	x
Hale					89%	82%	92%	74%	89%	71%	79%	84%
Hope						84%	85%	86%	100%	88%	89%	89%
Kerr							80%	78%	x	71%	71%	92%
Mance								86%	x	80%	80%	x
Phillips									x	83%	79%	83%
Reed										x	x	x
Rodger											90%	x
Walker												x
Wilson												

Table 5.3: Overall levels of agreement amongst the Justices in the UK Supreme Court 2009–13 (March).

Top 10 (11) Highest Agreement		No. of Times Sat Together	Top 10 (13) Lowest Agreement		No of times Sat Together
Hope – Reed	100%	21	Brown – Hale	62%	50
Dyson – Walker	97%	29	Hale – Rodger	71%	35
Clarke – Hale	95%	42	Kerr – Rodger	71%	31
Dyson – Hope	95%	38	Kerr – Mance	71%	40
Clarke – Dyson	94%	33	Brown – Kerr	72%	60
Collins – Kerr	94%	18	Hale – Phillips	74%	47
Brown – Dyson	93%	40	Brown – Clarke	75%	28
Dyson – Phillips	93%	30	Brown – Mance	78%	40
Hale – Mance	92%	52	Kerr – Phillips	78%	37
Clarke – Phillips	92%	37	Dyson – Hale	79%	28
Kerr – Wilson	92%	24	Dyson – Kerr	79%	38
			Hale – Walker	79%	52
			Phillips – Walker	79%	33

Table 5.4: Highest and lowest agreement rates amongst the Justices in the UK Supreme Court 2009–13 (March).

CHANGES OF MIND

How influential are the group-oriented judges in the final court? One test for the efficacy of dialogues and for those who engage in them most often—the group-oriented or tactician judges, is whether he or she can persuade one or more colleagues to share his point of view, particularly where this will result in a switch in votes or even a reversal of the existing majority position. Such successes do occur but can be hard to document. Indeed, some wonder if such changes of mind should be the subject of scholarly analysis. The contrary position—adopted in this work is that a willingness on the part of judges in the final Court of Appeal to change their minds at any stage in a case, on further reflection, or after engaging with their colleagues is to be applauded as being healthy in democracy, provided it is not taken to extremes.

As we have just seen, the final judgment cannot be taken at face value. My interviews with Law Lords 40 years ago indicated that most changes of mind took place during the hearing stage, but that they also occurred between the first conference and the final judgment—though not with the frequency with which they occurred in the US Supreme Court at this stage.[5] As one Law Lord of the time put it, 'It is unusual, though, of course, by no means unheard of ... for people to change their mind after ... the end of the oral hearing'. Another Law Lord admitted that he had changed his mind on several occasions after the first conference and that sometimes the majority even changed, but added that 'on the whole people are reluctant to change their positions after the first conference'. A third Law Lord said that in the cases he had sat in between 1971 and 1973 there had only been two instances of a Law Lord 'coming right round' and switching his vote after the first conference. Viscount Radcliffe indicated that he very rarely changed his position after the hearing and neither Lord Denning nor Lord Devlin could recall ever changing at this stage, while in the Lords. As we know, hearings in the Lords then lasted for roughly twice as long as those at the end of the Bingham era, giving much more time for dialogue with counsel and with one's peers during the hearing. In that time we witnessed a shift from a decision-making process that used to be largely oral to one that was significantly more in writing.[6] Did this have an effect on how and when vote switches took place? My interviews with the Law Lords of the Bingham era did not suggest that a great deal had changed.

> The great merit of the old system, where you knew very little about the case till you heard the oral argument, was that you could change your mind any number of times as the thing went on. (Lord Lloyd)

---

[5] See M F Berry, *Stability, Security and Continuity* (Connecticut, Greenwood Press,1978); J W Howard, 'On the Fluidity of Judicial Choice' (1968) 62 *American Political Science Review* 43; R Hodder-Williams, *The Politics of the United States Supreme Court* (London, George Allen Unwin, 1980); 103 and 106; and B Woodward and S Armstrong, *The Brethren: Inside the Supreme Court* (New York, Simon & Schuster, 1979) eg 69, 71, 260, 364, 403, 419, 420.

[6] See A Paterson, *Lawyers and the Public Good* (Cambridge, Cambridge University Press, 2012) at 167.

I did occasionally change my mind before I'd written and I certainly changed my mind once or twice when I was just going to concur or when draft opinions were circulating. So I did occasionally change my mind. I know Nick Browne-Wilkinson did. I doubt that Johan [Steyn] ever did. (Lord Millett)

Once there was a fairly clear decision in a discussion or a conference as to what people's views were and you had stated your view I rarely found, I think, that I changed my mind after that. (A Law Lord)

The factor which most often made me change my mind was simply when I'd gone away and thought about it and started to write. That's what caused me to change my mind rather than that I've been waiting for other people's judgments or I've received other people's judgments which have caused me to change my mind. However, changing one's mind when one has started to write is not uncommon. (A Law Lord)

I think by the time one had had the first conference in the committee room after the hearing (and most cases people would express a fairly definite view), I think one then knew quite clearly what the outcome was going to be. One had expressed one's own views and heard the views of one's colleagues … I don't think I, I can't remember a case where I then completely changed my mind after that, after having read a judgment from a colleague. (A Law Lord)

Minds change after the hearing and even after the discussion you find that people who were dissenting or likely to dissent are in the end persuaded to come along and agree. You sometimes find that what looked like a 3:2 case one way has turned into a 3:2 case the other way and then that can be quite awkward, but it does happen. (Lord Hope)

I think for all of us it is more common in the hearing. We don't often any of us change our mind from the position initially declared at the post-hearing conference. We do sometimes and there are some cases where we are more liable to negotiate afterwards than others. (Lady Hale)

By the time each person has written, those who write, they tend to become entrenched, it's quite difficult if you've written, it's about two or three days writing a reasoned judgment which comes to a conclusion, to then say 'Well, actually I think I've got it wrong'. (A Law Lord)

That's very difficult to answer numerically. I haven't really thought of trying to analyse that numerically, but I would think that people are less certain during the oral hearing. Usually they make up their minds, sometimes changing them, during the oral hearing. Once they've expressed a provisional view the general tendency is for people to stick with that provisional view, but there's a quite sufficient number of occasions on which people change their minds for one to be confident that people do think about cases substantially when they're writing judgments. (Lord Mance)

Lord Mance's observation is a telling one. Oral historians will not be surprised to learn that the Law Lords found it very difficult to put accurate estimates on numerical matters, eg the length of first conferences, the frequency of dissents or single majority judgments, how often they had been involved in close call decisions and on which side, or how often they completely changed their minds or votes in cases. Some lower court judges may be aware how often their decisions have been reversed or affirmed on appeal, but Law Lords and Justices do not count their successes in numerical terms or keep a running tally of their decision-making, far less that of their colleagues. It is easier for the researcher, provided there are objective data that can be counted. As we know there are no official records of the case conferences in the final court either in the UK or in the US, including their length.[7] What of vote switches? Many of these are documented in published judgments, but far from all.[8] In *The Law Lords* I showed that the judgments of around 30 years ago contained regular indications of Law Lords changing their views in cases, either as a result of further reflection, or further reflection and reading the judgment(s) of other Law Lords.[9] However, only a handful of cases a year contain such admissions.

There were also then cases where one or more Law Lords changed his opinion as to the outcome of the case but this was not apparent from the Law Reports. As we saw in chapter one Lord Reid—the senior Law Lord who sat on the House of Lords for 26 years, longer than any other Law Lord since it was created in its 'modern form' in 1876—donated 104 of his judicial notebooks to the Parliamentary records. Five boxes of notebooks are available, including almost every one of the major cases in which Lord Reid sat or presided. From this it emerges that in a significant number of the major cases in which he sat there was a change of vote between the first conference and the handing down of the judgments.

Amongst the significant cases where this may have occurred were *White and Carter (Councils) Ltd v McGregor*,[10] *Anisminic Ltd v Foreign Compensation Commission*,[11] *Home Office v Dorset Yacht Co*,[12] and *Cassell v Broome*.[13] One other

---

[7] In the US much has been gleaned from the private papers and diaries of certain Justices. In the UK far less has come to light although Lord Reid's notebooks from a range of significant cases have recently become available and a few of Lord Rodger's notebooks and rather more of Lord Bingham's case notebooks have been rescued.

[8] Baroness Hale told me that once a swing voter has swung he is often the staunchest member of the majority. In such cases, there may be a reluctance to admit to having had any doubts whatsoever in your speech. Again one Law Lord of the Bingham era had a reputation for agonising over close call cases but once his decision was made his speeches contained no evidence of hesitation or difficulty.

[9] Paterson, *The Law Lords* (London, Macmillan, 1982).

[10] [1961] UKHL 5. A controversial Scottish appeal about whether a contacting party could insist on a contract being implemented rather than accepting damages from the other party who wished to cancel the contract. It seems Lord Keith was undecided at the first conference and Lord Morton voted with the other members of the House to allow the appeal. Lord Keith's judgment came out for trenchantly dismissing the appeal and Lord Morton came over to vote with him. The case featured in Lord Sumption's dissent in *Geys*.

[11] [1969] 2 AC 147. A seminal public law case where Lord Pearson, having voted at the first conference to allow the appeal in the end, joins Lord Morris of Borth-Y-Gest in dissenting.

[12] [1970] UKHL 2, [1970] AC 1004. A major tort case on the duty of care owed by prison authorities for borstal trainees who escaped and caused damage to the property of persons in the locality. Lord Reid's notes show that Lord Diplock, the junior on the court, voted to allow the appeal at the first conference but his final judgment goes the other way.

[13] [1972] UKHL 3, [1972] AC 1027. A famous defamation case. In a highly charged appeal to see if a distinguished naval captain would be able to retain his damages in the case, the majority agreed that he should but it seems that Lord Wilberforce (one of the three dissenters in a 4:3 case) was originally with the majority at the first conference.

case involving Lord Reid in where a change of votes occurred was the celebrated tort case *Rookes v Barnard*,[14] where after the initial hearing Lord Devlin was in a minority of one (or possibly two) favouring the appellant. After a second conference and a reconvened hearing, he won them all round.[15]

Looked at as a whole the 104 notebooks of Lord Reid yielded only 70 cases in which the votes of the Law Lords at the first conference could be clearly identified. In 13 of the 70 (19 per cent) a change of vote by one or more Law Lords appears to have occurred between what is recorded as their position at the first conference and what appears in the published law report for the case. This is very likely to be an exaggerated figure since the 104 notebooks are from the more important cases on which Lord Reid sat, which are likely to contain more of the close calls.

In the ensuing years up to the Bingham era, other celebrated cases have witnessed similar late switches. In *Pepper v Hart*[16] the original court was split 4:1 against Lord Griffiths. However, having consulted *Hansard* Griffiths was able to persuade his brethren to re-hear the case in a seven-judge panel with the Lord Chancellor presiding. Although Lord Mackay ultimately dissented on the *Hansard* issue, Lord Griffiths was unrepentant and won over the remaining five members of the court to the proposition that *Hansard* should be able to be drawn on to establish the purpose of legislation. In one of the *Spycatcher* cases[17] Lord Brandon (the swing voter) changed his mind at the end of the argument, when, unusually, the Appellate Committee had agreed for special urgency reasons[18] to announce its decision (but not its reasoning) at the end of the first conference. Lord Bridge, who was presiding, was not best pleased to discover that he was now in the minority and even less so when his colleagues decided that contrary to his wishes, and his public announcement that the reasoning would not come until the end of the summer vacation, they proposed to provide their reasons almost immediately. Lord Bridge agreed with very bad grace as his speech makes clear.[19] Lord Ackner,

---

[14] *Rookes v Barnard* [1964] AC 1129. The case involved an issue as to when exemplary damages could be awarded. Interestingly, *Cassell v Broome* had to decide whether this part of *Rookes v Barnard* had been correctly decided.

[15] Lord Pearce was one of those who switched. His speech indicated the difficulty he experienced in the case and that he was persuaded by the speeches of Lords Reid and Devlin. It does not reveal that in fact he had initially written it in favour of the respondent but found it 'so feeble and wrong' that he then rewrote it the other way. Lord Evershed's speech seems to indicate that he was the last to switch. Apart from the Law Report itself my account of the case is derived from interviews with some of the Law Lords involved and from Sir Neville Faulks, *A Law Unto Myself* (London, William Kimber, 1978) at 103.

[16] *Pepper v Hart* [1992] UKHL 3. The issue at stake was whether the court in a case where the legislation they were scrutinising was ambiguous, could look at Hansard's records of the parliamentary debates to see if they offered any clarification of the ambiguity.

[17] *Attorney General v Guardian Newspapers Ltd* [1987] 1 WLR 1248.

[18] So that the Press, who were in something of a frenzy, could learn whether the injunctions restraining them from publishing in England and Wales the contents of Peter Wright's memoirs as an MI5 officer—which were widely available around the world, including Scotland—were to remain in force.

[19] *Attorney General v Guardian Newspapers Ltd* [1987] 1 WLR 1248. His outlook was unlikely to have been improved by Lord Oliver, his fellow dissenter, indicating in his speech that he had very nearly defected to the other side, as well.

in the majority, satisfied himself with some fairly intemperate remarks about the Press.

Two of the cases—both decided in 1997–98—involved Lord Hoffmann. In the first, the *Argyll Supermarket* case,[20] he began the case conference at the end of the hearing in a minority of one and thereafter engaged in a furious debate with the other four Law Lords led by the senior Law Lord, Lord Browne-Wilkinson. At stake was whether the law should punish those who, following an economic calculus, deliberately breach their contracts because it is cheaper to do so. Browne-Wilkinson—a classic 'parson'[21] since he tended to look at issues in moral terms—thought that it should. Lord Hoffmann—a 'pragmatic realist'—thought that damages were enough. After three months Lord Hoffmann had won them all round. The other case was *Kleinwort Benson v Lincoln Council*[22] (whether a taxpayer could recover tax paid pursuant to a legal rule which was subsequently struck down by the courts). This was Lord Goff's final case in the Lords, and the case was in his speciality area, restitution. Nevertheless at the first conference Lord Goff was in the minority, much to his dismay. However, this time it was Lord Hoffmann who changed his own mind, on further reflection, and since he was the swing voter, Lords Browne-Wilkinson and Tony Lloyd to their surprise unexpectedly found themselves dissenting. Lord Goff, however, was delighted.

Lord Hoffmann was a tactician and group-oriented, but he did not win every close call (as we have seen),[23] particularly in the aftermath of the Pinochet affair. In *Foskett v McKeown and Others*[24] Lord Hoffmann did end on the winning side in a 3:2 split, but the swing voter, Lord Browne-Wilkinson, whose relationship with Hoffmann had been severely strained by the Pinochet affair, goes out of his way to state that his change of heart (and vote) had come from reading Lord Millett's judgment (alone), in draft. Again in *R (on the application of Imperial Tobacco Ltd) v Secretary of State for Health*[25] Lords Hoffmann and Millett (both tacticians) thought they had a majority (with Lord Clyde) on a matter relating to the implementation of EU regulations on the tobacco industry. Over the summer vacation Lord Clyde went abroad on a speaking tour in the Far East, where he was lobbied (on the phone) by both factions—each of which thought that they were writing the majority judgment. To the chagrin of the Hoffmann/Millett camp, Lord Nicholls won Lord Clyde over at the last minute, leaving the former as dissenters.

---

[20] *Cooperative Insurance Society Ltd v Argyll Stores (Holdings) Ltd* [1998] AC 1.

[21] Lord Sumption has suggested that appellate judges can be divided into 'parsons' who instinctively look at issues in moral terms, 'pragmatic realists' who have an eye to consequences, and 'analysts' who focus relentlessly on legal principle. Interviews with the author, 2009 and 2012. See also his comments in M Engel, 'British Institutions: The Supreme Court', *Financial Times*, 19 April 2013.

[22] *Kleinwort Benson Ltd v Lincoln City Council* [1998] UKHL 38; [1999] 2 AC 349.

[23] See Table 4.2, in chapter four of this volume, above.

[24] *Foskett v McKeown and Others* [2000] UKHL 29.

[25] *R (on the application of Imperial Tobacco Ltd) v Secretary of State for Health* [2000] UKHL 38, [2001] 1 WLR 127.

THE BINGHAM ERA 2000–09

The last case brings us to the Bingham era. Here, again, we now have some harder evidence to bring to bear on Lord Mance's question. During the period 2000–04 Lord Bingham sat in 118 or so cases in the House of Lords. Due to great good fortune, before the House transferred to the Supreme Court, many of Lord Bingham's notebooks from that era were discovered.[26] These offer invaluable material for historians of Lord Bingham's notes on the argument in these cases. Thirteen of the notebooks contain loosely within the leaves of the notebooks, handwritten, draft judgments by Lord Bingham in the relevant case.[27] A further seven contain notes of his thoughts on the case, sometimes in cases where he did not ultimately write, eg *Etridge*.[28] More germane for current purposes, the notebooks contain in most cases Lord Bingham's notes of the first conference in the case. No record of these conferences was retained in the House of Lords, so these notebooks, those of Lord Reid and any kept by other Law Lords which have not yet surfaced, are the only known contemporaneous records of the seriatim presentations made by the Law Lords at the first conference.[29] Since Lord Bingham usually records which way the each Law Lord (apart from himself) proposes to vote, it is sometimes possible to identify apparent switches of vote between the first conference and the date that judgment was handed down. This provides the best evidence available to historians as to how often Law Lords changed their minds between the first conference and the final judgment. From the notebooks it appears that in around 15 of the 96 cases (16 per cent)—a remarkably close figure to that from Lord Reid's notebooks—there seems to have been a vote switch between the seriatim presentations being made and the publication of the judgments.[30] Given that the 96 cases represent 39 per cent of the 244 cases heard during the period from late 2000 to late 2004 we may surmise that the number of cases containing a change of vote in that period was probably nearer to 38 (16 per cent). By extrapolation, since 586 cases were decided by the House of Lords between 2000 and 2009 the number of cases with a vote switch in its final decade may be as high as 93. Further these are only the changes of vote that related to outcome. Changes of mind which

---

[26] In fact, the boxes contain notebooks relating to 96 cases in the House of Lords and two in the Privy Council. Amongst the 22 or so notebooks that are missing are all but one from 2000, *London Borough of Harrow v Qazi* [2003] UKHL 43, *Rees v Darlington Memorial Hospital NHS Trust* [2003] UKHL 52 and *A and Others v Secretary of State for the Home Department (Belmarsh)* [2004] UKHL 56.

[27] I was able to compare the draft judgments in two of the cases with the actual printed judgments in the Appeal Cases. Whilst there were differences between the two, they were generally not very substantial.

[28] *Royal Bank of Scotland v Etridge* [2001] UKHL 44.

[29] Unfortunately, apart from the *Etridge* case (which lasted over three hours) Lord Bingham did not record the start and finish times of the case conferences so the notebooks cast only an indirect light on the issue of the duration of case conferences. Nor does he record any deliberations or debates which took place at the first conference once each Law Lord had made their presentation.

[30] In those 15 cases, 19 Law Lords appear to have switched their vote after further deliberation or during the circulation of the judgments.

related to the reasoning (eg, during circulation following suggestions from others) must have been considerably more common. In sum, even if we leave aside the changes of mind that occur during the hearing stage, it seems clear that there was greater fluidity of opinion in the Bingham era, even after Law Lords had expressed a provisional view, than the Law Lords' interviews might suggest.[31] Of course, even if this is true, it says nothing about why the changes of mind took place. Here we remain dependent on the Law Lords' judgments and what they said in their interviews.

The first case from the Bingham era with a late vote switch appears to be *Bank of Credit and Commerce International SA v Munawar Al and Others*[32] (whether employee contracts survived a bank's liquidation) and Lord Bingham's notebook implies that Lord Nicholls, who was originally dissenting with Lord Hoffmann, switched to join the majority after the first conference. In *Johnson v Unisys*,[33] (whether common law contract claims can co-exist with a statutory unfair dismissal claim), Lord Steyn and Lord Nicholls changed their votes (in opposite directions) in a case which ended with Lord Steyn alone dissenting. Similarly in *Anyanwu v South Bank Student Union*[34] (racial discrimination claims in a University context) a first conference which saw the panel divided 3:2 was followed by a change of heart by both dissenters. Lord Millett switched sides and then Lord Bingham (not a great believer in solo dissents, until the end of his career) decided that his doubts could be accommodated by a *dubitante* judgment.[35] In this case the persuasion came from reading the majority's judgments. Lord Millett also switched his vote in *Banks v Chief Adjudication Officer*,[36] where he withdrew the speech that he had written when he read David Hope's.

> I was taking the completely opposite view to him, but when I saw his explanation of the regulations I realised that I was wrong and I phoned him up and went in to see him. I think I'd circulated mine as well—I just withdrew it and rewrote it, but that was very rare.[37]

In *Director General of Fair Trading v First National Bank*[38] (the fairness of a term in a consumer credit contract) it was Lord Steyn who was persuaded to change his vote between the first conference (where he was in a minority of one) and the

---

[31] Lord Bingham told me that it was unusual for his colleagues to change their minds during the circulation stage. 'People quite often at the discussion immediately after the hearing, would say "Well my view is tentative and at the moment I think X, Y and Z but I want to think about it further" but they almost always actually ended up in the same position, only more strongly. So it was not usual for people to express a provisional view *and then change it*, although sometimes people would express a provisional view and the majority went the other way and they wouldn't so to speak, press it'.

[32] *Bank of Credit and Commerce International SA v Munawar Al and Others* [2001] UKHL 8, [2001] 1 All ER 961, [2001] 2 WLR 735.

[33] *Johnson v Unisys Ltd* [2001] UKHL 13.

[34] *Anyanwu v South Bank Student Union* [2001] UKHL 14.

[35] The judgments of Lords Bingham and Millett support this account of the case. See para 18.

[36] *Stafford v Chief Adjudication Officer; Banks v Chief Adjudication Officer* [2001] UKHL 33; [2001] 1 WLR 1411.

[37] Interview with the author, 2009.

[38] *Director General of Fair Trading v First National Bank plc* [2001] UKHL 52.

handing down of his judgment making the decision unanimous.[39] In *Ashworth*,[40] (landlord and tenant) we have a not infrequent example of a 3:2 case in which there were no vote swings at any stage. *Twinsectra*,[41] however, which was 4:1 at the first conference and 4:1 when the judgment was published 153 days later (twice the average gap between the hearing and the handing down of the final judgment in all cases in 2002) was a rather more lively affair than it appears. The delay was caused because of a sustained campaign by Lord Millett to win over Lord Hoffmann to dismiss the appeal. Lord Hoffmann and his colleagues were arguing that the test for 'dishonesty' in financial transactions was a combined test of subjective and objective elements. Lord Millett asserted that the test was purely objective:

> The problem was Lennie because ... he has such influence that I knew that in order to persuade the majority I had to persuade him. If I could persuade him the rest would fall into line, or most of them. But he was absolutely adamant and I went in to see him several times. I went into his room and we discussed it and we circulated, but he never budged. I offered everything. I said 'If you are sorry for the defendant I am quite prepared to write in a way which will let him off the hook on the facts so long as you give me the law'. 'No'. Then I went away and eventually I came back and I said 'I'm prepared to write *dishonesty* right out of the equation and go back to *knowledge* provided you define it as actual knowledge' and define it the way Donald Nicholls had. Because this *dishonesty* is going to be a trap and he said 'I thought you'd come round to that view, Peter, but I'm not prepared to change my mind'. So that was a failure and I think the last thing I did after I'd circulated, I went and I saw him and I said 'You know, Lennie that your view means that you are going to draw a distinction between procuring a breach of trust and procuring a breach of contract and that is nonsense, especially as in this case they could have pleaded it as procuring a breach of contract as the trust was contractual', and his response to that? 'Yes, Peter, that's your best point'. Now it's not a best point, actually it's a devastating point. And inevitably they've changed their minds [in *Barlow Clowes*[42]], or the Bar certainly thinks that they've gone back to Nicholls and me in effect. (Lord Millett)[43]

Lord Millett in a self-deprecating way blamed his ineffectualness at persuading his colleagues for this unfortunate case, however his success rate in 'close calls' was the same as Lord Hoffmann's. He was twice as often on the majority side as on the minority.[44] Ironically, the Privy Council in *Barlow Clowes* revisits the whole question three years later. As Lee notes in a hard-hitting critique,[45] Lord Hoffmann in giving the judgment of the Council, effectively accepts that the test

---

[39] Ibid, para 38.
[40] *Ashworth Fraser Ltd v Glasgow City Council* [2001] UKHL 59.
[41] *Twinsectra Ltd v Yardley and Others* [2002] UKHL 12, [2002] 2 AC 164.
[42] *Barlow Clowes International Ltd v Eurotrust International Ltd* [2005] UKPC 37.
[43] Interview with the author, 2008.
[44] In part due to the frequency that both of them had switched to the majority side.
[45] J Lee, 'Fidelity in Interpretation: Lord Hoffmann and *The Adventure of the Empty House*' (2008) 28 *Legal Studies* 1.

laid down by Lord Nicholls in *Royal Brunei Airlines Sdn Bhd v Tan*[46] (which was the position supported by Lord Millett alone in *Twinsectra*), was right all long. Disappointingly, the judgment does not do this by the admission of error but by a bizarre assertion that Lords Hutton and Hoffmann did not mean what their words plainly said in *Twinsectra*.

In *Heaton v Axa Equity*[47] (concurrent and successive damages claims), however, it is Lord Rodger who, persuaded by the judgments of Lords Bingham and Mackay, abandoned his initial dissent at the first conference in favour of a *dubitante*.[48] Soon after, in the curious case of *Callery v Gray*[49] which visited the vexed territory of conditional fees, the court split 3:2 at the first conference. Lord Bingham assigned the lead judgment to the main dissenter, Richard Scott, something he did several times in the Lords, only for Lord Hoffmann then to switch sides (convinced by his own logic) leaving Scott on his own. Bingham's very next case, *Robinson v Secretary of State for Northern Ireland*[50] involved another 3:2 split where nobody changed their positions. This may have been in part because the issue—the validity of the election of the First Minister in Northern Ireland during the troubles—raised points of fundamental principle. The two principled analysts (Lords Hutton and Hobhouse) argued that the Court could not look at political issues or the consequences of what they were deciding, and the pragmatists (Lords Hoffmann and Millett) asserted that the Court could look at the purpose and political context of the Act. Lord Bingham, unusually, sided with the pragmatists, to make the casting vote. Two further 3:2 cases followed in swift succession: *Re L*[51] and *R (on the application of Sivakumar) v Secretary of State for the Home Department*.[52] In neither is there any evidence that any of the Law Lords had a change of heart after the first conference.

The next case did not involve Lord Bingham at all. It was the celebrated case where the BBC sought to censor the party political broadcast of the Prolife Alliance which featured pictures of aborted foetuses in a mangled and mutilated state, *R v BBC, ex parte Prolife Alliance*.[53] At the end of the hearing the smart money was on Prolife to have won with perhaps Lord Hoffmann on his own in dissent. In fact, Lord Hoffmann, who would have circulated his opinion very early, seems then to have been joined by Lord Nicholls and between them they then won over two others to make the result 4:1 for the BBC. Lord Millett, despite being 'for a long time of the contrary view' was persuaded by Lord Nicholls' judgment, and Lord

---

[46] *Royal Brunei Airlines Sdn Bhd v Tan* [1995] 2 AC 378.

[47] *Heaton and Others v Axa Equity & Law Assurance Society plc* [2002] UKHL 15.

[48] Ibid, para 86.

[49] *Callery v Gray* [2002] UKHL 28.

[50] *Robinson v Secretary of State for Northern Ireland and Others* [2002] UKHL 32.

[51] *Re L (a minor by his father and litigation friend); R v Governors of J School, ex parte L* [2003] UKHL 9, where the two seniors were outvoted by the three juniors.

[52] *R (on the application of Sivakumar) v Secretary of State for the Home Department* [2003] UKHL 14.

[53] *R v British Broadcasting Corporation, ex parte Prolife Alliance* [2003] UKHL 23.

Walker who admitted that 'his opinion on the matter had fluctuated', indicated that he had been helped to his final position by Lord Hoffmann's judgment.[54] As Lord Millett told me,

> When I read the papers I had no idea what the right answer was. I could see very strong arguments both ways and one had to beware of prejudice coming in. In the course of argument I probably wavered but eventually at some stage, probably as late as the opinions coming in that I didn't write, I went with the majority.

Lord Hoffmann was equally successful in the next close call, *R v Central Valuation Officer*,[55] where in close formation with Lords Millett and Scott (a trio of tacticians who are likely to have worked together at the stage when drafts were circulating) he outvoted Lords Bingham and Steyn. Interestingly, it seems that the position at the end of the first conference was 4:1 for the respondent and Lord Bingham assigned the lead judgment to Lord Millett. Lord Steyn then reflected further and 'in the light of the arguments presented by counsel for the appellant, the judgment of Dyson LJ and the speech of my noble and learned friend Lord Bingham of Cornhill',[56] switched his vote to the appellant, making the final outcome 3:2. The tacticians would not have minded—they only needed three votes to win.

Lord Hoffmann prevailed again in the next case, *Russell v Devine*,[57] a Northern Ireland appeal concerning the correct procedure for taking blood samples in drunk driving cases. The appeal by the accused (Mr Devine) was dismissed by 5:0, yet the notebook makes clear that at the first conference the two junior Law Lords, Hutton and Millett, voted for the appellant with Lords Bingham, Nicholls and Hoffmann for the respondent. Yet again Lord Bingham assigned the lead judgment with the facts to a dissenter, Lord Hutton (presumably because he was the Northern Ireland specialist). Ultimately, Lords Hutton and Millett joined the majority, making the case unanimous. Their judgments do not reveal these changes of heart or why they occurred, but of the majority only Hoffmann was a tactician.

The next vote switch occurred in an interesting case prompted by the incorporation of the European Convention on Human Rights into UK law. In Scotland an Article 6 challenge[58] had seen the office of temporary sheriff[59] declared incompatible with the Convention. In *Lawal v Northern Spirit*[60] the issue was whether the practice of allowing QCs to sit as part-time judges in the Employment Appeal Tribunal and also appear before such tribunals (which contained lay members with whom the barristers had sat when presiding in the EAT) was compatible with Article 6. This relatively narrow point, argued by a party litigant, provoked

---

[54] At para 142.
[55] *R v Central Valuation Officer and Another ex parte Edison First Power Ltd* [2003] UKHL 20.
[56] A triple dialogue in my analysis.
[57] *Russell v Devine* [2003] UKHL 24.
[58] *Starrs v Ruxton* 2000 SLT 42. Article 6 relates to the right to a fair and impartial hearing.
[59] A mid-ranking judge for which there is no English equivalent. These judges had almost unlimited civil jurisdiction and the power to deal with crimes attracting up to a five-year prison sentence. At the time of the action there were 230 temporary sheriffs.
[60] *Lawal v Northern Spirit Ltd* [2003] UKHL 35.

a fascinating debate as to what today's 'fair-minded and informed [lay] observer' would find acceptable in changing times. Curiously, this question is always (and necessarily) answered by judges, without access to any means of ascertaining what the informed public does indeed think. In this case the single report of the House in the name of Lord Steyn allowed the appeal, thus striking down the practice, but it did not indicate that both Lords Rodger and Steyn were initially hesitant as to which way to vote at the end of the first conference, or that Lord Millett voted for the respondent at the conference, only to subsequently acquiesce with the majority position.

In *R v Secretary of State for the Home Department, ex parte Anufrijeva*[61] Lord Bingham's reluctance to lobby for his position or to revisit his judgment worked against him, as it was to do in later cases.[62] The case itself revolved around whether the withdrawal of income support to the appellant, an asylum seeker, could be achieved by an internal note on a departmental file or whether it was required to be intimated (and explained) to the appellant. The Law Lords found this a very difficult question since the words of the legislation were plain and unambiguous and made no mention of notification being required. Further, this particular appellant was not perceived by them to have the strongest of cases in terms of the moral merits. On the other hand it had become clear in the hearing that the Home Office had a deliberate and systematic policy of delaying notification of their decisions to asylum seekers for up to four months. Lord Bingham's notebook indicates that Lord Scott began the first conference (as the junior) with the words, 'I've had several changes of mind and may change again' but ended by tentatively allowing the appeal. Lord Hoffmann was next, 'Originally I was going to allow the appeal but by the end of the argument I've decided to dismiss it'. Lord Millett agreed with Lord Hoffmann, leaving Lord Steyn to observe that although he was not very sure and had little sympathy with the appellant,[63] nonetheless he would allow the appeal. With votes tied 2:2 Lord Bingham had the casting vote. For him the clear words of Parliament must be given effect to, the appeal should be dismissed.

Lord Bingham wrote his judgment swiftly, as was his wont, setting out the facts and thinking it was to be the majority judgment. However, Lord Steyn, having reflected further on the case, produced a blisteringly powerful dissent referring to the Kafka-esque behaviour of the Home Office whose arguments ignored fundamental principles of UK law. 'It provides a peep into contemporary standards of public administration. Transparency is not its hallmark. It is not an encouraging picture'. This was enough to remove Lord Scott's doubts, to win round Lord Millett[64] and to make Lord Hoffmann revert to his original allegiance. Lord Bingham had lost his majority. True to form he did not fight for his position,

---

[61] *R v Secretary of State for the Home Department, ex parte Anufrijeva* [2003] UKHL 36.

[62] See the case described as *A v B* in chapter four n 12 of this volume, above

[63] 'I recognise, of course, that in some ways the appellant's case does not merit great sympathy' (para 36).

[64] See ibid, para 38.

although he did add a slightly puzzled[65] but very forthright rejoinder to his colleagues about giving effect to the clear words of statutes.[66]

In general Lords Bingham and Steyn were on the same side (92 per cent of cases) (see Table 5.1 above) so by the next close call, *Cullen v Chief Constable of the Royal Ulster Constabulary*,[67] they were once again together, but this time in dissent,[68] as they were outvoted by Lords Hutton,[69] Millett and Rodger. The point at issue was whether the failure of the RUC to give a detained suspect access to a solicitor in private under section 15 of the Northern Ireland (Emergency Provisions) Act 1987 gave rise to a claim for damages. The majority thought that it did not, at least where the accused had suffered minimal harm. Although Lord Rodger, speaking first as the junior Law Lord, expressed some hesitation[70] it seems that this was a 3:2 vote in which none of the Law Lords changed their minds after the hearing stage.

There then followed two close calls that weren't, but might have been. The first, *Burnett's Trustees v Grainger*,[71] as we will see in chapter six, was a very close run affair. A couple had bought a flat from a lady who was then made bankrupt after they had paid over the price. The trustee in bankruptcy managed to register title to the flat before the couple. In the Scottish courts the couple were held to have lost both the flat and their money, but they then appealed to the House. At the first conference Lords Hobhouse and Hoffmann were strongly for allowing the appeal and Lord Rodger shared some of their doubts. To the relief of the legal nationalists in Scotland Lord Rodger was able to convince himself, after researching the history of the field in depth, that the appeal should be dismissed, which had been Lord Hope's position all along. Lord Bingham, whatever his reservations, is understood to have taken the view that if two such experts in Scots law had agreed on what Scots law was, who was he to differ and gave his casting vote to the Scots Law Lords. Lords Hobhouse and Hoffmann with some reservations fell in line with Lord Rodger's opinion, ensuring that to the wider world the case appears as a 5:0 to dismiss the appeal. Appearances can be deceptive. The perceived inequities of the case had made it a much closer struggle than that.

Barber v Somerset County Council,[72] about an employer's liability for psychiatric illness caused by work-related stress, was also a close call that wasn't, since the final outcome was 4:1 for the schoolmaster appellant. Lord Rodger had expressed doubts about upholding the appeal at the first conference but he was won over by

---

[65] In our interview he told me, 'There are some cases where you think you are writing for the majority because you simply cannot believe that people are going to go the other way'.

[66] Ibid, para 20.

[67] *Cullen v Chief Constable of the Royal Ulster Constabulary* [2003] UKHL 39.

[68] Uniquely in the Lords, they produced a dissent in joint names.

[69] Writing the lead judgment as befits a former Chief Justice of Northern Ireland.

[70] As indeed he did quite regularly in his first year or two, according to Lord Bingham's notebooks.

[71] *Burnett's Trustees v Grainger* [2004] UKHL 8; 2004 SLT 513.

[72] *Barber v Somerset County Council* [2004] UKHL 13.

the detailed analysis in Lord Walker's opinion, leaving Lord Scott dissenting on his own and lamenting Lord Rodger's switch.[73] *Re McFarland (NI)*[74] related to a rather less sympathetic individual accused of indecent assault who learnt that the magistrate had told his counsel that if the accused continued to plead not guilty he was minded to remit the case to a higher court with greater sentencing powers. Having promptly pleaded guilty on hearing this news, the accused then discovered that a remittal to the higher court was not competent in his case and his conviction was quashed on appeal. His case for compensation reached the Lords by dint of leave being granted by Lords Steyn, Hope and Scott. At the first conference two of them, Lords Steyn and Scott (together with Lord Walker), were for allowing the applicant's appeal but eventually, all of them were won over by Lord Bingham who gave the leading judgment for dismissing the appeal (although Lord Steyn dissented on a secondary point).

R (on the Application of Razgar) v Secretary of State for the Home Department[75] was an asylum case where the applicant sought to use an Article 8 challenge (respect for private life) to prevent the Home Department from expelling him from the country. At the first conference the panel split, with Lady Hale, Lord Walker and Lord Carswell voting to allow the Home Department's appeal and Lords Bingham and Lord Steyn voting for the applicant. As was not infrequently the case Lord Carswell was the swing voter[76] and at the circulation stage he switched to join the senior members, thus reversing the outcome of the case.

Over the long vacation of 2004 the Law Lords wrestled with the second of several tricky causation cases which were to confront them in the final years. The claimant in *Chester v Afshar*[77] was a patient who reluctantly agreed to have an operation on her spine on the advice of her consultant surgeon. However, he failed to warn her that there was a small risk of severe neurological damage occurring if she had the operation. She had the operation—he was not negligent—but she nonetheless suffered nerve damage. She sued and won in the lower courts, leading the surgeon to appeal to the Lords with leave from Lords Hoffmann, Hope and Millett. At the first conference Lord Bingham's notebook suggests that Lords Bingham and Hoffmann had no doubts, the surgeon's appeal should succeed. The others were much less certain. Lord Walker, the junior, was hesitant but voted to dismiss. Lord Hope also found it a difficult case but sympathised with the claimant and ultimately dismissed the appeal. Lord Steyn, unusually, was undecided at

---

[73] His final words (para 16) contain a distinct barb: '[H]aving had the advantage of reading in advance the opinion of my noble and learned friend Lord Rodger of Earlsferry, I agree with everything he has said save his conclusion that the appeal should be allowed'.

[74] *Re McFarland (Northern Ireland)* [2004] UKHL 17.

[75] *R (on the Application of Razgar) v Secretary of State for the Home Department* [2004] UKHL 27.

[76] See ibid, para 78. In *Campbell v Mirror Group Newspapers Ltd* [2004] UKHL 22 Lord Carswell had also been the swing voter but despite the strength of Lord Hoffmann's dissent—the power of which he found very persuasive, in the end, by a whisker he voted to uphold the damages against the *Mirror*.

[77] *Chester v Afshar* [2004] UKHL 41.

the first conference. Unsure as to which way to go, he was tempted to follow the arguments of the Oxford don Honoré,[78] but in the end, he prevaricated. True to form, Lord Bingham made no effort to win over the swing voter, indeed, perhaps because the hearing finished three days before the long vacation, he did not even write straight away as he almost always did, but left the lead opinion to Lord Hope. Over the summer the drafts were circulated with little opportunity for discussion, and Lord Steyn made up his mind, he would be on the side of the angels:

> 24. Standing back from the detailed arguments, I have come to the conclusion that, as a result of the surgeon's failure to warn the patient, she cannot be said to have given informed consent to the surgery in the full legal sense. Her right of autonomy and dignity can and ought to be vindicated by a narrow and modest departure from traditional causation principles.

> 25. On a broader basis I am glad to have arrived at the conclusion that the claimant is entitled in law to succeed. This result is in accord with one of the most basic aspirations of the law, namely to right wrongs. Moreover, the decision announced by the House today reflects the reasonable expectations of the public in contemporary society.

During that same vacation Lord Bingham was involved in another close call: *AG's Ref (No 4) of 2002*.[79] Actually it was two conjoined appeals which raised the contentious issue of the reverse burden of proof that certain offences create. In these cases, instead of a presumption of innocence, the accused has to prove his or her innocence. In both cases the question was whether this reverse burden was compatible with the presumption of innocence guaranteed by Article 6(2) of the European Convention. In the Reference case the accused was charged with belonging to a proscribed organisation, contrary to section 11 of the Terrorism Act 2000. Lords Carswell and Roger had no difficulty at the first conference in agreeing with the Court of Appeal that the statute was compatible with the Convention. Lord Phillips was more tentative. He considered on balance, however, that the imposition of a legal burden of proof on the accused was incompatible with the Convention, that it could not be saved by 'reading down' the provision under section three of the Human Rights Act to treat it as imposing only an evidential burden and therefore that a declaration of incompatibility was the answer. Lord Steyn was equally tentative in coming to the same conclusion. However, by the stage of the published judgments, Lord Bingham gave the lead, concluding that whilst a legal burden would be incompatible with the Convention in this case, it could be rectified by treating it as imposing merely an evidential burden, without the need for a declaration of incompatibility. Lords Steyn and Phillips simply agreed, suggesting that they had been won over by Lord Bingham's lengthy opinion. On this occasion the lack of opportunity for discussion had worked in his favour. The two junior Law Lords (both former chief justices) stuck to their guns.

---

[78] The leading text on causation in English Law, *Causation in the Law* (Oxford, Clarendon Press, 1959) was written by Herbert Hart and Tony Honore, both of Oxford University.

[79] *Attorney General's Ref (No 4) of 2002; Sheldrake v Director of Public Prosecutions* [2004] UKHL 43.

In *Belmarsh*,[80] perhaps the most important national security case to come before the final court, the panel split 5:4 against the Government at the first conference, however, once Lord Rodger had circulated his speech, the votes began to peel away from the minority side until only Lord Walker was left in dissent.[81] *AG's Ref (No 4) of 2002* was the final close call in Lord Bingham's notebooks, however, there were, of course, many more cases in the Bingham era where there were vote swings. The ones known about are those to emerge from the Law Lords' judgments—especially in close call cases—or those mentioned in the Law Lords' interviews. First off in 2005 was the third causation case, *Gregg v Scott*.[82] Mr Gregg the appellant had had his cancer misdiagnosed for nine months due to the negligence of his doctor. However, although he probably had to endure considerably more pain and suffering from the misdiagnosis, the question facing the House was whether the loss of a chance of a cure, was actionable. It is clear that the panel agonised over the case, it took them 244 days from hearing to final judgment—four times the normal gap between the first conference and judgment in 2005. It is evident from Lord Hope's judgment that during the first conference and for many months thereafter it was completely unclear which side would prevail.[83] Lord Nicholls believed passionately that to deny the appellant would be unjust as, ultimately, did Lord Hope, but Lord Hoffmann was equally convinced that there was no coherent basis for extending causation to cover a possible loss that was not a probability. Lady Hale clearly sympathised with the appellant but could not in the end find a coherent way of extending liability to cover such a loss. Lord Phillips may well have demonstrated his usual ability to retain fluidity in his thinking for longer than most of his colleagues—he certainly wrote after Lords Hope and Nicholls—but ultimately he too balked at the incoherence of the proposed extension of liability.[84] It may have been Baroness Hale who at a relatively late stage swung against Mr Gregg, but it could also have been Lord Phillips. Nor is it clear what prompted the change of heart.

---

[80] *A and Others v Secretary of State for the Home Department* [2004] UKHL 56. Unfortunately, Lord Bingham's notebook from *Belmarsh* has not been recovered. A further discussion of this case appears in chapter 7 below.

[81] Lord Hoffmann's judgment was essentially a dissent also, even though he also voted against the Government.

[82] *Gregg v Scott* [2005] UKHL 2.

[83] At para 92 he states: 'This is an anxious and difficult case. It is only after many months of deliberation that it has become clear that the majority view is that the appeal must be dismissed. I have reached a different opinion. In agreement with my noble and learned friend Lord Nicholls of Birkenhead, I would allow the appeal and remit the case for further consideration and the assessment of damages. I have to confess that I would not have written at such length if at the time of writing the result of the appeal had been clear to me'. Lord Hoffmann, who was on the majority side subsequently remarked, '*Gregg v Scott* was a very close case'. See L Hoffmann, '*Fairchild* and After' in A Burrows, D Johnston and R Zimmermann (eds), *Judge and Jurist: Essays in Memory of Lord Rodger* (Oxford, Oxford University Press, 2013).

[84] Mr Gregg's misfortunes were compounded by the majority Law Lords identifying that had his lawyers acted differently he could have made a modest recovery against the doctor. Doubtless this conclusion helped those like Mr Gregg, in subsequent cases. It was, however, salt in the wound for Mr Gregg.

If Lord Hoffmann prevailed in *Gregg v Scott*, he lost the next close call *A v Home Secretary*[85] despite having the other two heavyweights in the Court (Lords Bingham and Nicholls) on his side. The issue at stake was the permissibility of using in a UK court evidence obtained by torture in a foreign country and on whom the onus lay to establish that evidence had or had not been obtained by torture. Despite the outrage of the three senior Law Lords at what they regarded as the watering down of the ban on the use of evidence obtained by torture, Lord Hope, as he was to do again,[86] led the charge of the four junior Law Lords against the heavyweight trio. It is a testament to his persuasive powers that he managed to win over and hold Lord Rodger[87] and Lord Carswell,[88] in the face of such trenchant opposition. Once again, we can see that Lord Carswell was the swing voter, and that Lord Bingham's reluctance to lobby for his position may have worked against him,[89] for all the power and status of the dissents.

The fourth causation case, *Barker v Corus*[90] revisited the territory originally staked out in the first causation case, *Fairchild v Glenhaven Funeral Services*.[91] There a unanimous Appellate Committee—essentially motivated by the perceived unfairness[92] of absolving a negligent employer from liability for exposing an employee to asbestos who had then contracted mesothelioma, simply because another party had also exposed the worker to asbestosis—created an exception to the normal 'but for' rule of factual causation rule. *Fairchild* had left it open whether the defendant found liable under the new test was liable for all damage suffered by a workman, or liable only in proportion to the risk caused by that defendant. In *Barker* it seems that Lords Hoffmann and Rodger, the only Law Lords left from the original panel in *Fairchild*, were at loggerheads from an early stage as to the interpretation to be given to the test developed in *Fairchild* and even as to the correct interpretation to be given to their own dicta in that case. It is understood that Lord Rodger felt that he had a majority of the panel in *Barker* on his side, when he was struck by a bout of flu. By the time he returned Lord Hoffmann had persuaded them all that his arguments in *Fairchild* had been accepted by the majority of the panel, when it is far from clear from the judgments

---

[85] *A v Secretary of State for the Home Department (No 2)* [2005] UKHL 71.

[86] See *Kay v Lambeth London Borough Council* [2006] UKHL 10, [2006] 2 AC 465.

[87] 'I have ultimately come to agree with your Lordships that the appeal should be allowed, but, I confess, I have found the issue far from easy' (para 128).

[88] 'After initially favouring the Bingham test, I have been persuaded that the Hope test should be adopted' (para 158).

[89] On this occasion Lord Bingham seems to have written and circulated his speech before Lord Hoffmann, who may also have relied on his draft opinion to win the day. (Lord Hoffmann told me that he preferred to rely on the circulation of his draft opinions to persuade his colleagues, rather than going to their rooms).

[90] *Barker v Corus (UK) plc* [2006] UKHL 20.

[91] *Fairchild v Glenhaven Funeral Services Ltd* [2002] UKHL 22.

[92] See Lord Nicholls: '[a]ny other outcome would be deeply offensive to instinctive notions of what justice requires and fairness demands'. See also L Hoffmann, '*Fairchild* and After' in A Burrows, D Johnston and R Zimmermann (eds), *Judge and Jurist: Essays in Memory of Lord Rodger* (Oxford, Oxford University Press, 2013).

that this was so.[93] Lord Rodger is understood to have been unimpressed at this re-writing of the judgment in *Fairchild* and the stinging tone of his dissent (which his colleagues steadfastly avoid engaging with) shows this clearly. It is to be doubted that his irritation would have been in any way diminished by Lord Hoffmann's much later confession[94] that he had indeed been indulging in 'some judicious re-writing of history' in the case (as Lord Rodger had asserted in his dissent), with a view to some pragmatic damage limitation in relation to the anomalies created by *Fairchild*).[95] (However, Lord Rodger was presumably comforted by the fact that Parliament partially reversed the decision of the majority in *Barker* within a few short months.)[96]

Barker involved several switches of positions and so too did *Stack v Dowden*,[97] a case about the proper distribution of the property of cohabitees whose relationship has come to an end. Lord Walker wrote his judgment early, as he occasionally did, concluding that equitable principles applied. When they had their delayed case conference Lord Hoffmann (who was presiding) and Lord Neuberger agreed with him, but Lady Hale and Lord Hope did not. It was agreed that Lord Walker's judgment would be the lead and that the other two could write if they wished. Lady Hale indicated that she wished to write on a Family point whilst reaching the same conclusion as Lord Walker. A month later when she circulated it, it did indeed reach the same answer but by a slightly different route. Lord Hoffmann then switched to agree with it and, very unusually, Lord Walker withdrew most of his judgment.[98] Lord Neuberger, now in a minority of one, spent much of the Easter vacation writing a long dissent but it was too late—the majority were not for turning.

Baroness Hale was not so successful in the next close call and Lord Neuberger, just about, remained with the majority. It was *YL v Birmingham City Council*,[99] where Lord Bingham and Baroness Hale combined in a long-awaited case over the applicability of the ECHR to residents of private care homes who are funded from the public purse. Unfortunately time did not permit much of a debate at the first conference and unusually Lord Bingham chose not to write immediately, asking

---

[93]   See J Lee, 'Fidelity in interpretation: Lord Hoffmann and the Adventure of the Empty House' (2008) 28 *Legal Studies* 1.

[94]   Ironically in a volume of essays in tribute to Lord Rodger. See '*Fairchild* and After', above n 92.

[95]   Whilst Lord Hoffmann is unrepentant about his role in *Barker* he does regret the *Fairchild* decision which he now feels is an example of a hard case making bad law, see '*Fairchild* and After', above n 92.

[96]   An intervention which has been criticised as ill-considered. See J Lee, 'Inconsiderate Alterations in our Laws' in J Lee (ed), *From House of Lords to Supreme Court* (Oxford, Hart Publishing, 2011) 71.

[97]   *Stack v Dowden* [2007] UKHL 17.

[98]   Ibid, para 14: 'I have had the advantage of reading in draft the opinion of my noble and learned friend Baroness Hale of Richmond. Having done so I have set aside as redundant most of the opinion which I had prepared'. Lady Hale told me, '[T]hat was a situation in which initially there was perhaps less enthusiasm for the line that I took than there was by the time we'd had some further chats about it. Eventually three of them subscribed to my line and one subscribed to a different line and that was the result of iterations of the argument'.

[99]   *YL v Birmingham City Council* [2007] UKHL 27.

Lady Hale to produce the lead judgment. When he did write their combined might was not enough, since the group-oriented Lords Mance and Scott seem to have been able to shore up a wavering Lord Neuberger, the swing voter. True to form, Tom Bingham would not lobby, leaving his opinion to speak for him. It was not enough.[100] It is difficult not to see this case as another where the chancery judges sought to resist the 'intrusion' of the ECHR into what they regarded as an area of private law.[101]

It is not clear there were any changes of vote in *YL*. However, *Somerville v Scottish Ministers*,[102] which turned on whether the Scotland Act 1998 (which adopted the European Convention of Human Rights into Scots law) contained a time limit for human rights challenges as the Human Rights Act 1998 did, did feature several changes of mind. From the judgments we can see that Lord Scott 'after much hesitation and an embarrassing number of changes of mind', votes to dissent with Lord Mance.[103] Equally, we can see that Lord Walker is the swing voter[104] who finally opts to go with the two Scots—Lords Hope and Rodger.[105] It is noticeable, however, that neither Lord Scott nor Lord Walker attributed the resolution to their indecision to the arguments of their colleagues. The case contains many dialogues between the Law Lords and counsel,[106] Law Lords and the court below[107] and between Law Lords and other Law Lords,[108] including Lords Hope and Rodger commenting on their own dicta in the Privy Council case of *R v HM Advocate*.[109]

On paper, *Smith v Chief Constable of Sussex Police*,[110] appears as a solo dissent by Lord Bingham, as to the circumstances in which the police might be liable under the common law for negligence in protecting the public. However, it is clear that of the majority, Lords Phillips and Brown were hesitant as to the outcome.[111] Had

[100] Lord Bingham told me, 'I'm told by those who were in the Court of Appeal that although *YL* failed [there] everybody in the Court assumed that it would get reversed in the House of Lords and indeed I was very surprised when it didn't ... I was very surprised at the view taken by the majority'.

[101] Eg *London Borough of Harrow v Qazi* [2003] UKHL 43, *Kay v Lambeth London Borough Council* [2006] UKHL 10 and *Doherty v Birmingham City Council* [2008] UKHL 57.

[102] *Somerville v Scottish Ministers* [2007] UKHL 44.

[103] See para 78.

[104] Para 163: 'The most important issue of law is as to the interaction of the Human Rights Act 1998 and the Scotland Act 1998. On that issue your Lordships are equally divided, with each side regarding the outcome as tolerably clear. I have to say that I have found this point much more difficult'.

[105] Para 166: 'I have however come to the conclusion that ... the alternative approaches canvassed by my noble and learned friends Lord Scott of Foscote and Lord Mance, face even greater difficulties than the views set out by my noble and learned friends Lord Hope of Craighead and Lord Rodger. I would therefore join with them in allowing the appeal on the first issue'. This choice has been labelled by some as an example of English deference to the Scots Law Lords in a Scots appeal.

[106] See eg, paras 71 and 132.

[107] See para 39.

[108] See eg, Lord Mance's speech or Lord Walker responding to the 'Swiftian strictures of my noble and learned friend Lord Rodger' (at para 164).

[109] *R v HM Advocate* 2003 SC (PC) 21.

[110] *Smith v Chief Constable of Sussex Police* [2008] UKHL 50.

[111] See ibid, paras 101 and 127.

Lord Bingham been more willing to engage with his colleagues after the circulation of his judgment or had a supporter who was less inhibited, the case might
have gone the other way. In a similar vein *Maco Door and Window Hardware (UK)
Limited v Her Majesty's Revenue and Customs*[112] did not involve any vote switching
so far as can be seen, despite turning on a narrow point of statutory construction.
In consequence there were narrow majorities all the way up (indeed the appellant
won in every court). Although it does not deal with any points of fundamental
principle, it contains pithy rejoinders. As Lord Scott observed:[113]

> My noble and learned friend Lord Neuberger of Abbotsbury has, in his opinion on this
> appeal (para 60), suggested that it would be surprising if section 18(2) served only to
> expand but not to limit the ambit of section 18(1). I must respectfully say that in my
> opinion that would not be in the least surprising.

On the other hand, the *Rent Service*[114] case, featuring the intricacies of housing
benefit law, contained much changing of minds. It began at the first conference
when the three junior Law Lords initially favoured dismissing the appeal, then the
two seniors spoke and the three juniors were won round to unanimously allowing
the appeal. Lord Neuberger was assigned and wrote the lead judgment, not without some difficulty and the two seniors (Lords Hope and Scott) agreed with it.
Lord Rodger then reverted to dismissing the appeal[115] and Lord Walker, having
read Lord Rodger's judgment came round to favouring dismissal of the appeal
as well.[116]

Moore Stephens[117] is a much more celebrated close call. A 'shell' company
was abused by a fraudster and the auditors failed to detect the fraud when they
might have done. The question for the House was whether the auditors could
escape liability by the use of the maxim '*ex turpi causa non oritur actio*' (from a
dishonorable cause an action does not arise). Lords Walker and Brown supported
ex turpi causa and Lord Mance favoured holding the auditors liable. Lord Scott
wavered but came down with Lord Mance, indicating in his judgment that he had
found the case a very difficult one.[118] Lord Phillips also seems to have found it a
particularly difficult case and is thought to have changed his mind on more than
one occasion at the writing stage which lasted 166 days, nearly twice the normal
gap between the first conference and the judgment. In the end he plumped for
ex turpi causa. Several Law Lords later told me that they would have voted against

---

[112] *Maco Door and Window Hardware (UK) Ltd v HM Revenue and Customs* [2008] UKHL 54.
[113] Ibid, para 11.
[114] *R (On the Application of Heffernan) v The Rent Service* [2008] UKHL 58.
[115] See para 10: 'At the conclusion of the hearing I was inclined to favour a construction ... along
the lines of Lord Neuberger. On further consideration, however, I have come to the view that it
introduces too many elements which are not to be found in the text'.
[116] See para 31: 'I have had great difficulty in the resolution of this appeal ... Like my noble and
learned friend Lord Rodger of Earlsferry, I was at the end of the hearing inclined to think that the
appeal should be allowed. But further reflection, and in particular study of Lord Rodger's opinion ...
have led me to the conclusion that the appeal should be dismissed for the reasons set out in Lord
Rodger's opinion'.
[117] *Moore Stephens (a firm) v Stone Rolls Ltd* [2009] UKHL 39.
[118] Ibid, para 88.

the auditors had they been sitting. I encountered a similar response to the equally notorious Chagos Islands close call, *Bancoult*,[119] in the Autumn before. It is thought that it was cases like these that persuaded Lord Phillips to push for the much greater use of seven- and nine-judge panels in the Supreme Court, because it was too easy to argue that close call cases turned on which judges were on the hearing panel.[120]

In sum, a review of vote changes in the Bingham era, at or after the first conference, indicates that they occurred rather more frequently than the Law Lords themselves recalled. This is a testament to the judicial dialogues that occurred in the court at that time. Group-orientation seems to have been a significant factor as we have seen. Moreover it seems that some Law Lords were more likely to change their vote than others. One Law Lord was thought to have changed his ultimate opinion six times in 2008, Lord Millett switched six times in five years and Lord Walker changed his vote on five occasions in the cases we have been examining. Lords Hoffmann, Rodger and Steyn switched on four occasions, a finding that will surprise those Law Lords who told me that Lords Hoffmann and Steyn hardly ever changed their vote at that stage. Lord Nicholls changed three times, and Lord Carswell twice. Curiously, Lord Scott, who in two cases indicated that he had changed his mind on an embarrassing number of occasions, only appeared to change position after the first conference on one occasion, as did Lords Bingham, Hutton, Hobhouse and Neuberger. On the other hand, Lords Brown, Hope, Mance and Lady Hale appeared to have a change of heart after the first conference relatively rarely. Those Law Lords who appeared to be the most successful in winning round their colleagues at that stage in the proceedings were Lords Rodger (6), Hoffmann (4), Hope (3), Bingham (3), Lady Hale (2) and Lord Steyn (2). Interestingly, two of the most successful, Lord Rodger and Lord Bingham relied on the power of the written dialogue—their judgments—rather than on a more group oriented approach or oral persuasion. Lords Hoffmann, Hope and Steyn, however were task leaders or group-oriented Law Lords, as we saw earlier.

THE UK SUPREME COURT 2009–13

We know that the move to the Supreme Court was accompanied by several initiatives designed to change the culture of decision-making in the Court. More sittings with large panels,[121] transmission of oral hearings and judgments to

---

[119] *R (Bancoult) v Secretary of State for Foreign and Commonwealth Affairs (No 2)* [2008] UKHL 61.

[120] For an argument along these lines see B Dickson, 'Close Calls in the House of Lords' ch 13 in J Lee (ed), *From House of Lords to Supreme Court* (Oxford, Hart Publishing, 2011) at 302. '

[121] In the Bingham era there were 12 enlarged courts (eight with seven Law Lords and four with nine Law Lords). In the Supreme Court up to August 2013 there had been 57 enlarged courts (43 with seven Justices and 14 with nine Justices). For an argument that the Supreme Court may have gone too far in sitting in enlarged panels as frequently as it has, see A. Burrows, 'Numbers sitting in the Supreme Court' [2013] 129 *LQR* 305.

increase transparency, pre-meetings, and greater use of technology in relation to permissions, electronic bundles (materials) and email for discussion of drafts being circulated. Less immediately visible has been the encouragement for more single judgments and fewer concurrences, as we saw earlier. Together these developments have led to more team-working,[122] especially from 2012 onwards, than was ever the case in the Lords.

In practice the principal thrust for team-working now takes place after the hearing, when the judgments are circulating. Either a dissenter will get in early to pre-empt the lead judgment when it arrives or those responding to the lead judgment will contact the lead writer to engage with that judgment. If there is an error in the judgment, the response will probably be in private to save embarrassment, but otherwise the response may be a general circulation by email saying, 'Look, there are three points here. I am very happy about two but on the third I am not happy for this reason.' Again sometimes a Justice might say, 'I am happy with this judgment but I know there is at least one possible dissent, so I will wait to see what the dissenter says.' Some Justices will prefer to preface their general response with an individual approach to the lead judgment writer. If a personal approach saying that you agree with most of the judgment but can't agree with one additional point makes no headway with the lead writer, the next step is a general email. It might set out a general agreement with the lead judgment except for the one point, accompanied by an indication that the responder will not dissent if he or she is on their own. This will elucidate whether others in the team share the responder's doubts and clarify to the whole panel where the balance of opinion lies. In turn, this may encourage the lead writer to modify his or her position. Equally, an astute lead writer can overcome the doubts of a potential dissenter by altering the lead judgment to take account of the points that are causing concern. Thus Lord Neuberger in *Zakrzewski*,[123] speaking last at the first conference in that case indicated that he had two reservations with the position supported by the rest of the panel, which would lead him reluctantly to dismiss the appeal. As he recounted ruefully rather later,[124] Lord Sumption, the writer of the lead judgment slightly recast the appellant's case and in so doing dealt with the two points thus undermining his potential dissent.

In this case, as he did in some others, Lord Neuberger had formed a view as to how the outcome of the appeal should go and then tried to work his reasoning backwards to justify his instinctive take on the case. As he said,

> I think virtually every judge does that. It's like construing a document. You look at it and you think this is what it means and then you go round the circle again and again … I almost always have an idea of what I want to find either because it instinctively feels right or it seems to go with the merits or my feeling is that it is in line with the principles as I think they are.

---

[122] As one Justice put it in our interview, 'I believe that what we are doing is not a series of individual decisions, but a corporate decision.'

[123] *Zakrzewski v Regional Court in Lodz, Poland* [2013] UKSC 2.

[124] Interview with the author, 2013.

Lord Sumption agreed,[125]

> Yes, I do have an instinctive feeling [for the outcome of cases]. I think everybody does. How hard it is to shift me of it, depends entirely on what sort of case it is and how much I know about the subject matter … How often I am persuaded my initial instinct is just completely wrong in principle, well probably not very often. When it happens it tends to be in cases on subject areas which I am not so familiar with as some of my colleagues

He added,

> If you start with the answer and work backwards it is very important to know when to recognise defeat. Some of us never recognise defeat and some of us give up at our first problem, though not many. I think the ideal is to penetrate some way down the road and when you find that you can't in any intellectually honest way get to where you thought you should be going, you change your mind.

He was not alone. For a number of Justices the greater engagement amongst them has led to more awareness of minds changing at the circulation stage.[126]

> It seems to me, looking at it, if anybody does change his mind it's more likely to be at the stage when they circulate drafts, written drafts where you can see the thing set out very clearly in writing. (A Justice)

> We think we change our minds throughout the case, more often than people might think. (Lord Clarke)

> I have changed my mind. It is usually when I have read a judgment. That has happened quite a few times … generally the deliberation tends to be held so soon after the hearing that people haven't really got terribly hardened. They are prepared to wait and see what it looks like when somebody writes something and then react to it and then decide whether they are going to dissent or be persuaded and sometimes we then have a second meeting to discuss matters further. (Lord Reed)

The first close call in the UK Supreme Court to involve changes of mind and position—indeed several of them at different stages—was the *Jewish Free School* case discussed in the last chapter.[127] It took 152 days from hearing to judgment—well in excess of the norm for the time—probably because of the splits in the Court. Lord Kerr told me that his mind had changed several times during the hearing stage and another Justice observed that there had been some changes of opinion at the circulation of judgments stage. Lord Phillips indicates in his judgment[128] that that he changed his mind and his vote on the key issue of direct discrimination. This seems likely to have been the vote swing which took the case from a 5:4 majority for indirect discrimination, with Lord Hope doing the lead judgment,[129]

---

[125] Interview with the author 2012.
[126] One told me that he had found that his colleagues changed their minds 'a surprising amount' at this stage.
[127] *R (on the application of E) v Governing Body of the Jewish Free School and Admissions Panel of the Jewish Free School* [2009] UKSC 15. See ch 4 n 52 above.
[128] Ibid, para [33].
[129] Not only does he have the fullest statement of the facts, he also deals with the issue of costs (with which his colleagues all agree), which is unusual in a dissenting judgment.

to a 5:4 majority for direct discrimination. However, Lord Phillips did not attribute his change of heart to the influence of any of his colleagues. It seems more likely that it can be put down to his ability to retain a flexible mind rather longer than most of his colleagues, as illustrated eg, in cases like *Moore Stephens*.[130]

The final case of 2009 *Secretary of State for the Environment v Meier*[131] (relating to trespassing travellers and orders for possession) took even longer than the *JFS*[132] case to come out—172 days. No explanation was given but it may be in part because there was at one stage a split in the Court. Originally Lord Collins had been persuaded of a point by counsel in the hearing but at the circulation of the judgments stage he seems to have decided that the point was unnecessarily bold and switched to support the majority.[133] There is nothing to indicate that in the next close call, *Martin*[134]—the first in the following year—there was any change of votes although it is believed that Lord Rodger was not pleased to find his friend and ally Lord Brown deserting him for a temporary alliance with Lord Hope.

In the next one, *R (Sainsbury's Supermarkets Ltd) v Wolverhampton City Council*[135] (a fascinating struggle between Tesco and Sainsbury's to develop the same site in Wolverhampton) the Court seems to have been fairly unanimous at the first conference, with Lord Collins writing the lead. However, it is understood that one by one the three senior Justices (including the President and Deputy President) came over to Tesco's side and Lord Collins, who was himself vacillating, was left writing furiously (as befits a task leader) to keep his majority for allowing the appeal.[136] In the next close call, *R (on the application of Smith) v Secretary of State for Defence*,[137] it is unclear what swings of vote there might have been before the final divide between the more socially liberal Justices (Hale, Mance and Kerr) against six of their colleagues. At stake was the applicability of the ECHR in relation to serving personnel in the Middle East. Lord Phillips might technically have been the lead judgment writer as President, but arguably the most influential Justice for the majority was Lord Collins, once more playing the role of task leader.[138] Nor is there any evidence that *R (on the application of the Electoral Commission) v City of Westminster Magistrates Court and UKIP*,[139] was ever anything other than a 4:3 close call in which the three dissenters were and remained Lords Rodger, Walker

---

[130] *Moore Stephens (a firm) v Stone Rolls Ltd* [2009] UKHL 39.

[131] *Secretary of State for the Environment, Fod and Rural Affairs v Meier and Another* [2009] UKSC 11.

[132] *R (on the application of E) v JFS Governing Body and Admissions Panel* [2009] UKSC 15.

[133] Ibid, para 96. Confirmed in interview with the author.

[134] *Martin v HM Advocate; Miller v HM Advocate* [2010] UKSC 10.

[135] *R (on the application of Sainsbury's Supermarkets Ltd) v Wolverhampton City Council* [2010] UKSC 20.

[136] Lord Collins seems to have had to fight hard as task leader to retain the majority in several cases.

[137] *R (on the application of Smith) v Secretary of State for Defence* [2010] UKSC 29.

[138] See eg ibid para 91(Lord Hope), para 111 (Lord Rodger), para 131 (Lord Walker). Although a group-oriented Justice, Lord Collins, like Lord Bingham appears to have relied primarily on his draft written judgment to persuade his colleagues.

[139] *R (on the application of the Electoral Commission) v City of Westminster Magistrates Court and The United Kingdom Independence Party* [2010] UKSC 40.

and Brown,[140] who had already dissented together in the *Jewish Free School* case and were to do so again in *Adams* later in the year.[141]

It is unclear whether *Radmacher (formerly Granatino) v Granatino*[142] (the enforceability of ante-nuptial agreements case) where Baroness Hale's dissent points to the possibly gendered nature of the outcome, ever contained a larger split than the 8:1 with which it ended up. Certainly, it took 211 days for the judgments to emerge—twice the norm for that year, which is sometimes an indication of a larger split on the Court.[143] *R (on the application of Coke-Wallis) v ICAEW*[144] (a challenging case because the moral merits were strongly against the appellant) on the other hand was definitely a close call that wasn't. It seems that Lord Rodger was leaning towards the respondent at the first conference[145] and Lord Collins, fighting his doubts all the way, only voted for allowing the appeal because he could not find a principled basis for dissenting. Both in the end voted to uphold the appeal, making the decision unanimous.

Lord Dyson played a significant role in the next close call, *Lumba v Secretary of State for the Home Department*,[146] a fearsomely tricky problem with multiple issues relating to the false imprisonment and detention pending deportation of foreign national prisoners released after serving their period of imprisonment in this country. Lord Dyson was allocated the lead judgment and wrote the longest judgment he had ever written (169 paragraphs) because of all the issues. It was worth it, however, since he managed to keep a solid majority on most of the issues—usually 6:3. It involved some considerable debate and (rather unusually) a second case conference, ensuring that the gap from hearing to judgment was 126 days. *Jones v Kaney*[147] (on the immunity from suit of expert witnesses) was the very next case. It was clearly a close call since the panel split 5:2 as to whether this was an area where the judges could develop the law, or whether it should be left to Parliament. It is unclear whether anyone on the case had doubts or a change of heart, but there was an interaction effect, however. Thus Lord Hope (one of the two dissenters) got his judgment out very, very quickly, a tactic that

---

[140] They were close friends with geographically contiguous rooms.

[141] *R (on the application of Adams) v Secretary of State for Justice* [2011] UKSC 18. With Lords Rodger and Brown dissenting together also in *R (on the application of GC) v Commissioner of Police of the Metropolis* [2011] UKSC 21 *and SK (Zimbabwe) v Secretary of State for the Home Department* [2011] UKSC 23 also in the next few months.

[142] *Radmacher (formerly Granatino) v Granatino* [2010] UKSC 42.

[143] See Table 3.14 in chapter three, above.

[144] *R (on the application of Coke-Wallis v Institute of Chartered Accountants in England & Wales* [2011] UKSC 1.

[145] See Lord Hope, 'Lord Rodger's Notebooks' chapter 9 in A Burrows, D Johnston and R Zimmermann (eds), *Judge and Jurist: Essays in Memory of Lord Rodger of Earlsferry* (Oxford, Oxford University Press, 2013).

[146] *Walumba Lumba v Secretary of State for the Home Department* [2011] UKSC 12.

[147] *Jones v Kaney* [2011] UKSC 13.

sometimes worked for Lord Hoffmann; however, not on this occasion. As Lord Dyson recalled,[148]

> What it did as far as I was concerned, it gave me something to argue against. I had already provisionally come to a conclusion, the opposite conclusion, but seeing the way that they put it, far from causing me to change my mind, it just gave me something to assess, to argue against.

Baker v Quantum Clothing Group[149] also featured Lord Dyson, although the lead came from Lord Mance.[150] At stake was the liability of employers in the knitting industry of Derbyshire and Nottingham for hearing loss sustained by employees. At the first conference it seems that there was no clear majority, with Lord Kerr on the side of the angels, Lord Clarke probably partially undecided, and Lords Mance and Dyson favouring the employers who had complied with the then prevailing Code of Practice. Lord Saville, who was presiding, eventually cast his lot with Lord Mance (and Dyson), and Lord Clarke joined Lord Kerr.

R (on the application of Adams) v Secretary of State for Justice[151] concerned three accused from Northern Ireland whose convictions had been quashed following investigations by the Criminal Cases Review Commission. In each case the question was whether there had been a miscarriage of justice such as to justify the payment of compensation. In two cases a paper thin majority led by Lords Phillips and Kerr overcame the 'outraged' dissents of Lords Judge, Rodger, Walker and Brown[152] to rule in favour of the accused and compensation even though they could not be shown to be innocent. As Lady Hale observed:[153]

> I do sympathise with Lord Brown's palpable sense of outrage that Lord Phillips' test may result in a few people who are in fact guilty receiving compensation. His approach would of course result in a few people who are in fact innocent receiving no compensation. I say 'a few' because the numbers seeking compensation are in any event very small. But Lord Phillips' approach is the more consistent with the fundamental principles upon which our criminal law has been based for centuries.

If there were no vote swings in *Adams*, there was one in *GC v The Commissioner of the Metropolitan Police*.[154] The case concerned Article 8 of the ECHR and the retention of fingerprint and DNA information of persons who have been cleared of committing any offence. At the first conference the split was 5:2 with Lords Rodger and Kerr in the minority (favouring retention) and Lord Brown the lead

---

[148] Interview with the author. Lord Collins was no more convinced, using the case, as was his wont, to provide an excursus on what the American case law had to contribute on the point.

[149] *Baker v Quantum Clothing Group Ltd and Others* [2011] UKSC 17.

[150] Although agreeing with Lord Mance, Lord Dyson, as he was prone to do, preferred a slightly simpler route to the outcome.

[151] *R (on the application of Adams) v Secretary of State for Justice* [2011] UKSC 18.

[152] The absence of a recognised task leader amongst the dissenters may help to explain why they were unable to persuade Lord Phillips, known for his willingness to retain an open mind long into a case, to their cause.

[153] Ibid, para 116.

[154] *R (on the application of GC) v The Commissioner of Police of the Metropolis* [2011] UKSC 21.

judgment writer. Lord Rodger got his dissent out quickly and it immediately had its desired effect because Lord Brown was persuaded to change sides, leaving the majority without a lead writer. As in *Jones v Kaney*, however, it also stirred up Lord Dyson (to whom counter-punching seems to have come naturally) by giving him something to argue against. In the end he took over the lead judgment and stemmed the haemorrhaging away from the majority position (indeed he seems to have won Lord Kerr over from the other side).[155]

The pairing of Lady Hale and Lord Kerr which had dissented in *Smith* and again in *A v Essex County Council*,[156] but succeeded in *Lumba*, *Adams* and *GC*, also ended in the majority in *SK (Zimbabwe)*.[157] This is hardly surprising since *SK (Zimbabwe)* was actually heard (but not decided) before *Lumba* had even been given permission to appeal. Once permission had been given, and the decision taken to have nine Justices on the panel, it was agreed that *SK (Zimbabwe)* should be held over until the outcome of *Lumba* was known (because both cases raised similar issues, namely the legality of the detention of foreign national prisoners where the Secretary of State has not complied with the terms of the published policy relating to detention). As in *Lumba*, once again the dissenters included Lords Rodger and Brown, and the majority included Lord Hope as well as Lady Hale and Lord Kerr. Hardly surprising that there were no signs of a change of heart by any of the protagonists. The liberals' run of success, however, came to an abrupt halt in *R (on the application of G) v The Governors of X School*[158] where a school assistant was denied a solicitor to represent him in a school disciplinary hearing, the result of which might have prevented him from ever working again in a school. Lords Hope, Walker, Brown and Dyson outvoted Lord Kerr in holding that there was no breach of Article 6(1) of the ECHR.

Lord Dyson wrote the lead judgment in *R (on the application of G) v The Governors of X School*. Rather more interestingly he also wrote the lead judgment in *Al Rawi v The Security Service*,[159] which concerned whether it was possible at common law to replace public interest immunity ('PII')—whereby a judge decides whether in the public interest certain material should be excluded from a hearing—with a closed material procedure where the parties are excluded from the hearing where classified material is involved except through special advocates. At the first conference it seems that a majority considered that the common law could evolve to include provision for a closed material procedure in certain unusual circumstances, and Lord Clarke was assigned the lead judgment. Lord Dyson then wrote a dissent arguing that the establishment of a closed material procedure was for Parliament. Gradually the majority crumbled and Dyson became

[155] See ibid, paras 82 and 85.
[156] *A v Essex County Council* [2010] UKSC 33.
[157] *Shepherd Masimba Kambadzi (previously referred to as SK (Zimbabwe)) v Secretary of State for the Home Department* [2011] UKSC 23.
[158] *R (on the application of G) v The Governors of X School* [2011] UKSC 30.
[159] *Al Rawi and Others v The Security Service* [2011] UKSC 34.

the lead judgment.[160] Lord Phillips—not for the first time—developed an idea of his own which accorded with neither the majority nor minority positions, and Lord Clarke was left with Lord Mance and Lady Hale as his only supporters.[161]

The next close call, *R v Maxwell*,[162] was unusual in a somewhat analogous way to *SK (Zimbabwe)* inasmuch as its publication was held up for over a year.[163] The case involved murder convictions obtained by gross prosecutorial misconduct and whether a retrial could be ordered or whether the misconduct was so egregious that a retrial was inappropriate. At the end of the first conference Lords Rodger, Brown and Collins had a slender majority over Lords Dyson and Mance, in favour of no retrial. Lord Dyson then circulated his draft dissent which won over Lord Rodger to his side.[164]

In neither *Davies*[165] nor *Quila*[166] (the next two split cases) are there any indications that the sole dissenter was ever more than on his own. Lord Mance, as dissenter in the former, did indeed get his dissent out rather more quickly than the lead judgment of Lord Wilson, but it failed to bring over any votes. *Edwards*,[167] however, was a close call. It turned on whether a common law suit for damages continued to lie in a case of unfair dismissal. There were no vote switches, although Lord Dyson (who wrote the lead judgment) must have feared for his 4:3 majority (against common law damages) when, having initially adjusted his judgment in response to suggestions from his colleagues, found Lord Phillips changing his position substantially (and his reasoning, though not, ultimately, his vote) on reading the judgments of Lady Hale and Lord Kerr as dissenters.[168]

Lord Dyson, despite his evident success as a task leader, was not always in the majority. In *Gnango*,[169] a fiendishly difficult criminal case about the intent to kill of gangsters firing at each other in a car park and killing an innocent passer-by, the original split at the first conference was 5:2 for holding the gangster liable for murder. Lord Dyson was in the minority but after much internal doubt he was won over by the majority position.[170]

---

[160] This is clear from the positioning of his judgment on the Court website and the words of the official press release. However, it also clear that originally the lead lay with Lord Clarke, because the statement of the facts is in his judgment, not Lord Dyson's. Further, Lord Phillips in his final paragraph (para 197) refers to 'Lord Dyson's dissent from that part of Lord Clarke's judgment'—a further indication of the original position.

[161] Lord Rodger died before he could produce a judgment in this case, but he had indicated that he would have been with Lord Dyson and his old friend Lord Brown in dismissing the appeal.

[162] *R v Maxwell* [2010] UKSC 48.

[163] Heard in July 2010 with the decision (without reasons) given in November 2010, the judgments in this case were not released until July 2011, one year to the day after the end of the hearing.

[164] Ibid, para 39. This was Lord Collins' one and only dissent in two years on the Supreme Court.

[165] *R (on the application of Davies and Another) v Commissioners for HM Revenue and Customs* [2011] UKSC 47.

[166] *R (on the application of Quila and Another) v Secretary of State for the Home Department* [2011] UKSC 45.

[167] *Edwards v Chesterfield Royal Hospital NHS Foundation Trust* [2011] UKSC 58.

[168] Ibid, para 70.

[169] *R v Gnango* [2011] UKSC 59.

[170] See ibid, para 103. (Won over by Lords Phillips and Judge).

2012 saw a series of close calls, including two that weren't. The first was the *Lehman Brothers* case[171] (arising from the crash of Lehman Brothers) where much to their dismay, Lords Hope and Walker having initially held a majority at the first conference, later found themselves outgunned by the three juniors, Lords Clarke, Dyson and Collins after a change of votes which yet again saw Lord Dyson's circulated dissent become a lead judgment.[172] This was the fourth time in which Lord Dyson ended up with the lead judgment when it had originally been elsewhere. No other Justice could match this degree of task leadership on the Supreme Court in this period.

In *In re Peacock*[173] the issue was whether a convicted drug trafficker who on release made considerable sums of money legitimately, could retrospectively be hit by a confiscation order from these assets. At the first conference the outcome was unclear but thereafter there seems to have been a degree of changing of minds, with Lord Hope departing from his original position[174] to vote with Lady Hale to object to the order and Lord Wilson finding himself as the last Justice to vote,[175] opting to uphold the order. The changes of mind seem to have come about from 'further reflection'. *Sugar v BBC and Another*[176] featured the Freedom of Information Act 2000 (the FOIA) and a report commissioned by the BBC. It was not a close call in the end but it seems to have been so at the first conference. There, it is understood that the initial roll call had the Court split 3:2, with the lead judgment with Lord Wilson. Subsequently two of the majority changed to join the minority, leaving Lord Wilson on his own, but still with the lead judgment. For Lord Wilson the information was exempt from the FOIA if it was held *predominantly* for the purposes of journalism, art or literature. His colleagues, however, indicated that they would have been satisfied that the report was outside the FOIA even if it was held only *partly* for the purposes of journalism, art or literature.

Sugar contained two changes of mind, as did *Flood v The Times*.[177] The latter was, it would seem, also a close call that wasn't, since the two Justices who originally voted to dismiss the appeal at the first conference eventually joined the majority in favour of allowing the appeal. The struggle entailed that a gap of 155 days elapsed between the hearing and judgment—twice the norm in that year.

In the *Atomic test veterans*[178] case a large number of service personnel who had served in the South Pacific between 1952 and 1958 when the British Government had carried out 21 thermonuclear explosions in the atmosphere, claimed

---

[171] *In re Lehman Brothers International (Europe) (in administration) and In re the Insolvency Act 1986* [2012] UKSC 6.
[172] It appears that the original lead judgment writer was Lord Walker.
[173] *In re Peacock* [2012] UKSC 5.
[174] See ibid, para 71.
[175] Ibid, para 43.
[176] *Sugar (Deceased) v British Broadcasting Corporation and Another* [2012] UKSC 4.
[177] *Flood v Times Newspapers Ltd* [2012] UKSC 11.
[178] *Ministry of Defence v AB & Others* [2012] UKSC 9.

subsequently to have been harmed by exposure to low level radiation. Establishing the causal link between exposure and the illnesses, which developed many years later, had been a major stumbling block for the veterans. However, in this case the key question was the rather different one, of whether the veterans had acted quickly enough following the emergence of knowledge and information which might have helped to establish causation, to defeat the three-year time limitation which runs in relation to all personal injury actions. Not surprisingly, the Supreme Court was split down the middle on this emotive topic. At the first conference those that favoured allowing the veterans' action to continue for a little longer (even though all were agreed they would ultimately fail on causation) seem to have been in a majority, although a bare majority of 4:3. Lord Phillips as President appears to have considered it was a judgment that he should do, and it looks very much as though that it was the first to be circulated, since most of the others respond to it. It certainly contains the fullest account of the factual background and runs to 71 paragraphs, easily the most substantial judgment in the case. It seems that Lord Wilson then wrote for the minority faction in dissent, objecting strongly to the 'heretical' concept that 'knowledge', for the purposes of the limitation acts, had not necessarily been established by the stage at which the claimants had commenced litigation. This trenchant analysis seems to have done the trick because after the dust had settled the case was now 4:3 against the veterans and Lord Wilson's judgment was the lead,[179] leaving the fuller account of the facts to Lord Phillips' judgment which only appears 90 paragraphs from the start of the case.

Several months later came the equally famous *Assange v Swedish Prosecution Authority*,[180] where the Wikileaks founder sought, unavailingly as it turned out, to defeat a European Arrest Warrant from Sweden. Although, as we saw earlier, Lord Dyson and his colleagues rejected four out of five of the arguments put forward by Lord Phillips in the lead judgment for dismissing Assange's case, they did accept the fifth argument, however peripheral Lord Phillips may have considered it. There is no reason to believe that the split in the court was ever anything different from the 5:2 that it proved to be at the date of judgment.

The following month came three extradition cases where young children were involved. The split in the Court is far from evident from the final judgments where only Lady Hale dissents in one of the cases *PH v Deputy Prosecutor of the Italian Republic, Genoa*.[181] One suspects that the split was rather closer at the first conference—possibly even in favour of the child—since there are signs that Lady Hale's judgment started out in the majority. The opposition probably featured Lords Judge and Wilson if the length and tenor of their judgments is anything to

---

[179] In situations such as this when the lead judgment ends up in the minority group, the decision as to which of the former minority group is to be the lead is likely to be a matter for negotiation with the presiding Justice.

[180] *Assange v Swedish Prosecution Authority* [2012] UKSC 22.

[181] *PH v Deputy Prosecutor of the Italian Republic, Genoa* [2012] UKSC 25.

go by. If so, they succeeded in persuading all but Lady Hale that the interests of young children in such situations, whilst important, were not sufficient to trump the public interest in extraditing parents back to Italy who had been accused of smuggling cannabis into that country.

The next close call was similarly opaque. It involved the majority of the Court changing their vote, with the result that the case appears as though it was a 5:0 decision. This was the *Oracle* case.[182] In a complex trademarks case it seems that the panel was split 3:2 at the first conference to dismiss the appeal. The lead judgment was assigned to one of the majority but the first judgment circulated was by one of the dissenters, Lord Sumption, who in some respects has begun to take on the mantle of Lord Hoffmann for his speed of thought and writing and the clarity of his vision. After a second conference it was agreed that Lord Sumption's judgment would be adjusted in two ways that dealt with the original majority's concerns, leaving it as the lead judgment, allowing the appeal, with the support of the whole Court.

With his promotion to Master of the Rolls, the summer of 2012 was Lord Dyson's swansong in the Supreme Court. True to form he went out leaving his mark, even if it is not apparent on the face of the decision. The case was *R (on the application of Alvi) v Secretary of State for the Home Department*.[183] Although it is clear that he won over several colleagues on a small point, it is not apparent that it was only after a struggle that he persuaded the whole Court to go with him in what appears as a unanimous 5:0 decision.

There is no evidence of any changes of heart in the 3:2 equal pay case of *Birmingham City Council v Abdulla*[184] or the joint tenancy case of *Solihull MBC v Hickin*,[185] although there is the curious irony in the latter of the two English Justices in dissent calling for Parliament to assimilate the tenancy laws in England with Scotland and Lord Hope for the majority seemingly unconcerned at the discrepancy between the two regimes in this area. *R v Waya*,[186] on the other hand, was a case with multiple switches throughout its long sojourn in the final court. A case involving a relatively minor mortgage fraud[187] coupled with a Proceeds of Crime Act confiscation order, it was originally heard before seven Justices in 2011. Since they could not agree on the outcome of the case, it was re-heard before

---

[182] *Oracle America Ltd v M-Tech Data Ltd* [2012] UKSC 27.

[183] *R (on the application of Alvi) v Secretary of State for the Home Department* [2012] UKSC 33.

[184] *Birmingham City Council v Abdulla* [2012] UKSC 47.

[185] *Solihull Metropolitan Borough Council v Hickin* [2012] UKSC 39.

[186] [2012] UKSC 51.

[187] The borrower seems to have given an over-inflated figure for his salary in the loan application. Since this was before the mortgage bubble burst it is possible that had he given his correct salary he would still have been given the mortgage, though perhaps not on such advantageous terms. The problem for the courts was what figure to set the confiscation order at. Was it the level of the mortgage? Was it the level of the flat at the outset? The loan was repaid on a re-mortgage deal two years later, but this time without any fraudulent element in the application. Was the confiscation order the increased value of the flat less the re-mortgage? Was it the value of the flat when Waya was arrested (2005), when he was convicted (2007), or when the confiscation order was made (2008)?

an expanded panel of nine in March 2012. After the first conference (really the second conference) the Justices were once again unable to produce a majority position. Lord Phillips suggested that they put their thoughts on paper and eventually a majority position emerged. Lord Reed, who had come in for the second hearing thought that the confiscation order should be set at zero. He laboured long and assiduously to produce his dissent and circulated it before the majority. When the latter came, their position had changed to take account of his dissent. Lord Reed then agreed on a joint judgment with Lord Phillips and withdrew the bulk of his dissent. In all it took 288 days from the second hearing to the final judgment. In part this was a product of the team-working of today's Supreme Court which eventually produced a conjoined majority and a conjoined minority judgment. However, if the same case had arisen in Bingham's time it might well have been a case where he approved of a single judgment in order to provide guidance to the lower courts.

Fittingly, the last close call in 2012 was *R (on the application of Gurja) v Crown Prosecution Service*[188] which revolved round the ability of the CPS to take over private prosecutions which they had not initiated and to abandon them because the CPS was of the opinion that the case has a less than 51 per cent chance of success. The case appears to have been finely balanced at the first conference however but by a 3:2 vote the majority, including the normally libertarian Lord Kerr, decided that this was acceptable, even though it would allow the CPS to get rid of prosecutions which for policy or evidential reasons they were reluctant to pursue. Not surprisingly, Lord Mance and Lady Hale were to be found united in dissent. Lord Neuberger confesses to have wavered on one point but not by the end.

2013 was to see its fair share of close calls, and in at least four of them there was a second conference. As we saw earlier, the *Lloyds Bank* case,[189] was a close call that wasn't since a 3:2 split at the first conference then became a 5:0 when the judgments were handed down. One of the most striking close calls in the year, however, was on the substantive issue in the *Bank Mellat* cases.[190] This was an Iranian bank which in the past had unwittingly had dealings with organisations which were linked to the nuclear proliferation programme in that country. The Treasury had taken action against the Bank without warning or consultation. Lord Sumption, writing the lead judgment for a majority of 8:1 at the first conference, ruled that the Treasury's action was not proportionate and should be struck down. Lord Reed, the dissenter, after a tour de force of exposition on the nature of proportionality, argued powerfully that the benefit of the doubt should be given to the interests of the country in resisting nuclear proliferation rather than the property rights of an Iranian bank which had had dealings (albeit unwittingly) with those involved with nuclear proliferation in that country. He won round the President, the Deputy President and the Master of the Rolls but couldn't quite win over the

---

[188]   *R (on the application of Gurja) v Crown Prosecution Service* [2012] UKSC 52.
[189]   *Lloyds TSB Foundation for Scotland v Lloyds Banking Group plc* [2013] UKSC 3.
[190]   *Bank Mellat v Her Majesty's Treasury (No 2)* [2013] UKSC 39.

other wavering Justice (Lord Carnwath).[191] The other major close call at the same time was *Smith v the Ministry of Defence*,[192] where the families of several servicemen who had died in IRAQ due to the alleged fault of the Ministry of Defence in failing to properly equip the troops, brought actions claiming breach of Article 2 of the ECHR (the right to life). The Court, by 4:3, allowed all three sets of claims to proceed to trial, but it is understood that despite the feelings aroused on each side of the case as to whether the decisions would make it harder for UK armed forces to operate abroad in the future, there were no changes of vote in this case.

CONCLUSION

This excursus strongly suggests that there is little to choose between the early years of the UK Supreme Court and the last decade of the House of Lords when it comes to changes of position. Vote changes occur and with some regularity. Whilst many are during the hearing stage when minds are more flexible, the particularly interesting ones are when the judgments are circulated. Although some Law Lords and Justices make up their minds relatively early in the hearing and are rarely shifted away from this, eg Lords Hoffmann, Steyn, Kerr and Wilson, others can remain remarkably flexible right up to very late in the circulation process. Lord Phillips was one such, which could at times test some of his less flexible colleagues. Lord Phillips was also a very imaginative lawyer who could see novel approaches to cases which did not occur to others on the panel. In this respect he rather resembled Lord Scott and the unsettling effect which he occasionally could have on his fellow Law Lords on the Bingham court. Nonetheless, it is submitted that a willingness on the part of the Justices to reconsider their decisions even at the stage of circulating judgments, after reflection and engagement between the Justices is healthy for the Court and for democracy,[193] especially when it occurs in a transparent manner.

That said, the degree of flexibility of thinking within both courts strongly suggests that explanations of decision-making in the final court will have to rely not only on values or social ideology but also on the social aspects of decision-making. Brice Dickson and others are right to point to the importance of the composition of the panel to hear any given case. However, this is not simply because of the outlook of the individual members of the panel but because of their approach to collective decision-making, to mutual persuasion, group interaction and tactical calculations. Lord Phillips refused to accept that in the appointments to the Supreme Court assessments of merit could be anything other than individual merit. Lord Bingham however, took 'merit' in the relevant section

---

[191] Ibid [133], [197] and [202]. Sir Humphrey would call *Mellat* a 'brave decision'.

[192] [2013] UKSC 41.

[193] As one Justice put it, 'I think this is what should happen because it is part of the whole collegiate approach of exchanging views and it seems to me a much more healthy way of doing things'.

of the Constitutional Reform Act as broad enough to include the needs of the court as a collective whole (including diversity). One distinctly new way of working which has emerged on the Supreme Court is to treat the panel as a team and to encourage team-working such as collaborative drafting of a single judgment (*Pinnock*)[194] or dividing up a judgment into different parts (*Société Général*)[195] or using trenchant dissents as a way of pushing the majority into adjusting their position, eg *Waya* and *Stack v Dowden*. There is also far more engagement with each other's arguments.[196] It is also clear that in a team context, task and social leadership are important skills. The question, to which we will return in the final chapter, is whether team working and group orientation should be harnessed as assiduously as it now is in the pursuit of single majority judgments in the 76 per cent of cases which are not split or close call cases.

---

[194] *Manchester City Council v Pinnock* [2010] UKSC 45, [2011] 2 AC 104.

[195] *Société Générale, London Branch v Geys* [2012] UKSC 63.

[196] 'I think the interlocking of the Supreme Court judgments, even when they are concurring judgments, is very important. It is terribly difficult for the profession to see what the points of agreement and disagreement are, unless there is a positive engagement with [each others' judgments].' Lord Wilson, interview with the author.

6

Wider Dialogues Old and New

THE DIALOGUE WITH THE COURT OF APPEAL

WHILST, AS WE have seen, the most significant dialogues in relation to judicial decision-making in the final court are those which take place between its judges, and between the judges and counsel, other dialogues do have an influence. One long-standing dialogue is that between the final court and the Court of Appeal. This is hardly surprising, since the overwhelming majority of Law Lords and Justices have been members of the Court of Appeal. They therefore know most of its members—certainly its senior ones—and have shared with them the intense experience of treadmill collegiality which is the hallmark of the contemporary Court of Appeal.[1]

Despite this, there appear to have been only two or three topics on which there have been major exchanges between the two courts in the last 20 years. They related leave to appeal, multiple judgments and the selection of Supreme Court Justices.

Leave to appeal was probably the most important in terms of long-term impact. As we saw in chapters two and three, 30 years ago 70 per cent of cases came to the House of Lords with leave from the court below. Today it is the other way round. Around 90 per cent get permission from the Supreme Court. This change came about because, it is thought, the leaders of the House persuaded the leaders of the Court of Appeal that they should only grant leave to appeal to the House in exceptional cases, since 'their Lordships preferred to dine à la carte'.[2] Although the role of the final court is not to deal with all cases where it considers that the Court of Appeal has gone astray, those that raise a point of public importance *and* are thought by the final court to be problematic in their reasoning or in their guidance to lower courts are more likely to be reviewed. Whether permission to appeal is granted or not, the Supreme Court's decision sends a message to the Court of Appeal, even if it is no more subtle than that the final court thinks there may be a problem with aspects of the lower court's decision.[3] Equally, on the rare occasions

---

[1] See P Darbyshire, *Sitting in Judgment* (Oxford, Hart Publishing, 2011) ch 14.

[2] This aphorism is usually attributed to Lord Bingham, and it certainly featured in our interview in 2009.

[3] Since only 50% of appeals are successful, by granting permission to appeal the final court is not necessarily indicating that it thinks that the lower court decision should be reversed.

when the Court of Appeal itself now grants leave to appeal, it is sending a clear message to the final court that the matter is one that needs their urgent attention. Despite this there is no evidence that the final court is more likely to uphold such appeals than those in which permission is granted by the final court itself. However, the fact that the judgment(s) of the Court of Appeal will appear in the documentation supporting the permission to appeal application can encourage dissenters in that court to engage in a dramatic dialogue with the final court,

> [One course] is to write your own judgment in effect as a dissent which is intended to influence the House of Lords and I did that in one case recently where I found myself dissenting. I felt very strongly about the case and when we came to grant leave to appeal (we don't basically, that's a big changing practice over the years), I said 'well, I agree that leave to appeal should be refused', because it was primarily for their Lordships House to decide which cases they take, 'but I hope they will take this case, such is the injustice of the majority decision that if it is the law it ought to be decided by the highest court'. (A Lord Justice)[4]

Another Lord Justice noted that where the Court of Appeal is split, its members may engage in a dialogue with the final court and with the Court of Appeal at the same time,

> You are writing for superior courts, in other words you are writing defensively to a certain extent to armour plate yourself against appeal. You may also be writing in answer to other members of your own court who disagree with you, so that's both a question and defence.

The second topic, of multiple judgments, stems from the Court of Appeal's desire—repeated on a number of occasions—for clearer guidance from the final appeal court. Matters came to a head in the *Doherty*[5] case, where Lord Justice Carnwath, ironically in a concurring judgment, chided the House of Lords in *Kay*[6] for giving multiple opinions with no clear majority *ratio*. As he subsequently put it, he had spent a weekend wrestling with a piece of self-assembly furniture—until he realised that IKEA had given him the wrong instructions leaflet. The problem with the House of Lords was that they had given him six different sets of instructions for the same case. His exasperation can be heard in the postscript to his concurrence,[7]

> Was it necessary for the opinions of the House to have come to us in the form of six substantive speeches, which we have had to subject to laborious comparative analysis to arrive at a conclusion? Could not a single majority speech have provided clear and straightforward guidance, which we could then have applied directly to the case before

---

[4] Interview with the author, 2008. Counsel made sure that the terms of the dissent were prominent in the leave to appeal petition, and leave was granted by the Appeal Committee of the House.

[5] *Doherty v Birmingham City Council* [2006] EWCA Civ 1739.

[6] *Kay v Lambeth London Borough Council* [2006] UKHL 10.

[7] *Doherty v Birmingham City Council* [2006] EWCA Civ 1739 at para 63.

us? Although we would not normally think it appropriate to comment on the working practices of a higher court, this case seems to us exceptional.

Yet, ironically, as we saw in chapter four, the majority Law Lords in the *Kay* case, led by Lord Hope, had met three times to try to settle on their *ratio* and they had agreed a joint paragraph.[8] When *Doherty* came to the House,[9] Lord Hope, now in the chair, paid heed to Carnwath's *crie de coeur* and convened several meetings to improve on the wording of the *Kay* decision without success, the more they met the worse it got.[10] Interestingly, the House did not respond openly to Carnwath's comments and in the months that followed several of his colleagues in the Court of Appeal, including the Master of the Rolls, endorsed his critical remarks.

The issue resurfaced in the judgments of the Court of Appeal in *Secretary of State for the Home Department v AF and others*.[11] Neither the majority (the Master of the Rolls and Waller LJ) nor the minority (Sedley LJ) were happy with the lack of clarity afforded them by the multiple judgments given by Law Lords in *Secretary of State for the Home Department v MB and AF*.[12] The majority expressed elliptical bemusement, 'While we have tried to interpret the views of the majority in *MB and AF*, there is undoubtedly scope for argument on the question whether our interpretation is correct',[13] before granting leave to appeal to the House without being asked to do so. Lord Justice Sedley's trenchant dissent starkly points to the impasse inherent in the *SSHD v MB and AF* case and the failure of the Law Lords to provide clear guidance to the lower courts,

> To suggest that the highest court of this country has by two concurring opinions, neither of which purports to do so, given the force of law to what is clearly a third member's aside is to go beyond even divination. Unless and until the new Supreme Court changes the mode of giving judgment, lower courts and lawyers ought in my respectful view to be able to assume that when their Lordships, or a majority of them, intend to make new law, they say so.

On this occasion the pleas of the lower court were listened to, if only because of an intervening decision of Strasbourg's Grand Chamber, although Lord Phillips as presiding Law Lord referred to Lord Brown's opinion in *SSHD v MB and AF* as being thought by some to be even more 'enigmatic' than Baroness Hale's.[14] Lady Hale, although not Lord Brown, accepted that the 'enigmatic' epithet had some justification, in her opinion in the *AF* case.[15]

---

[8] [2006] UKHL 10, para 110.

[9] *Doherty v Birmingham City Council* [2008] UKHL 57.

[10] The gap between the hearing and judgment in *Doherty* was 138 days (twice the normal average at that time) even though the case was unanimous as to the outcome. For the aftermath to *Doherty* see 'The Dialogue with Strasbourg' later in this chapter.

[11] *Secretary of State for the Home Department v AF and others* [2008] EWCA Civ 1148.

[12] *Secretary of State for the Home Department v MB and AF* [2007] UKHL 46.

[13] [2008] EWCA Civ 1148, para 103.

[14] *Secretary of State for the Home Department v AF* [2009] UKHL 28, para 18.

[15] [2009] UKHL 28, para 100.

As we saw in chapter three the Court of Appeal's campaign for fewer multiple judgments from the final court is now paying off with 55 per cent of cases in the first half of 2013 being single majority judgments. Irrespective of the merits of this development—it is a testament to the fact that the final court can be receptive to the concerns of the Court of Appeal. However, one factor which partly accounts for the outcome of the dialogue is that over the last four years 11 Supreme Court Justices have been appointed, eight of whom have come from the Court of Appeal (including Lord Carnwath and the former Master of the Rolls, Lord Clarke). Those who supported multiple judgments who transferred from the House of Lords have gradually retired, leaving the viewpoint from the Court of Appeal in the ascendancy.

The third dialogue related to a narrower, but related topic: appointment to the Supreme Court. The initial proposal that Jonathan Sumption QC should be appointed to the Supreme Court direct from the Bar provoked a backlash from the Court of Appeal. There, voices were raised against the prospect of direct appointments to the final court on the grounds that it would discourage good applicants from working their way through the High Court and the Court of Appeal. It may be that their unhappiness had a temporary impact but shortly thereafter the appointment panel, rightly, concluded that the statutory criteria for the appointment to the Supreme Court very clearly envisage that outstanding candidates can be appointed directly from the Bar, and Lord Sumption was duly appointed.

However, in relation to individual cases the dialogue between the courts has been less fruitful than might have been anticipated. Partly the problem stems from the geographical separation of the two courts. Members of the Court of Appeal will lunch and dine at their Inns on a regular basis. However members of the final court lack the time to travel to the Inns for lunch and only some of them are active members of their Inns in the evenings.[16]

Partly again the problem is the conventions on discourse that are adhered to by members of both courts, which inhibit any serious discussion of a case that is moving from the Court of Appeal to the final court until the outcome of that case in the final court. Now that almost all of the appeals which emanate from the Court of Appeal go by the leave of the final court rather than the Court of Appeal, Lord Justices may not know that a case of theirs is going to be heard by the final

---

[16] As against this, Lord Neuberger and to a lesser extent Hoffmann, would go to work in the Court of Appeal even after they were in the final court, and Lords Neuberger and Judge sat in the final court from time to time in especially important cases. Lord Hoffmann was caught out in 2008 when the most interesting patent case for years to come before the Court of Appeal appeared and Lord Hoffmann calculated that by the time it got to the House he would be retired, so he stepped down to sit on the panel in the Court of Appeal. However the credit crunch meant that the Law Lords unexpectedly caught up with their backlog before they transferred to the Supreme Court and Lord Hoffmann was still in Lords when the appeal came to House. Of course, he could not sit. However, the deference by his colleagues to his judgment in the court below was almost sycophantic. One wonders why the appellant thought it was worth the effort.

court. Even if they do, there is a natural reluctance on the part of a Lord Justice to raise a current case in conversation for fear of appearing to lobby or to self-justify. Instead, all that occurs is a jokey reference to 'you made a meal of that one' and other exchanges in a similar vein. Generally, therefore, with a few exceptions as we have seen, the oral dialogue with the Court of Appeal is a rather stilted one, with little value as a feedback mechanism. That said, the written dialogue between the courts is an everyday occurrence with the Court of Appeal judgments appearing prominently in the authorities bundles read by the final court and frequently referred to in counsel's arguments oral and written. A scrutiny of the judicial notebooks of Lords Reid and Bingham reveals that although frequently cited by counsel, the Court of Appeal judgments are not that frequently mentioned expressly in the first conference by the judges. On the other hand, references to the Court of Appeal judgments are commonplace in the final court judgments and often they are relatively complimentary.

In sum, whilst the oral dialogue between the Court of Appeal and the final court has probably declined in the last 40 years, the written dialogue has remained as important now as it was then.

THE DIALOGUE WITH ACADEMICS

The other long-standing dialogue is that with academe. Forty years ago relatively few academics had the opportunity to interact regularly with the Law Lords. Mainly dons at Oxbridge, with perhaps a few in London. Most of the Law Lords did not read even the prestige law journals in any depth or with any great frequency. Nor did they write their opinions in cases with academics in mind.[17] Moreover academic criticism of the House tended to be fairly muted.[18] It seems that the general editor of the *Modern Law Review* in 1950 was summoned by the Law Lords and solemnly reproved for publishing an article by Professor Gower that included a criticism of the judicial attitude towards academics.[19] But whatever may have been the case 20 years before, the Law Lords in 1972 were not particularly sensitive to, or likely to be influenced by, academic comment. One

---

[17] See A Paterson, *The Law Lords* (London, Macmillan, 1982) 10.

[18] When he was editor of the *Law Quarterly Review*, Professor Goodhart is reputed to have had a policy of preventing stringent comment on the performances of the Law Lords on the grounds that it would offend the Law Lords, most of whom he thought (erroneously) regularly read the journal. Intriguingly, Francis Reynolds, his successor in 1990, at a time when more of the Law Lords *did* read the *LQR*, is said to have operated a similar policy to Goodhart. Thus, when sent an article on the public law philosophy of Law Lords, Reynolds is understood to have submitted it to several Law Lords to see that it met with their approval, rather than jeopardise their willingness to read the Review by publishing something of which they did not approve. The article was published as D Feldman, 'Public Law Values in the House of Lords' (1990) 106 *LQR* 246–76.

[19] See LCB Gower, 'Looking Back' (1978) 14 *Journal of the Society of Public Teachers of Law* 155. The comment in question appears in Gower, 'English Legal Training' (1950) 13 *Modern Law Review* 137, 198.

Law Lord of that era indicated that he very seldom found the law journals of any assistance in their comments or criticism because they were not critical enough. He went on,

> I'd much sooner have a more detailed criticism than what one gets—the sort of notes which are couched in very respectful language, are not particularly helpful, to us at any rate. I would much sooner have a more robust thing of much greater length.

The Law Lords were soon to have their wish granted, as their sustained run of unhappy decisions continued in the criminal law field. *R v Caldwell*[20] was assailed by the leading scholars of the day, Professors JC Smith[21] and Glanville Williams and by various judges. Although it survived when challenged by an appeal to the House in *R v Reid*[22] 10 years on the House was persuaded, in *R v G*,[23] in part by the 'reasoned and outspoken criticism by the leading scholars of the day',[24] to overrule *Caldwell*.

The academics did not have to be so patient in *R v Shivpuri*.[25] The printers' ink was barely dry on the judgment of the House in *Anderton v Ryan*[26] (on that fertile topic of the impossibility of attempts—is trying to kill a dead person a crime?) when it was being challenged in *Shivpuri*. Shortly after the hearing in that case Professor Glanville Williams published a critique[27] which was undoubtedly robust. He began,

> [T]he tale I have to tell is unflattering of the higher judiciary. It is an account of how the judges invented a rule based upon conceptual misunderstanding; of their determination to use the English language so strangely that they spoke what by normal criteria would be termed untruths; of their invincible ignorance of the mess they had made of the law; and of their immobility on the subject, carried to the extent of subverting an Act of Parliament designed to put them straight.

In the 50-page article that follows he accuses the House of producing its two worst decisions on a point of law in the twentieth century, of juvenile errors of logic, institutional obduracy, ignoring and discriminating against the Law Commission, acting in an idiosyncratic and autocratic way, and verging on incompetence. Astonishingly, not only did Lord Bridge in *Shivpuri* read the article, he acted on it and used it to justify overruling *Anderton* rather than distinguishing it,[28] and persuaded his colleagues to follow him in this regard, despite the 'lack of moderation' in the article's language.

---

[20] *R v Caldwell* [1982] AC 341.
[21] '[A] withering contemporary criticism', as Lord Steyn described it in para 47 of *R v G* [2003] UKHL 50.
[22] *R v Reid* [1992] 1 WLR 793.
[23] *R v G* [2003] UKHL 50.
[24] Lord Bingham, ibid, at para 34.
[25] *R v Shivpuri* [1986] UKHL 2, [1987] AC 1.
[26] *Anderton v Ryan* [1985] UKHL 5, [1985] AC 560.
[27] Glanville Williams, 'The Lords and Impossible Attempts, or Quis Custodiet Ipsos Custodes?' (1986) 45 *CLJ* 33.
[28] As Glanville Williams predicts (in the article) would be the outcome of *Shivpuri*.

Glanville Williams and John Smith undoubtedly knew some of the Law Lords personally, and scholars in other fields such as William Wade and Stanley de Smith, Roy Goode, Guenter Treitel, Tony Weir, Francis Reynolds and the redoubtable Peter Birks, did as well. However, the overwhelming majority of the hundreds of other legal scholars that now existed around the country in the 1980s and 1990s, did not know them, other than the occasional chance meeting at a law school moot, a learned society conference or a lecture. Their hopes of engaging in a dialogue with the final court as opposed to a misfiring monologue rested with getting a case note into one of the key journals and hoping it might be noticed.[29] As Braun argues, in the UK as opposed to much of continental Europe, academe is not a community with which the final court engages collectively. True, Law Lords of that time, as now, frequently spoke at the Society of Public Teachers of Law (now Society of Legal Scholars) annual conference, attended the annual President's Reception, or Oxford Law Faculty dinners, yet their exposure was and is only to a relatively few individuals at these events. Further, the Law Lords of 40 years ago and the Justices of the last few years whilst they might occasionally refer to the weight of academic opinion, far more often engage(d) with individual academics whom they knew than those they did not. That said the circle of academic acquaintances of today's Justice is likely to be broader than 40 years ago. Then as now the Oxbridge influence remains, but new networks have emerged. Three of the current Court[30] worked at the Law Commission—an environment which exposed them to multiple academic contacts. An increasing number of senior judges today have been academics earlier in their careers[31] and retain links with former academic colleagues. Finally, although little discussed, a handful of academic scholars and counsel in the last fifteen years have joined with Law Lords, Lord Justices and now Justices on week-long conferences with senior judges (and the occasional practitioner and academic) from Canada, Germany, Israel, and South Africa (both at home and away) to discuss comparative developments in the law.[32] Such visits can cement very strong links between academics and members of the final court.

For the vast majority of academics today, however, as twenty years ago, any suggestion of dialogue has to come from writing in learned journals and hoping that the Justices will read them, either because counsel cite them, or the Justices (with or without the help of their judicial assistants) find them of their own accord.

---

[29] In this they were hampered by the approach of the Case Notes Editor of the *Modern Law Review* in the 1990s whose policy was not to publish case notes after the Court of Appeal decision but only after that in the House of Lords when it was too late to influence the Court. See N Duxbury, *Jurists and Judges: An Essay on Influence* (Oxford, Hart Publishing, 2001) at 107, fn 222.

[30] Lady Hale, Lord Carnwath and Lord Toulson.

[31] Eg Lord Goff, Baroness Hale, Lord Collins, Lord Rodger, Kay LJ, Buxton LJ, Elias LJ, Hooper LJ, Beatson LJ, Cranston J and Singh J.

[32] This can include papers on topics which are likely to come before the courts, as well as universal topics such as terrorism and human rights, judicial independence and politics, and the separation of powers.

At least the House and now the Supreme Court have long since abandoned the old rule that a work of a living author could not be cited in the final court because he was not an authority.[33] Indeed, the influence exercised by an academic article on the Law Lords' decision in *Oppenheimer v Cattermole* in 1973 would make many a continental academic writer envious. The article[34] led not only to two re-hearings before the House and a referral back to the Commissioners of Taxation but also to a majority of the House deciding the appeal contrary to the way they would have done had the article not come to their attention. The changed attitude of the House to academic writings was epitomised by Lord Diplock in a tribute to AL Goodhart,

> In contrast to the judicial attitude in my early days at the Bar, judges no longer think that the sources of judicial wisdom are confined to judgments in decided cases and, exceptionally, some pronouncement of the illustrious dead. In appellate courts, at any rate, when confronted with a doubtful point of law we want to know what living academic jurists have said about it , and we consider that counsel have not done their homework unless they come equipped to tell us about it.[35]

Johan Steyn agreed:[36] 'It became a much more open place. Much more attention has been paid to academic literature generally in the House of Lords in recent years'. Similarly, in a lecture in 2005 Lord Hope confirmed that 'references to academic literature are far more common than they used to be ... Appellate judges are particularly conscious of the good work that has been by academic lawyers to reveal weaknesses in the existing law and to explore new territory'.[37]

Certainly the Bar gradually learned to cite relevant legal scholarship in its written materials provided before appeals in the final court, and even to draw on them from time to time in their oral arguments. However, simply dumping a mass of undigested academic writings on the judges was not well received. As one senior QC recalled,

> [I remember a case] with a mass of materials and my opponents who were the Appellants said we've got five bound volumes of academic commentaries (this was just towards the end of July) and I remember Lord Rodger saying 'Well what are we supposed to do, take it on holiday with us and read it on the beach? What are you saying about it?' And of course they had just put it in and they hadn't distilled it.

---

[33] As Lord Reid observed, 'In the House of Lords ... we turn a blind eye to the old rule that an academic writer is not an authority until he is dead, because then he can no longer change his mind'. See Reid, 'The Judge as Law Maker' (1972) 12 *Journal of the Society of Public Teachers of Law* 22. For a discussion of the application of this rule 40 years ago in the House, see *The Law Lords* (London, Macmillan, 1982) at 17. For a more recent discussion of the 'rule' see J Beatson, 'Legal Academics: Forgotten Players or Interlopers?' ch 40 in A Burrows, D Johnston and R Zimmermann (eds), *Judge and Jurist: Essays in Memory of Lord Rodger of Earlsferry* (Oxford, Oxford University Press, 2013).

[34] FA Mann, 'The Present Validity of Nazi Nationality Laws' (1973) 89 *LQR* 194. For its influence, see *Oppenheimer v Cattermole* [1976] AC 249, 268.

[35] Lord Diplock, 'A.L.G.: A Judge's View' (1975) 91 *LQR* 457, 459.

[36] Interview with the author, 2009.

[37] Lord Hope of Craighead, 'Writing Judgments' Annual Lecture 2005, (London, Judicial Studies Board, 2005).

When counsel fail to refer to relevant academic writings, and the Justices are aware of the literature, they will note the omission and may even mention it in their judgments as they did in *Jones v Kernott*.[38] That case was taken to the Supreme Court in part because of the considerable amounts of criticism—including academic criticism—which had been aimed at *Stack v Dowden*.[39] Despite this, counsel made no reference to the academic literature. The Justices did. As Lord Walker and Lady Hale observed in their consolidated judgment,[40]

> The decision in *Stack v Dowden* has also attracted a good deal of comment from legal scholars, which we have read although it was not referred to by counsel (who took a sensibly economical approach to the presentation of the appeal).

Whether this reference was sufficient to placate the disgruntled academics who had written on the issue or the Court of Appeal who had, unusually, granted leave to appeal must be doubted. There is a considerable difference between presenting the critical observations of an academic to the whole Court in open forum, which forces all of them to engage with the argument—even those not expert in the field—and one or two specialist Justices reading the same remarks on their own. Lord Diplock might not have approved.

Jones v Kernott reveals the gatekeeper role that counsel perform in the Supreme Court with respect to the citation of relevant academic literature, and that the Justices can get round this, even if not necessarily entirely satisfactorily. However, the dialogue between academics and counsel is, if anything, even more remote than that between academics and Justices. Most counsel do not consult academics before arguing an appeal in the final court unless they are in one of several high-profile chambers where academic lawyers have become part-time tenants. True a few elite professors do make the ranks of Honorary Benchers but these aside, encounters between academics and senior counsel may be even less frequent than with the senior judiciary.

If one was to go by the recent comments of the Chief Justice of the US Supreme Court,[41] we would conclude that law review articles are not of value to the bench because their focus is so far removed from the issues that trouble the courts.[42] Yet recent empirical research has shown that over the last 50 years the US Supreme Court used scholarship in 32 per cent of its decisions at an average of one article per decision and that Roberts CJ uses legal scholarship in 23 per cent of the opinions he writes. Moreover the research found that statistically the Court disproportionately uses scholarship when 'cases are either more important or more

---

[38] *Jones v Kernott* [2011] UKSC 53. For earlier cases containing critiques to counsel for omitting to refer to academic writings see those cited by Duxbury, *Jurists and Judges* (above, n 29) at 106.

[39] *Stack v Dowden* [2007] 2 AC 432.

[40] [2011] UKSC 53, para 2.

[41] Roberts CJ.

[42] L Petherbridge and DL Schwartz, 'An Empirical Assessment of the Supreme Court's Use of Legal Scholarship' (2012) 106 *Northwestern University Law Review* 995.

difficult to decide', eg where the Court is sharply divided, a precedent is being departed from, or a law is being held unconstitutional.[43]

In the UK's final court the comments from the judiciary are much more positive about the significance of academic writing for decision-making in that court. But what of the practice? The summaries of counsel's arguments which appear in Appeal Cases reveal that references to academic literature is far more common now than it was 40 years ago. As in the US this seems particularly true in close call cases where the Court is sharply divided.

Such developments are not enough to guarantee a successful dialogue between the academic author and the senior judiciary. The issue is not that the judges will not read such references—almost all of them will today. Rather, it turns on the purpose for which the citation is used. As Keith Stanton's stimulating essay[44] shows, citation of academic literature may serve several functions in the judgments of the final court, eg to provide the historical background to the field, to provide a convenient summary of the basic law in a field, to state the law authoritatively, and to provide suggestions as to what the law ought to be. Only the last two could really claim to be part of a dialogue which influences judicial decision-making, or as some have put it (eg Lords Reid[45] and Goff[46] and Peter Birks),[47] part of a partnership in law-making between the academics and the final court.[48] As Lord Hope reflected, thoughtfully,

> [Sometimes] you are dealing with a very interesting area of law which is largely the product of research by academics which comes before us and you're then having to choose [whether] to move it on, often with academic stimulus behind you. It may be uncharted territory, on the other hand if you don't do that the law's not going to develop and so it requires a certain amount of courage as to whether you're prepared to do that. Unless you do it the law is not going to move on and academics I feel sometimes need the support of the judges who are prepared to speak out a bit and nudge the thing on so that they can feel the law is open to discussion instead of just being sterile.

Stanton shows, there have been numerous examples of the Law Lords in the Bingham era referring to academic literature in their judgments but mostly they have related to the first two functions rather than the last two.[49] There have, of

---

[43] Ibid.

[44] K Stanton, 'Use of Scholarship by the House of Lords in Tort cases' ch 10 in J Lee (ed), *From House of Lords to Supreme Court* (Oxford, Hart Publishing, 2011).

[45] See Lord Reid, 'The Judge as Lawmaker' (1972) 12 *Journal of the Society of Public Teachers of Law* 22.

[46] See his comments in *Spiliada Maritime Corp v Cansulex Ltd* [1987] AC 460, 488 '[J]urists are pilgrims with us on the endless road to unattainable perfection; and we have it on the excellent authority of Geoffrey Chaucer that conversations among pilgrims can be most rewarding'.

[47] P Birks, 'The academic and the practitioner' (1998) 18 *Legal Studies* 397.

[48] See also A Braun, 'Judges and Academics: Feature of a Partnership' ch 11 in J Lee (ed), *From House of Lords to Supreme Court* (Oxford, Hart Publishing, 2011).

[49] In keeping with this, a scrutiny of the judicial notebooks of Lord Reid and Lord Bingham did not reveal many occasions when the arguments of academics were referred to in the first conference between the Law Lords at the end of the hearing.

course been modern instances of the last two functions, eg the impact of Newark's 'The Boundaries of Nuisance'[50] on nuisance cases in the House, the use of Hart and Honoré's work on causation[51] to influence the famous series of causation cases in the Lords and the Supreme Court,[52] and the impact of Goff and Jones and Peter Birks on the development of the law of unjust enrichment through decisions of the House of Lords and the Supreme Court[53]—often by Law Lords and Justices known to the authors, eg Lord Goff and Lord Millett.[54]

Nevertheless, such clear cut instances of the influence of the jurist, like those of Glanville Williams and JC Smith that we discussed earlier, remain isolated examples. As Duxbury argued over a decade ago, more often the influence of academic writings is nuanced and gradual.[55] Citation is not the same as influence. The judge may not agree with the academic writings or may find that they add little to the existing authorities. Thus, against the success of the academics in *R v G*[56] and *R v Shivpuri*,[57] we could just as easily have looked at the extensive academic writings cited to the House in the cases of *Knuller v DPP*,[58] *R v Hyam*,[59] and *DPP v Majewski*,[60] in each of which the House was being asked to depart from one of its earlier decisions. In each the critical comments of the academics were acknowledged by the Law Lords and in each politely dismissed. Sometimes citation is merely a useful form of background support for a decision which the judge has come to on other grounds. Sometimes it is the polite genuflection of the modern judge paying belated tribute to an education long past, or to demonstrate, as Lord Rodger put it, that he too 'has got the academic tee-shirt'.[61] Yet sometimes also it is a testament to a relationship with an academic, usually at Oxbridge or London to whom the Justice has turned for advice.[62]

---

[50] FH Newark, 'The Boundaries of Nuisance' (1949) 65 *LQR* 480.

[51] Hart and Honoré, *Causation in the Law*, 2nd edn (Oxford, Clarendon Press, 1985). See, K Stanton, 'Use of Scholarship by the House of Lords in Tort Cases' in J Lee (ed), *From House of Lords to Supreme Court* (Oxford, Hart Publishing, 2011) at 221.

[52] Dealt with in chapters 4 and 5 of this volume above.

[53] See eg *Benedetti v Sawiris and others* [2013] UKSC 50 where Lord Clarke in the lead judgment indicates that the case has involved a 'wide ranging discussion of the principles relevant to an aspect of unjust enrichment which has been the subject of lively debate among academics.' The three main judgments in the case are littered with references to the leading academic writers on unjust enrichment.

[54] On the influence of unjust enrichment scholars see G Virgo, 'The Law of Unjust Enrichment in the House of Lords: Judging the Judges' ch 9 in J Lee (ed), *From House of Lords to Supreme Court* (Oxford, Hart Publishing, 2011). For other instances of influential writings by academics which were aimed at the final Court of Appeal see J Beatson, 'Legal Academics' above n 33 at 534.

[55] *Jurists and Judges* (above, n 29) at 22.

[56] *R v G* [2003] UKHL 50.

[57] *R v Shivpuri* [1986] UKHL 2, [1987] AC 1.

[58] *Knuller v Director of Public Prosecutions* [1973] AC 435.

[59] *R v Hyam* [1975] AC 55.

[60] *Director of Public Prosecutions v Majewski* [1977] AC 443.

[61] Lord Rodger, 'The Form and Language of Judicial Opinions' (2002) 118 *LQR* 226 at 237.

[62] *Jurists and Judges* (above n 29) at 105 fn 213.

My interviews with members of the final court did not suggest that this was an everyday event. Most Law Lords and Justices consider(ed) it improper or unwise to seek such advice. As one former Law Lord remarked,

> Not talked to, but obviously welcomed and read many times articles. I have on a number of occasions spoken to a number of academics and said the time we want you to write please is before we've written, not afterwards. No, I have always felt some inhibition about doing that because I think that that's really rather like consulting with somebody else without counsel knowing. I felt really inhibited about doing that.

Even those who did it were somewhat circumspect. Lord Steyn was one, 'I would have felt free during a House of Lords case to ask an academic for material and I have frequently done that, but I would not have asked him for his opinion about the case'.[63]

Nevertheless, by the Bingham era and even more so in the Supreme Court, most Law Lords and Justices skimmed journals which regularly feature cases either going to or that have been to the final court of appeal, such as the *Law Quarterly Review, Cambridge Law Journal* or *Public Law*, when they could get their hands on them. Most of them also, when asked whom they wrote their judgments for, would mention academics along with other audiences, although some academics and some journals (notably the *Law Quarterly Review*) were particularly favoured. However, Lord Millett was probably alone in seeing academia as his primary audience:[64]

> In a way it would be the academics, I was probably more of an academic lawyer than most of my colleagues. I certainly had in mind not just my colleagues and obviously the profession and the future if you like … but in a way it was the academics I wanted. Especially in my own, or the subject I had made my own, because it wasn't originally restitution. I kept very much abreast of the academic work on the subject and where there was a division of view between say Peter Birks and Andrew Burrows, for example, I had to make up my mind which to back and which was right. I tried to work out a coherent scheme for myself, and then I plugged it.

Nevertheless, the friendships between Professor Peter Birks of Oxford University and Lord Rodger, Lord Goff and Lord Millett were very real and discussion of on-going cases was not off limits. As Lord Millett jokingly complained to Peter Birks, 'Peter, you keep changing your mind … you say something and you persuade me completely, I adopt it in a judgment, then you change your mind and you leave me stranded'.[65] Moreover, strong Oxford connections with Andrew Burrows and others continued even after Peter's untimely death. Indeed Lords Bingham, Brown, Mance, Reed and Rodger have all held senior positions in the governance of Oxford University or its colleges. Understandably, judges in the final court have

---

[63] Interview with the author, 2009. Lord Reed told me he had on occasion discussed the principles applicable to a case with an academic without revealing the details of the case.

[64] Interview with the author, 2009.

[65] Interview with the author, 2009.

generally found some academics' writing more influential than others and it tends to be that of those whom they know.

At its best the relationship between judge and jurist in the final appeal court can in certain cases resemble a partnership in law-making, even though the judges are inevitably the senior partners. This has led some academics of a more optimistic outlook to express the hope that the passing of the enabling legislation in the Crime and Courts Act 2013[66] will bring about the creation of part-time positions in the UK Supreme Court for which leading academics might apply. We may be sure that such a development would be even less well received in the Court of Appeal than direct appointments from the Bar. It would certainly strengthen the links with academe. For the present, however, it would seem that while the dialogue between jurist and judge on the final court has deepened in the last 40 years, its contribution to judicial decision-making still generally falls below that of the dialogues between counsel and judges and between the judges themselves, which we discussed in chapters two–five above.[67]

DIALOGUES WITH COURTS OVERSEAS

One of the strategic objectives of the UK Supreme Court is to develop appropriate relationships with courts in Europe, throughout the Commonwealth and in other countries, especially those which share the Court's common law heritage. This was not a radical departure from the House of Lords, whose members had been taking part in judicial exchanges for many years. In addition to links to other Commonwealth courts through the Commonwealth Magistrates' and Judges' Association and links with the Australian High Court and the Canadian Supreme Court, the Law Lords had been sending one of their number for a month a year to sit on the Hong Kong Final Court of Appeal since the time of that jurisdiction's handing back to China. In Europe there were formal links with the European Court of Justice (ECJ) in Luxembourg and the European Court of Human Rights (ECtHR) in Strasbourg. A number of individual Law Lords also had personal links with judges in Europe eg Lords Goff, Slynn, Hoffmann,[68] Bingham and Mance.

Nevertheless, the establishment of the UK Supreme Court has certainly acted as a catalyst for a steady stream of overseas judicial visitors as its Annual Reports attest. As far as common law countries are concerned the most frequent visitors have been from the Australian High Court and to a lesser extent the South African Constitutional Court. The regular, usually triennial, judicial exchange programme[69]—now scaled back on resource grounds, has included Canada,

---

[66] Schedule 13 Part 1 2.(2)(b).

[67] Duxbury in *Jurists and Judges* (above, n 29) at 115 is of the opinion that the dialogue between jurist and judge in England and Wales is no more significant than that between jurist and judge in most of continental Europe and the USA.

[68] Lord Hoffmann exchanged patent judgments with the German federal patent court.

[69] Involving Supreme Court Justices, academics and other senior judges.

Israel, Germany and South Africa. Thus, a delegation from Israel visited the Supreme Court in 2010, with a reciprocal visit in 2013 and there was a high-level Indian judicial delegation led by the Chief Justice in 2012. Lord Walker sat for a month in Hong Kong in most years 2009–13 and Lord Clarke went in 2013. Unconnected with this, there was a major visit by four Supreme Court Justices to China in 2011. Judicial contact with the US Supreme Court has been rather limited. Only Baroness Hale goes there relatively regularly and Justice Ginsberg is the only US Supreme Court Justice to visit the UK Supreme Court since 2009. However, the judicial assistants visit the US Supreme Court each year and the Temple Bar scholars contain several law clerks from the US Supreme Court who visit the UK Supreme Court for a week serving as visiting judicial assistants during that period.

With respect to Europe there are networks of European Supreme Court judges and Presidents of European Supreme Courts, which have led to a number of visits to the Court. Moreover, the formal links with the ECJ and the ECtHR remain, with annual meetings of members of each court—and with annual visits to meetings between members of the courts. In addition in 2012, Lord Hope led a delegation of Supreme Court Justices on a three-day visit to the German Constitutional Court.

The UK Supreme Court has therefore been involved in a very wide range of judicial dialogues in its first four years. Not all of them, however, are likely to have had much of an impact on the judicial decision-making role. Of the common law countries the links with the Australian High Court remain strong and references to Canadian Charter decisions of their Supreme Court appear regularly in UK Human Rights cases. The links with the US Supreme Court, as befits two institutions divided by a common legal language and culture, are enduring but sometimes less deep than might be expected.[70] When Lord Collins was sitting in the Supreme Court he noted how rarely counsel chose to refer to US authorities. Again, in debates surrounding judicial appointment and Senate confirmation hearings, UK judicial awareness tends to be limited to the high-profile hearings in 1987 (Bork) and 1991 (Thomas) rather than anything more recent.

The Dialogue with Strasbourg

Of the dialogues with European courts much the most influential is that with the European Court of Human Rights. It should be stressed, however, that in this book the dialogue with Strasbourg does not have the technical meaning used by

---

[70] It may only be coincidental but whilst there has been no formal meeting of the UK and US Supreme Courts between 2009 and 2013, the US Supreme Court had its first formal meeting with the Strasbourg Court at Washington on 1 March 2012. See C McCrudden: ukconstitutionallaw. org/2012/03/12/christopher-mccrudden-comparing-the-european-court-of-human-rights-and-the-united-states-supreme-court/.

constitutional scholars when discussing the relationship between the two courts,[71] but the wider sense of dialogue used throughout this work. Clearly the framework is the European Convention on Human Rights itself and the Human Rights Act 1998 (HRA) and the Scotland Act 1998 (which implemented the European Convention in Scotland—with a few differences). However, since the Convention is a living instrument and the conception of what the Convention requires is an evolving one, it was inevitable that the final court in the UK would have to engage with Strasbourg as to the issue of precedent and the authoritative interpretation of the Convention.

Fifty years ago the House of Lords was the unquestioned final court of appeal for the UK. Then came our accession to the EU and with it the requirement that on points of EU law the Luxemburg-based European Court was paramount. Its decisions had to be followed by our courts. The incorporation of the European Convention on Human Rights into our domestic law through the Human Rights Act 1998 was done in a different way. The legislation left open the extent to which our final courts could refuse to follow the interpretation given to the Convention by Strasbourg, and the issue continues to divide our senior judiciary.

The extent to which these legislative differences have impacted on the relationship between these courts and our final court must be a matter for conjecture. However, differences there are. With Luxembourg the links are few. Every year one or possibly two of the Justices attends the annual meeting between the EUCJ and national supreme courts but other than that there does not seem to be much by way of intellectual exchange. To the common law judge the outputs from the Luxembourg court are short, stilted and enigmatic, adhering to a civilian style which appears as though drafted by a committee with no spark of individualism.[72] Therefore, while debates on EU points will be referred from our courts (including the final one) to the European Court for resolution, as the law requires,[73] otherwise

---

[71] For a useful discussion of dialogue and deference as it is understood by public law scholars see J King, 'Deference, Dialogue and Animal Defenders International', Constitutional Law Group blog, 25 April 2013: ukconstitutionallaw.org/2013/04/25/jeff-king-deference-dialogue-and-animal-defenders-international/. See further on deference and dialogue, M Hunt, 'Sovereignty's Blight: Why Contemporary Public Law Needs a Concept of Due Deference' in Bamforth and Leyland, *Public Law in a Multi-Layered Constitution* (Oxford, Hart Publishing, 2003); A Kavanagh, 'Defending Deference in Public Law and Constitutional Theory' (2010) 126 *LQR* 222; A Young, 'In Defence of Due Deference' (2009) 72 *Modern Law Review* 554; J King 'Institutional Approaches to Judicial Restraint' (2008) 28 *Oxford Journal of Legal Studies* 409, and *Judging Social Rights* (Cambridge, Cambridge University Press, 2012) Part II; TRS Allan, 'Human Rights and Judicial Review: A Critique of "Due Deference"' (2006) 65 CLJ 671; T Hickman, *Public Law after the Human Rights Act* (Oxford, Hart Publishing, 2010); A Brady, *Proportionality and Deference under the UK Human Rights Act* (Cambridge, Cambridge University Press, 2012).

[72] No dissents or concurrences are permitted.

[73] Article 267 of the Treaty on the Functioning of the European Union requires the Supreme Court to ask the CJEU to give preliminary rulings on the interpretation of the Treaties and the validity and interpretation of acts of the institutions, bodies, offices or agencies of the Union, where such a question is raised in proceedings before the Supreme Court and it considers that a decision on the question is necessary to enable it to give judgment.

the dialogue between the courts is more akin to sequential monologues and almost always in writing.[74]

With Strasbourg the dialogue is quite different.[75] Egged on by the Presidents of both courts,[76] there is far more interaction—oral and written—between the two courts than there is with Luxembourg.[77] Members of each court visit the other and discussions ensue of actual cases and points of debate.[78] Written exchanges are also frequent, and not just in judgments[79] but also through lectures,[80] and even occasional emails.

The ambiguity over the autonomy of UK courts as regards the Convention has manifested itself in two related questions: whether our final courts are bound by Strasbourg's decisions and whether our courts can be out of step with Strasbourg jurisprudence. As to the former, the position established in the Human Rights Act 1998 is that our courts must 'take into account' any judgment of the Strasbourg Court[81] and that our institutions (including our courts) cannot act in a manner inconsistent with the Convention unless required to do so by primary legislation which cannot be read or given effect in a manner compatible with Convention

---

[74] Alison Young, in a blog on the UK Constitutional Law Group website 12 February 2012: 'Whose Convention Rights are they anyway?' describes the dialogue with Luxembourg as a silent one, reminiscent of the cold war.

[75] V Bogdanor, 'Courts and the Making of Public Policy–The Conflict between Government and the Judges', p 4: www.fljs.org/sites/www.fljs.org/files/publications/Bogdanor.pdf.

[76] See Lord Phillips in *R v Horncastle* [2009] UKSC 14, para 11 and Nicolas Bratza in *Al Khawaja and Tahery v United Kingdom* (2012) 54 EHRR 23, para O-I2 2 and in N Bratza, 'The relationship between the UK courts and Strasbourg' [2011] *European Human Rights Law Review* 505, 511–12. Both Lord Bingham and Lord Phillips endeavoured to keep regular lines of communication open between Strasbourg and the final court of appeal in the UK.

[77] Or, for that matter, with the Scots or the Court of Appeal.

[78] Some of these meetings are recorded in the Annual Report of the UK Supreme Court. In January 2011, Lady Hale took part in a seminar to mark the opening of the judicial year at the European Court of Human Rights, Strasbourg, and in May 2011 Lord Hope and Nicolas Bratza took part in a seminar together in Edinburgh organised by the Public Law Group on the topic of the relationship between Strasbourg and the national courts.

[79] The 'telephone tag' exchange of judgments between the Courts with respect to the repossession of social housing (see below) is but the clearest example of this. Lord Walker describes Strasbourg's judgment in *Pretty v United Kingdom* (2002) 35 EHRR 1 as 'an example of a real dialogue between our final appeal tribunal and the Strasbourg Court' in 'The Indefinite Article 8', Thomas More Lecture, Lincoln's Inn, 9 November 2011 at 10.

[80] See, for example, the interlocking lectures by the President of the ECtHR, N Bratza, 'The relationship between the UK courts and Strasbourg' [2011] *European Human Rights Law Review* 505, Lord Walker, 'The Indefinite Article 8', Thomas More Lecture, Lincoln's Inn, 9 November 2011, Lady Hale, '*Argentoratum Locutum*: Is the Supreme Court supreme?' Nottingham Human Rights Lecture 2011, 1 December 2011 and Lord Kerr 'The UK Supreme Court. The modest underworker of Strasbourg?', 2011 Clifford Chance Lecture.

[81] Section 2 Human Rights Act 1998. This formulation was deliberate. Attempts to amend the legislation as it proceeded through Parliament to say that our courts should be bound by the decisions of the ECtHR or alternatively that they might take them into account were both rejected by the Government. See Lord Kerr, 'The conversation between Strasbourg and the National Courts—Dialogue or Dictation', John Maurice Kelly Memorial lecture, University College Dublin, 20 November 2009; Lord Irvine, 'A British Interpretation of Convention rights', Lecture to the Bingham Centre for the Rule of Law, 14 December 2011; and Lord Kerr, 'The UK Supreme Court. The modest underworker of Strasbourg?', 2011 Clifford Chance Lecture.

rights.[82] In Lord Bingham's time this was taken to mean that our final courts were bound by decisions of Strasbourg if there was a clear and constant jurisprudence on the point[83] which was not based on a misunderstanding of domestic law. Custom and practice evolved such that decisions of the Grand Chamber are treated as more authoritative than those of one of the Sections. This can have a dramatic effect on decisions in our final courts. Thus in *Secretary of State for the Home Department v AF*[84] a nine-judge Appellate Committee of the House of Lords was all set to reaffirm its decision in the previous year on control orders in *Secretary of State for the Home Department v MB*[85] when the ECtHR, one week before the hearing, handed down a decision in another case[86] that departed from the House's 2008 decision. Although not compelled to follow the ECtHR ruling, the Law Lords, with varying degrees of good grace, reluctantly accepted the jurisprudence of the ECtHR in preference to their own, even if some of them did not believe that the ECtHR had got it right.[87] As Lord Rodger memorably put it, '*Argentoratum locutum, indicium finitum*— Strasbourg has spoken, the case is closed'.[88]

Lord Phillips (Bingham's successor) shared his view that in the light of the HRA if there is a clash between a domestic court and the ECtHR, 'Strasbourg is going to win'.[89] However, Lord Judge LCJ at the same evidence session before the Constitution Committee said:

> I would like to suggest that maybe Strasbourg should not win and does not need to win ... I myself think it is at least arguable that, having taken account of the decisions of the court in Strasbourg, our courts are not bound by them. They have to give them due weight; in most cases obviously we would follow them but not, I think, necessarily.[90]

---

[82] Section 6 HRA.

[83] See Lord Slynn's obiter dictum in R (*Alconbury Developments Ltd) v Secretary of State for the Environment, Transport and the Regions* [2001] UKHL 23, [2003] 2 AC 295, para 23, subsequently endorsed by Lord Bingham (and his colleagues) in R (*on the application of Ullah) v Special Adjudicator* [2004] UKHL 26, [2004] 2 AC 323, para 20.

[84] *Secretary of State for the Home Department v AF and another* [2009] UKHL 28.

[85] *Secretary of State for the Home Department v MB* [2008] 1 AC 440. A case in which the House had according to Lady Hale 'performed heroic feats of interpretation ... and read the Prevention of Terrorism Act to mean precisely the opposite of what Parliament had intended'. Lady Hale, 'Argentoratum Locutum: Is the Supreme Court supreme?' Nottingham Human Rights Lecture 2011, 1 December 2011 at 1.

[86] *A v United Kingdom* (Application No 3455/05), BAILII: [2009] ECtHR 301.

[87] *Secretary of State for the Home Department v AF and Another* [2009] UKHL 28 Lord Hoffmann did not mince his words. 'I think that the decision of the ECtHR was wrong ... Nevertheless your Lordships have no choice but to submit ... To reject such a decision would almost certainly put this country in breach of [our] international obligation[s]'.

[88] Para 98. Words which have eclipsed the import of the case. His untimely death only reinforced his brilliance and wit to his colleagues who have now begun to rework them—see Lord Kerr, 'The UK Supreme Court. The modest underworker of Strasbourg?', 2011 Clifford Chance Lecture at 39 'Argentoratum locutum, nunc est nobis loquendum—Strasbourg has spoken, now it is our time to speak'. For the President of the ECtHR the words were positively unhelpful since they are 'not the way in which I or my fellow judges view the respective roles of the two courts'. N Bratza, 'The relationship between the UK courts and Strasbourg' [2011] *European Human Rights Law Review* 505, 512.

[89] Evidence to the HL Constitution Committee pp 4–5 on 19/10/2011 .

[90] Lord Irvine the mover of the Human Rights Act 1998 agrees with Lord Judge on this point, and not with the House of Lords in *AF*. See Lord Irvine, 'A British Interpretation of Convention rights', Lecture to the Bingham Centre for the Rule of Law, 14 December 2011.

As is well known, the Supreme Court appeared to take a similar stance in the *Horncastle*[91] case (a Fourth Section case where there was no sustained and consistent jurisprudence) and reinforced this in *Pinnock*.[92] In the latter case Lord Neuberger on behalf of a unanimous Supreme Court subtly restated the position by asserting that,

> This court is not bound to follow every decision of the European Court ... as it would destroy the ability of the court to *engage in the constructive dialogue* with the European Court which is of value to the development of Convention law ... Of course, we should usually follow a clear and constant line of decisions by the European Court ... But we are not actually bound to do so or (in theory at least) to follow a decision of the Grand Chamber (emphasis added).[93]

Horncastle involved several dialogues with Strasbourg. First, the UK Government persuaded the ECtHR to postpone the hearing of an appeal which they themselves had referred to the Grand Chamber in the *Al-Khawaja*[94] appeal until after the *Horncastle* judgment was out.[95] This enabled the Supreme Court to engage in a sustained dialogue with Strasbourg in their *Horncastle* judgment which was written consciously as a form of advocacy.[96] The dialogue with Strasbourg did not stop there. As Lady Justice Arden observed in her 2009 Sir Thomas More Lecture, informal dialogues between Strasbourg judges and judges of the national courts have a valuable role to play whether in quiet conversations, seminars or plenary meetings of judges.[97] There are clear signs that with the disquiet of No 10 Downing Street over certain decisions of the ECtHR only too well known in Strasbourg,[98] the ECtHR took particular care with the eventual decision in *Al-Khawaja*,[99] which went a long way towards meeting the Supreme Court's concerns.

---

[91] *R v Horncastle* [2009] UKSC 14, [2010] 2 AC 373.

[92] *Manchester City Council v Pinnock* [2010] UKSC 45, [2011] 2 AC 104.

[93] Ibid at para 48. See now *R (on the application of Chester) v Secretary of State for Justice* [2013] UKSC 63 [27], [137].

[94] *Al-Khawaja & Tahery v United Kingdom* (Application no 26766/05) (2009) 49 EHRR 1.

[95] According to Lord Kerr in his Dublin lecture (2009) (see above, n 81) the House was informed by Strasbourg that they were delaying their handling of the *Al-Khawaja* case until the outcome of the *Horncastle* appeal to the Lords was known—a gesture which Strasbourg described as, and Lord Kerr considered to be, an example of the dialogue between the House and Strasbourg at work.

[96] Lord Phillips, in delivering the collective judgment of the Court, expressed the 'hope that in due course the Strasbourg Court may also take into account' the judgment. In this he was fortified by the fact that the Crown was represented in *Horncastle* and *Al-Khawaja* by the same counsel, David Perry QC. Lady Hale in 'Argentoratum Locutum: Is the Supreme Court supreme?', Nottingham Human Rights Lecture 2011, 1 December 2011, states explicitly that the *Horncastle* judgment was aimed at Strasbourg.

[97] Arden LJ, 'Peaceful or Problematic? The relationship between national Supreme Courts and Supranational courts in Europe', 10 November 2009, Lincoln's Inn, at paras 36 and 38.

[98] See Joshua Rozenberg's interview with the President of the ECtHR, 31 January 2012, *The Guardian*, 'Bratza bemused by UK's disdain for Strasbourg' and N Bratza, 'The relationship between the UK courts and Strasbourg' [2011] *European Human Rights Law Review* 505.

[99] It is understood that the announcement of their decisions was originally scheduled for July 2010 but postponed until 15 December 2011.

Horncastle was not the first case where our final court had difficulties with Strasbourg. Lord Bingham in *R v Spear*[100] suggested that the ECtHR in an earlier case, *Morris v United Kingdom*,[101] had misunderstood UK domestic law in relation to Court Martials. Strasbourg in the unanimous Grand Chamber decision of *Cooper v United Kingdom*[102] promptly reversed their decision in *Morris*, convinced by the dialogue with Lord Bingham. As he told me,[103]

> One knows the huge pressures that they're under and there are certainly cases in which having expressed one view in one case and then found it's had a very critical reception they've rather modified their position. *Osman*[104] is a classic case but there's also an entirely different authority about court martials. In one case they had held that the junior officer on a court martial was not an independent, impartial tribunal because he was subject to military discipline and therefore was liable to be ordered by senior officers as to how he should decide whether or not this actually happened. My own view very clearly was that this was a view that could only be held by somebody who had absolutely no understanding of court martials ... So we expressed very clear disagreement with their view on the subject and in the next case they had they modified their position and just simply accepted our view on this.

Strasbourg do not resent such exchanges, on the contrary they positively welcome them.[105] Their Annual Report is entitled *Dialogues between Judges* for just that reason. In the 2006 Report Lord Justice Sedley,[106] in a piece that presaged Lord Phillip's later words in *Horncastle*,[107] explains that where lower courts question the reasoning of the Grand Chamber, it is not an act of insubordination, but 'a constructive dialogue between national and supranational courts' which has seen Strasbourg become more supportive of the doctrine of precedent and more willing to adopt the British model of full exposition of the law and facts in their judgments.

However, the most fascinating dialogue between Strasbourg and our final courts related to the use of Article 8 as a defence to housing repossession actions. In a series of fraught exchanges reminiscent of trench warfare, a group within the House of Lords which was opposed to the Convention destabilising a key part of the common law relating to property, took on an opposing group in the House,

---

[100] *R v Spear and Hastie; R v Boyd; R v Saunby and Others* [2002] UKHL 31, [2003] 1 AC 734.

[101] *Morris v United Kingdom* (Application no 38784/97) (2002) 34 EHRR 52.

[102] *Cooper v United Kingdom* (Application no 48843/99) (2004) 39 EHRR 8.

[103] Interview, 2009.

[104] *Osman v United Kingdom* (1998) 5 BHRC 293.

[105] N Bratza, 'The relationship between the UK courts and Strasbourg' [2011] *European Human Rights Law Review* 505, 511–12.

[106] Sedley LJ, 'Personal reflections on the reception and application of the Court's case-law' *Judicial Dialogue* (Council of Europe, 2006) at 63. Lady Justice Arden similarly describes the judgments of UK courts as a 'very important means of dialogue' in 'Peaceful or Problematic?' at (n 97 above) at para 39–40. Lord Neuberger MR in his lecture of June 2010, 'The incoming tide of European law' (Court of Appeal website) called for a more robust dialogue between Strasbourg and London.

[107] *R v Horncastle* [2009] UKSC 14; [2010] 2 AC 373, para [11].

and the majority voice in Strasbourg. It all began with *Qazi*,[108] where a tenant whose Islamic wife and family had left him, sought to avoid eviction from a local authority tenancy of a family home, through reliance on Article 8. The two senior Law Lords on the appeal, Lord Bingham and Steyn, had no difficulty in giving the Convention purchase in the situation but the private lawyer majority (Lords Hope, Millett and Scott) excluded reliance on Article 8 to defeat a proprietary right to possession on the basis that Parliament had already offered equal and effective protections in such cases. Qazi tried to take his case to Strasbourg but his case was deemed to be inadmissible. The following year Strasbourg decided *Connors v United Kingdom*[109] for reasons incompatible with *Qazi*. When the issue next came before the House in *Kay v Lambeth*,[110] Lord Bingham sat with a panel of seven Law Lords with a view to reconsidering *Qazi*,[111] however, again he was defeated, this time by 4:3. Again it was Lords Hope and Scott who contrived to frustrate Strasbourg, this time with the help of Lady Hale and Lord Brown. Bingham, who wrote the main dissent, was joined by Lords Nicholls and Walker.

Lord Hope explicitly saw the saga as a dialogue with the ECtHR,[112]

> You get a case like *Kay* about housing law where we have this problem of people having strong views about particular aspects of an issue in the law. It's really a dialogue with Strasbourg—in a case where some of us are trying to resist the Strasbourg authority in a way that … can be followed simply by the lower courts. There are others who have issues of principle which they don't find easy to reconcile with that approach.

Others, less charitably, have described the exchange as an 'unedifying game of ping pong'.[113] In *McCann*[114] the ECtHR pointedly endorsed Bingham's dissent in *Kay*, handing down its decision just as the hearing in *Doherty*,[115] the third case on the topic to reach the House of Lords, was about to proceed. The five-Law Lord panel (Lords Hope, Scott, Rodger, Walker and Mance) declined to re-convene as seven in order to review *Kay* and *Qazi*. This time the refuseniks won by 4:1 (Lord Mance dissenting, and Lord Walker expressing grave disquiet while concurring only because he felt bound by the principles of stare decisis to do so), claiming that they did not need to follow the ECtHR decision in *McCann* because it was impossible to derive clear guidance from the judgment.[116]

---

[108] *Qazi v Harrow London Borough Council* [2003] UKHL 43.
[109] *Connors v United Kingdom* (2004) 40 EHRR 189.
[110] *Kay v Lambeth London Borough Council* [2006] UKHL 10, [2006] 2 AC 465.
[111] See p 1 of his opinion.
[112] Interview with the author, 2008. Lord Walker also saw it as a dialogue with Strasbourg, 'The Indefinite Article 8' Thomas More Lecture, Lincoln's Inn, 9 November 2011 at 23.
[113] HHJ Madge, 'Article 8—la lutta continua', 9 March 2009: www.nicmadge.co.uk/Art_8_-_after_Doherty.php.
[114] *McCann v United Kingdom* (2008) 47 EHRR 913.
[115] *Doherty v Birmingham City Council* [2008] UKHL 57.
[116] *Doherty*, ibid, Lord Hope at para [20].

The whole point of the reasoning of the majority [in *Kay*] was to reduce the risks to the operation of the domestic system by laying down objective standards on which the courts can rely. I do not think that the decision in McCann has answered this problem.

It was their last victory, for the unsuccessful appellants in *Kay* took their case to Strasbourg,[117] and the feeling was growing that the Court could not continue to refuse to follow a 'clear and constant' line of decisions at Strasbourg.[118] As Lord Neuberger MR observed in a lecture at the time, the time for the Supreme Court to reconsider its stance in *Qazi*, *Kay* and *Doherty* seemed to have arrived.[119] The opportunity did not present itself for two years, but when it did, in *Pinnock*,[120] a nine-Justice panel of the Supreme Court (including Lord Hope) unanimously voted to allow Article 8 to be used to defend housing eviction actions, with the sole opinion of the court written by none other than Lord Neuberger. Three months later came the last case in the saga, *Powell*.[121] Strasbourg had indeed won.

The autonomy of UK courts as regards the Convention has also arisen with respect to the related question: Can our courts be out of step with Strasbourg jurisprudence? Our starting point, of course, is Lord Bingham in *Ullah*[122] and the 'mirror principle':

[T]he Convention is an international instrument, the correct interpretation of which can be authoritatively expounded only by the Strasbourg court. From this it follows that a national court subject to a duty such as that imposed by section 2 should not without strong reason dilute or weaken the effect of the Strasbourg case law … It is of course open to member states to provide for rights more generous than those guaranteed by the Convention, but such provision should not be the product of interpretation of the Convention by national courts, since the meaning of the Convention should be uniform throughout the states party to it. The duty of national courts is to keep pace with Strasbourg jurisprudence as it evolves over time: no more but certainly no less.

He elaborated his view on Strasbourg and the Convention when I interviewed him in 2009,

My own belief was always that if domestic effect was given to the Convention we would fare very much better than we had done up to then in our rate of success with the cases that did go to Strasbourg because they would at least have, one hoped, a sensible judgment by a British court giving what they conceived to be the right answer. I thought and hoped that the Strasbourg court would take quite a lot of notice of what we thought

---

[117] *Kay v United Kingdom* (Application no 37341/06) [2011] HLR 2, ECtHR, 21 September 2010.

[118] In '*Argentoratum Locutum*: Is the Supreme Court supreme?', Nottingham Human Rights Lecture 2011, 1 December 2011, at 17 Lady Hale indicates that 'we had to give in' with respect to the repossession of social housing and Article 8 because of the clear and constant line of decisions in Strasbourg.

[119] 'The current legal challenges facing social landlords: A judge's perspective', Social Housing Law Association Annual Conference, 27 November 2009.

[120] *Manchester City Council v Pinnock* [2010] UKSC 45, [2011] 2 AC 104.

[121] *Hounslow London Borough Council v Powell* [2011] 2 WLR 287.

[122] *R (on the application of Ullah) v Special Adjudicator* [2004] UKHL 26, [2004] 2 AC 323, para 20 (endorsed by his colleagues).

about these things. I also myself was quite enthusiastic about being very loyal to their jurisprudence. Now I think this has worked out pretty well. We've had some reverses in cases that were heard here but very many fewer than there had been and they have been really on the whole very polite about our approach to their jurisprudence. [Several Strasbourg judges] … have expressed a gratitude for the care and depth with which we had gone into all this and sometimes said that we've analysed their cases much better than they have done themselves.

The first rider to the *Ullah* principle came three years later in *Al Skeini*,[123] a case in which Lord Bingham did not sit, where Lord Brown famously replaced 'no more but certainly no less' with 'no less but certainly no more'. Lord Brown's pragmatic reformulation stemmed from the fact that if the House is overly restrictive of an applicant's Convention rights, they can always take the case to Strasbourg. However, if the House goes beyond Strasbourg then the Government cannot take its case to Strasbourg.

In recent times the mirror principle has attracted more attention. Lord Hope voiced his endorsement of it in *Ambrose v Harris*,[124] whilst Lord Kerr in his dissent in the same case, observed,[125]

I greatly doubt that Lord Bingham contemplated—much less intended—that his discussion of this issue should have the effect of acting as an inhibitor on courts of this country giving full effect to Convention rights unless they have been pronounced upon by Strasbourg. I believe that, in the absence of a declaration by the European Court of Human Rights as to the validity of a claim to a Convention right, it is not open to courts of this country to adopt an attitude of agnosticism and refrain from recognising such a right simply because Strasbourg has not spoken … If the much vaunted dialogue between national courts and Strasbourg is to mean anything, we should surely not feel inhibited from saying what we believe Strasbourg ought to find in [the future]. Better that than shelter behind the fact that Strasbourg has so far not spoken and use it as a pretext for refusing to give effect to a right that is otherwise undeniable. I consider that not only is it open to this court to address and deal with those arguments on their merits, it is our duty to do so.

Lady Hale, having seemingly embraced Lord Bingham's approach with Lord Brown's gloss in *Al Skeini*,[126] came close in a lecture in late 2011[127] to endorsing Lord Kerr's line of argument, as did Lord Brown himself in *Rabone*:[128]

---

[123] *R (on the application of Al-Skeini) v Ministry of Defence* [2007] UKHL 26, [2008] 1 AC 153, para 106.

[124] *Ambrose v Harris (Procurator Fiscal, Oban)* [2011] UKSC 43, para 20.

[125] Ibid, paras 128 and 130. Lord Kerr has elaborated on his views on *Ullah* in his Clifford Chance Lecture 2011, 'The UK Supreme Court. The modest underworker of Strasbourg?'.

[126] *R (on the application of Al-Skeini) v Ministry of Defence* [2007] UKHL 26, [2008] 1 AC 153, para 90.

[127] 'Argentoratum Locutum: Is the Supreme Court supreme?', Nottingham Human Rights Lecture 2011, 1 December 2011.

[128] *Rabone and Another v Pennine Care NHS Trust* [2012] UKSC 2, para 112.

Nobody has ever suggested that, merely because a particular question which arises under the Convention has not yet been specifically resolved by the Strasbourg jurisprudence, domestic courts cannot determine it—in other words that it is necessary to await an authoritative decision of the ECtHR more or less directly in point before finding a Convention violation. That would be absurd. Rather what the *Ullah* principle importantly establishes is that the domestic court should not feel driven on Convention grounds unwillingly to decide a case against a public authority (which could not then seek a corrective judgment in Strasbourg) unless the existing Strasbourg case law clearly compels this.

In an affirmation that the *Ullah* principle is closely related to our earlier discussion as to the import of section 2 of the Human Rights Act 1998, Lord Brown also observed in *Rabone*,[129]

> In saying that the courts '"must take into account" any judgment of the ECtHR', Parliament left it open to the courts to decide how far they should be influenced by a Strasbourg judgment in any particular circumstances. I do not believe the *Ullah* principle … in any way offends section 2. On the contrary, it operates to my mind to promote each of two frequently expressed aims: *engaging in a dialogue* with Strasbourg and bringing rights home (emphasis added).

However *Ullah*'s days may be numbered, for in *Sugar v BBC*[130] Lord Wilson (with the concurrence of Lord Mance) indicated that,

> [he] would welcome an appeal, unlike the present, in which it was appropriate for this court to consider whether, of course without acting extravagantly, it might now usefully do more than to shadow the ECtHR in the manner hitherto suggested—no doubt sometimes in aid of the further development of human rights and sometimes in aid of their containment within proper bounds.

Moreover, the mirror principle has been attacked, implicitly by Lady Hale,[131] and explicitly by Lord Irvine[132] and by the President of the ECtHR [133] for suggesting an overly deferential relationship between the courts which obstructs effective dialogue between them. Even Lord Phillips has indicated that his views have changed on the issue.[134] Lord Bingham did not see the relationship in that way, as we have seen—but he was not living in an era when No 10 was seeking to alter

---

[129] Ibid, para 114.

[130] *Sugar v British Broadcasting Corporation* [2012] UKSC 4, para 59.

[131] 'Argentoratum Locutum: Is the Supreme Court supreme?', Nottingham Human Rights Lecture 2011, 1 December 2011.

[132] 'A Court which subordinates itself to follow another's rulings cannot enter into dialogue with its superior in any meaningful sense': See Lord Irvine, 'A British Interpretation of Convention rights', Lecture to the Bingham Centre for the Rule of Law, 14 December 2011.

[133] N Bratza, 'The relationship between the UK courts and Strasbourg' [2011] *European Human Rights Law Review* 505, 512.

[134] Lord Phillips, 'Strasbourg Has Spoken' ch 12 in A Burrows, D Johnston and R Zimmermann (eds), *Judge and Jurist: Essays in Memory of Lord Rodger of Earlsferry* (Oxford, Oxford University Press, 2013), 118.

the powers of Strasbourg and to free our Supreme Court from the need to follow the rulings of that court.

In sum, the dialogue with Strasbourg is clearly dynamic and vibrant. Lord Phillips was just as supportive of the HRA as Lord Bingham, but along with others on the Supreme Court was keen to develop the dialogue with Strasbourg in a way that gave greater room for manoeuvre than the slightly unedifying and sulky response of the House in *AF*. Cynical observers of the Court familiar with Mr Dooley's famous aphorism concerning the US Supreme Court that 'The Court reads the election results' might be tempted to attribute the resistance of the Court in *Horncastle* in part to the Conservative Party threat to repeal the HRA if they won the 2010 general election. Certainly Strasbourg has shown signs of being aware of the Tories' distaste for Strasbourg (eg, over prisoners' voting rights, and the deportation of alleged terrorists). Not only did Strasbourg meet the Supreme Court half way in *Al Khawaja* but later decisions eg, over 'kettling',[135] political advertising[136] and even over prisoners' votes,[137] arguably show their awareness of the Conservative Party and UKIP threat to repeal the HRA and the UK's commitment to the ECHR. Strasbourg seems as keen to enter into dialogue with the Supreme Court as the Supreme Court is with Strasbourg. Indeed, the Draft Protocol No 16 to the ECHR currently being worked on following the Brighton Ministerial conference and Brighton Declaration[138] in 2012 has been described by one ECHR judge as 'the protocol of dialogue' between the highest national courts and Strasbourg.[139] The relationship between Strasbourg and the Supreme Court has undoubtedly improved since *AF*, but there are still occasional blips. In *Re E*[140] the Supreme Court sought to avoid the potential danger from a Strasbourg decision to the Hague Convention policy of returning a child taken illegally out of a country as soon as possible to that country. The President of the ECtHR, speaking extra-judicially, indicated that Strasbourg wasn't attacking the Hague principle. However, from *Re S*[141] it would appear that in a subsequent decision Strasbourg has reinforced the original threat. Moreover, following a change in the President of the ECtHR, the decision of the Grand Chamber to assert that all prisoners sentenced to imprisonment for the rest of their lives should have a review mechanism at some stage,[142] was delivered in more robust language than of late, and may suggest that Strasbourg is now reconsidering its more placatory stance to No 10.

Nevertheless, as one UK Supreme Court Justice recently observed,[143]

---

[135] *Eweida and Others v United Kingdom* [2013] ECHR 37.
[136] Animal Defenders International 22 April 2013. [2013] ECHR 362.
[137] *Greens and MT v United Kingdom* [2010] ECHR 1826 (23 November 2010).
[138] High Level Conference on the Future of the European Court of Human Rights, 19–20 April 2012.
[139] Noreen O'Meara, 'Reforming the European Court of Human Rights through Dialogue?' UK Constitutional Law Group blog: ukconstitutionallaw.org/2013/05/31.
[140] *Re E (Children)* [2011] UKSC 27, para 25.
[141] *Re S (A Child)* [2012] UKSC 10, para 38.
[142] *Vinter and others v United Kingdom* (Grand Chamber: application nos 66069/09, 130/10 and 3896/10).
[143] Interview with the author.

[Our relationship with Strasbourg] has probably improved since this Court has become more assertive. I frankly think the same would happen with Luxembourg as well. They pay far more attention to the Bundesverfassungsgericht—I think ... because it is liable to disagree with them. So, under Nicholas Phillips, we have in a number of senses developed a dialogue with the Strasbourg Court both in terms of writing judgments here which contain a well reasoned critique of Strasbourg case law and also having quite a good programme of meetings with the Strasbourg judges, so we can get to know them and they can see we are not actually hostile to them at all. We try on occasion to explain to them that preconceptions based on French or German law may need to be revised when they are looking at a system that works in a fundamentally different way. That is a quite a productive relationship which was helped by Costa[144] actually. He was a very good ambassador for the Court and keen to engage with other Supreme Courts ... We haven't got the same relationship with Luxembourg at all.

SCOTS APPEALS AND LONDON: A FRAUGHT RELATIONSHIP?

It would be fair to say that from time to time the dialogue between the final court of appeal and the Scots has been a fraught one. Surprising as it may seem, it has never been entirely clear—even today when the Supreme Court has replaced the House of Lords—whether the final court when hearing appeals from Scotland is sitting as a UK court or as a Scottish court.[145] If that ambiguity has done nothing for nationalist sensitivities, neither did the ambiguities in Articles 18 and 19 of the Treaty. The former ensured that the integrity of Scots private law was enshrined in the terms of Union but opened the door to the harmonisation of public and commercial law in the UK. The latter, as is now known, consciously left open the possibility of both civil and criminal appeals to London and it was many years before it was definitively established that whilst civil appeals might go South (and in many cases without leave) criminal appeals could not, even if some considered criminal law to be more public than private in character.[146] It was the Scottish legal community which effectively resolved the ambiguity in Article 19; indeed they chose to swamp the House of Lords as a court with civil appeals. Thus between 1794 and 1807, 84 per cent of appeals[147] presented were Scots and as late as 1833–65, 53 per cent of appeals to the House were Scots. It was not until the third quarter of the nineteenth century that the number of English appeals consistently exceeded those from Scotland. The picture in the last century has been very different. Less than 10 per cent of the caseload of the final appeal court has

---

[144] Jean-Paul Costa (President of European Court of Human Rights 2007–11).

[145] See Neil Walker, *Final Appellate Jurisdiction in the Scottish Legal System* (Scottish Government, January 2010).

[146] Philip Brodie, 'From Scotland and Ireland: Scotland after 1707' in Blom Cooper et al (eds), *The Judicial House of Lords 1876–2009* (Oxford, Oxford University Press, 2009) ch 17; Walker (above, n 145); AJ MacLean, 'The 1707 Union: Scots Law and the House of Lords' (1984) 5 *Journal of Legal History* 50.

[147] 419 out of 501. See Paterson, 'Scottish Lords of Appeal 1876–1988' [1988] *Juridical Review* 235. Even as late as 1833–65, 53% of appeals to the House were Scots.

emanated from Scotland. Only very rarely between 1930 and 2009 did the number of Scots appeals determined by the House[148] exceed 10 a year. Interestingly the Supreme Court has changed that. After a slow start in 2009, Scots cases arrived in London in a steady stream, achieving double figures each year, ensuring that 17 per cent of the Court's decided cases[149] up until the end of March 2013 were from North of the border.

It might have been thought that the absence of Scots law experts in the House would have deterred the gadarene rush to London in the first 150 years of the Union, but not at all. First, an appeal bought appellants time since the House had decided—probably erroneously—that marking an appeal acted as a stay of the Court of Session decision.[150] Secondly, the fact that the judges in the House were untainted by Scottish tribal politics was a positive attraction to Scots appellants, and thirdly (in part, perhaps because of one and two), appellants had a better than even chance of winning if the case was determined by the House. As late as 1856 the Scottish legal profession was still divided as to whether the lack of Scots-trained judges in the House was a bad thing. Lord Justice Clerk Hope[151] was in the 'anti' camp—indicating that in the 11 years he had been Lord Advocate the suggestion of having a Scots-trained judge in London had never been raised by anyone. The first Scots law-trained judicial peer, Lord Colonsay, did not begin to sit in London until 1867 and the first Scots Lord of Appeal, not until 1876.[152] From 1913 onwards there have almost always been two Scots-trained Lords of Appeal—augmented by occasional Scots judicial peers. However, since the House sat normally with five Law Lords in Scots appeals, in the overwhelming majority of cases the Scots were in the minority.[153]

As is well known the almost complete lack of a specialist Scots input into the judicial work of the House before 1867, coupled with the fact that most of these cases were argued by English counsel citing English authorities—or perhaps more

---

[148] Indeed, even if determinations of Scottish devolution issues by the Privy Council were to be classified as Scots appeals, the combined figure would still be below 10 a year. See the appendices of N Walker, *Final Appellate Jurisdiction in the Scottish Legal System* (January 2010).

[149] 35 out of 207 cases.

[150] Lord Hope, 'Taking the case to London—is it all over?' [1998] *Juridical Review* 135, 139; Philip Brodie, 'From Scotland and Ireland: Scotland after 1707' in Blom Cooper et al (eds), *The Judicial House of Lords 1876–2009* (Oxford, Oxford University Press, 2009) ch 17.

[151] An ancestor of the Law Lord and Justice, Lord Hope.

[152] Benjamin Disraeli was sure there would be no trouble in filling the first Lord of Appeal position with a Scots judge because the salary on offer 'was enough to make a Scotsman's mouth water'. In fact the first two Scots to be offered the post turned it down. Lord Gordon was the third choice. A Paterson, 'Scottish Lords of Appeal 1876–1988' [1988] *Juridical Review* 235.

[153] In the 20 years up to 2012, there have been 12 Scots cases where three of the five Law Lords on the panel were Scots-trained judges, eg *Herd v Clyde Helicopters Ltd* 1997 SC (HL) 86, *Girvan v Inverness Farmers Dairy* 1998 SC (HL) 1, *Redrow Homes Ltd v Bett Brothers plc* 1998 SLT 648. Most were in the period 1993–2002 and there have been no such cases in the Supreme Court. Ironically, three Scots-trained judges have sat in more than one English appeal and one of the Scots cases had no special Scottish features.

bizarrely Scots counsel citing English cases in preference to Scots[154]—undoubtedly led to the Anglicisation of parts of Scots law in the eighteenth and nineteenth centuries. Either deliberately, or through misunderstanding or unwarranted concessions from Scots counsel, English judges in the House would regularly harmonise English and Scots cases along the line preferred in English cases, much to the disgust of twentieth-century academics such as TB Smith,[155] Dewar Gibb[156] and David Walker.[157] The most infamous instance, of course, was the dicta of Lord Cranworth LC in *Bartonshill Coal Co v Reid*,[158] where he set out the English law of common employment before applying it in a Scots appeal with the words 'But if such be the law of England on what grounds can it be argued not to be the law of Scotland?' adding two lines later, 'I think it would be most inexpedient to sanction a different rule to the North of the Tweed to that which prevails to the South'.[159] But the Anglicisation thesis can be overdone. *Donoghue v Stevenson*[160]—arguably the most influential private law appeal to come to the Lords—harmonised the law of tort and delict in the two countries along non-English lines. Again, the law on the fiduciary duties of agents and directors was harmonised along Roman law and civilian lines[161] in a trilogy of cases[162] coming to the Lords over a century. In each case a panel of English judges reversed decisions of the Court of Session which had set the law on an unhelpful path. Moreover, there were some decisions of the House in Scots cases, eg *Robertson v Fleming*,[163] of which the legal nationalists were inordinately proud, which on consumer protection grounds should have been abandoned many years earlier than they were.

The eventual arrival of Scots judges in London did not satisfy the legal nationalists[164]—either because there were not enough of them or because there

---

[154] See P Brodie, 'From Scotland and Ireland: Scotland after 1707' in L Blom Cooper et al (eds), *The Judicial House of Lords 1876–2009* (Oxford, Oxford University Press, 2009) ch 17 at 291, A Paterson, 'Scottish Lords of Appeal 1876–1988' [1988] *Juridical Review* 235, 236.

[155] TB Smith, 'English Influences on the Law of Scotland' in *Studies Critical and Comparative* (Edinburgh, W Green, 1962) 122–24.

[156] AD Gibb, Law from over the Border: A Short Account of a Strange Jurisdiction (Edinburgh, W Green, 1950).

[157] D Walker, 'Walker on the Scottish Legal System' (Edinburgh, W Green, 1976) 371.

[158] *Bartonshill Coal Co v Reid* (1858) 3 Macq 266.

[159] For argument that Bartonshill not as clear cut from of imperialism as it looks see Philip Brodie 'From Scotland and Ireland: Scotland after 1707' in L Blom Cooper et al (eds), *The Judicial House of Lords 1876–2009* (Oxford, Oxford University Press, 2009) ch 17. The reference to harmonisation is an interesting one. If the House is a UK court then Article 18 of the Treaty of Union provides ample justification for it seeking to harmonise the laws of the UK in commercial matters—including employment. The objection is in the method of harmonisation—always following the English solution.

[160] *Donoghue v Stevenson* [1932] AC 562.

[161] As Laura McGregor showed in 'An Agent's Fiduciary Duties' (2010) 14 *Edinburgh Law Review* 121.

[162] *York Buildings v Mackenzie* (1795) 3 Pat App 378; *Aberdeen Railway Co v Blaikie* (1854) 1 Macq 461; *McPherson's Trustees v Watt* (1877) 5 R (HL) 9, 3 App Cas 254. Ironically in *Aberdeen Railway Co v Blaikie* the same Lord Cranworth resorted to Justinian's Digest to put Scots law onto a fairer footing.

[163] *Robertson v Fleming* (1861) 4 Macq 167.

[164] Those in the Scottish legal community committed to retaining the purity of Scots law free from external (particularly English) influence.

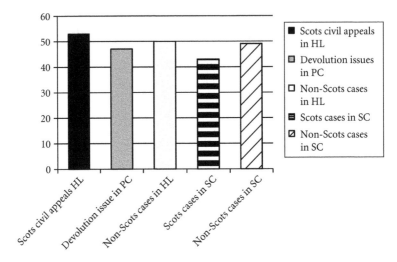

Table 6.1: Comparison of success rates of Scottish and Non-Scottish cases in the Privy Council, House of Lords and UK Supreme Court 1993–2013 (July).

were too many. The latter criticism arose since some Scots—even the greatest of all, Scott Reid—were accused of losing touch with their heritage whilst the absence of others was lamented because they (eg, Alan Rodger and David Hope) were the best minds of their generation. However, in the last 50 years allegations of cultural imperialism by the English Law Lords in civil appeals have appeared less frequently.[165] That is, until Devolution. Perhaps not surprisingly, the legal nationalists in the judiciary and academia did not anticipate that a constitutional reform that was intended to devolve power from London would lead instead to London acquiring hegemony over aspects of Scots criminal law—something that had been rejected in the eighteenth century.[166] However, those who believe that London judges have intervened too readily in Scots appeals in the last two decades receive little support from the statistics. Despite most Scots civil appeals coming as of right and English appeals and devolution issues requiring leave, the success rate between 2000–09 for Scots civil appeals, for devolution issues cases to the Privy Council and for non-Scots appeals to the House of Lords were all very similar (see Table 6.1).

---

[165] *Sharp v Thomson* 1997 SC (HL) 66 of course stands out as an exception seared on the hearts of the legal nationalists (even though there were three Scots judges on it).

[166] Devolution brought with it the requirement that the devolved governments and politicians should behave in accord with the provisions of the European Convention on Human rights. The Scotland Act 1998 enabled breaches of this obligation to be raised in Scottish courts and—to avoid different applications of the ECHR in the different parts of the UK—appeals to go to the Privy Council in London. These cases were described as ones which raised devolution issues.

The advent of the Supreme Court has produced a surprising change—with the success rate in Scots cases falling to 43 per cent whilst that for non-Scots cases remained steady at 49 per cent. It would be fair to add however, that Lord Hope is on record as indicating that part of his role in London is to resist the natural desire of the non-Scots that the law on each side of the Border should be the same,[167] and to inhibit them from making the occasional excursus on an aspect of Scots law which reveals that they haven't quite got the right end of the stick.

Deference

Ironically, in the last 20 years the charge levelled against non-Scots Law Lords in Scots appeals has been less of interventionism but of neglect. As various commentators have argued,[168] in this period we have more often seen the non-Scots judges deferring to their Scots counterparts as the specialists in the field rather than writing their own thoughts on Scots law points or providing an excursus on how English law would solve the problem. Given that in 118 of the 133 Scots cases[169] heard in that period the Scots judges constituted a minority of the panel and in 31 of these cases there was only one Scots judge on the panel (see Table 6.2) there might appear to be some truth to the critique which has been voiced from time to time that in this period the decisions of three or more Scots in the Inner House[170] or the High Court were effectively being reviewed by a panel with only one or two Scots on it, with the other judges not knowing much about Scots law, particularly common law with the exception of negligence.

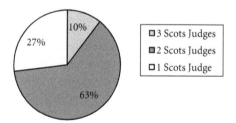

Table 6.2: Scottish cases in the Privy Council, House of Lords and UK Supreme Court with Scottish judges sitting during 1993–2013 (July).

---

[167] Lord Hope, 'Taking the Case to London—is it all over?' [1998] *Juridical Review* 135; P Brodie, 'From Scotland and Ireland: Scotland after 1707' in L Blom Cooper et al (eds), *The Judicial House of Lords 1876–2009* (Oxford, Oxford University Press, 2009) ch 17.

[168] Paterson, above, n 147; J Chalmers, 'Scottish Appeals and the Proposed Supreme Court' (2004) 8 *Edinburgh Law Review* 4.

[169] Including 20 devolution issues cases heard by the Privy Council, 78 Scots civil cases heard by the House of Lords and 29 Scots cases determined in the Supreme Court up until the end of July 2013.

[170] This is the Scottish Court of Appeal.

However, when the deference critique is scrutinised, it does not hold up that well,

1) First, some of the writings in this area treat Scots appeals as though they were all uniformly alien territory for non-Scots judges. In fact, as Neil Walker in his report[171] recognises, most Scots appeals in the last 20 years relate to areas which do not concern aspects of Scots common law. There is no reason why a non-Scot could not write on a tax or employment statute or a Human Rights issue—and they do. Indeed in 10 per cent of all Scots appeals in the period the lead judgment came from a non-Scot and none related to an area of pure Scots law.

2) If the critique exaggerates the arcane nature of the Scots law caseload to the final court, it also exaggerates the specialist expertise of the judges in the Inner House. This is because the objection to two Scots in London sitting in judgment on three in the Inner House is somewhat diluted once it is accepted that the three may not all have been specialists in the area of the appeal, in which case they may have been showing deference to their own colleagues in the Inner House.

3) Thirdly the critique can only apply to those cases in which the Scots judges on the final court are outnumbered by non-Scots on the panel. In 15 of the 133 Scots cases which went to London in the last 20 years a majority of those sitting were Scots trained, so it is only the other 118 to which this critique might apply;

4) As can be seen from Table 6.3 whilst Scots judges have written on 77 per cent of the occasions in which they sat on Scots appeals to the House and Privy Council, and on 78 per cent of the occasions in such cases in which they sat on the Supreme Court,[172] non-Scots judges recovered from a poor start during the years 1993–2002 of writing on only 24 per cent of occasions in which they sat in Scots cases, to 44 per cent in the next decade which is much more respectable, even if it has fallen back to 30 per cent in the Supreme Court.

   Moreover, the most criticised scenario—when a sole opinion from a Scots judge overrules a decision in Scotland—has happened on only six occasions in 127 cases (five per cent).

5) The critique that the non-Scots didn't write in Scots cases out of deference to the specialist Scots judges largely stemmed from that 24 per cent figure (which was 17 per cent if we only look at civil cases) which has now much improved, in part because there were fewer pure Scots civil law cases coming to the Court in the Supreme Court era than in 1993–2002—so the non-Scots could be expected to write more. But the critique was also flawed because it stems from looking at the output of the court—namely its judgments and

---

[171] N Walker, *Final Appellate Jurisdiction in the Scottish Legal System* (Scottish Government, January 2010): www.scotland.gov.uk/Resource/Doc/299388/0093334.pdf.
[172] In the case of Lord Hope it was an astonishing every case but one.

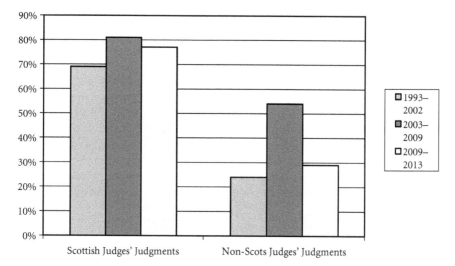

Table 6.3: Scottish appeal participation rates in the House of Lords, Privy Council and Supreme Court during 1993–2013 (July).

not at the circumstances in which the output was arrived at or the process by which it was arrived:

a. Thus between 1993–2002 and 2003–2009 there was a substantial shift in the attitude to multiple judgments in the court. As can be seen from Table 3.2[173] (in chapter three above) in the period 1993–2002 single judgments of the court were commonplace. However, in the period 2003–2009—the era of Bingham—multiple judgments were back in favour—much to the disgust of the Court of Appeal, so more judgments could be anticipated, and that is what happened. Finally when the Supreme Court was established there was a push for more single judgments, so again the number of concurring judgments from the non-Scots should have declined.

b. Secondly, to judge the input of the non-Scots judges by the opinions produced at the end of the day, is to overlook their input at the earlier stages. All the Law Lords since Bingham's era read the printed Cases submitted in advance,[174] and all took part in the oral argument, and the format of the first conference at the end of the case was that all of the participating judges were expected to give an account of their thinking in the case, starting with the most junior. Further, under Bingham the junior was

---

[173] See Fig 4.8 in A Paterson, *Lawyers and the Public Good* (Cambridge, Cambridge University Press, 2012) at 182. In Paterson, above, n 147, I argued that the prevalence of single opinions in the Lords would exacerbate the phenomenon of opinion deference.

[174] Lord Rodger was said to be a partial exception.

encouraged to speak for longer than the others at that first conference and it would not have been considered acceptable for the non-Scottish juniors to say 'I don't understand Scots private law so I'll wait to see what David Hope and Alan Rodger say'—they all had to express a considered opinion based on what they'd read and heard. A scrutiny of Lord Bingham's judicial notebooks does indeed confirm that non-Scots Law Lords expressed detailed views at the first conference, in Scots cases. Finally, on input, just because the only judgments in a case have the name of a Scots judge attached to them does not mean that a non-Scots judge has not contributed passages in the judgment. A very clear example of a non-Scot making a telling intervention in a Scots appeal (without writing a judgment) was *RBS v Wilson*[175] and Lord Walker's emperor's new clothes question: 'why when the statute says "shall" do you always apply it as if it said "may"?'.[176]

c. Speaking bluntly there is another reason why English Law Lords did not say a great deal in some Scots appeals in the last 20 years. It was because, as in certain overseas Privy Council cases, they felt privately that the case should never have got to London. The Law Lords have grown used to determining which cases merit being heard by them, and for how long.[177] The Scots privilege of taking final appeals to London without leave from anywhere (except certification from two counsel[178] that the appeal was reasonable), contrasts sharply with the position in most English appeals, which have to survive the scrutiny of the Law Lords in Appeal Committee and Justices in PTA committees certifying that they raise a point of public general importance. In cases which really shouldn't have come to London it should not be a surprise if the non-Scots decline to write.[179]

All this is not to deny that 'opinion deference', as it has been described,[180] goes on in the final Appeal Court—quite appropriately, since there are several forms

---

[175] *Royal Bank of Scotland v Wilson* [2010] UKSC 50.

[176] See Lord Hope, 'Scots Law seen from South of the Border', Scottish Young Lawyers' Association address, April 2011, n at 20

[177] See chapter 2 of this volume above.

[178] Who might have an interest in taking the appeal to London. At the time of writing this book, the Scottish Government was consulting to see whether appeals should henceforth only go to the Supreme Court with leave from the Inner House or the Supreme Court itself.

[179] Over the years there have been a number of such cases. In *Wilson v Jaymarke* 2007 SLT 958, Lord Hope, echoing the dicta of Lords Hoffmann and Brown in *Buchanan v Alba Diagnostics* three years earlier, sent a clear message (which was again endorsed by his English colleagues) to the effect that the appeal should not have been brought and that counsel should take the responsibility of certifying the appeal as reasonable seriously, if the current set up was to continue. Lord Hope also referred to another issue that troubled the Law Lords in recent years in relation to Scots appeals and some Privy Council cases. The estimates of Scots counsel as to the amount of time required for argument were in the past often in excess of those that the Law Lords considered justified. In *Wilson* the argument could never have taken more than a day, yet counsel had asked for (and got) four days.

[180] See C Palley, 'Decision-making in the Area of Public Order by English Courts' in *Public Order*, II, parts 1–5 (Bletchley, Open University, 1972) at 58 and A Paterson, 'Scottish Lords of Appeal 1876–1988' [1988] *Juridical Review* 235.

of deference and some are quite unobjectionable. Thus over the years there have been some truly great Law Lords, eg Scott Reid (the greatest of them all), Tom Bingham and Lennie Hoffmann, and Law Lords who were doubtful as to which way to go in an appeal would occasionally follow the statesman-like lead which these greats could offer. That is a perfectly acceptable form of deference. Again in areas where a Law Lord is a known and respected specialist, eg Lord Walker in Tax cases, Lord Hoffmann in patent cases, Lord Neuberger in Landlord and Tenant, other Law Lords would take what they had to say in these areas very seriously. As one said to me, '[Y]ou disagree with Lennie Hoffmann on a patent case with very great caution I have to say'. So in many cases the willingness of the non-Scots Law Lords to defer to the Scots is simply another form of deference to specialists. Lord Rodger and Lord Hope were hugely respected by their colleagues. As another Law Lord observed,

> I think in Scots cases involving Scots law particularly, almost all the Scottish cases will have both David Hope and Alan Rodger on them. If they agree and it's not an English law point as well, I think it would be quite difficult to disagree. [B]ut when there's a difference between them ... then you can make a decision in the same way as anyone else.[181] However, I think when they are both agreed on something ... I will probably just say 'I agree with both judgments' or if one of them writes I will agree with one of them. However, one has to remind oneself that it's your decision for the case.[182] Nevertheless, I think above all on Scots law there is a strong inclination to follow two of them if they are agreed.

By and large in areas of pure Scots law this seems reasonably unexceptionable, the more so if the alternative is for the non-Scots to outvote the two Scots in a Scots case. This has almost never happened in the last 20 years, although some cases have come pretty close to it. Lord Edmund-Davies gave a delightful example of such deference in *Fotheringham v Passmore*,[183]

> Several moons have waxed and waned since your Lordships concluded the hearing of these appeals relating to the Scots law governing salmon fishing in a stretch of the River Tay ... With the diffidence becoming one whose regrettable ignorance of Scots law as to salmon fishing at least equals that of English judges born east of the Severn regarding the admirable code of Welsh law on the same subject ... I have naturally studied with great care the speeches prepared by my noble and learned brethren. My Lords, I wish I could say that I have found their cogency compelling, but I regretfully cannot ... in so specialised a branch of the law the tyro must necessarily be heavily influenced by the fact that the noble and learned Lords, Lord Fraser of Tullybelton and Lord Keith of Kinkel, in particular share the same view as to the proper outcome of these Scots appeals. And, since all of your Lordships are not united on the point, my only seemly course is

---

[181] See the devolution issue case of *Martin v HM Advocate* 2010 SLT 412, where Lords Hope and Rodger did indeed part company.

[182] At least one Justice told me that he wanted to reflect on whether he had been too reticent to write in Scots cases.

[183] *Fotheringham v Passmore* 1984 SLT 401, 408.

to suppress my doubts and formally concur in allowing both appeals and in the orders proposed by your Lordships.

Lord Bingham's approach was just as gracious if somewhat less poetic in the finely balanced appeal of *Burnett's Trustee v Grainger*[184] on a difficult aspect of pure Scots private law. With two English Law Lords strongly of the opinion that the House was being asked to affirm a manifestly unfair outcome and one of the Scots wavering it took Tom Bingham to say at the end of the first conference, 'if two such experts on Scots private law are agreed as to what the law of Scotland requires, who am I to disagree with them' to settle the matter.[185] In the end both the non-Scots wrote of their concerns but went along with the two Scots and Bingham. Lord Hope attributes that to deference to Lord Bingham[186] but it is probably an example of double deference. Intriguingly, Lord Bingham did not sit in many Scots civil appeals—only eight in nine years—and only gave an opinion in three. But this unwonted reticence did not extend to devolution issues. Here he sat 11 times and gave a judgment in seven.[187]

The Devolution Issues Jurisdiction

Lord Bingham may not have felt at home in the intricacies of Scots private law but he had no such compunction when it came to the cross-over between Scots public and criminal law which is the devolution issues jurisdiction.[188] His sensitive political antennae would have told him that he could safely stay away from Scots private cases without comment, but that devolution issues were an area of political sensitivity where harmonisation between the two jurisdictions against a shared backdrop of the European Convention on Human Rights could be contemplated, but only with care. It all began with the Scotland Act 1998 ushering in the concept of a 'devolution issue'. Once again, this was an ambiguous term which was resolved by the Scots legal community in a surprisingly broad way[189] albeit that it was the Privy Council that ultimately decided on the meaning of the

---

[184] *Burnett's Trustee v Grainger* 2004 SC (HL) 19.

[185] Account drawn from Lord Hope, 'Scots Law seen from South of the Border' Scottish Young Lawyers Association lecture, 1 April 2011, at 20.

[186] Lord Hope, 'Scots Law seen from South of the Border', 1 April 2011, SYLA lecture.

[187] The discrepancy must have been deliberate. Lord Bingham's unfamiliarity with Scots law and his willingness to defer to the Scots Law Lords seem to have made Lord Bingham reluctant to sit in 'ordinary' Scots appeals delegating them, instead, to the second senior Law Lord, Lord Nicholls. The latter chaired the panel in 13 Scots cases between 2002 and 2007.

[188] Although for 200 years the House of Lords could not hear appeals in Scots criminal cases, following the Scotland Act 1998, the Privy Council could hear appeals on points of law relating to the Devolution settlement, including the incorporation of the European Convention on Human Rights into Scots law. This led, unexpectedly to significant numbers of Scots criminal appeals raising Human Rights issues to go to the Privy Council.

[189] See N Walker, *Final Appellate Jurisdiction in the Scottish Legal System* (Scottish Government, January 2010) Appendix at 40: www.scotland.gov.uk/Resource/Doc/299388/0093334.pdf.

phrase. As we have seen, this was not welcomed by the legal nationalists. Neither was it well received in certain judicial circles, as can be seen from the unusual and unexpected decision of the senior Scots judiciary to submit written evidence to the Calman Commission on Scottish Devolution[190] attacking the development, even though there was no consensus amongst the judges as to how to resolve the problem. The judges disliked the enforced harmonisation of UK laws on the impact of delay by prosecutors in *Spiers v Ruddy*,[191] and the series of the disclosure cases.[192] The judges were, of course, notoriously joined by an outraged SNP government,[193] after the cases of *Cadder* and *Fraser*.[194]

Lord Hope replied in a spirited fashion,[195] demonstrating that as far as devolution cases were concerned all of them had to come to the Privy Council or the Supreme Court (after 2009) with the leave of either the High Court of Appeal (20 in all)[196] or London (only nine). Lord Hope added that London had differed from the Appeal Court on the question of leave on only nine occasions and in only five of them had London upheld the appeal. The barbed riposte of the First minister was that just one case that turned the Scots system upside down was one too many. The case, of course, was *Cadder*.[197] Many in the English legal community found it hard to understand the difficulty which this case caused north of the border. To them it was a great surprise that the Police and Criminal Evidence Act (PACE)

---

[190] Submission by the Court of Session Judiciary to the Calman Commission, 10 October 2008.

[191] *Spiers v Ruddy* [2008] 1 AC 873. The case involved the harmonisation of the impact of delay in prosecutions on both sides of the Border which was the culmination of several cases where the English and ultimately Strasbourg allowed the pragmatism of their infrastructural needs to triumph over the more principled position of the Scots. See *R v HM Advocate* [2002] UKPC D3 and *AG's ref No 2 of 2001* [2003] UKHL 68.

[192] *Holland v HM Advocate* 2005 1 SC (PC) 3; *Sinclair v HM Advocate* 2005 1 SC (PC) 28; *McDonald v HM Advocate* 2010 SC (PC) 1; *HM Advocate v Murtagh* 2010 SC (PC) 39; *Allison v HM Advocate* 2010 SC (UKSC) 19, [2010] UKSC 6; and *McInnes v HM Advocate* 2010 SC (UKSC) 28, [2010] UKSC 7.

[193] Following the *Fraser* case, the First Minister, Alex Salmond stated on 26 May 2011 that the 'increasing involvement of the UK Supreme Court in second-guessing Scotland's highest criminal court of appeal' was totally unsatisfactory. He further accused the Supreme Court of 'intervening aggressively' in Scotland's independent legal system and then in an interview with Mandy Rhodes of the *Holyrood* Magazine on 13 June 2011, accused Lord Hope and the Supreme Court of 'routinely interfering in criminal appeals in Scotland' and the Privy Council of reaching a decision which was 'the very antithesis of Scots law'. Mr MacAskill the Justice Secretary then accused the Supreme Court of being an 'ambulance-chasing court' and its non-Scots members of knowing no more of Scotland than they picked up on their visits to the Edinburgh Festival. He then threatened to cut the Scots funding for the Court. D Leask, 'MacAskill threat to end Supreme Court funding', 31 May 2011, *The Herald*.

[194] *Cadder v Her Majesty's Advocate* [2010] UKSC 43; *Fraser v Her Majesty's Advocate* [2011] UKSC 24. The ire of the Nationalist Government was first raised by *Somerville v Scottish Ministers* [2007] UKHL 44, where the majority (including the two Scots) held that there was no time bar for claims under the Scotland Act 1998. Alex Salmond blamed the Scots Law Lords for this decision rather than the English. See M Rhodes interview (above, n 193).

[195] Lord Hope, 'The Impact of Europe on Criminal Justice in Scotland: The Role of the Supreme Court of the United Kingdom', Address to SASO Annual Conference, 19 November 2011.

[196] Strictly speaking six of them were references by the Appeal Court rather than leave cases.

[197] *Cadder v Her Majesty's Advocate* [2010] UKSC 43. The case involved the rights of suspected persons to be interrogated at police stations without access to the advice of the lawyer.

did not exist in Scotland and they were convinced, like JUSTICE, that *Salduz*[198] and Strasbourg was right. But there are several reasons why *Cadder* was an unfortunate case:

1) It is almost alone in being a decision in the last 30 years which overturned an enlarged court in Edinburgh of seven judges;

2) It demonstrated starkly that the implementation of the ECHR in the Scotland Act had been done in a much more brutal way than in the Human Rights Act. Infractions of the latter lead to acts being declared unlawful or statutes declared to be incompatible with the Convention. This leaves the authorities leeway to fashion an appropriate response after due reflection. Under the former, infractions are not only unlawful, they are a nullity and incompatible statutes are struck down forthwith. Neither outcome provides the authorities with leeway or time for reflection. This can have a devastating impact on a legal system and *Cadder* nearly did—had not Lord Hope and his colleagues found a way to make their decision non-retroactive, 600,000 cases might have been overturned as opposed to the 1,000 that were actually lost. 'Let justice be done though the heavens fall' is admirable rhetoric but cold comfort to the now hundreds of victims whose cases were lost or abandoned following *Cadder*;

3) The marked contrast with the *Horncastle* case;[199]

4) It involved the court in deciding a polycentric problem,[200] which some consider are best left to Parliament.[201]

Be that as it may, those in the legal and political communities who disliked *Cadder* were as angry with the Scots Justices in the Supreme Court as with the non-Scots ones. This illustrates the 'Catch-22' of the legal nationalist's critique. If the decision is that of a majority of non-Scots then it's cultural imperialism from London. If the decision is the work of the two Scots it is attributable to a misplaced deference from the non-Scots. It's a clear case of 'heads I win, tails you lose'.[202] London cannot win in this game and if they are wise they will not try.

All this, of course is to see the position of Scots appeals and Scots final appeal judges through the optic of Scots legal nationalism. The legal unionist would not

---

[198] *Salduz v Turkey* (2009) 49 EHRR 19. This was the Grand Chamber decision of the ECtHR that established the requirement for those interrogated at police stations to be advised that they were entitled to legal advice before answering any police questions.

[199] *R v Horncastle* [2009] UKSC 14 [2010] 2 AC 373. This English case, which affected the narrow area of hearsay, provoked more concern in the English legal community and consequent clamour aimed at Strasbourg than the *Cadder* case, with its far greater impact on Scotland, ever did.

[200] The *Cadder* case involved the pragmatic package of measures which protect accused persons in Scotland, namely, the time limits for police detention, the right to silence and requirement for corroboration of evidence. In Cadder the Supreme Court was forced to deal with one element in the package leaving the other elements to unravel.

[201] See chapter 7 of this volume below.

[202] For an articulation of this 'Catch-22' see Alex Salmond's interview with Mandy Rhodes in the *Holyrood* Magazine, 13 June 2011.

find it difficult to point to Scottish appeals to the final court where the law of Scotland has been considerably enhanced by the appeal, ranging from *Donoghue v Stevenson*[203] to *Axa General Insurance Ltd v The Lord Advocate*.[204] Indeed, taking the perspective of English legal nationalism would provide a rather different focus altogether. The first thing a non-Scot would say is: 'what are the Scots complaining about?' Look how powerful and unbiquitous Scots Law Lords and Justices are. It's the West Lothian question all over again. They are appointed younger; they stay longer; they are generalists so they can sit in lots of cases; they got to be senior or presiding Law Lord so often that the English at times had to resort to devices to delay the promotion of the Scot to that role. If non-Scots have given the lead judgment in 10 per cent of Scots cases in the last 20 years, Scots judges have given the lead judgment in 15 per cent of non-Scots Supreme Court cases and about the same in non-Scots House of Lords cases. Scott Reid sat in the Lords for 26 years (1948–75) and presided in cases there for 14 years. Lord Hope was incredibly industrious: from 1996 when he first began as a Lord of Appeal until June 2013 when he retired he sat in around 500 cases and wrote a judgment in around 75 per cent of them. Since 2009 he has given the lead judgment in all types of cases more often than any other Justice as we can see from Table 3.1 in chapter 3 of this volume, above. In short, looking at these figures the right epithet might be 'Scottification', not Anglicisation.

Conclusion

To the legal nationalists, especially the legal academics, the fear of a perennial desire of the non-Scots judges to harmonise the law on both sides of the border—and too often by bringing Scots law in line with English law rather than vice versa—has been a running sore. It is also the case that legal academics in Scotland have been split over the products of London's devolution issues jurisdiction, thus creating an unlikely alliance between some Scots academics and some English judges both wishing to restrict the easy access of Scots cases to London. In the eyes of some legal nationalists the London courts have shifted from intervention to deference, perhaps as a response to the concerns of the Scottish legal community, but neither approach has won them many supporters in Scotland. The Scottish Government may have been the last grouping to express concern as to the activities of the London courts but it has made up for this by the vehemence of its critique of these courts. (There is little likelihood of the London jurisdiction surviving a 'Yes' vote in the independence referendum). This too, has provoked a response from the Court—with Lord Hope providing, quite unusually, an interview with *The Times* and tackling what he termed a 'corrosive anti-English

---

[203] [1932] UKHL 100, 1932 SC (HL) 31.
[204] [2011] UKSC 46.

sentiment' in a series of speeches in Scotland in the winter of 2011–12. It would be fair to conclude, however, that the relationship between the Scots and London has become mired in the wider ramifications of the independence referendum, and accordingly, like the dialogue with Strasbourg, is one that is being influenced by the political 'elephant in the room'.

Were the referendum to produce a 'Yes' vote, this would be far too negative an epitaph to the Scots contribution to the final court of appeal. The contribution of Scots Law Lords to the House of Lords and the Supreme Court has been immense. Although specialists in Scots law, they are much more generalist than most of the Law Lords from England and Wales or Northern Ireland. As a result they are peculiarly attractive to the listing officers for the House of Lords and the Supreme Court, because of their versatility. In the English legal world Lord Reid of Drem is still spoken of in the same adulatory terms as Lord Bingham, and he had 26 years of influence to look back on. Moreover, Scots Law Lords have disproportionately held the office of senior Law Lord in frequency and duration. They have also held the office of Lord Chancellor (a largely English role) far more often than might have been predicted for Scots lawyers.[205] Lord Mackay of Clashfern might have made the same mark as Lord Reid on the House, had he not been elevated, unexpectedly, by Mrs Thatcher to Lord Chancellor. Although his acts in that office were controversial at the time, he is now regarded in many quarters as amongst the most effective Lord Chancellors in the twentieth century. Lord Keith (senior Law Lord 1986–96) played a major role in reversing the growth of Tort liability following *Anns v Merton LBC*, and Lord Rodger's formidable intellect, his influence on his colleagues (detailed in chapter five above and demonstrated repeatedly in *Judge and Jurist*[206]) his pithy asides and wicked sense of fun are rapidly attaining legendary status. Finally, Lord Hope, although denied the opportunity to be President or senior Law Lord, is widely recognised as playing a major leadership role in the transfer to the Supreme Court and the early years of that Court—and not just in the frequency of cases sat in and judgments written (set out above), which outstripped his English colleagues, or in his role in bringing in and nurturing the new institution of judicial assistant. A balanced assessment, then, might well conclude that the Scots, in sending some of their best brains to serve in London, have made a disproportionate contribution to the United Kingdom's final court of appeal, to the considerable benefit of both England and Scotland.

---

[205] Since 1900 six have been Scots—Haldane, Finlay, Maxwell Fyfe, Mackay, Irvine and Falconer—serving for a total of 33 out of 113 years (29%), a far higher proportion than population alone would merit.

[206] A Burrows, D Johnston and R Zimmermann (eds), *Judge and Jurist: Essays in Memory of Lord Rodger of Earlsferry* (Oxford, Oxford University Press, 2013).

THE DIALOGUE WITH JUDICIAL ASSISTANTS

The newest, most rapidly changing, and in some sense one of the most problematic dialogues for the final court is that with the judicial assistants. The practice of recruiting very bright young lawyers in the early years of qualification to shadow appellate judges is one that first emerged in the US Supreme Court in 1882—receiving legislative sanction in 1919[207]—and thereafter has spread through the common law jurisdictions[208] and beyond.[209] In the House of Lords the post of judicial assistant emerged under the aegis of Lord Bingham when he was translated from the position of Lord Chief Justice into that of senior Law Lord by Lord Irvine LC. He was assisted in his decision by the fact that Lord Hope had experience of working with a judicial assistant as Lord President,[210] and was happy to take on the responsibility of resolving the practical challenges of implementing the decision in 2001 to bring them into the House of Lords, as well as the main role in the recruitment of the judicial assistants.

The first challenge was accommodation. As we have seen the House suffered from chronic space constraints—the only room to be found for the judicial assistants was in a *Hogwarts*-like turret in the roof of the House of Lords reached by a winding staircase from the Law Lords' corridor, which was surrendered by a generous Black Rod. The cramped conditions were compensated for by the stunning view. However, its relative inaccessibility reduced the assistants' contact with other Law Lords than those to whom they were assigned.[211] Since there was only space for four judicial assistants, one was assigned to each of the four senior Law Lords (Bingham, Slynn, Nicholls and Steyn) as their lead judge and the remaining Law Lords (excluding Lord Hoffmann, who chose never to have a judicial assistant) took a share of what was left by the seniors. In this respect some Law Lords were more equal than others, and when the move to the Supreme Court came in 2009, the requests of some of the more junior Law Lords for their own judicial assistant or a larger share of one were able to be accommodated. The open plan space on the third floor of the new Court provided ample room for eight judicial assistants and (were it ever necessary) a similar number of law reporters. As we saw in chapter four above, geography matters in the final court of appeal. The decision to locate some of the main support functions (the secretarial office, the judicial assistants and the law reporters) on the third floor along with nine of

---

[207] A Ward and D Weiden, *Sorcerers' Apprentices: 100 Years of Law Clerks at the United States Supreme Court* (New York, New York University Press, 2006).

[208] See R Munday, 'Of Law Clerks and Judicial Assistants' (2007) 171 *Justice of the Peace* 455 and G Coonan, 'The Role of Judicial Research Assistants in Supporting the Decision-Making Role of the Irish Judiciary' (2006) 6 *Judicial Studies Institute Journal* 171–96. Judicial assistants or their equivalents exist in the Australian High Court and the Canadian Supreme Court.

[209] In January 2013 a European judicial assistant was appointed to the Supreme Court for three months in a pilot exercise which would give the Court greater familiarity with civilian systems.

[210] A post that combines the role of Master of the Rolls and the Lord Chief Justice in Scotland.

[211] Most Law Lords chose to summon the assistant by phone rather than make the trek upstairs in the hope of finding them.

the Justices (and the tea room) has affected the decision-making practices of the Supreme Court because it means that four of the more junior Justices are located on the second floor and slightly detached from the rest of the Court. The judicial assistants were the net gainers, since there is far more passing traffic of Justices through the judicial assistants' space than ever there was in House of Lords. This can be exaggerated, however. Key conversations between Justice and assistant continue by telephone as they did in the past; increasingly both parties resort to email; and confidential discussions about on-going matters and the stimulating 'coaching sessions', so graphically described by Tetyana Nesterchuk in 'The View from Behind the Bench',[212] are reserved for the Justices' rooms.

Lord Hope's main challenge was to devise and operate a recruitment process that left the Court with four (now seven)[213] judicial assistants of high intellectual calibre but balanced in terms of diversity and professional background, who would complement each other (in terms of legal specialism) and be able to get on with each other as well as their judges. Overall he was remarkably successful in meeting this challenge. The annual team[214] selected from over 200 applicants, 40 long-listed candidates and 20 interviewees usually had a gender balance,[215] often a balance between solicitors and barristers, and a measure of ethnic or cultural diversity through (usually) the appointment of a Scot and regular selections from wider afield, eg Mauritius, Ireland and Australia. That was the easier part. As Nesterchuk notes, the real success was the extent to which Lord Hope would pair the judicial assistants to fit with the personalities of his colleagues. Lord Bingham's were often Oxbridge graduates with a First in an Arts subject. Lord Rodger appreciated candidates with a civilian background, whilst Lord Hope himself frequently chose a Scottish solicitor. Interestingly, personality and background was preferred to matching the specialism of the assistant with the specialism of the Justice.[216] Even more interesting, and a point we will return to, no attempt was made to link candidates and Justices in terms of philosophical outlook.

The Job of the Judicial Assistant

The title speaks for itself. The role of the judicial assistant is to assist the judges. Since different judges want different things from their assistants we should expect the experience of the judicial assistants to vary—and so it has. To begin with

---

[212] See T Nesterchuk, 'The View from Behind the Bench' ch 11 in A Burrows, D Johnston and R Zimmermann (eds), *Judge and Jurist: Essays in Memory of Lord Rodger of Earlsferry* (Oxford, Oxford University Press, 2013).

[213] The eighth judicial assistant, Ms Penelope Gorman, unlike the others who serve for 12 months, is a permanent, part-time member of the staff. She came to the Court with Lord Phillips and has continued after his retirement.

[214] Lord Hope regarded himself as selecting a team of assistants which would complement each other—see Nesterchuk, above, n 212.

[215] 2012–13 the first year in which Lord Kerr had taken over running the recruitment process from Lord Hope, yielded the very unusual result that all seven (other than Ms Gorman) were male.

[216] Some Justices prefer to have a judicial assistant whose specialism is not the same as their own so that they can provide research support in areas with which the Justice is less familiar.

their primary role was to assist with the growing burden of managing petitions to appeal (PTAs). As a team the judicial assistants were, and are, expected to provide neutral petition memos summarising in three or four pages what each application is about, and providing a road map linking the documents and their key arguments to the petition. The judicial assistants who wrote the memos will then attend the PTA hearing (which are almost always now in private without the benefit of oral argumentation by counsel) where the three Justices will decide whether to admit these appeals or not, as we saw in chapter two above. The standard pattern was that the Law Lords would read the papers for each application to the Appeal Committee as well as the petition memos and once they had reached their decision following the judges' presentations and deliberations, the judges would invite the author of the relevant memo to put their own views. This remains the norm in the Supreme Court. There was folklore in the House that an impassioned plea by an assistant once persuaded a unanimous Appeal Committee to reverse itself and admit the petition. The story may not be entirely apocryphal, since the rule of thumb is that it only takes one judge's vote to admit, and the appeal will be admitted. However, where there is a split on the Appeal Committee or the PTA the practice of the judges is to seek to reach a rapprochement and it is not always in favour of admitting the appeal. The dissenter can prevail but may have to be pretty determined to do so. Nesterchuk implies that in the Supreme Court assistants have had the occasional triumph at PTA hearings, but it has not been a common occurrence. That is not to say that their influence on PTAs has not grown since the earliest days. Increasingly, some of the Justices have been asking their own judicial assistants to review the applications for leave in order to assist the Justice in preparing for the PTA, and as part of that they will be asked to provide a short written note as to whether the application should be granted.[217] In this respect the role of the judicial assistant has begun in a minor way to resemble that of the law clerk in the US Supreme Court. There, the bulk of the work associated with sifting through the 10,000 certiorari petitions—the American version of applications for permission to appeal—received by that court in a year (as compared with 250 in the UK Supreme Court) is done by the law clerks.[218]

Following the move to the Supreme Court the judicial assistants acquired a new task. The assistant of the Justice delivering the lead judgment was expected to assist in drafting the press release to go on the Court website and to be handed down with the judgment. This responsibility taxes the assistant's ability to write for the intelligent layperson, to encapsulate a balanced account of the Court's ruling (including the views of dissenters) and to do it preferably in two pages. In some cases the assistants are also asked to do the first draft of the lead Justice's statement at the handing down of the judgment in open court, which is broadcast on Sky and now YouTube. This is a severe test of the assistant's ability to do justice

---

[217] See Nesterchuk, 'The View from Behind the Bench', above, n 212.

[218] In reality, as we in chapter 2 above, these figures exaggerate the difference in potential caseload between the two courts since around 80% of the certiorari petitions are 'in forma pauperis' where the petitioner (often a prisoner) has no lawyer and no means. Very few of these are admitted.

to the intricacies of the Court's ruling whilst writing in plain English. The judicial assistants' third Court-facing task is to prepare answers to general inquiries from the public and the press which are passed on to them by the press office or the CEO or Registrar.[219] As an extension, assistants may occasionally be asked to assist when foreign dignitaries are being shown around the Court or even to assist when there is a conference linked to the Court.

However, the largest single commitment of the assistant—in terms of time—is to shadow their principal judge like a pupil barrister, by attending the hearing in which they are involved, sitting behind the Justices.[220] Although the assistant is encouraged to make notes, unlike the petition memos these have no formal status. The notes are not used to add to what is recorded in the judicial notebooks, neither are they used to assist the law reporter, nor do they serve as a back-up record of the interaction between counsel and the Justice should an issue arise as to what was argued—as occurred in the *Assange*[221] case. Their only role is to serve as an aide memoire if the Justice should ask the assistant to follow up a point that arose in the argument, or to refresh the memory before a discussion of the case with the Justice.

Almost all of the Law Lords or Justices would ask their assistant to research points of law or fact, drawing on databases, academic literature and perhaps foreign authorities, whether for a lecture or for a case. As Lord Saville put it, 'normally we'll identify a particular aspect of the case and give the judicial assistants an open-ended request to investigate eg "Are there any other cases which touch on this?", or "Has anyone written on this?"'. Since the assistant is attending the hearing in which their Justice is sitting it is easy for them to understand a request coming out of the oral debate as to whether, say, recklessness in a criminal context is the same in a civil context, and to know how the research should be framed. Lord Collins, however, tended to have an unusual slant on case law. Either he would ask for details of American authorities not mentioned in the printed Cases, or for details of more marginal cases in the same area as those already cited in the Cases, since he found 'over-citation' of cases to be helpful when he was in an unfamiliar area of law. Especially in the early days in the House of Lords when only a minority of the Law Lords were computer literate, one skill looked for in the assistants was a facility in interrogating legal databases, and that remains the case.

However, here the commonality of experience begins to break down. Lords Bingham, Hope and Rodger saw their assistants every morning (at 7.45 am, 8.30 am

---

[219] However, judicial assistants are not expected to deal with the press or the public—that task falls to the Communications Officer .

[220] The drawback of this is that the assistants cannot, as they could in the House of Lords, see their judge's face in the oral argument thus depriving them of instant feedback on the effect of some pre-discussed question to counsel.

[221] *Assange v Swedish Prosecution Authority* [2012] UKSC 22.

and 9 am respectively)[222] when the Court was sitting, to discuss the case that was coming up that day. The assistant would always be asked for their views on the case, and sometimes what points might be made to counsel, but for the main part the role of the assistant was to act as a sounding board for the judge to bounce ideas and questions off. Success for the judicial assistant was if their suggestions were used by the judge in questioning counsel. Lord Hope stressed that the judges benefit from these half-hour sessions as well as the assistants,[223]

> You see one of the things that one is trying to do is to marshal your own thoughts and sometimes when you start speaking you realise your thoughts are going off in the wrong direction, and bouncing ideas off people at an early stage in the case is very helpful. I'm interested in the assistant's reaction. Sometimes we sense that we disagree but sometimes we agree and then we go into the hearing and realise we were both wrong because it's very narrow sometimes and then the following morning on a two-day case we realise things have developed to a different pitch and then there's bits of research that I ask them to do, bits that haven't really come through the hearing which I need some extra work done on and they do that in the knowledge of what we were actually talking about.

Lord Kerr agreed,[224]

> [I]if we can find the time it's good to have a discussion before the case is heard. Any discussion with an informed observer is beneficial in that it either confirms views that you may have tentatively formed, or the best judicial assistants will challenge views that you have provisionally made and very often they can also come up with an angle or a perspective that hadn't occurred to you.

Similarly, Lord Dyson added,[225]

> [M]y way of clarifying my thinking is to talk. I find that having an intelligent person who sat in on the case and knows what it is about, just to bounce ideas off, I find it helps me to sharpen my own thinking.

I asked the judges what the dialogue with the assistants offered over and above that which they had with counsel—with the inference that it might begin to replace their dialogue with counsel. Indeed already some Justices seem to get more from their assistants than they do from some counsel. Others appear to feel just the reverse. Lord Hope saw it as a new dialogue that offered opportunities to test out ideas in private. Lord Kerr pointed to the greater informality of the dialogue with the assistant, which takes place in a less challenging atmosphere than the hearings, and one in which neither party has an agenda[226]—unlike counsel who,

---

[222] In the year or two before he retired Lord Bingham relaxed his schedule to the extent of seeing his assistant at 8 am or even 8.15 am.

[223] Interview with the author, 2009.

[224] Interview with the author, 2009.

[225] Interview with the author, 2010.

[226] In the US Supreme Court, however, this is not an assumption than can so easily be made. Sometimes both the Justice and the law clerk will have an agenda—usually the same one but very occasionally, different. See E Lazarus, *Closed Chambers: The Rise, Fall and Future of the Modern Supreme Court* (New York, Penguin Books, 1999).

understandably, wish to persuade you to a particular point of view. Lord Dyson saw no intrinsic difference from the dialogue with counsel—'except that you can't just have a little chat with counsel and you can't speak to them when you are writing a judgment and you have suddenly got a thought'. Another Justice, however, described the dialogue with the assistant as quite different from that with counsel, 'It is much more of a personal, targeted sort of exchange'.

A further benefit from the morning discussions with assistants was that in the House, and the Supreme Court before pre-hearing meetings were introduced, some judges would ask their assistants whether any of the other judges had expressed an opinion about a case before the hearing had begun. Such an inquiry seemed perfectly natural, since in those days an assistant was shared with two other judges and inevitably when closeted together in their turret the assistants would exchange some of their hard-earned information. Indeed, the sessions with the judges continued as the case progressed and whatever was gleaned from your Law Lord would usually be shared with the other assistants and vice versa. That said, as Nesterchuk notes, some elements of the 'tutorial with the pupil-master' were considered confidential unless the judge had indicated that it was not. It might be thought confidentiality issues or even conflict of interest issues might arise if two of an assistant's judges were dissenting from each other but this does not seem to have given rise to particular problems.

Nevertheless not all assistants have the same experience. The relationship with the individual Justice is so personal that it varies not only between Justices but between years and the same Justice. So much depends on the strengths of the assistant and the working habits of the Justices. Some Justices have daily tutorials with their assistants whilst others see them less regularly and use them to research points arising from the hearings or for their judgments. Most will discuss what happens at the first conference at the end of the hearing, but some will not. Most will show occasional examples of their draft judgments to their assistants, as Lord Hope did, but not always expect much by way of comment. Others still give their own drafts to their assistant and ask them to be as critical as possible of it, an invitation which surprisingly—since lawyers are often better at criticism than praise—some assistants find harder than others. Lord Wilson had the opposite experience with a particularly bright assistant. Prone to putting his judgments through repeated revisions he was surprised to find that she frequently came up with new points or embellishments even after his revisions were at an advanced stage. With such an assistant the sounding board discussions become more of a two-way exchange of ideas about the appeal. Yet in the case of at least one Justice there are never any discussions of cases or judgments with the assistant. At the other extreme Lord Rodger was particularly forthright with his assistants, discussing all aspects of the case with them, including what his colleagues were thinking, and discussing not only what he was intending to put in his own judgment but sharing with them the drafts being circulated by other Justices. Thus Nesterchuk records that on occasion she was asked to write a brief memorandum outlining the differences between the concurring draft judgments, which was then passed to the Justices concerned. In a similar vein one Justice will discuss the circulated drafts with his assistant and if he considers that, for example, the analysis of some of the case law is insufficiently developed he may ask his assistant to do some further analysis and, depending on the quality of the result, may suggest that it be included in the judgment.

Leaving aside the diversity of experience of individual assistants when it comes to the relationship with their Justice, there are signs that the role of the judicial assistant is continuing to evolve: first with respect to team-working and secondly with respect to their input to the decision-making process. Both affect their dialogue with the Justices. As to the first, in individual cases—particularly where the judges who shared a judicial assistant were sitting together—the tutorial sessions with the judicial assistant have occasionally involved more than one judge. As Darbyshire noted[227] when she visited the Supreme Court in 2009, 'two of the Justices were making heavy use of their judicial assistant, a tax solicitor in a tax case[228] in which they were sitting. He was called in to discuss it with them. "We discuss the issues. I like bouncing ideas off him. He's very bright"', remarked one of the Justices. In these 'coaching sessions', as Lord Rodger dubbed them,[229] the 'coach' was the judicial assistant, and the role was to be a sounding board for the Justice(s). But the assistant was also expected to put forward his or her own views and these would be tested to destruction by Lords Rodger and Brown, as Nesterchuk graphically recounts. Certainly, she speculates, their mutual dialogue with the assistant seems only likely to have brought the Justices closer together.[230] Similarly in the *Axa* case[231] in 2011 three of the Justices would meet in the afternoons after the hearing to discuss where the case had got to and what avenues they wanted the judicial assistant to research. As one recalled, '[J]ust speaking out loud forced you to form your ideas in articulate language'.

As to the growing input of judicial assistants, in 2001 at the inception of the role, no judicial assistant was expected to have any contribution as to which appeals would be admitted by the Appeal Committee, other than through the neutral petition memoranda. Today, as we saw above, some are emulating their transatlantic counterparts in the US Supreme Court by being asked to express views to their Justices as to which appeals might be admitted. Whilst it was thought that some Law Lords would discuss their thinking with their assistants during the hearings, it may be doubted that it was foreseen that occasionally an assistant will help prepare their Justice for the first conference. Thirdly, in 2001 it was not expected that a judicial assistant would have any role in respect of the

---

[227] Darbyshire, *Sitting in Judgment* (Oxford, Hart Publishing, 2011) at 384.

[228] Probably *Grays Timber Products Ltd v Revenue and Customs* [2010] UKSC 4.

[229] See Nesterchuk, above, n 212.

[230] As we saw in chapter 4 of this volume the two judges voted together in 92% of the cases in which they sat with each other in the House of Lords and the Supreme Court, and 97% of the time in the 29 cases in which they sat together in the Supreme Court in the last year of Lord Rodger's stint as a Justice (June 2010–May 2011).

[231] *Axa General Insurance Ltd and Others v Lord Advocate and Others (Scotland)* [2011] UKSC 46.

draft judgments, and no provision was made for them to receive them. The Law Lords and the Justices were well aware that, in the eyes of the US law clerks at least, the latter have a significant input to the first drafts of most Justices' judgments in the US Supreme Court. This was not thought to be a good precedent to follow. Yet over the years the brilliance of some of the UK assistants has begun to push the boundaries. Discussions as to what happened at the first conference in key cases was the first to go (at least in the case of some Law Lords and Justices) leading—on occasion—to more general discussions of what other Justices were saying in their draft judgments, and the strengths and weakness of the same. The informality of the Court was such that the more inquisitive assistants would come to see, without any impropriety, some or all of the circulating drafts. From an early stage some Law Lords asked their assistants from time to time to research some factual or even legal issue for use in their judgments. Perfectly naturally, it was not unknown for the results of this work to find their way into the judge's final judgment even in the Lords, as can be seen in *Ghaidan v Godin-Mendoza*.[232] In the Supreme Court, armed with the circulating drafts, some assistants may now find themselves expected not only to critique their own Justice's judgment but also to comment on the drafts of other Justices. Of course, this is not the same as drafting the judgments, but the input is growing. One of the questions facing today's Supreme Court is how much further these developments should go. Doubtless, some will argue that since the judicial assistants attend the PTA hearings without problem, and since they tend to learn what transpires in the first conference anyway, is there not a case for them to attend the first conference, perhaps even to keep a record of what was agreed? Such a suggestion has never made any headway in the US Supreme Court, where the Justices jealously guard the restriction of the conference to themselves alone.[233] Of course, the US law clerks are every bit as assiduous as their counterparts in other final appellate courts, in gleaning from their Justices their account of what happened in the conference room. Their recollections, in time, have appeared along with the contents of the Justices' papers recording the details of the conferences, in a plethora of books on decision-making in the Supreme Court.[234] However there has always been a cooling off period. Moreover, the mere presence of outside observers may have a

---

[232] *Ghaidan v Godin-Mendoza* [2004] 2 AC 557, para 39, Lord Steyn pays tribute to the research of his assistant Laura Porter whose research into cases invoking s 3 of the Human Rights Act 1998 he had included as an Appendix to his judgment.

[233] In consequence the junior Justice has the duty to answer the door should any message arrive during the meeting.

[234] E Lazarus, *Closed Chambers: The Rise, Fall and Future of the Modern Supreme Court* (New York, Penguin Books, 1999); J Rosen, *The Supreme Court: The Personalities and Rivalries that Defined America* (New York, Times Books, Henry Holt & Company, 2006); A Ward and D Weiden, *Sorcerers' Apprentices: 100 Years of Law Clerks at the United States Supreme Court* (New York, New York University Press, 2006); T Peppers, *Courtiers of the Marble Palace* (Stanford CA, Stanford University Press, 2006); JC Greenburg, *Supreme Conflict: The Inside Story of the Struggle for the Control of the United States Supreme Court* (New York, The Penguin Press, 2007); J Toobin, *The Nine: Inside the Secret World of the Supreme Court* (New York, Anchor Books, 2008).

Heisenberg effect on the behaviour of the Justices. Since there are already signs that follow-up case conferences can become occasions where personal feelings are engaged, the presence of observers would only be likely to exacerbate this.

The ultimate issue, of course, is whether judicial assistants should play any role in the writing of the first drafts of judgments. This is not a role assigned to judicial assistants or their equivalents in the UK Supreme Court, the Australian High Court or the Canadian Supreme Court.[235] Nor was it part of the original role of US Supreme Court clerks. However, an unintended consequence of a well-intentioned reform by Chief Justice Vinson in the 1940s,[236] which tried to equalise workloads on the Court in terms of judgment writing, led to some Justices asking their clerks to be responsible for the first draft of their judgments. The accounts of their role given by the law clerks over the last 20 years have a natural tendency to exaggerate the influence of the clerks, and those by the Justices, to do the reverse. The truth is probably somewhere in the middle. It certainly seems to be the case that all or almost all of today's US Supreme Court Justices routinely allow their clerks (they have four each except the Chief Justice who has five) to do first drafts of judicial opinions, or to revise and edit such drafts.[237] According to the authors of *Sorcerers' Apprentices*, a book on the influence of Supreme Court clerks, about 30 per cent of the opinions issued by the Supreme Court are almost entirely the work of law clerks. The clerks also do the great bulk of the research and analysis in certiorari petitions, the US equivalents of permission to appeal applications. The Justices, however, point to the fact that 80 per cent of a Supreme Court judgment is a formulaic mixture of relevant facts and legal analyses which the clerk will only embark on after detailed instructions from their Justice as to what should be in it. The key dispositive 20 per cent of the opinion will be tightly controlled by the Justice. Moreover, most Justices claim to rewrite the draft extensively, as Scalia says, 'I'll put it up on my screen and take it apart and put it back together'.[238] In truth, human nature being what it is, the pressures that drove the Justices to delegate drafting to the law clerks in the first place will ensure that there is a limit to the extent to which the Justices will actually revise each first draft in the way Scalia suggests, especially if it is not the majority judgment. Nonetheless, although there have been repeated allegations that some Justices in the last 20 years have allowed their clerks to have too great an input into the drafting process, the key decisions are the votes in conference. These are the responsibility of the Justices however much the clerks may have worked on preparing the Justice for the oral hearing and the conference and drafted the 'disposition memorandum'[239] to inform the Justice in the run up to the votes on appeals or on certiorari petitions.

---

[235] See J Heydon, 'Varieties of Judicial Method in the Late 20th Century' (2012) 34 *Sydney Law Review* 219.

[236] See R Munday, 'Of Law Clerks and Judicial Assistants' (2007) 171 *Justice of the Peace* 455, 459.

[237] T Peppers, *Courtiers of the Marble Palace* (Stanford CA, Stanford University Press, 2006) at 205.

[238] See C-SPAN interview at 57.

[239] The description is Justice Thomas's, taken from his C-SPAN interview published in B Lamb et al (eds), *The Supreme Court* (New York, Public Affairs, 2010) at 90.

There is a further protection for the Justices from the 'rogue' or ambitious clerk. Most Justices run their chambers like a law firm with the clerks as members of the team, with mutual self-checking. In addition, it has become commonplace for Justices to hire clerks that share their general philosophical stance, eg originalist, strict construction, black-letter, purposive or the like. Justice Thomas even uses a 'specific ideological litmus test'.[240] As he somewhat unflatteringly observed, 'I won't hire clerks who have profound disagreements with me. Its like trying to train a pig. It wastes your time and aggravates the pig'.[241] On the other hand, Thomas is far more inclusive of recruits from non-elite law schools than his colleagues who tend to recruit very heavily from the elite, Ivy League schools.

The changes in the role of the law clerk in the US Supreme Court in the last 60 years pose a warning to the other common law jurisdictions. Justice Heydon of the Australian High Court is not a fan of the 'over-sophistication' which he feels comes from the employment of research staff who he somewhat waspishly describes as 'not only academically brilliant, but also conscious of that fact'.[242] Heydon's unstated argument is that law clerks, however intelligent, lack the understanding of a Supreme Court Justice and may have the overconfidence of youth—a potentially dangerous combination. He has no doubts that for judges to start delegating the task of writing reasons for their decisions would be wrong. Interestingly, not every federal judge in the US is a fan of using law clerks to write opinions. Richard Posner, an acutely insightful and reflective scholar judge, con-sidered the delegation of opinion writing to law clerks to be ill-advised, since he felt that it had already led to a loss of quality in Supreme Court opinions, greater length, more footnotes, more concurring opinions, and a blandness that negated the idiosyncratic style which was the hallmark of the great Justices of the past. More practically, he pointed to the dangers of an inexperienced law clerk being reluctant to tell his Justice that the draft opinion will not write and ploughing on regardless, whereas the Justice herself would have known that when an opinion will not write that is often an indication that the decision is wrong.[243]

All this seems very far removed from the judicial assistants of the UK Court. At present the consensus that their role does not and should not encompass the writing of judgments seems robust.[244] But doubtless the same was true 70 years ago in the US Supreme Court. Already the job description for the Law Clerk to the Lord President[245] includes 'preparing draft text which is suitable for possible inclusion in the Opinions issued by the Court of Session and the High Court of

---

[240] See J Toobin, *The Nine*, above, n 234, at 100.

[241] J Toobin, *The Nine*, above, n 234, at 101.

[242] J Heydon, 'Varieties of Judicial Method in the Late 20th Century' (2012) 34 *Sydney Law Review* 219, 226.

[243] R Posner, 'Judges' Writing Styles (And Do They Matter?)' (1995) 62 *University of Chicago Law Review* 1421.

[244] 'The rule is they don't draft judgments for us. They don't see a draft judgment of ours until after we have written it'. Lord Sumption, interview with the author, 2013.

[245] Scotland's equivalent of the Lord Chief Justice and the Master of the Rolls.

Justiciary'.[246] Moreover, as their input to the decision-making process continues to grow, and as more Justices come to see the assistant as part of the judicial decision-making team ('Two heads are better than one'), so it will become more likely that the Justices will want a say in the recruitment of their own assistant, as in the US Supreme Court, and if that happens a form of cloning effect may develop. Should this come about assistants will tend to become protective of their own Justice and the occasional tensions between Justices will be reflected in their assistants. Any tendency to polarisation is to be avoided. The bitter and searing account by Edward Lazarus, of his experiences as a liberal clerk in the US Supreme Court in an era of unremitting defeats by the conservative bloc of Justices and their clerks, makes salutary reading.[247]

Fortunately the communal spirit amongst the assistants which is supported by the open plan office and the collective work arrangements, eg over petition memos, which Lord Rodger and Lord Hope did so much to foster, will work against such factionalising tendencies. So too will the reunions and the growing esprit de corps of this, the newest and most interesting community to engage in dialogue with the judges of the final court.

---

[246] Advertisement in May 2013.

[247] See *Closed Chambers*, above, n 234, Greenburg, *Supreme Conflicts: The Inside Story of the Struggle for the Control of the United States Supreme Court*, at 76 recounts an unseemly instance of a law clerk to Justice Kennedy (the swing vote in 1988, as he often is today) boasting to other clerks that he had persuaded his Justice to vote with the conservatives, in a 1988 case, by telling Justice Kennedy that he was being taken advantage of too often by Justice Brennan, the leading liberal on the Court.

7

The Dialogue with the Other Branches of Government

SETTING THE SCENE

T HE FINAL DIALOGUES are those between the Court and the other two arms of government—Parliament and the Executive. The paradox is that whilst these are the 'powers' that the purer separation of powers implemented by New Labour sought to keep separate, nonetheless a complete separation would lead to gridlock. For a state to function effectively there has to be a measure of communication between the different branches of government through which the checks and balances which delimit the parameters of the powers of each can be regularly fine-tuned. In this chapter we will examine first the dialogue with Parliament and then the dialogue with the Executive. However, this is to a certain extent artificial since the interconnection between Parliament and the Executive in the UK is such that dialogue with one will often impact on the dialogue with the other.

THE DIALOGUE WITH PARLIAMENT

So long as there has been a division of labour based on the separation of powers between final courts of appeal and legislatures there has always been a tension— not necessarily an unhealthy one—between what is the proper role for the courts and what should be left to the Parliament when it comes to developing or reforming the law. Articulating the traditional formula that Parliament creates the law and the judges apply the law made by Parliament is simply another way of re-stating the problem without solving the definitional or historical problems that the formula masks. This is the territory of legal and political philosophy but we will eschew these tempting byways, restricting our focus to the dialogue between the Court and Parliament and the question as to what role, if any, that dialogue plays in the decision-making of the final court in the UK.

With respect to cases turning on statutory interpretation, there is clearly a sense in which the Court is grappling with the intention of Parliament on every occasion, however artificial that concept may be. Yet as often as not it is a case of making sense of a monologue rather than engaging in a dialogue, symbolic or otherwise, with Parliament. Even when resort is had to *Hansard*,[1] the Court is more often embellishing the monologue than responding to it. Of course, that is not to deny that the final court engages in law-making in the statutory sphere through the concept of a statute as a living instrument as in *Fitzpatrick v Sterling Housing Association Ltd*[2] and *Yemshaw v London Borough of Hounslow*[3] or in other cases where a precedent enshrining a decision based on statutory interpretation is being departed from. However, here—as in the common-law field—the dialogue is almost entirely indirect, symbolic and asynchronous.[4] Nonetheless, whether statutory or common law in focus the dialogue has become more problematic as the power of the Court has grown in the last decade and more, through the expansion of the judicial review jurisdiction and the passing of the Human Rights Act 1998 (HRA),[5] as we shall see.

Judicial Activism and its Drawbacks

Commentators in the field of judicial law-making not infrequently refer to the differences in judicial temperament of the participants who engage (or fail to engage) in this pursuit. Famously, Lord Denning distinguished between the bold spirits who are willing to develop the law and the timorous souls who are not. This was and is an oversimplification—even if we accept Denning's basic thrust that some judges are more adventurous law-makers than others, there is clearly a continuum rather than a dichotomy on the matter. Equally, some judges are more or less willing to be creative depending on the field of law in which the case arises. This brings us to the concept of judicial activism. Historically this has been contrasted with judicial restraint and the parallel with Lord Denning's dichotomy

---

[1] The official record of the proceedings of the UK Parliament.

[2] *Fitzpatrick v Sterling Housing Association Ltd* [1999] UKHL 42. The issue here was what the word 'family' meant in the Rent Acts for the purposes of succession to a deceased tenant. The majority Law Lords held that 'family' in the statute did not have a technical meaning but only its ordinary language meaning. In 1950 the courts had held that 'family' for the security of tenure purposes did not include cohabiting couples—even of 20 years duration. Lord Denning reversed this decision in 1976 on the grounds that by then, at least, 'family' included longstanding cohabitants. In *Fitzpatrick* the majority Law Lords held that by 1999 'family' could include a same sex relationship of longstanding, although the partners could not be treated as spouses for the purposes of the Act.

[3] *Yemshaw v London Borough of Hounslow* [2011] UKSC 3. Under the homelessness legislation a person could claim to be in need of accommodation if they had been driven out of their home by domestic violence. The question in this case was whether 'domestic violence' included 'abusive psychological behaviour'. The Court (Lord Brown *dubitans*) held that using a living instrument approach to the legislation, it did.

[4] A rare exception was the case of *R v Chaytor* [2010] UKSC 52, where the Court was ruling on the extent of parliamentary privilege—a dialogue that was real and relatively direct, although not in person. As Lord Phillips said in para 16, 'although the extent of parliamentary privilege is ultimately a matter for the courts, it is one on which the courts will pay careful regard to any views expressed in Parliament by either House or by bodies or individuals in a position to speak on the matter with authority'.

[5] Especially s 3 on interpreting statutes in keeping with the ECHR.

is clear. Again, the dangers of over-simplification bedevil easy analysis. Brice Dickson's edited volume on *Judicial Activism in Common Law Supreme Courts*[6] was partly intended to show that 'judicial activism' is a term which has been used to mean several different things. While it could signify how heavy a caseload a court has and the number and length of the judgments it issues, much more often judicial activism is used to refer to how willing the judges are to develop the law.[7] On this analysis, judges who find liability by applying existing principles where none has been found before, eg where a solicitor has negligently drafted a will thereby depriving the beneficiaries of their entitlements, are being activist. But what of the judges who, after serious consideration, decided that a mother who gave birth to a healthy child (because of a negligently performed vasectomy on her husband), could not recover damages for the wrongful birth of the child?[8] Under the existing principles of law there was a strong argument that she should have been entitled to damages. Was that an example of creative activism or simply a form of restraint? Brice Dickson in his eponymous contribution to *Judicial Activism in Common Law Supreme Courts*[9] used a more precise definition, namely,[10]

> an approach to adjudication which seeks to locate the particular decision in the context of a wider legal framework, pointing out what the consequences of the decision are likely to be for fact situations which are different from those currently before the court and explaining how the reasoning underlying the decision fits with the reasoning underlying other related rules and principles already set down by Parliament or by previous judges.

On this approach, the activism stems from a refusal to confine the reasoning supporting the decision to the narrow facts of the particular case and an insistence on coherence and consistency in the judicial development of the law. Coherence, consistency and consequentialism—the three 'c's of judicial law-making are widely admired, but Dickson added a fourth 'clarity', a fifth 'cogency' and a sixth 'considered' in his next assessment of the achievements of the Bingham Court. Perhaps the three new 'c's made a difference to the analysis, for his verdict on the quality of law-making in the 1995–2007 Court[11] is rather more critical than that on the Court's record from 2000–08.[12] Dickson is undecided as to the quality

---

[6] B Dickson (ed), *Judicial Activism in Common Law Supreme Courts* (Oxford, Oxford University Press, 2007) ch 9 'Judicial Activism in the House of Lords 1995–2007'.

[7] As such, as with judicial legislation, it is a pejorative term in the mouths of more conservative judges.

[8] See *Macfarlane v Tayside Health Board* [1999] UKHL 50.

[9] B Dickson (ed), *Judicial Activism in Common Law Supreme Courts* (Oxford, Oxford University Press, 2007) ch 9 'Judicial Activism in the House of Lords 1995–2007'.

[10] Ibid, 370.

[11] 'Unadventurous in some areas and assertive in others, but patchy overall' (ibid, 414).

[12] See B Dickson, 'A Hard Act to Follow: The Bingham Court, 2000–08' in L Blom-Cooper, B Dickson and G Drewry, *The Judicial House of Lords* (Oxford, Oxford University Press, 2009) at 270 'Consistently of high quality'.

of the Bingham Court's decision-making on human rights, swinging between disappointment over the timidity of *Belmarsh* and *Bancoult* and praising the Court's assertiveness in the field. Other commentators' assessments of decision-making in the European Court of Human Rights are similarly divergent. Theresa May would be astounded at the English public law scholars who rail at its timidity in developing the human rights jurisprudence. Perhaps this is the key. Activism is too much in the eye of the beholder to serve as a useful mechanism for discrimination. Everyone cannot be right. As such it is best avoided as a term to cast light on the dialogue between the final court and Parliament.

In *The Law Lords* a rather similar dialectic to activism and restraint was highlighted—that between the drive for stability and certainty in the common law on the one hand and individuated justice and fairness on the other.[13] This tension between justice and certainty is in some respects another way of putting the age old tension between the moral merits and the legal merits of a case. In the interviews, the Law Lords and Justices were asked whether the moral merits made any difference at the level of the final court of appeal. Interestingly, the majority answered in the affirmative. Even senior judges are not immune to the attractions of what appears fair to the neutral bystander. True, the law reports are littered with expressions of judicial sympathy, from *Purdy* (assisted dying) to *Jones v First Tier Tribunal and Criminal Injuries Compensation Authority*[14] (a road accident victim seeking compensation under the Criminal Injuries Compensation Scheme), whilst the court firmly rules against the appellant. However, in situations where the legal merits are finely balanced on either side the perceived just outcome may have an impact, although where the court is split it is not unknown for each side to be influenced by different perceptions as to where the moral merits lie.[15] Lord Sumption made a related point in our interview. As we saw in chapter five of this volume[16] he considers that appellate judges fall into three categories: 'parsons' who tend to look at issues in moral terms, 'pragmatic realists' (who have an eye to consequences) and 'principled analysts' who want a principle that will covers the generality of cases and looks at the full range of relevant law. In his eyes,

> Of course the merits [matter, but] ... the question that I ask myself is not what are the merits of this individual case, but do the merits of this individual case warrant a general rule which would encompass it ... It has got to be a principle that covers the generality of cases and looks at the full range of relevant law.

A practical example of a significant case in the UK Supreme Court where the moral merits and the legal principles appeared to pull in different directions

---

[13] A Paterson, *The Law Lords* (London, MacMillan, 1982). Lord Reid in 'The Judge as Law Maker' (1972) 12 *Journal of the Society of Public Teachers of Law* 22, 26 said 'People want two inconsistent things; that the law shall be certain, and that it shall be just and shall move with the times. It is our business to keep both objectives in view'.

[14] *Jones v First Tier Tribunal and Criminal Injuries Compensation Authority* [2013] UKSC 19.

[15] See eg *Geys v Société Générale London Branch* [2012] UKSC 63.

[16] At n 21.

was *Prest v Petrodel Resources Ltd*[17]where a multimillionaire and his wife were divorcing. Most of the husband's property had been held for some time in limited companies which he owned and controlled. For the divorce court to award any property to Mrs Prest would require it to 'pierce the corporate veil' and look behind the companies to see who controlled them. Since it was accepted that they were not sham companies and that there was no question of fraud, such an action by the divorce court appeared to breach accepted principles of company law. However, not to pierce the veil would have appeared to open the door for wealthy spouses in the future to hide their resources in companies which they controlled. In a case where the two family judges were balanced by two chancery judges, interestingly, it was Lord Sumption who came up with a third way that avoided a decision which might have caused lasting damage to either family law or company law.

Hard Cases Make Bad Law

One of the sobering truths which militates against giving greater weight to the moral merits is the celebrated aphorism that 'hard cases make bad law'. That is that courts which allow their hearts to rule their heads can end up distorting the law for other cases. Several examples can be given. The first is the historic fraud case of *Derry v Peek*.[18] There a court of common law Law Lords was persuaded by clever advocacy that (a) the directors of the company who had made an untrue statement in the company's prospectus were Victorian gentlemen (b) that 'you don't shake hands with a man who has been guilty of fraud' and (c) therefore the directors were not guilty of fraud.[19] Neil Duxbury in *Jurists and Judges*[20] demonstrates graphically how long it took and how much effort by Sir Frederick Pollock it took to get the House to gradually reduce the influence of *Derry v Peek*.

Equally notorious, at least in modern times, was the case of *Pepper v Hart*.[21] Here, Lord Griffiths was in a minority of one after the original hearing. However, having consulted *Hansard* unofficially, he formed the view that it contained a statement from the relevant Minster which answered the case in a different way than the majority were proposing. His passionate conviction as to the equities of the case eventually persuaded his colleagues to go to a re-hearing with seven judges, with the Lord Chancellor (Lord Mackay) presiding. In the end he won over all bar one of his colleagues to modifying the existing rule that *Hansard* could not be used to establish the purpose of legislation. This change might seem more democratic and more transparent in terms of the dialogue with

---

[17] [2013] UKSC 34
[18] *Derry v Peek* (1889) 14 App Cas 337 (HL).
[19] See *The Law Lords* (above, n 13) 54.
[20] N Duxbury, *Jurists and Judges* (Oxford, Hart Publishing, 2001) at 84ff.
[21] *Pepper v Hart* [1992] UKHL 3.

Parliament. However, Lord Mackay dissented on the grounds that the change was like Pandora's Box—in practice the relaxation would be unworkable. Many judges now agree with him considering that abandoning the old rule has led to much increased expense and very little practical benefit. Hints can be found in the judgments of the final court in recent years suggesting that *Pepper v Hart* will have to be reconsidered. This experiment in opening up the dialogue with Parliament may not, after all, have led to more effective decision-making in the Court.

Finally, the celebrated series of causation cases, and *Fairchild*[22] in particular.[23] In that case, the Law Lords, moved by the plight of mesothelioma sufferers who could never recover under the existing law on causation—the 'but for' test— fashioned a new causation test for them. Lord Hoffmann's contribution to the Lord Rodger memorial volume[24] graphically describes how in a series of subsequent cases the House tried desperately to put the brakes on the *Fairchild* anomaly before its logic swept away the whole of the established law on causation in the tort of negligence. His conclusion is that it would have been better if the Law Lords had steeled themselves to the unfairness in *Fairchild* and left it to Parliament to sort out. Lord Brown's rebuke that 'the law tampers with the "but for" test of causation at its peril'[25] strongly suggests that he is at one with Lord Hoffmann on this. In each of these *cause célèbres* an original decision based on a perception of manifest inequity has come to be seen as a misfortune which is difficult to depart from. It seems that where the final court feels compelled by the moral merits to act rather than to leave the issue to Parliament, a 'supertanker effect' kicks in which makes it difficult for the Court to change course.

Justice, Certainty and Fairness

Clearly, the temptation to act in cases of great injustice is one to which even final courts are not immune. This tension between certainty and fairness was one that the Law Lords of 40 years ago felt keenly.[26] Yet in the period 1957–62—dubbed by Robert Stevens as the era of 'Substantive Formalism'—Lord Simonds as senior Law Lord ensured that 'justice as certainty' prevailed in the House of Lords since most of the Law Lords generally favoured precedent to principle, refining rather than rationalising the law, and applying the law as it was, not as they might wish it to be.[27] Law reform was for the legislature.

Substantive formalism constituted the apotheosis of the declaratory theory. The latter had the democratic advantage that judges did not develop or reform

---

[22] *Fairchild v Glenhaven Funeral Services Ltd* [2002] UKHL 22.
[23] See chapter 5 of this volume above.
[24] 'Fairchild and After' in A Burrows, D Johnston and R Zimmermann (eds), *Judge and Jurist: Essays in Memory of Lord Rodger of Earlsferry* (Oxford, Oxford University Press, 2013).
[25] *Sienkiewicz v Grief* [2011] UKSC 10, [186].
[26] *The Law Lords* (above, n 13) 124ff.
[27] Ibid, 132.

the law, but merely declared what it had always been. However, it was not without its shortcomings. It provided no guidance in 'hard' cases where the applicable law was unclear—or indeed, like the steady state theory of the Universe, of how the common law/ Universe could have evolved originally. Further, in those situations where the courts did develop the law or overrule lower court precedents, however longstanding they were, the theory required that the new ruling had always been the law. Unlike legislative change, such common law reversals were always retrospective.

However, a minority of Simonds' colleagues (Lords Reid, Radcliffe, Denning and MacDermott) were unconvinced by the declaratory theory. By 1962 the pressure on the remaining Law Lords to accept that the Court had a role to play in keeping the common law in touch with the society in which it operated, was becoming a force that could no longer be ignored. Lords Radcliffe and Devlin provided the solution—dissimulation—or 'the façade approach'. In Lord Radcliffe's striking words,[28]

> If judges prefer the formula—for that is what it is—that they merely declare the law and do not make it, they do no more than show themselves wise men in practice. Their analysis may be weak, but their perception of the nature of the law is sound. Men's respect for it will be the greater, the more imperceptible its development.

In his subsequent address to the Harvard Law Faculty his preference for dissimulation in the dialogue with the legislature was equally apparent,[29]

> We cannot run the risk of finding the archetypical image of the judge confused in men's minds with the very different image of the legislator … Personally, I think that judges will serve the public interest better if they keep quiet about their legislative function.

Indeed the following period in the House 1962–66 was one marked by numerous instances of judicial law-making—albeit under the guise of dissimulation eg *Hedley Byrne v Heller*,[30] *Ridge v Baldwin*,[31] *Gollins v Gollins*,[32] *Burmah Oil Co v Lord Advocate*,[33] *Rookes v Barnard*[34] and *Myers v DPP*.[35] Overt references to policy-considerations in these cases were unusual even where—as in Lord Devlin's exegesis on exemplary damages in *Rookes v Barnard*—the judgment was a purely policy based one.[36] It was, however, an era which was marked by a less reverential attitude to precedent culminating in the celebrated adoption of

---

[28] Lord Radcliffe, *The Law and Its Compass* (London, Faber and Faber, 1961) at 39.
[29] Lord Radcliffe, 'The Lawyer and His Times' in A Sutherland (ed), *The Path of the Law from 1967* (Cambridge MA, Harvard University Press, 1968) 14–15.
[30] *Hedley Byrne & Co Ltd v Heller & Partners Ltd* [1964] AC 465.
[31] *Ridge v Baldwin* [1964] AC 40.
[32] *Gollins v Gollins* [1964] AC 644.
[33] *Burmah Oil Co Ltd v Lord Advocate* [1965] AC 75.
[34] *Rookes v Barnard* [1964] AC 1129.
[35] *Myers v Director of Public Prosecutions* [1965] AC 1001.
[36] Lord Devlin indicated as much to me in interview and his colleagues agreed.

the 1966 Practice Statement on Precedent[37] in the House of Lords. The Practice Statement—which freed the House from following its own precedents—was a statement to Parliament just as it was to the legal community in general. In future, the House decreed, it would no longer require an act of Parliament to get rid of a precedent of the House which had outlived its 'sell by date'. As the more detailed accounts of the making of the Practice Statement reveal,[38] the Law Commission of Scotland and the Lord Chancellor played significant roles in its promulgation, but Parliament was not consulted. The Lord Chancellor presiding in the House had created the original practice of the House being bound by its own decisions in 1898[39] and the Lord Chancellor with the support of most of the Law Lords[40] revoked that practice in 1966 without any greater input from the legislature than the rule that Parliament cannot bind its successors—the Lords being the Upper Chamber of Parliament in constitutional theory.

Lord Reid, now senior Law Lord, had launched a series of attacks on the 1898 rule in the run up to the 1966 announcement.[41] His support was essential to the adoption of the new practice and he provided the guidelines as to when the Practice Statement should be exercised in a series of deliberate pronouncements in relevant cases.[42] Essentially these were that the freedom to depart from a precedent of the House should be exercised sparingly and should rarely be used in situations where parliamentary reform would be more suitable, eg (1) where it would upset contracts or expectations based on the old decision, (2) where the precedent turned on statutory construction, (3) where the consequences of changing the law could not be estimated or (4) where the area was one which required comprehensive reform. However, a decision should be overruled if it caused great uncertainty to advisers or it was considered to be unjust and out of touch with modern conceptions of public policy. In keeping with this balanced approach he was of the view that the role of the House as the final court should be 'to clear up the messes of which there are many and occasionally to be a bit bold and innovate a bit'.[43] He considered that in a democratic society the legitimacy of such judicial legislation had to be confronted head-on. Not for him the 'façade'

---

[37] Practice Statement on Precedent [1966] 3 All ER 77.

[38] See Paterson, *The Law Lords* (above, n 13) 146–53 and L Blom-Cooper, '1966 and All That: The Story of the Practice Statement' ch 9 in Blom-Cooper, B Dickson and G Drewry (eds), *The Judicial House of Lords 1876–2009* (Oxford, Oxford University Press, 2009) 128ff.

[39] *London Tramways Company v London County Council* [1898] AC 375. Often cited as *London Street Tramways Company v London County Council* but an erratum slip in the Reports indicates that the 'Street' is erroneous.

[40] The prime mover was Lord Reid. The suggestion (see L Blom-Cooper, '1966 and All That', above, n 38) that Lord Simonds had recanted his earlier resolute opposition to changing the practice of the House on this matter does not fit with the interviews given to me by his former colleagues in the early 1970s. See *The Law Lords* (above, n 13) 150–51.

[41] See *The Law Lords* (above, n 13) 146–53.

[42] Particularly *Jones v Secretary of State for Social Services* [1972] AC 944. See Paterson, *The Law Lords* (above, n 13) 156ff. Lord Reid conceded to me that he had tried to set guidelines for his colleagues.

[43] Interview with the author, 1972.

approach of Lords Radcliffe and Devlin. As he stated in his seminal lecture on judicial law-making,[44]

> There was a time when it was thought almost indecent to suggest that judges make law—they only declare it … But we do not believe in fairy tales any more. So we must accept the fact that for better or worse judges do make law, and tackle the question how do they approach their task and how should they approach it.

From the roll call of significant 'hard' and close call cases decided in the House at around the time when Lord Reid made this speech: *Conway v Rimmer*,[45] *Indyka v Indyka*,[46] *Anisminic v FCC*,[47] *Home Office v Dorset Yacht Co Ltd*,[48] and *British Railways Board v Herrington*,[49] it can be seen that he practised what he preached. Indeed, so effective a leadership role did Lord Reid play in relation to the limits of judicial law-making and to the use of the 1966 Practice Statement that his views on these matters continued to have currency 30 years later when Lord Bingham was senior Law Lord.[50] A detailed examination of the 29 cases in which the 1966 Practice Statement was raised by counsel[51] or Law Lords between 1966 and 1980 shows that Lord Reid's guidelines as to the appropriate use of the Practice Statement were very largely adhered to by his colleagues during that period.[52] Subsequent analyses[53] of the Practice Statement and its use in the House of Lords also indicate the efficacy of Lord Reid's guidelines in encapsulating the substantial consensus amongst his colleagues and successors as to the use of the Practice Statement. Eight overrulings in the first 14 years and less than 25 in the first 43 years suggests that the injunction that it be used 'sparingly' has indeed been taken seriously. However, there is also evidence that in the early days at least, the availability of the Practice Statement encouraged the Court or a majority of its members to get round unhelpful precedents rather than tackling them head on. Thus of the 29 cases raising the 1966 freedom between 1966 and 1980, there were 10 in which the precedent was distinguished rather than departed from or expressly overruled.[54]

---

[44] See Lord Reid, 'The Judge as Law Maker' (1972) 12 *Journal of the Society of Public Teachers of Law* 22.

[45] *Conway v Rimmer* [1968] AC 910.

[46] *Indyka v Indyka* [1969] 1 AC 33.

[47] Anisminic Ltd v Foreign Compensation Commission [1969] 2 AC 147.

[48] Home Office v Dorset Yacht Co Ltd [1970] AC 1004.

[49] British Railways Board v Herrington [1972] AC 877.

[50] See eg Lord Bingham's dictum in *Horton v Sadler* [2006] UKHL 27, para 29.

[51] In the decade after 1966 until Lord Reid's guidelines were established, counsel tended to invoke the Practice Statement every time a precedent of the House was against them. Thereafter there was a marked decline in speculative invocations by counsel. See *The Law Lords* (above, n 13) 162.

[52] Ibid.

[53] A Paterson, 'Lord Reid's Unnoticed Legacy—A Jurisprudence of Overruling' (1981) 1 *Oxford Journal of Legal Studies* 375 and L Blom-Cooper, '1966 and All That' ch 9 in Blom-Cooper et al (above, n 35) 128ff.

[54] *The Law Lords* (above, n 13) 163.

UK Supreme Court watchers were initially kept in the dark as to its approach to its own precedents and those of the House of Lords.[55] It gradually emerged that one of the criteria for having a panel of seven Justices was that it was a case where the Court was being asked to reconsider a precedent of its own or of the House. However it was not until *Austin v The Mayor and Burgesses of the London Borough of Southwark*[56] that Lord Hope speaking on behalf of the Court, revealed that not only did the Practice Statement carry over from the House of Lords but so too did the jurisprudence[57] as to its use. A Practice Direction was then issued,[58] repeating Lord Hope's words and indicating that counsel at the permission stage should make it clear if they wished to ask the Court to depart from a precedent of its own or that of the House, but leaving unanswered the tantalising question as to why nothing on the issue had been in the original Practice Directions of the Court. Certainly, if anything, the Court has been even less willing than the House of Lords to use the freedom. The Statement had been raised overtly by counsel[59] or the Justices in only a handful of cases by the start 2013 and in none of them has the Court purported to exercise it.[60]

However, as with the House, there have been a number of cases in which the panel or a majority of it has appeared to use the availability of the Practice Statement as an encouragement to get round precedents of its own or the House. Thus in *Pinnock*,[61] Lord Neuberger with judicious help from Strasbourg, in what was effectively a judgment of the Court, discarded the authorities of *Qazi*,[62] *Kay*[63] and *Doherty*[64] with hardly a mention that they were all precedents of the House which in their time had been fought over like the opposing armies around the forts of Verdun.[65] Again, Lord Dyson in the sole judgment in *R (Munir) v Secretary of State for the Home Department*[66] (on the immigration rules) sidestepped a 2009 House of Lords decision by treating the relevant aspects as *obiter dicta*. In *Jones v Kaney*[67] (the expert

---

[55] On this and on the general issue of the 1966 Practice Statement and the Supreme Court I am indebted to the helpful paper by James Lee, 'Precedent and the Supreme Court' presented at the Supreme Court conference in October 2012.

[56] *Austin v The Mayor and Burgesses of the London Borough of Southwark* [2010] UKSC 28.

[57] Including, it would seem Lord Reid's guidelines, which are all contained in decisions of the House.

[58] Supreme Court Practice Direction 3, *Applications for Permission to Appeal*, para 3.1.3.

[59] In *Botham v Ministry of Defence* [2011] UKSC 58 counsel for the respondent suggested in his written Case that a precedent of the House *Johnson* [2001] UKHL 13 should be departed from but he did not develop the argument orally or in writing. See para 1. Ironically the three dissenters plus Lord Phillips dropped hints to the effect that a challenge to *Johnson* might have been appropriate.

[60] A lower strike rate than had pertained in the House.

[61] *Manchester City Council v Pinnock* [2010] UKSC 45, para 49.

[62] *Harrow London Borough Council v Qazi* [2003] UKHL 43.

[63] *Kay v Lambeth London Borough Council* [2006] UKHL 10.

[64] *Doherty v Birmingham City Council* [2008] UKHL 57.

[65] See Lord Mance's judgment in *Doherty*, ibid, at para 125. Indeed in the hearing of *Doherty* efforts by the appellants and the Secretary of State as an intervener to persuade the House to depart from *Qazi* and *Kay* had been rejected by the House without the need to convene a panel of seven Law Lords.

[66] *R (on the application of Munir) v Secretary of State for the Home Department* [2012] UKSC 32.

[67] *Jones v Kaney* [2011] UKSC 13.

witness immunity case) the majority Justices largely ignored a Scots decision of the House of Lords which the minority Justices (Hale and Hope) felt was directly on point and required the Practice Statement if it was to be departed from. James Lee supports this view, arguing also that *Jones v Kernott*[68] (the *Stack v Dowden* sequel on the property rights of cohabitants) and *R (KM) v Cambridgeshire County Council*[69] (about resource allocation constraints on local authorities) are further examples of the Supreme Court using distinguishing techniques rather than the more direct Practice Statement to avoid precedents of the House. In short, the tendency of the Supreme Court to date has been to pursue indirect methods of removing unhelpful precedents of the House rather than direct ones—a practice which Lords Devlin and Radcliffe would have approved of, though not Lord Reid. The House of Lords by contrast, despite the continuing attractions of distinguishing precedents of its own,[70] overtly exercised the Practice Statement on almost 25 occasions between 1966 and 2009—a clear indication that the Law Lords were 'occasional legislators', as Richard Posner[71] would put it, and shared the burden of law reform with Parliament on a significant number of occasions in the last 40 years.

Drawing the Line

Returning to the broader theme of judicial law-making, Lord Bingham approved of Lord Reid's critique of the declaratory theory and his rejection of the façade approach since he, too, took the view that the modern appellate judge inevitably makes law and that therefore the key question was where to draw the line between what the Law Lords could do and what should be left to the Parliament.[72] Most of his colleagues and the Justices in the Supreme Court shared his view:

> Well I'm definitely of the Bingham school of thought ... I think Radcliffe said that you shouldn't reveal the mystery. Well I think that that's undemocratic and rather arrogant really ... On the other hand, I think that very often the issues which we have to decide do involve the question of what it is appropriate for judges to decide as opposed to Parliament and this is often a very subtle question. It's not sometimes obvious that this is a matter which should be dealt with by Parliament. (Lord Hoffmann)

---

[68] *Jones v Kernott* [2011] UKSC 53.Counsel did not suggest using the 1966 power in their written Case or in their oral argument.

[69] *R (on the application of KM) v Cambridgeshire County Council* [2012] UKSC 23.

[70] Brice Dickson in 'Judicial Activism in the House of Lords 1995–2007' (above, n 9) 414 concludes that in the later years of the House it tended to use distinguishing of its own precedents in preference to overruling them. In fact, the House has always done that but it still—even towards the end—chose to tackle two of its own precedents head on in the space of three years. See Blom-Cooper, '1966 and All That' ch 9 in Blom-Cooper et al (above, n 38) at 144.

[71] R Posner, *How Judges Think* (Cambridge MA, Harvard University Press, 2008) 81ff.

[72] Lord Bingham, 'The Judge as Lawmaker' in *The Business of Judging* (Oxford, Oxford University Press, 2000) 25–34.

Lord Neuberger, however, added that there was more of a spectrum of positions.

> Nobody is completely declaratory. Nobody is a completely out and out reformer … I think some judges are prepared to be much more creative in some areas than in others but I'm afraid I don't think there is a great principle here, I just think it's a question of degree.

In chapters four and five above we explored the scope for collective decision-making in the final court and the extent to which the judges changed their minds at different stages of the process, especially in close calls or divided cases. Does the fact that the judges can disagree as to what is the appropriate answer to a case indicate that in the final court the judges perceive themselves as having a certain degree of room for manoeuvre or judicial discretion, or merely that getting to the 'right answer' can be inherently difficult in some cases coming before the final court? The interviews with the judges did not yield a definitive answer to this question. Forty years ago when, as now, close calls existed in about 11 per cent of cases and there was at least one dissent in 22 per cent of cases the overwhelming majority of Law Lords considered that in at least 20 per cent of cases the decision could go either way with reasonable legal justification. Curiously, despite the fact that in the last decade and more (as we have seen) the final court has taken much greater control of the cases which it hears, and despite the passing of the Human Rights Act 1998 (which many commentators consider provides today's final judges with more overt value choices to make than their predecessors), the interviews with Law Lords and Justices in the last five years produced a very similar figure for the percentage of cases which could go either way.

Again, the interviews of 40 years ago showed clearly that the Law Lords saw themselves as making choices in many of the cases coming before them for resolution.[73] Thirty years later, little seemed to have changed. As Lord Bingham observed,[74]

> But the inescapable fact is that they do have to make choices, and unless superseded by Act of Parliament their choice determines what the law shall be.

In interview, four years on, he added,

> I think we do spend our time asking ourselves, 'Do I go this way or do I go that way?', the unstated assumption being that one could go either way and if you take a case like *Smith*[75] … obviously one weighed up the consequences of going this way or that way but I clearly felt that the majority outcome represented a considerable injustice to *Smith* and I also did not accept the view that it was going to make the job of the police intolerable … but it would be very difficult to say there wasn't a choice … I think in an awful lot of cases there's a choice even where one's not in much doubt about what one's own personal choice is.

---

[73] *The Law Lords* (above, n 13) 194–95.
[74] Lord Bingham, 'The Judges: Active or Passive?', The British Academy Maccabean Lecture for 2005.
[75] *Smith v Chief Constable of Sussex Police* [2008] UKHL 50.

Lord Hope agreed,

> Well you do have a choice and often it is a choice between moving the law on or staying with a result which you feel uncomfortable with because you feel you haven't got the courage to move on.

Another Law Lord added,

> These sort of choices are age old aren't they? They happen in all these cases, as between certainty and flexibility, as between this value and that value, as between the needs of immigration control and the sympathy one has for various classes of immigrant whatever it may be, these are all choice cases, cases in which there's ultimately a choice to be made.

However, as a descriptive term, 'choice' is ambiguous. Thus a strong minority of interviewees rejected this description of decision-making even at the level of the final court because in their minds it was associated with forms of arbitrary decision-making such as coin-tossing or dice rolling. Lord Neuberger observed,[76]

> Normally I don't feel free in the sense that I just say well this is what I want to decide. So in that sense you're not free. You've got to weigh up the arguments and come to what you think is an intellectually honest conclusion.

Lord Bingham did not mean 'choice' in that sense, but he was all for intellectually honest conclusions. This renowned champion of the rule of law[77] was not a closet legal realist, far less a supporter of the post-modern judging. That most eloquent of modern American judge commentators, Richard Posner,[78] would doubtless characterise him as belonging to the largest grouping within the American federal judiciary—'constrained pragmatists'—who decide cases primarily on the effects or consequences that they are likely to have. Lord Bingham certainly would take account of consequences, but he was also a strong believer in principled decision-making—what Posner would classify as legalism (albeit of a sophisticated form). Moreover, Bingham's pursuit of the appropriate resolution to appellate cases, and close calls in particular was not, in his case, a Dworkinian search for the single right answer to be found in the rules and principles of the law, like a hunt for buried treasure.

Yet subtly, views were changing. Some Law Lords and Justices were equally happy to describe their decisions as the product of choices, whilst insisting that there was only one right answer to cases, based on the competing rules, principles and policies. Thus Lord Hoffmann, in many ways closer to Posner's archetypal pragmatist judge than Bingham, viewed 'close call' cases as evidence that the Law Lords made choices but added,

---

[76] Interview with the author, 2008.

[77] Tom Bingham, *The Rule of Law* (London, Allen Lane, 2010).

[78] Richard Posner, a distinguished federal appellate judge in the United States has encapsulated his views on judging from an internal perspective in *How Judges Think* (Cambridge MA, Harvard University Press, 2008).

[W]hen you look at the outcome of a case from the point of view of the judge who's deciding it, he thinks there is a right answer, he doesn't think that his colleagues are simply exercising their discretion in a different way to arrive at an equally legitimate answer, he thinks that his answer's right and theirs is wrong.

Lord Millett, so often Lord Hoffmann's sparring partner,[79] agreed with him on the 'single right answer' issue but was more wedded to solutions which were coherent and consistent with the wider legal context.

I wouldn't use the language of choice, I was innocent or naïve enough to think that there was a right answer if only I could work it out and if I found it difficult that was because I hadn't managed to analyse it to my own satisfaction … I was always very keen not only to decide the instant case and get it right but also to make certain that the decision would then fit in with the rest of the law.

Lord Kerr also jibbed at the use of the 'choice' word, except in the rare cases where he experienced the legal merits as very evenly balanced, a view that Lord Collins shared, 'It is only a choice if you think that the arguments are on the absolute knife-edge. If you don't, then of course whichever way it goes is the right view'.[80]

Yet, 40 years ago the great majority of the Law Lords were unconvinced by the proposition that there was a single right answer to all or the great majority of the cases coming before the final appeal court.[81] As one said,

No, things are very seldom as simple as that, unfortunately; in most cases there is a conflict, sometimes between the merits of a particular case and the merits of a particular rule, and whether we should change something or leave it to legislation; that is the interest here, there are many choices open.

Lord Reid was also characteristically forthright,

Well, of course there isn't [a single right answer] … it's not that legal principles cannot solve cases … legal principles normally lead you in the same direction but sometimes they don't, and you have to choose between them, and public policy comes in more than perhaps we would like to admit.

What accounts for the difference between Lord Reid's era and the Supreme Court today? In part the modern response is a more nuanced one. Lord Carnwath, for example, recalled that,[82]

[G]oing back to my Law Commission experience, most legal issues can be presented in a number of ways and they can be rationalised in a number of ways, at least by the time that they get to this level … I think that a lot of the cases involve an intellectual analysis which may lead you to a single conclusion which you feel is the only one you can properly conclude in law. More often, however, there is a policy element where

---

[79] *Twinsectra Ltd v Yardley and Others* [2002] UKHL 12.
[80] Interview with the author, 2009.
[81] Usually attributed to the legal philosopher Ronald Dworkin in his seminal treatise, *Taking Rights Seriously* (Cambridge MA, Harvard University Press, 1978).
[82] Interview with the author, 2013.

you are … deciding where should the law be going or to what extent should the Supreme Court take it in that direction.

Several other Justices including Lords Reed, Saville[83] and Sumption took and take the view that there are only right answers to a minority of cases coming before the court, but that there is a better answer based on the relevant legal rules and principles in most cases. However, they also accepted that in 'close call' cases what one Justice considered to be the better answer was often not accepted by other Justices—who preferred their own better answers, making it difficult to assert that there are objectively better answers in such cases other than the arbitrary tally of the votes. Moreover, as Lord Sumption noted,[84] a Justice's concept of the better answer in hard or close call cases is likely to reflect the philosophical base of that Justice,

> No I don't [think there is a single right answer in each appeal], I think there certainly is in some cases. I think that there may be a variety of satisfactory answers which are satisfactory to different degrees from different points of view and obviously a lot depends on your basic instinct, which is likely to colour your approach to cases generally which are the most important considerations. If you take the view, as I do, that the object of this Court is to produce a result that is coherent in relation to the generality of cases in relation to other cognate areas of law, then it seems to me you may come to a different conclusion than if you [take a different philosophical stance].

Thus it may be that those Law Lords and Justices who endeavour(ed) to devise a principle for a case which would reflect their instincts about the morality of the case, are more likely to think that there is a right answer to the case than judges who are more pragmatically inclined to look for the most sensible and realistic answer in the circumstances. The latter are more likely to see the solution to a finely balanced situation as one where there are several plausible answers, which can best be resolved by how the cost–benefit calculus comes out. As one Justice put it,

> I am a pragmatist as much as a realist. One deals with a case and attempts to form a realistic, pragmatic and intellectually defensible view on it … I don't have a black and white intellectual position on many legal issues. In most cases that reach this level the law turns out to be inherently imprecise in some respects and so there is often room for manoeuvre.

A further possibility—which we will return to later—is that, as with the exercise of the 1966 Practice Statement, the Supreme Court prefers to be less overt in their law-making than the House was in Lord Reid's era, precisely because the more formal separation of powers, its control of its caseload and the concomitant

---

[83] 'In a large number of cases there is no definitive, single answer and it's very dangerous to try and look for this holy grail of the complete unanswerable, unarguable answer because life isn't like that. Cases aren't like that. So … in many cases you end up with what, for the reasons you've thought through, is the better answer'. Interview with the author, 2008.

[84] Interview with the author, 2013.

growth in its Human Rights jurisdiction has given it more power vis à vis the other branches of the state than the House had in Reid's time. Minimising one's profile in such situations, even re-discovering the attractions of the declaratory theory,[85] has certain advantages, even if it does mean a more nuanced dialogue with Parliament.

Who Really Draws the Line?

Whatever may be the explanation for the apparent coyness of the Supreme Court to date in relation to judicial law-making as compared with certain eras of the House of Lords, such differences do not necessarily entail that there are real differences between them in relation to where they actually drew the line between what was deemed appropriate for the final court to do and what must be left to Parliament. This issue lies at the core of the intra-governmental dialogue between the Court and Parliament. On a day-to-day basis the definition as to where the dividing line is to be drawn, and what the respective institutional competencies of the two bodies are to be, is a matter for the Court. Parliament, so long as parliamentary sovereignty prevails, sets most of the larger parameters—as in the case of the Human Rights Act 1998, but even legislation reversing a decision of the Court is not necessarily an assertion that the Court has drawn the boundary incorrectly.[86] True, in *Jackson*[87] and elsewhere[88] a few Law Lords have boldly asserted that in the event of Parliament abolishing judicial review or voting to abolish elections the courts might not uphold this, but so far the sober voice of Bingham has prevailed. Most Justices might well consider legislation which seeks to alter fundamental or constitutional rights to be lacking in legitimacy, and as such subject it to extremely close scrutiny, but in the end accept that that is the law.[89] As Matthew Engel records,[90] when he asked several of the Justices what they would do if Parliament passed an Act which was too obnoxious to countenance, they all replied in similar terms,

---

[85] One Justice told me in 2013, 'Yes, the declaratory theory is back again in full force'.

[86] A situation where the Court has declined to reform the law and Parliament chooses to do so is equally compatible with the Court's definition of the boundary being viewed by the Parliament as correct and incorrect.

[87] *Jackson and Others v Her Majesty's Attorney General* [2005] UKHL 56, [2006] 1 AC 262 at [101]–[102] Lord Steyn, [104] Lord Hope, and [159] Baroness Hale. Discussed in Lord Neuberger MR, 'Who are the Masters Now?', Second Lord Alexander of Weedon lecture, 6 April 2011 (Court of Appeal website).

[88] See Lord Woolf, 'Droit public—English style' [1995] *Public Law* 57 at 69, Lord Phillips, Interview, The Today Programme, *BBC Radio 4*, 2 August 2010; and Sir John Laws in 'Law and democracy' [1995] *Public Law* 622, 628 and 635.

[89] See Lord Hoffmann in *R v Secretary of State for the Home Department, ex parte Simms* [2000] 2 AC 115, 131.

[90] M Engel, 'British Institutions: The Supreme Court', *Financial Times*, 19 April 2013.

Try to find a less harsh interpretation of Parliament's intention. If that fails, either support the law or resign.

Lord Sumption, in keeping with his Mann lecture similarly commented,[91]

At the moment, I am inclined to think that there are some things which it is illegitimate for Parliament to do but if it does them, that is the law. I believe that was also Lord Bingham's view ... The problem with an unwritten constitution is that constitutional propositions about the limitations on Parliament's sovereignty would, if laid down by the ultimate court of appeal, be beyond democratic amendment. I think that the concept of a Court devising a constitutional principle beyond democratic amendment is profoundly suspect.

Nevertheless, generally it is the Court which tries to find the boundary and sometimes appears to give up the struggle to find a coherent or consistent position. As Lord Goff once asserted,[92]

I feel bound however to say that, although I am well aware of the existence of the boundary, I am never quite sure where to find it ... Much seems to depend upon the circumstances of the particular case.

The latter formulation, as Lord Dyson observed in a 2012 lecture,[93] is the 'traditional refuge of the judge who is unable to articulate a principle and wishes to retain maximum flexibility'. If resorted to with too great frequency, it is likely to be viewed by commentators—and parliamentarians—as insufficiently transparent. Ronald Dworkin is not the only commentator to argue that the rule of law requires judges to give reasons for their decisions which appear rooted in principles of law rather than in public or legal policy. However, sufficient Law Lords and Justices have admitted to making policy choices in their decision-making[94] to make us question the value of this bright line divide. Yet consistent and coherent reasons must be given, especially when judges are setting the boundaries for the other branches of government and ruling on their competencies (and thereby their legitimacy). This may explain the steady stream of lectures by distinguished judges[95] (though, interestingly, never addressed directly to a parliamentarian audience) grappling with varying degrees of success with this thorny and intractable subject.

---

[91]   Interview with the author, 2013. On the Mann lecture see n 244 below.

[92]   *Woolwich Building Society v Inland Revenue Commissioners* [1993] AC 70, 173.

[93]   Lord Dyson, 'Where the Common Law fears to tread', 2012 Alba Lecture, 6 November 2012 (Court of Appeal website).

[94]   Often in interviews, but also in other fora.

[95]   Eg Lord Dyson, 'Where the Common Law fears to tread' (above, n 93); Lord Justice Etherton, 'Liberty, the Archetype and Diversity: A Philosophy of Judging' [2010] *Public Law* 727; Baroness Hale, 'Law Maker or Law Reformer: What is a Law Lady for?', John Maurice Kelly Memorial Lecture (University College Dublin Faculty of Law); Lord Bingham, 'The Judge as Lawmaker' in *The Business of Judging* (Oxford, Oxford University Press, 2000) 25–34; Justice Heydon, 'Limits to the powers of ultimate appellate courts' (2006) 122 *LQR* 399, Lord Reid, 'The Judge as Law Maker' (1972) 12 *Journal of the Society of Public Teachers of Law* 22.

Where Should the Lines be Drawn?

Lord Justice Etherton, in characteristically insightful fashion, notes that the traditional approach of British judges in this area has been anti-intellectual and pragmatic. Typically they appeal in their judgments to a series of nostrums which sound comforting and possibly soothing to the parliamentary ear but in the end offer little clear guidance to the wider world as to where to draw the legislative demarcation line. Lord Reid was a great believer in the virtue of common sense as a yardstick and Bingham liked 'sound judgment' and each of them saw a place for 'reasonableness'. Yet, as Etherton pithily observes, in hard cases each side could appeal to any of these with equal conviction.

Lord Reid offered other yardsticks,[96] with a view to providing certainty in the law whilst achieving justice in individual cases. As with Law Lords and Justices after him,[97] he was happier to countenance different degrees of judicial creativity in some areas of law than others.[98] 'Lawyers' law' topics, eg contract law, tort, restitution and public law were generally fair game for judicial law-making, though in areas such as property law, trusts and criminal law (where public reliance tends to be high) he generally preferred certainty to flexibility. Areas of public controversy, eg assisted dying, same-sex marriages and abortion, were best left to Parliament. In his era, his views were generally shared by his colleagues, but the advent of the Human Rights Act 1998 changed everything. Before the Act, the House of Lords unanimously ruled that a same-sex couple could not be living together as spouses for the purposes of the Rent Acts.[99] Five years later, with the HRA in force, the House was to be found concluding the complete reverse (by a 4:1 margin).[100]

Lord Reid's indication that the judges should avoid law-making in areas of public controversy was rooted both in notions of institutional competence[101] and legitimacy. An unelected judiciary should defer to the elected Parliament on such matters. The symbolic dialogue with Parliament was clear. However, in *Ghaidan* the House could recognise same-sex spouses despite public controversy because the HRA mandated it and, of course, Parliament had legitimated judicial discretion, even in relation to statutory interpretation, through section 3(1) of the HRA.

Lord Reid's next guideline—shared by Lord Bingham—that areas of law requiring a detailed and comprehensive review were best left to Parliament was again rooted in notions of comparative institutional competence. However, it was less clearly rooted in legitimacy considerations, which may explain that while it

---

[96] See *The Law Lords* (above, n 13) 170ff.

[97] Including those bold enough to offer lectures on the subject, see n 95 above.

[98] For a similar argument, see Lord Neuberger, 'Has Equity had its day?' Lecture in Hong Kong, 12 October 2010.

[99] *Fitzpatrick v Sterling Housing Association* [1999] UKHL 42. They were, however, held to be 'family' for the purposes of the Rent Acts.

[100] *Ghaidan v Godin-Mendoza* [2004] UKHL 30.

[101] What Lord Dyson has referred to as 'how well equipped the courts are' to develop the law: 2012 Alba Lecture on 'Where the Common Law fears to tread', 6 November 2012.

has been followed in some celebrated cases, eg *Morgans v Launchbury* (the family car insurance case)[102] it has been rejected in others, eg *Donaghue v Stevenson* (product liability) or *Hall (Arthur JS) & Co v Simons*[103] (the advocate's immunity case). This guideline was closely connected to another which Lord Reid also espoused, as to the desirability of judges being able to foresee the consequences of their decisions if they were going to reform the law. What were seen as polycentric problems were not for the courts to resolve.[104] This guideline commanded a large measure of acceptance by his contemporaries.[105] Parliament, especially if it was implementing a well-researched and consulted on proposal from the Law Commission, was in a better position than the Court to divine what the consequences of a reform one way rather than the other would amount to. As with the last guideline, it is clearly based on an assessment of comparative institutional competence but not so clearly on issues of legitimacy. Support for consequentialist reasoning has come not only from legal philosophers[106] but from pragmatist Law Lords and Justices. However, it is not a 'knock down' argument. It may have succeeded in *Morgans v Launchbury* and *Caparo*[107] (third party liability of auditors for negligently conducted audits) but it did not in *Hall*. Indeed, a version of the consequentialist guideline, that if the final court upholds liability in a case it will open the floodgates for other litigants (the floodgates argument) was seen as a makeweight argument[108] in Lord Reid's time, by both counsel and Law Lords alike. Interestingly the argument may have acquired greater weight in the dialogue with Parliament in modern times now that allegations of 'a compensation culture'[109] have become part of political and parliamentary discourse.

Arguments from Parliamentary Activity and Inactivity

Amongst the most interesting guidelines from the perspective of the dialogue with Parliament that have been put forward by various Law Lords over the years—though to only a very limited extent by Lords Reid and Bingham—relate to parliamentary activity or inactivity. These arguments take different forms, as we shall see, but all are based on action or inaction by the Court being justified by the activity or inactivity on the part of Parliament. As such, the arguments relate more to questions of legitimacy rather than institutional capacity or competence.

---

[102] *Morgans v Launchbury* [1973] AC 127, a decision criticised for its timidity by Lord Dyson in the 2012 Alba Lecture on 'Where the Common Law fears to tread', 6 November 2012.

[103] *Arthur Hall & Co v Simons* [2000] UKHL 38, [2002] 1 AC 615.

[104] It has since been argued that most legal problems are polycentric and that this guideline is misconceived. See J King, 'The pervasiveness of polycentricity' [2008] *Public Law* 101.

[105] See *The Law Lords* (above, n 13) 177.

[106] Eg Neil MacCormick, *Legal Reasoning and Legal Theory*, (Oxford, Clarendon Press, 1978).

[107] *Caparo Industries plc v Dickman* [1990] UKHL 2.

[108] Ie, to support a course of action which had been decided on, on other grounds.

[109] See J Hand, 'The Compensation Culture: Cliché or Cause for Concern' (2010) 37 *Journal of Law and Society* 569. See now the consequentialist arguments in *Woodland v Essex County Council* [2013] UKSC 66.

They clearly see the Court as having a law reforming role but as a lesser partner to Parliament—as 'occasional legislators', as Posner would put it. Arguments relating to parliamentary activity have taken two main forms:

1) Version 1 of the argument runs as follows: This is a subject of current legislative activity, therefore the courts should not act.[110] It makes admirably good sense but is not always adhered to. Thus, Lord Millett as the unhappy dissenter in *Ghaidan*,[111] took the view that the majority in *Ghaidan* had reversed the interpretation of the law given by the House three years earlier, even although a Bill dealing with the point was in the House.

2) Version 2 is deceptively similar: This is an area where Parliament has recently legislated, it did not alter the existing judge-made law, therefore it must be happy with it, and accordingly it would be wrong for the courts now to change it. In Lord Reid's era most Law Lords said this was a makeweight argument carrying little real weight,[112] in part because there may be no evidence that Parliament ever considered the point. The recent practice of the final court has varied. The argument also did not succeed in *Hall*, perhaps because the legislative opportunity in question was 10 years earlier.[113] However, it did persuade Lord Hope and Baroness Hale not to overrule a precedent of the House of Lords in the Supreme Court case of *Austin v The Mayor and Burgesses of the London Borough of Southwark*[114] despite both of them expressing dissatisfaction with the current state of authorities. Again, a variant of the argument was used by the majority of the Supreme Court in the *Prudential*[115] case, to justify not extending legal professional privilege to tax accountants.

Arguments from parliamentary inactivity have taken rather more forms and are in some ways more interesting in relation to the dialogue with Parliament since, as we saw earlier, it is the Court that determines the demarcation line between it and Parliament, on a day-to-day basis.

1) Version 1 of the argument on parliamentary inactivity is the one most frequently articulated: This is an area where Parliament has not legislated over the years, therefore it must be happy with what courts are doing, therefore we can continue doing so. This is felt to be more potent if the area of law in question relates to 'lawyers' law' areas of traditional activity by the courts.

2) Version 2 is more or less the obverse of the second argument on parliamentary activity: Parliament has had a chance to reform the law, hasn't done so, so

---

[110] See Lord Bingham, 'The Judge as Lawmaker' in *The Business of Judging* (Oxford, Oxford University Press, 2000) at 25–34.

[111] *Ghaidan v Godin Mendoza* [2004] UKHL 30.

[112] See *The Law Lords* (above, n 13) at 180. Lord Reid regarded the argument as 'too expedient'.

[113] The Courts and Legal Services Act 1990.

[114] [2010] UKSC 28.

[115] *R (on the application of Prudential plc and Another) v Special Commissioner of Income Tax* [2013] UKSC 1 at [52], [68]–[69], [90], [112].

it is acceptable for the court to act. On its own, the Law Lords of Lord Reid's and Lord Bingham's era seemed to regard it as little more than a makeweight argument. Thus, where the courts have given a statutory provision a certain meaning and Parliament then passes subsequent legislation using the same words, judges who like the earlier courts' decisions say Parliament was clearly happy with that and those who don't, say Parliament may or may not have intended it but it's for us to decide.[116] As Lord Radcliffe put it,

> People will use these points in order to support something which they want to decide anyway. You'd be fantastic, I think, to argue that because Parliament hasn't moved, therefore the legislature agrees with you … It's a sort of bad point thrown in.

3)   Version 3 is more controversial: There is no likelihood of Parliament acting in the near future therefore the Court ought to. Lord Mance has observed that there are certain areas of lawyers' law (where there are few votes) where the Court is justified in acting because 'regrettably, Parliament just doesn't have the time to think about [them]'.[117] In practice, the Law Lords and Justices have been more willing to run this argument if Parliament has had the opportunity to act and appears to have chosen not to. Thus in *Stack v Dowden*,[118] the majority led by Baroness Hale were prepared to deal with the area of separating cohabitants' property because they believed (correctly, as it turned out) that Parliament was not going to act on the Law Commission's Report on the issue, and also that it was an area of judge-made law in any event. Lord Neuberger (in dissent) felt that it was premature to conclude that Parliament wasn't going to act and that in any case it was an area of public controversy best left to Parliament. Four years later, by the time of *Jones v Kernott*[119] in the Supreme Court, little had changed except that Government had produced another excuse for not implementing the Law Commission's recommendations. Accordingly the Justices further developed the law on cohabitants' property.

Again, in *Sempra Metals*,[120] the case on the awarding of compound interest, the Lords had said twice in a period of about 150 years that this was a matter for Parliament and Parliament had done nothing. Accordingly, the House of Lords felt able to act because Parliament looked like it never would. Here we see that the dialogue with Parliament has moved on a phase. Parliament has failed to respond to promptings from the House, therefore the House can take action on its own. This can be seen as the pragmatic conclusion of a subordinate legislator—it might also be seen as the courts trespassing on areas where Parliament has implied that the status quo should prevail.

---

[116]   Example drawn from interview with Lord Neuberger in 2008.
[117]   Interview with the author, 2008.
[118]   *Stack v Dowden* [2007] UKHL 17.
[119]   [2011] UKSC 53.
[120]   *Sempra Metals Ltd v Her Majesty's Revenue & Customs* [2008] 1 AC 561; [2007] UKHL 34.

4) Version 4 is the most controversial of all: Parliament is unable to act, therefore the Court has a licence to act. Given that this version implies that the democratic process is incapable of working, it is surprising that this argument has appeared on a number of occasions. One of the earliest was *Woolwich Equitable Building Society v IRC*,[121] where the Inland Revenue acting under ultra vires regulations, had unlawfully demanded (and obtained) money from taxpayers. As the case law stood, they could not get their money back since it had not been obtained by coercion. However, Lord Goff stimulated by academic writings on restitution,[122] was able to persuade two of his colleagues that this was a case in which the House could develop the law, on the grounds (it is thought) that in this area, no Parliament was ever going to force the Treasury to return the funds. Since Parliament could not act, the House could. Lords Keith and Jauncey in dissent, indicated that this was taking judicial legislation too far, but several other Law Lords agreed with the decision.[123]

The next three cases, *Airedale NHS Trust v Bland*[124] (withdrawal of life-sustaining treatment from a Hillsborough disaster victim who was in a persistent vegetative state), *Pretty v DPP*[125] and *Purdy v DPP*[126] (guidance concerning assisted dying), all related to sensitive areas concerning the sanctity of human life where Parliament has been very reluctant to go. Indeed, in *Purdy* Baroness Hale starts her judgment[127] by describing the debate which was proceeding in the House of Lords legislative chamber at the same time as the *Purdy* case on the topic of legalising assisted dying. The attempt to reform the law was defeated. Although the parliamentary inability argument is not expressly raised in the judgments in these cases,[128] it may well have had an influence in the first and third of them, where the House did indeed step in to change the law.[129]

However, in *R v Clegg*,[130] the House unanimously refused to act even though the case related to the mandatory life sentence for murder, which was

---

[121] *Woolwich Equitable Building Society v Inland Revenue Commissioners* [1993] AC 70.
[122] Some of which were his own.
[123] Including Lords Hoffmann and Hope. Interviews with the author.
[124] *Airedale NHS Trust v Bland* [1993] AC 789.
[125] *R (on the application of Pretty) v Director of Public Prosecutions* [2001] UKHL 61; [2001] 1 AC 800.
[126] *R (on the application of Purdy) v Director of Public Prosecutions* [2009] UKHL 45.
[127] At para 57.
[128] Indeed in *Pretty* Lord Hobhouse asserts, at para 120, 'that both the nature of the questions raised by assisted suicide and the formulation of any new policies must under our system of parliamentary democracy be a matter for the Legislature not the Judiciary'.
[129] In *Purdy* the House departed from its earlier decision in *Pretty*. Although widely applauded at the time the *Purdy* case was excoriated by the eminent jurist John Finnis as the Court lending itself with 'unwarrantable and unlawyerly enthusiasm, to a propaganda polemic' which undermined the rule of law. His objection does not appear to relate to anything to do with the parliamentary inability argument, which he does not discuss. J Finnis, 'Invoking the Principle of Legality against the Rule of Law' [2010] *New Zealand Law Review* 601.
[130] *R v Clegg* [1995] 1 AC 482.

an area where Parliament had demonstrated over the years that it was unable
to reform the law, perhaps through fear of the *Daily Mail*'s likely response.[131]
One or two Law Lords felt strongly that there should not have been a murder
conviction in the case, but despite repeated calls for reform by the House,
and the Law Commission in 2006, Parliament has failed to change the law. It
may be that the Supreme Court in this area will be attracted by version 3 or 4
of the parliamentary inactivity argument above, but more likely the tension
between a final court that *can't* act (and who can blame them given the track
record of the House over provocation cases) and a legislature that *won't* seems
likely to continue.

Yet in two cases in its final years the House of Lords did appear to embrace
the argument on parliamentary inability. The first, *Total Network*,[132] concerned a carousel fraud in Europe which took advantage of the UK VAT laws.
The easiest solution was to make all the transactions in the circle (both in the
UK and in Europe) subject to VAT in the UK. However, that solution was not
open to the UK Parliament, since it was beyond its competence to impose VAT
on transactions in other Member States, and neither the European Parliament
nor the European Commission would countenance such a change. With
Parliament unable to act, the House divided 3:2 on whether it was open to
the Law Lords to create a common law remedy in the VAT field to enable the
money to be recovered by the Revenue. Lord Hope, who accepted the use
of the 'inability' argument in *Woolwich*,[133] was not open to using it in *Total
Network*. However, Lords Scott, Walker and Mance combined to produce a
common law remedy.

Equally striking was *Re P*,[134] which concerned adoption by unmarried
couples in Northern Ireland. In the rest of the UK, legislation had been
introduced to permit such adoptions, but not in Northern Ireland. Baroness
Hale and a majority of her colleagues concluded that the HRA required that
such adoptions should be permitted. Although it is not expressly stated in the
judgments, what appears to have influenced Lady Hale's thinking was that the
Northern Ireland Assembly was unable to act because of the religious beliefs
of a majority of its members.[135] Lord Walker, who did not agree, nevertheless used an argument based on parliamentary inactivity, indicating that
the Assembly should be given one more chance, but only one, to solve the

---

[131] The case was headline news. A soldier in Northern Ireland during the troubles was manning a
checkpoint when a stolen car drove towards him at great speed. The shots fired at the car to prevent it
from hitting the soldiers were justified in terms of self-defence but the shot fired at the departing car,
which hit and killed a passenger in the back was considered to be excessive force. The House held that
this had to be murder not manslaughter.
[132] *Total Network SL v Her Majesty's Revenue and Customs* [2008] UKHL 19.
[133] Interview with the author, 2008.
[134] *In Re P and Others (Northern Ireland)* [2008] UKHL 38
[135] See Baroness Hale, 'Law Lords at the Margin', JUSTICE Tom Sargant memorial lecture, 15
October 2008.

problem. Some Law Lords agreed with majority's approach but others took the view that a deliberate decision not to change the law by the Assembly should be respected.

The argument from parliamentary inability is amongst the most fascinating in the dialogue between final court and Parliament since it lies on (and possibly over) the constitutional fault line which delimits the institutional competencies of the two branches of government. Here the Court is undeniably in the realm of politics with a small 'p'. In cases where the Court chooses to act on the basis of the argument it is openly embracing the role of surrogate legislator. In the light of the maxim that nothing succeeds like success it is telling that to date Parliament has chosen not to reverse any of the cases where the parliamentary inability argument appears to have prompted the Court into action. Perhaps this demonstrates the validity of the Court's assessment of the political realities in these cases. It is equally noteworthy that the Supreme Court, with its lower profile on judicial law-making, has yet to deploy the argument from parliamentary inability in its decisions.

Arguments from parliamentary activity and inactivity are one thing but what about the activity or inactivity of the Law Commission? In *Smith v Chief Constable of Sussex Police*[136] Lord Phillips of the majority who had waivered in the case, was comforted in his decision not to reform the law by the thought that the Commission had just produced a report on the relevant issue which would go to Parliament.[137] Similarly, Baroness Hale uses the fact that the Law Commission is working on reform recommendations in the field as a reason for not reforming the law on pre-nuptial agreements in *Radmacher*,[138] but the argument did not convince her eight male colleagues. However, as we saw earlier, the presence of Commission recommendations which Parliament has not acted on, did not prevent her and most of her colleagues from developing the law in *Stack v Dowden* and *Jones v Kernott*. Lord Hope in *Jones v Kaney*[139] (a case concerning the immunity from being sued enjoyed by expert witnesses) used the fact that there had been a recent report by the Law Commission on expert witnesses which had not raised the immunity issue, to justify leaving the issue to the Commission and Parliament.[140] Lady Hale agreed with him but the majority of the Court did not. It would seem therefore that arguments from the activity or inactivity

---

[136] [2008] UKHL 50.

[137] Ibid, para 102.

[138] *Radmacher (formerly Granatino) v Granatino* [2010] UKSC 42. As she observes at para 134, 'The Commission can research and review the law over the whole area, not just the narrow section which is presented by the facts of an individual case. It can consider such research as there is into the use and abuse of marital agreements of all kinds. It can commission research into the experience and attitudes of practitioners and the public. It can identify and discuss the full range of policy arguments, including a detailed examination of the experience of legislative reform in other common law countries'.

[139] [2011] UKSC 13.

[140] Ibid, para [173].

of the Law Commission carry no more weight than those from the activity or inactivity of Parliament, and probably less. Nevertheless, arguments from the activity and inactivity of Parliament and the Law Commission are used regularly by the judges—and not always in dissent. While some variants of the arguments may be thought less weighty than others nonetheless they do appear to be part of an on-going dialogue between the final court and Parliament (and the Law Commission). This dialogue, however, is almost entirely symbolic and sufficiently asynchronous as to appear more like a monologue in which Parliament appears not to hear the Court and the Court sometimes responds by developing the law where normally they would not.

Lines of Communication

There are several explanations for the relationship between the final court and Parliament sometimes appearing to resemble more of a monologue than a dialogue. First, public law scholars have typically confined their discussions of the dialogue between final courts and legislatures to reading down statutes in terms of section 3 of the Human Rights Act and declarations of incompatibility under section 4 of the Human Rights Act.[141] As to the latter, such declarations *by the final court* have been relatively uncommon in the UK,[142] in part because decisions of the House of Lords confirmed that Convention compliant interpretation of legislation under section 3 of the Human Rights Act is the primary remedial measure, rather than a declaration of incompatibility.[143] Although the reading down of legislation under section 3 *can* involve departing from the clear intention of Parliament in a piece of legislation, it must still not be inconsistent with

---

[141] See S Fredman, 'From dialogue to deliberation' [2013] *Public Law* 292; P Hogg and A Bushell, 'The Charter Dialogue Between Courts and Legislatures' (1997) 35 *Osgoode Hall Law Journal* 75.

[142] The most celebrated was *Belmarsh, A and Others v Secretary of State for the Home Department* [2004] UKHL 56. Other cases where a declaration of incompatibility has been made by the final court include *R v Anderson* [2002] UKHL 46, *Bellinger v Bellinger* [2003] UKHL 21, *R (Hindawi) v Secretary of State for the Home Department* [2006] UKHL 54, *Wright v Secretary of State for Health* [2009] UKHL 3, *R (on the application of F) v Secretary of State for the Home Department* [2010] UKSC 17, and *Salvesen v Riddell* [2013] UKSC 22. However, there have also been cases where the final court has overturned declarations of incompatibility by lower courts, eg *Matthews v Ministry of Defence* [2003] 1 AC 1163, *Wilson v First County Trust Ltd (No 2)* [2004] 1 AC 816 and *R (Alconbury Developments) v Secretary of State for the Environment, Transport and the Regions* [2003] 2 AC 295. For a useful and extended account of declaration of incompatibility cases in the top court see B Dickson, *Human Rights and the United Kingdom Supreme Court* (Oxford, Oxford University Press, 2013) ch 3.

[143] *Ghaidan v Godin-Mendoza* [2004] UKHL 30, [2004] 2 AC 557 and *Sheldrake v Director of Public Prosecutions* [2004] UKHL 43, [2005] 1 AC 264, [28]. Other cases involving a read down under s 3 HRA include in *R v A* [2001] UKHL 25 (questions of prior sexual conduct in a rape case), *Manchester City Council v Pinnock* [2010] UKSC 45 (whether housing eviction governed by the HRA), *Principal Reporter v K* [2010] UKSC 56 (on the rights of unmarried fathers) and *R (on the application of GC) v Commissioner of Police of the Metropolis* [2011] UKSC 21 (retention of DNA records). See again B Dickson, *Human Rights and the United Kingdom Supreme Court* (Oxford, Oxford University Press, 2013) ch 3.

a fundamental feature of the legislation or 'go against the grain of the legislation' or change the substance of the legislation completely.[144] As a result, Parliament has rarely felt it necessary to re-legislate to tackle a reading down under section 3 with which it disagrees.

Secondly, there is a much more frequent opportunity for dialogue between the final court and Parliament, namely when the former is called on to interpret and apply a complex statutory provision to a set of circumstances that the legislature appears not to have anticipated. In that situation the Court will interpret the statute using the implicit argument that they are seeking to be faithful to what Parliament had intended, but if Parliament disagrees then as the ultimate authority they will be able to reverse the decision. In practice occasions where Parliament has passed legislation or delegated legislation to respond to or reverse judicial decisions of the House of Lords or the Supreme Court (whether relating to a declaration of incompatibility or not) are not that common,[145] and instances where the final court has then interpreted that legislation, eg as in the control orders cases,[146] *Axa*,[147] the *FII* case[148] or immigration regulations have been even rarer.

The third reason is that, even before the establishment of the Supreme Court and moving out of the House of Lords, there were no official lines of communication and now there are very few unofficial lines of communication between the final court and the legislature. It is true that the President of the Supreme Court

---

[144] To paraphrase the words of Lord Bingham in *Sheldrake v DPP* [2004] UKHL 43, [2005] 1 AC 264, [28].

[145] Cases in the final court which Parliament has responded to with legislation have included: *Beswick and Beswick* [1967] UKHL 2 (on third party rights under a contract to which they are not a signatory), reversed by the Contracts (Rights of Third Parties) Act 1999; *Barker v Corus* [2006] UKHL (a causation case which was reversed by s 3 of the Compensation Act 2006 with respect to victims of asbestosis related mesothelioma); *YL v Birmingham City Council* [2007] UKHL 27, [2008] 1 AC 95 (which as we saw in chapter 5 above, held that residents in a private care home whose care was paid for by the public purse were not protected by the HRA). This was partially reversed in the Health and Social Care Act 2008 (s 145) but a gap remains, see S Hosali and H Wildbore, 'Closing the loophole' ukhumanrightsblog.com/2013/05/22; *Rothwell v Chemical and Insulating Co Ltd* [2007] UKHL 39, [2008] 1 AC 281, a decision denying recovery in pleural plaques cases, was reversed by legislation in Scotland—but not in the rest of the UK—in the Damages (Asbestosis Related Conditions) (Scotland) Act 2009—this Act in turn was challenged unsuccessfully in the *Axa* case [2011] UKSC 46; *R v Davis* [2008] UKHL 36 a decision on witness anonymity, was reversed in the Criminal Evidence (Witness Anonymity) Act 2008.

[146] *Secretary of State for the Home Dept v JJ* [2007] UKHL 45, *Secretary of State for the Home Dept v MB and AF* [2007] UKHL 46, *Secretary of State for the Home Dept v E* [2007] UKHL 47, *Secretary of State for the Home Dept v AF (No 3)* [2009] UKHL 28.

[147] *Axa General Insurance Ltd and Others v Lord Advocate and Others (Scotland)* [2011] UKSC 46.

[148] *Test Claimants in the Franked Investment Income Group Litigation v Inland Revenue Commissioners* [2012] UKSC 19 (hereafter FII). Following *Woolwich Equitable Building Society v Inland Revenue Commissioners (No 2)* [1993] AC 70 (repayment of tax paid to the IRC in error) the Government passed legislation in the Finance Acts 2004 and 2007 designed to introduce a limitation period on such claims, since £5 billion in overpaid tax was involved. The Supreme Court in *FII* held that the provision in the Finance Act 2004 was incompatible with EU law, but the provisions of the 2007 Finance Act split the Court, leading to a reference to the EUCJ.

has appeared before the Constitution Committee on an irregular basis[149] but these sessions do not discuss individual cases. As we saw in the last section, there are not infrequent occasions when members of the final court call on Parliament to act. One of the most recent was in *Gow v Grant* (a Scots Supreme Court appeal on cohabitants' property) where Baroness Hale in a judgment with which Lords Wilson and Carnwath agreed, called on Parliament to introduce a statutory remedy for England and Wales akin to that existing in Scotland.[150] Another case which was part of a long running saga was *R v Powell and Another*,[151] where Lords Mustill and Steyn expressly called on Parliament to intervene in the area of homicide.[152] However, history suggests that such calls are frequently ignored by Parliament and the fact that there was and is no mechanism to ensure that the judges' pleas reach the ears of anyone in Parliament cannot help.

Curiously there is not even a line of communication to the Law Commission. The Law Lords hoped that their judgments were read by law reformers but rarely did anything to ensure that they were; nor did the Law Commission.[153] At the time of my second interviews, a Law Commissioner indicated in a public meeting that the Commission did not systemically monitor the judgments of the final court for reform issues. The protocol that the Government must endorse each new project of the Law Commission makes it even less likely that the final court will influence the Commission.[154] The Law Lords and Justices, in interview, did not object to some more formal line of communication with the Law Commission but thought that any link to Parliament would be unwise. As one put it, 'the politicians will inevitably ask well if we were to put the law this way would you [accept] it and we can't, we really can't get into that'[155]—a point to which we will return in the next section.

---

[149] Lord Neuberger has offered to appear before the Constitution Committee on an annual basis in the same way that the Lord Chief Justice does, but has indicated that meetings should not be more regular than this.

[150] *Gow v Grant* [2012] UKSC 29, paras 44–56.

[151] *R v Powell and Another* [1997] UKHL 57; [1999] 1 AC 1.

[152] Lord Mustill concluded his judgment with 'Once again, an appeal to this House has shown how badly our country needs a new law of homicide, or a new law of punishment of homicide, or preferably both. The judges can do nothing about this being held fast by binding authorities on the one hand and mandatory statute on the other, only parliament has the powers if it will choose to exercise them'.

[153] It is possible that the lack of formal communication channels stems from the era when, in the criminal law field at least, the House appeared to ignore most of what the Law Commission had to say—see G Williams, 'The Lords and Impossible Attempts, or *Quis Custiodiet Ipsos Custodes*?' (1986) 45 *CLJ* 33, 44.

[154] Brice Dickson has suggested that the Commission should keep a register of such calls for action, (see *Judicial Activism* (above, n 9) 398) but it is the Executive that ought to be expected to respond.

[155] Thus the House gave no indication as to what constraints would be in order in *Belmarsh, A and Others v Secretary of State for the Home* Department [2004] UKHL 56. Again Lady Hale in *Wright v Secretary of State for Health* [2009] UKHL 3, para 39 specifically states in the sole judgment in the case that she is not expressing an opinion as to how the incompatibility might be resolved since 'It is not for us to attempt to rewrite the legislation' and the balancing of the competing interests in the case was so delicate that it should 'be struck in the first instance by the legislature'.

Conclusion

Even before the passing of the Human Rights Act which made it clear beyond peradventure, no one since the substantive formalists 50 years ago seriously doubted that the final court played a law-making role. As the Law Lords recognised, the switch from a substantial diet of tax cases (30 per cent) to a heavy public law and human rights caseload (47 per cent) has only enhanced the scope for judicial law reform albeit of a subordinate nature. The debate relates to when and how. Successive judicial leaders have sought with greater or lesser degrees of conviction to articulate a boundary between the final court's role and that of Parliament which a majority of their colleagues could live with. In practice, Parliament has been happy to leave the 'junior legislative branch' to set the boundary, safe in the knowledge that in the minds of most of the constitutional community it retains the whip hand. Yet the sharper separation of powers of New Labour and the Supreme Court has done little to improve the functionality of a relationship between the two branches of the state where dialogue is more often replaced by unheard and unheeded monologue.

When it comes to law-making, Parliament has the authority and the power to act, but it sometimes lacks the will. The Supreme Court, on the other hand, cannot decide not to decide.[156] Despite its much heralded transparency, it seems more reluctant to showcase its law-making activities than some of its predecessors perhaps because its power has grown without a growth in democratic accountability. A more effective dialogue between the Court and Parliament would involve mutual recognition of the institutional competencies of each when it comes to legislation. Parliament should accept that courts may act if Parliament cannot, through lack of time or votes. The Court should recognise the limits to its law-making abilities, eg (a) that the adversarial system is not best suited to logical law reform,[157] (b) that section 3 of the Human Rights Act is only about interpretation, it does not allow the Court to legislate by completely re-writing the statute,[158] and (c) and that in hard cases there are few right answers—it partly depends on the outlook of the Justices hearing the case.

One reason that the UK Supreme Court began to sit in many more enlarged panels than the House did, is because Lord Phillips and most of his colleagues were of the opinion that in close calls the outcome depended to a significant extent on the views of the individual judges. This is the same point as Lord Sumption made in relation to right answers and different judicial philosophies.[159] From here it is

---

[156] See Baroness Hale, 'Law Maker or Law Reformer: What is a Law Lady for?', John Maurice Kelly Memorial Lecture (University College Dublin Faculty of Law)

[157] See Lady Hale (ibid) and Lord Dyson lecture (above, n 93).

[158] Two separate Law Lords told me in interview that they considered that in *R v A* [2001] UKHL 25 (questions of prior sexual conduct in a rape case) the House had gone too far in law-making by forging a completely new exception to a statutory provision, which was not in the Act, relying on section 3. The case was widely criticised, and not only by feminists.

[159] See n 84 above.

a short step to Terry Etherton's point that hard cases call for a balanced court—in terms of outlook and philosophy.[160] Lord Gardiner, when Lord Chancellor and faced with making more than one appointment to the House of Lords, said that he would consciously select those with divergent judicial philosophies to maintain a balance on the Court,[161]

> Basically you want different types ... if there are two outstanding lawyers, and one is rather rigid and the other is too flexible, well then have both and they will even things out.

Benjamin Cardozo famously penned a similar observation,[162]

> The eccentricities of judges balance one another ... one is timorous of change, another dissatisfied with the present: out of the attrition of diverse minds there is beaten something which has a constancy and uniformity and average value greater than its component elements.

Similarly, Lord Neuberger considers that in cases involving a tension between the legal and the moral merits the best panel is one that balances black-letter lawyers with those of a more liberal persuasion. Lord Bingham, when writing about appointment to the UK Supreme Court, said: 'Merit ... directs attention to proven professional achievement as a necessary condition, but also enables account to be taken of wider considerations, including the virtue of gender and ethnic diversity'.[163] Here, Bingham is pointing to the desirability of taking account of the needs of the court when selecting Justices. His support for diversity in appointments stemmed from his belief in the merit in balance on the Court. By arguing for a diverse Supreme Court bench he was supporting one that is more representative of society than the predominantly white, male, middle class cadre that has dominated its ranks to date. As I have argued elsewhere, greater diversity on the Supreme Court would increase legitimacy and therefore accountability.[164]

THE DIALOGUE WITH THE EXECUTIVE

This is the last of the dialogues and one that is among the most problematic for the Law Lords and Justices. Today, direct forms of the dialogue are largely forbidden. Yet several centuries ago the Lord Chief Justice sat in the Cabinet and even in the twentieth century the Lord Chancellor could sit in Cabinet and the Appellate

---

[160] See Lord Justice Etherton, 'Liberty, the Archetype and Diversity: A Philosophy of Judging' [2010] *Public Law* 727.

[161] See *The Law Lords* (above, n 13) 200.

[162] *The Nature of the Judicial Process* (New Haven CT, Yale University Press, 1921) 177.

[163] T Bingham, 'The Law Lords: who has served' in L Blom-Cooper, B Dickson and G Drewry (eds), *The Judicial House of lords 1876–2009* (Oxford, Oxford University Press, 2009) 126. For a very powerful and impressive statement of the importance of diversity in the judiciary see E Rackley, *Women, Judging and the Judiciary: from Difference to Diversity* (London, Routledge-Cavendish, 2012).

[164] A Paterson, *Lawyers and the Public Good* (Cambridge, Cambridge University Press, 2012) and A Paterson and C Paterson, *Guarding the Guardians?* (London, Centre Forum and CPLS, 2012).

Committee.[165] But that was then and this is now: 'The past is a foreign country, they do things differently there'.[166] Over the last 15 years, the final court and the Executive have been moving further apart. Lord Bingham insisted that the Lord Chancellor should not sit in the Appellate Committee, once he was appointed as senior Law Lord, even although the Lord Chancellor who appointed him to that post, Lord Irvine, wished to retain the privilege. Nor was the Lord Chancellor or his Permanent Secretary any longer to be allowed to dictate which Law Lords were to sit in a case. Further, Lord Bingham persuaded his colleagues that they should cease to speak in debates in the House of Lords which related to topics on which they might be asked at a later date to rule in their judicial capacity. However, the biggest change, of course, has been to take the final court out of the House of Lords and to re-locate it across the square as the Supreme Court.[167] Its powers are much the same as those of the Appellate Committee, although the opportunity was taken by its new members to make a range of minor but nonetheless telling changes to enhance transparency, which the procedures of Parliament inhibited or prevented.[168] Moreover, the Justices who are life peers are not permitted to return to the Chamber of the House even to listen to debates and their participation on other parliamentary committees likewise came to an end.[169] All of these changes have made the dialogue between the Court and the Executive (intentionally) more distant, more symbolic and less dynamic than in the past. What may strike the layperson in the street as odd about this is that this is the dialogue between two branches of government. In a mature democracy, why should two arms of government not talk to each other? Doesn't joined up government require that there should be some form of dialogue, albeit a rather stilted one?

Intra-governmental Relations

Perhaps the most regular dialogue between the Court and the Executive today relates to running the Supreme Court. The UK, like New Zealand and South Africa, opted for a complete makeover of an existing building rather than a new build from scratch. Each were symbolic statements—with South Africa's

---

[165] Modern Lord Chancellors who sat in both did not, as Lord Halsbury is understood to have done, start an appeal to the Privy Council with him presiding, wander out of Number 1 Downing Street to attend the Cabinet in Number 10 and walk back again several hours later to resume the presider's chair although the appeal had carried on without him.

[166] LP Hartley, The Go-Between (1953).

[167] For a detailed account of the process by which the Supreme Court came about, see A Le Sueur, 'From Appellate Committee to Supreme Court: A Narrative' ch 5 in L Blom-Cooper et al, *The Judicial House of Lords* (Oxford, Oxford University Press, 2009) at 64ff.

[168] These included an impressive website with details of current, future and decided cases, televised hearings, televised summaries of the judgment being delivered, an ability to deliver conjoined judgments, easier identification of the lead judgment and refinements to the permissions process.

[169] Retired Justices can return to the House and take part in its legislative activities, and Lord Brown has done this.

decision to make a Supreme Court out of the prison that once housed Ghandi and Mandela easily taking the palm. However, each was still expensive[170] and the cost of running a Supreme Court is much more expensive than staying in the House of Lords because IT, security, catering, printing and other services cannot be shared with a wider body. In times of austerity, this poses major problems for the President of the Court, since much of his budget is locked into judicial and staff salaries with little room for manoeuvre.[171] Further, the proposals designed to ring-fence the Court's funding put forward by Lord Falconer were not acceptable to the Treasury and the Constitutional Reform Act 2005 which established the Supreme Court leaves much within the control of the Ministry of Justice. Lord Phillips did not consider that in practice the funding system had worked well in the initial years. He also sensed a desire from some within the Ministry to have a say in the appointment of the CEO of the Court, making that person accountable to the Minister rather than the President.[172] That dispute was only resolved, in the President's favour, in 2013.

The dialogue[173] which probably attracts the most day-to-day attention, is that between the final court and different parts of the Executive who appear before the Court in litigation. Here there can be a real and direct dialogue in the exchanges between Government lawyers (Crown Counsel, Treasury juniors etc) and the judiciary. Forty years ago, the Government was a regular litigant in the House of Lords, in part because of the significant number of criminal (23 per cent) and tax (15 per cent) cases in its caseload.[174] An interesting study by Hanretty[175] indicates that between 1969 and 2003 central government was much more likely to win its cases than any other type of litigant before the House of Lords, and that overall, central government won in 65 per cent of its cases.[176] By the decade from 2000–09, criminal and tax cases had fallen to 17 per cent and five per cent respectively and

---

[170] The UK Supreme Court cost £77 million to establish and the NZ Supreme Court $80.7 million NZ dollars.

[171] The option of not filling a judicial vacancy, which would save £200,000 or so, was not available to him until 2013 when the Crime and Courts Act allowed the Executive to choose not to fill vacancies. Lord Phillips' willingness to allow Lord Sumption to delay taking up his post for several months after his appointment had been announced may have been influenced by the savings that would accrue to the Court.

[172] Lord Phillips, 'Judicial Independence and Accountability: A view from the Supreme Court'. Lecture to UCL Constitution Unit, 8 February 2011.

[173] Here again I should stress that I am not using 'dialogue' in the technical sense embraced by public law scholars when discussing the relationship between the different arms of the state or government.

[174] See chapter 2 of this volume above. Between 1952 and 1968 26% of the caseload in the House related to tax matters.

[175] C Hanretty, 'Haves and Have-Nots before the Law Lords', Working Paper, published 30 November 2011, available at: chrishanretty.co.uk/blog/wp-content/uploads/2011/11/article.pdf. An updated version of the study is shortly to appear in *Political Studies*. I am grateful to Mr Hanretty for an opportunity to see the proofs of this article in advance of publication.

[176] As appellant the Government won in 57% of cases—as compared with the normal success rate for all appellants from 1967–96 of 44%, and as respondent it won in 70% of cases—as compared with a normal success rate for respondents of 56%.

in the Supreme Court criminal and tax cases account for only seven and four per cent of the caseload respectively, whilst the combined Human Rights and public law caseload is around 47 per cent. Interestingly, the success rate of central government (whether as appellant or respondent) had fallen to 57 per cent in the House (from 2006–09) and then to 54 per cent in the early years of the Supreme Court.

Lord Falconer, the Lord Chancellor, tasked with bringing in the Supreme Court, observed in a radio broadcast:[177]

> The Supreme Court will be bolder in vindicating both the freedoms of individuals and, coupled with that, be more willing to take on the Executive.

Lord Bingham demurred on the same programme, and other senior judges and commentators agreed with Bingham.[178] Despite the considerably higher profile embraced by the Supreme Court than its predecessor body, as we saw earlier in this chapter, the Supreme Court has kept a low profile in its law-making activities. Could that be the same in relation to cases in which the Government has been a party?[179] The figures set out above suggest that any greater willingness to find against central government started before the Supreme Court came into existence. The drop in the Government's success rate in the final years of the House as compared with that in the Supreme Court may not be significant. However the change from the success rate between 1969 and 2003 reported by Hanretty, probably is. So is this an indication that the House became more willing to find against the Executive under Lord Bingham? Not consciously, is the answer. The contrast with the earlier years of the House is more likely to be a result of a substantial change in the case mix of the Supreme Court as compared with the House. The dramatic fall in crime and tax cases from 40 years ago—areas where traditionally the central government has tended to be successful in the final court may be the main explanation. As we saw in chapter two,[180] the success rate of the central government varies with the type of case. It still tends to win in tax and criminal cases. In extradition cases they are also successful, winning in 11 out of 13 cases (83 per cent) of such cases in the House of Lords, and eight out of 10 (80 per cent) of such cases in the Supreme Court. Even in human rights cases, as we saw in chapter two above, the success rate of the central government was 15 out of 24 cases (63 per cent) in the Supreme Court (up until March 2013). Yet in public law cases—at least in the Supreme Court, the central government has been experiencing something of a losing streak—winning 11 (39 per cent) and losing 17 (61 per cent).

---

[177] In J Rozenberg, 'Top Dogs: Britain's New Supreme Court', *BBC Radio 4* broadcast, 8 September 2009. Quoted in K Malleson, 'The evolving role of the Supreme Court' [2011] *Public Law* 754.

[178] See A Kavanagh, ch 3 'From Appellate Committee to United Kingdom Supreme Court: Independence, Activism and Transparency' in J Lee (ed), *From House of Lords to Supreme Court* (Oxford, Hart Publishing, 2011).

[179] Kavanagh argues that judicial activism can have two meanings: being willing to be creative in developing the law or being willing to stand up to the Executive and Parliament, ibid at 40.

[180] See ch 2 n 190 above.

Perhaps the two most interesting areas when it comes to the litigation dialogue with the central government relate to immigration and asylum on the one hand and national security on the other. As far as immigration and asylum are concerned, the Government's success rate in the Bingham Court was 21 out of 37 (57 per cent) (equal to the overall norm for all central government cases at that time). Although successful in the preponderance of these cases, the Government did suffer from notable rebuffs during the Bingham era. In *R v SSHD ex parte Anufrijeva*[181] (where the Government covertly withdrew Income Support from asylum seekers) the majority was won round (as we saw in chapter five above)[182] by a blistering critique of the Government's kafka-esque behaviour by Lord Steyn. This left Lord Bingham in puzzled isolation, since, whatever he may have thought of the Government's behaviour, he was acutely conscious that the plain and unambiguous words of the statute allowed the Government to do what they had done.[183] In the following year the Home Secretary lost an Article 8 (respect for a family life) challenge by an asylum seeker endeavouring to expel him from the UK, in *R (on the Application of Razgar) v Secretary of State for the Home Department*[184] by the closest of margins—3:2—when the swing voter switched sides after the first conference. There was no doubt in the Court about the next Article 8 challenge, in *EM (Lebanon)*.[185] Here a mother who had divorced her Lebanese husband because of his violent behaviour, fled to the UK with her young son to prevent him being returned to her abusive former husband in accordance with Islamic law. Her claim to asylum was upheld unanimously by the House on the basis of Article 8. Another unanimous defeat for the Government occurred in *Adam*,[186] where the asylum seekers were being denied financial support, and in 2006 came a further rebuff—over refugee status and female circumcision.[187] Finally, in one of his last cases before retirement, Lord Bingham upheld the challenge to the Home Secretary in a case concerning asylum seeking cousins from Kosovo who were treated differently because of a woeful and unexplained delay in handling the application of one of them.[188] In general, however, the House was understanding of the difficulties that Home Secretaries find themselves in, in immigration and asylum cases, and the Government won nearly 60 per cent of such appeals to the House.

Yet in the Supreme Court the Government's success rate in immigration and asylum cases has fallen dramatically to seven out of 19 (37 per cent) (as against an overall norm in Government cases of 54 per cent). The Government lost five of the first six immigration and asylum cases to come to the Supreme Court,

---

[181] *R v Secretary of State for the Home Department, ex parte Anufrijeva* [2003] UKHL 36.
[182] At n 61.
[183] Ibid, para 20.
[184] *R (on the Application of Razgar) v Secretary of State for the Home Department* [2004] UKHL 27.
[185] *EM (Lebanon) v Secretary of State for the Home Department* [2008] UKHL 64.
[186] *R v Secretary of State for the Home Department ex parte Adam* [2005] UKHL 66.
[187] *Secretary of State for the Home Department v K* [2006] UKHL 46.
[188] *EB (Kosovo) v Secretary of State for the Home Department* [2008] UKHL 41.

hardly an auspicious start. The sixth was the most celebrated. It involved two homosexual men, HJ and HT,[189] seeking asylum in the UK because of the risk of persecution in their home countries if they were forcibly returned there. The Supreme Court ruled unanimously that homosexual persons are protected by the Convention Relating to the Status of Refugees and that to compel such a person to pretend that their sexuality does not exist is to deny him his fundamental right to be who he is. As Lord Rodger famously observed in his judgment,[190]

[J]ust as male heterosexuals are free to enjoy themselves playing rugby, drinking beer and talking about girls with their mates, so male homosexuals are to be free to enjoy themselves going to Kylie concerts, drinking exotically coloured cocktails and talking about boys with their straight female mates. Mutatis mutandis—and in many cases the adaptions would obviously be great—the same must apply to other societies. In other words, gay men are to be as free as their straight equivalents in the society concerned to live their lives in the way that is natural to them as gay men, without fear of persecution.

A few months later the Government lost an Article 8 challenge from a Tanzanian mother[191] who had formed a relationship with a British citizen whilst seeking asylum in the UK and had two children with him. When the children were 12 and nine, her final claim for asylum failed and deportation loomed. However, the Supreme Court ruled unanimously that her appeal under Article 8 should succeed in the light of a proper assessment of the best interests of the children. The next reverse for the Government was a major rebuff, at least on the surface. In *Walumba Lumba (Congo) v Secretary of State for the Home Department*[192] a foreign national who had been sentenced to four years' imprisonment for various offences was served with an order for deportation at the end of his term in prison. The order purported to be made under the existing published policy, where there was a presumption against deportation, whereas it was actually made under a 'secret' blanket detention policy which had been implemented covertly by the Home Office in 2006, after adverse publicity against the published policy. Lord Dyson, in a lengthy majority judgment, upheld Mr Lumba's public law claim for false imprisonment but also held that he was only entitled to nominal damages because the initial judge had held that as a matter of fact Mr Lumba would have been detained under the published deportation policy, in any event. Critics of the decision argued that the sting of the rebuff to the Government for illegally detaining a person (for five years in Mr Lumba's case) had been greatly undermined by the low award of damages, which they claimed would act as an open incentive to arbitrary detention by the Government in the future. The Court was unrepentant and in the following case[193] upheld a somewhat less meritorious claim for false

---

[189] *HJ and HT v Secretary of State for the Home Department* [2010] UKSC 31.
[190] At [78].
[191] *ZH (Tanzania) v Secretary of State for the Home Department* [2011] UKSC 4.
[192] *Walumba Lumba (Congo) v Secretary of State for the Home Department* [2011] UKSC 12.
[193] *SK (Zimbabwe) v Secretary of State for the Home Department* [2011] UKSC 23.

imprisonment—though this time it was only by a 3:2 vote. Equally irritating for the Home Secretary was the next reverse a few months later in *Quila*.[194] This raised the vexed issue of forced marriages. In an endeavour to stem the flow of young couples into the UK where one was thought not to have consented fully to the marriage, the Home Office raised the minimum age for a married person's visa to 21. Mr Quila (a Chilean national) wished to marry a 17-year-old UK national. Even though the marriage was fully consensual the couple were denied a visa. So Mr Quila brought an Article 8 challenge and succeeded in the Supreme Court by 4:1, in the teeth of a trenchant dissent by Lord Brown who observed,[195]

> Article 8 is a difficult provision which has already led to some highly contentious, not to say debatable decisions. Upon that I am sure we would all agree. In a sensitive context such as that of forced marriages it would seem to me not merely impermissible but positively unwise for the courts yet again to frustrate government policy except in the clearest of cases. To my mind this cannot possibly be regarded as such a case.

Ironically, only two of the 17 immigration and asylum cases decided in the Supreme Court before April 2013 turned on an Article 8 challenge—so Lord Brown's strictures were not entirely apposite as far as the final court was concerned. Indeed, the Government won five of the last seven immigration cases to be decided by the Supreme Court by July 2013. However, the two it lost were significant. The first, *Alvi*,[196] concerned the Home Secretary's use of a Code of Practice which contained guidance and rules for the determination of which skilled immigrant workers were entitled stay in the UK. The Code purported to supplement the Immigration Rules, which had been placed before Parliament, although the Code had not. Mr Alvi persuaded the Supreme Court that the Code could only be used to exclude him if it had been laid before Parliament, thus considerably extending the amount of material which the Home Secretary would be required to lay before Parliament before being able to rely on it to exclude skilled immigrants.

Finally in *KM (Zimbabwe)*[197] came the sequel to *HJ (Iran)*. This time the applicants were not homosexuals, but persons whose political beliefs were such that, if known, and they were returned to their own country, they would suffer violence and persecution, unless they were prepared to pretend to be supporters of the Government. In keeping with the decision in *HJ (Iran)* the Supreme Court held that if people who had political beliefs were required to conceal them in order to avoid persecution in their own country then that was a justification for granting them asylum in the UK.

This excursus on immigration and asylum cases in the final court shows that in this area at least, always a sensitive one with the Home Office, the Supreme Court has very definitely set down a marker. The Government's success rate is well

---

[194] *R (on the application of Quila) v Secretary of State for the Home Department* [2011] UKSC 45.
[195] Ibid, [97].
[196] *R (on the application of Alvi) v Secretary of State for the Home Department* [2012] UKSC 33.
[197] *RT (Zimbabwe) v Secretary of State for the Home Department* [2012] UKSC 38.

below its norm in all cases and has halved in immigration cases from the Bingham era. Lord Falconer seems to have been right, after all. Quite why there has been such a turnaround is unclear, however, it has not been due to the bane of Home Secretaries—Article 8—the right to a family life. What the Supreme Court has done in this particular sector of its dialogue with the Executive is to make it clear that whatever the Government's margin for appreciation the benefit of the doubt in any given case will lie with the asylum seeker.

The final sector of the Court's dialogue with the Executive relates to national security cases. Here numbers are small but the pattern is very similar between the House and the Supreme Court. Under Bingham the House dealt with 10 cases raising national security issues and the Executive won only three of them (30 per cent), a surprising outcome given the oft-stated view of constitutional commentators that this is an area where deference to the Executive is appropriate. The first was *Rehman*.[198] Here the House very definitely deferred to the Home Secretary on the issue of deportation and national security, perhaps not surprisingly, since it was decided shortly after the 9/11 atrocities in New York. As Lord Hoffmann added in a postscript to his judgment,[199]

> I wrote this speech some three months before the recent events in New York and Washington. They are a reminder that in matters of national security, the cost of failure can be high. This seems to me to underline the need for the judicial arm of government to respect the decisions of ministers of the Crown on the question of whether support for terrorist activities in a foreign country constitutes a threat to national security. It is not only that the executive has access to special information and expertise in these matters. It is also that such decisions, with serious potential results for the community, require a legitimacy which can be conferred only by entrusting them to persons responsible to the community through the democratic process. If the people are to accept the consequences of such decisions, they must be made by persons whom the people have elected and whom they can remove.

This powerful statement points not just to the 'deference' due by the Court to the Executive in national security matters, but also to the importance that such decisions are made by democratically accountable persons.

In the following national security case, *Sivakumar*,[200] the threat to UK interests was considerably less apparent. Here the asylum applicant was a Tamil, a member of an ethnic group involved in terrorism against the Sri Lankan state. Although not apparently engaged in terrorist activities, he was arrested on several occasions in Sri Lanka and tortured there. He was refused asylum because his case did not fall within the Refugee Convention however, the House, by a 3:2 majority, took the view that the asylum request should be reconsidered, since insufficient weight had been given to the torture suffered by the applicant. Nonetheless, Lord Bingham,

---

[198] *Secretary of State for the Home Department v Rehman* [2001] UKHL 47.
[199] Ibid, para 62.
[200] *R v Secretary of State for the Home Department (ex parte Sivakumar)* [2003] UKHL 14.

anxious lest the wrong message should go to the Government,[201] stressed that the decision did not establish a blanket provision or presumption.

The next case, *Belmarsh*,[202] was much more pertinent. Indeed, Lord Bingham (who was presiding over the appeal) regarded it as the most important case that he had had to decide in his career and, unusually,[203] he assigned nine Law Lords to hear it. It concerned whether the indefinite detention without trial of foreign nationals suspected of terrorism was compatible with the Human Rights Act 1998. As we have seen, it was not the first national security case to come before the House in Bingham's time but it was the first serious challenge to the Government's anti-terrorism strategy to come to the House. Lord Bingham wanted the House to do it justice. Rather than take the case in July when energies were flagging he opted instead for an October hearing—a decision he subsequently regretted. The Government, however, initiated the preliminary skirmish, by writing to Lord Bingham as senior Law Lord to suggest that Lord Steyn, who they felt had expressed a view on the central issue in a lecture,[204] should recuse himself. This was a highly unusual occurrence but in the end the request was acceded to. Whether it was a wise start to the dialogue between the House and the Executive in the case must be doubted.

In a hard fought contest neither side could land the crucial blow. To the neutral observer the sides seemed evenly balanced by the end of oral hearing and indeed they were. A particularly powerful submission for the Secretary of State, showing that in International Law foreign nationals could be treated differently from domestic nationals, swung some votes in the Government's direction and at the end of the first conference the vote was only 5:4 against the Government. Unfortunately, no special provision had been built in for writing time and almost uniquely in his tenure in the House, Lord Bingham's schedule did not permit him to write his opinion for nearly six weeks. With Lord Steyn recused, the mantle for circulating quickly would normally have fallen to Lord Hoffmann, but perhaps because his mind was moving in the direction of his ultimate 'dissent',[205] it is not clear that he was first into print. Lord Walker did probably get his out early but he was not in the majority. Lord Rodger was also among the early circulators, and to good effect, as gradually the votes won by the Government's submissions slowly ebbed away. Lord Carswell's views, which had moved about a bit in the

---

[201] Ibid, [2].

[202] *A v Secretary of State for the Home Department* [2004] UKHL 56. The account of this case is largely taken from A Paterson, *Lawyers and the Public Good*, (Cambridge, Cambridge University Press, 2012) by kind permission of Cambridge University Press.

[203] Between 2000 and 2009 623 were heard in the Lords. Of these, only 13 were enlarged sittings of the House, five of which were with nine Law Lords.

[204] Lord Steyn, 'Guantanamo Bay: The Legal Black Hole', 27th FA Mann Lecture, 25 November 2003.

[205] Lord Hoffmann alone of the nine (although two had sympathy with his argument) concluded that there was 'no emergency threatening the life of the nation' as was required by the Human Rights Act before a derogation order could be competently promulgated. He considered this less extreme than calling the Government irrational.

case, came down against the Government and Lord Walker found himself in a minority of one, which had not been the position at any of the earlier stages in the appeal. In the eyes of the majority, the Government's decision to treat foreign terrorist suspects differently from home-grown ones, was an irrational one. As Lord Rodger pithily observed, 'If a man is holding a gun at your head, it makes no difference whether he has a British or a foreign passport in his pocket'.[206]

At the end of the conference Lord Bingham had indicated that he would write and deal with the facts and whether it was the first to be written or not; his judgment by tradition was the first to be delivered in the Chamber of the House and also in the Law Reports. Inevitably, posterity has come to see it as the lead judgment. Although Lord Bingham's prose was as pellucid as ever, his tone as one former colleague put it, was flat as a pancake. This was a deliberate strategy on Lord Bingham's part. As he recalled later:[207]

> My opinion in *Belmarsh* was very deliberately written in very low key and extremely unin-flammatory language with no big rhetorical high spots because one knew perfectly well it was going to be extremely unpopular with the powers that be. I didn't want it to sound like a political speech of a hostile kind so I myself made a clear decision to make it very low key and unrhetorical in tone ... My recollection is that when delivering judgment on the floor of the House we decided that it would be a good idea for each of us to make a very short statement summarising; very unusually, it would be a very short statement, sort of three or four sentences explaining why we were reaching the decision we were. This certainly was directed to the public because we knew that this was going to be televised.

In *Belmarsh* Lord Bingham was engaging in a conscious dialogue with the Executive, steering a masterly course 'between the shoals of political deference and the reefs of judicial supremacism' as Stephen Sedley memorably put it.[208] He wished to lay down clear parameters to the Executive's anti-terrorism powers, which inevitably took the courts into the political territory of publicly curbing the powers of the other two branches of government. Bingham was well aware of the damage caused by highly publicised spats between Home Secretaries and the courts. He was also aware that judges were non-elected, as Lord Hoffmann's dicta in *Rehman* had highlighted. Nevertheless, he had no truck with the Attorney General suggesting that judicial decision-making was in some way undemocratic, and told him so. However, despite the provocation in the Attorney General's argument and in the prior challenge to Lord Steyn, Lord Bingham deliberately downplayed the rhetoric in order (successfully) to avoid the media headlines which in the recent past had soured relations between two branches of the state.[209]

---

[206] Ibid, para 161.

[207] Interview with the author, 2009.

[208] Sir Stephen Sedley, 'The Long Sleep' in Mads Andenas and Duncan Fairgrieve (eds), *Tom Bingham and the Transformation of the Law* (Oxford, Oxford University Press, 2009) at 183.

[209] Such headlines have emerged again with David Cameron's slightly intemperate remarks in February 2011 about the Supreme Court's ruling on the right of a sex offender to have their position on the sex offender's register reviewed. See D Pannick, 'The Prime Minister and the Home Secretary should know better', *The Times*, 24 February 2011.

The House had handed the Executive a rebuff but done it in a manner that minimised the hurt.[210]

The sequel to *Belmarsh* came the following year when some of the foreign nationals suspected of terrorist links following 9/11 who had challenged their treatment in *Belmarsh* then took a direct challenge to their detention to the Special Immigration Appeals Commission (SIAC).[211] SIAC reviewed the detentions and upheld them all. In one case they were alleged to have relied on evidence obtained by torture in a foreign country. SIAC claimed that as long as the UK authorities were not complicit in the alleged torture the evidence could be looked at without breaching the UN Convention against Torture. This was challenged in the courts and the House of Lords held that irrespective of where the torture took place and whether the UK authorities were involved in it or not, evidence obtained by torture could not be relied on by SIAC, since there was no express power to allow this in the relevant legislation. The three most senior Law Lords of the seven deciding the case (including Lord Bingham) went on to add that the onus of showing that the evidence had been obtained by torture should not lie on the 'accused'—since the test would then become largely meaningless—being next to impossible for the accused to establish. However, Lord Hope leading a group of the four most junior Law Lords on the appeal, concluded that it was sufficient to reduce the standard of proof for the accused to meet from 'beyond reasonable doubt' to 'on the balance of probability'. The senior Law Lords and other critics were not slow to note that what should have been a resounding re-affirmation of the common law's abhorrence of evidence obtained by torture had been undermined and that the practical message to the Executive was considerably less robust that it should have been.

The *Belmarsh* case had another sequel, this time it was the next element in the dialogue between the Court and the Executive on post 9/11 national security. In response to the declaration of incompatibility of parts of the Anti-Terrorism, Crime and Security Act 2001 in that case, the Government passed the Prevention of Terrorism Act 2005, which replaced indefinite detention with a regime of control orders (curfews) with electronic tags, which moved the alleged foreign terrorists to other parts of the country and required them to spend between 12 and 18 hours a day in their new homes, with constraints on visitors and communications. Charles Clarke, the then Home Secretary, sought to develop the dialogue with the Government further by requesting a meeting with Lord Bingham where he could seek guidance on how many hours of curfew would be considered acceptable under the ECHR, but the latter was too canny to agree to the meeting. Thereafter, in a series of four cases coming together before the House in 2007 the Court held

---

[210] In so doing, Lord Bingham demonstrated the restraint that Vernon Bogdanor has declared to be necessary in order to maintain the compromise between parliamentary sovereignty and the rule of law which was enshrined in the Human Rights Act. See *The New British Constitution* (Oxford, Hart Publishing, 2009) 69.

[211] *A and Others v Secretary of State for the Home Department* [2005] UKSC 71.

that control orders with a curfew of 14 hours or less were acceptable but that 18 hours was too great a deprivation of liberty to be compatible with Article 5 of the ECHR.[212]

These were not the last of the challenges to control orders. As Lord Phillips (Lord Bingham's successor as senior Law Lord in 2009) pointed out in *AF*,[213] the 38 individuals to be subject to control orders up until May 2009 gave rise 'to an extraordinary volume of litigation'. In *AF* whose case went to the House twice, it was held on the first occasion[214] by 4:1 that the control order should be re-considered by the Administrative Court and whether a closed material hearing[215] in the circumstances of the case could be compatible with the requirement of Article 6 of the ECHR (the right to a fair trial). On the second occasion,[216] a nine-judge Appellate Committee presided over by Lord Phillips was asked to rule on the acceptability of closed hearings in which the controlee has no information as to the charges made against him. A week before the oral hearing the Grand Chamber of the ECtHR in *A and Others v United Kingdom*[217] ruled that the controlee must be given sufficient information about the allegations against him to enable him to give effective instructions in relation to those allegations. The Law Lords, with varying degrees of ill-disguised irritation, accepted that this decision was binding on the House and that therefore the appeals all had to be allowed, even if this might threaten the whole regime of control orders. Having stuck their necks out in the first *AF* case, to try to make the control order approach work so that the Government had a viable alternative to indeterminate detention, they were faced with the possible collapse of the whole scheme because of the ECtHR's intervention. In sum, we can see that the Court's approach to the dialogue with the Government in national security cases was to engage constructively with the Government to safeguard the liberty of the citizen, at the same time as trying to protect the safety of the country. Although the Government won only 30 per cent of these cases before the Bingham Court, in each case care was taken by the House not to rub the Executive's nose in the dirt and to soften the blow where it could.

What of the Supreme Court? The first national security case was *HM Treasury v Ahmed*.[218] Following 9/11 the UN Security Council passed resolutions requiring member states to freeze the assets of those involved in international terrorism. To assist in the process the UN Security Council produced a list of alleged international terrorists. Those included on the list were not notified of their inclusion on the list or given the opportunity to challenge it. The UK Treasury duly implemented the

---

[212] See B Dickson, *Human Rights and the United Kingdom Supreme Court* (above, n 142) 171.

[213] *Secretary of State for the Home Department v AF* [2009] UKHL 28, [6].

[214] *Secretary of State for the Home Department v MB and AF* [2007] UKHL 46.

[215] Such hearings are closed not only to the public but also to the controlee. His interests are looked after by 'a special advocate' who sees the hidden material including the charges and evidence against the controlee, but may not pass such information to the controlee.

[216] *Secretary of State for the Home Department v AF* [2009] UKHL 28, [6].

[217] *A and Others v United Kingdom* (Application No 3455/05), [2009] ECHR 301.

[218] *Her Majesty's Treasury v Ahmed* [2010] UKSC 2.

asset freeze through Orders in Council which were not subject to any parliamentary scrutiny. In response to a challenge from one of those on the list, the Supreme Court, by 6:1, struck down the Orders in Council as being beyond the powers of the Executive under the relevant legislation. Lord Phillips, in the chair, stressed that the Court's decision vindicated the primacy of Parliament, as opposed to the Executive, in determining in what circumstances fundamental rights might legitimately be restricted. This was a rather different message to the Executive to that sent by the Bingham Court, which was further underlined when the Executive asked that the unfreezing of the assets should be postponed for a month to give the Executive a chance to take further steps to prevent the assets returning to potentially dangerous hands. This was in keeping with the position on the continent, but with the exception of a ringing dissent from Lord Hope, the Court gave it short shrift and allowed the unfreezing to go ahead at once. Had Parliament been in recess this ruling could have been potentially damaging to the security of the country by allowing potential terrorists access to funds with which to further their cause, as the *Daily Telegraph* was quick to point out.

This was then followed by another control order case, *Secretary of State for the Home Department v AP*.[219] Here the Supreme Court held that some of the terms associated with the control order were unreasonable. The curfew was 16 hours, and the 'accused's new 'home' was in a Midlands town 150 miles from his immediate family, where he had no friends or relations. The Court took account of the earlier control order cases and of the fact that his family found it very difficult to visit him. The Court again rebuffed the Government and this time used a combination of Articles 8 and 5 to rule that the control order was not proportionate. The Home Secretary was unlikely to have been amused.

The following year brought more distress for the Government. Detainees following 9/11 had begun to raise civil actions against the Security Services for complicity in their alleged detention, rendition and mistreatment by foreign authorities in overseas locations (including Guantanamo Bay). The Security services argued that they could only defend themselves if they were allowed to utilise security sensitive material. To do this the Court would have had to agree to hearing some evidence under a 'closed material procedure' ie behind closed doors and in a manner that excluded the detainees from hearing that evidence, although special advocates acting on their behalf (but not on their instructions) would be able to examine the material. The Supreme Court after the first conference was prepared to allow some sort of closed material procedure to be used in an ordinary civil claim for damages, with Lord Clarke writing the lead judgment. However, as we saw in chapter five above, Lord Dyson's powerful dissent attracted enough votes for him to become the writer of the lead judgment. His view, which the majority of his colleagues endorsed, was that there was no power at common law[220] to

---

[219] *Secretary of State for the Home Department v AP* [2010] UKSC 24.
[220] This case was decided on the common law, not the Human Rights Act.

introduce 'a closed material procedure' into the civil courts—if it was to be done it must be left to Parliament. Here again the Court handed a rebuff to the Executive whilst at the same time asserting that they were showing respect for Parliament. In other words the negative outcome of the dialogue with the Executive was attributed to the need to have due regard to the dialogue with Parliament.

The same nine Justices on the same day handed down their judgment in *Home Office v Tariq*.[221] In this case an immigration officer was suspended and his security clearance revoked apparently because his brother and cousin had been arrested in connexion with a terrorist attack on transatlantic flights. Mr Tariq brought proceedings against the Home Office in the Employment Tribunal on the grounds of alleged discrimination. The Home Office sought to have part of the hearing before the Employment Tribunal by 'closed material procedure' so that information from members of the security services could be led in evidence. The Supreme Court held that such a hearing would not be in breach of Article 6 of the ECHR in the light of the case law in Strasbourg (the ECtHR). The difference from *Al Rawi* was that in relation to the Employment Tribunal, Parliament had already approved regulations permitting evidence to be heard by closed material proceedings. The two decisions were therefore not inconsistent with each other.

W (Algeria) v Secretary of State for the Home Department[222] came a few months later, and once again the Government suspected the opponents (Algerian nationals) to be terrorists. The Secretary of State therefore proposed to deport them to Algeria, a country where torture was systematically practised by state officials. The appellants took their case to the Special Immigration Appeals Commission (SIAC), which utilises closed material procedures and special advocates. In this case, unusually, it was the appellant (not the Secretary of State) who wished evidence to be led under conditions of extreme confidentiality, from a witness with knowledge of the security position in Algeria. The witness would only give evidence if SIAC gave an absolute guarantee of confidentiality with respect to the witness's identity and evidence. The Secretary of State objected because this would prevent her from communicating the witness's evidence to the Algerian Government. The Supreme Court unanimously upheld the appellant's request for an anonymity and confidentiality order, handing another rebuff to the Government (based on Articles 2 and 3 rather than Article 8).[223]

If *W (Algeria)* was a decision with a message to the Government it is rather less obvious what was being sent and to whom by the Court in the *Rahmatullah* case.[224] The latter was detained by British forces in Iraq in an area controlled by US forces. R was therefore handed over to the US forces who transferred him to

---

[221] *Home Office v Tariq* [2011] UKSC 35.

[222] *W (Algeria) v Secretary of State for the Home Department* [2012] UKSC 8.

[223] Of course, the Home Secretary was not being treated like other litigants coming before the SIAC, because she would hear all the evidence and have a chance to challenge it, without the need for special advocates.

[224] *Secretary of State for Foreign and Commonwealth Affairs v Rahmatullah* [2012] UKSC 48.

the Bagram detention facility in Afghanistan (the new Guantanamo Bay) without informing the UK Government. Under a diplomatic agreement between the two countries the UK could ask for the return of detainees whom they had handed over to the US Government, and the latter had agreed that they would return them forthwith at the request of the UK Government. The Court of Appeal issued a writ of habeus corpus requiring the UK Government to seek R's return or state why it wasn't possible. The Foreign Office then wrote to the US Secretary of State for Defence asking for R's transfer back to the UK and was politely fobbed off. R appealed to the Supreme Court asking the UK Government to be more resolute with their US counterparts and the Foreign Secretary appealed the Court of Appeal's issuing of a writ of habeus corpus. The Supreme Court (by 7:0) rejected the latter, robustly asserting that this was not an intrusion into the area of foreign policy. However, they also rejected (by 5:2) R's appeal. The Court indicated that scope for deference by the Court to the Executive in the key areas of foreign and national security policy was narrower than some constitutional commentators may have thought. However, their response to R also shows a preference for pragmatism over pointless legalism.

Al-Sirri v Secretary of State for the Home Department[225] was as inconclusive as *Rahmatullah*. It related to a rarely invoked provision in the Geneva Convention on the Status of Refugees (Article 1F(c)), which excludes from its protections anyone for whom there is serious cause to believe that they have been 'guilty of acts contrary to the purposes and principles of the United Nations'. Al-Sirri was refused refugee status on this ground and challenged the finding in the Supreme Court. Although classified as a victory for the Government since Al-Sirri did not technically win his appeal to be declared eligible to be a refugee, he did succeed in persuading the Supreme Court to adopt a restrictive approach to article 1F(c), to insist that the conduct had an international dimension and that the standard of proof be set at a level that was to his advantage. In the eyes of the Court, therefore, there was a sense in which he had not lost his appeal either. In a parallel appeal, *DD v Secretary of State for the Home Department*,[226] the appellant failed (unsurprisingly) in his bid to argue that being engaged in fighting a UN mandated peace keeping force was not enough to engage Article 1F(c). This was an obvious win for the Government but even here the Supreme Court took with one hand what it had given with the other, by requiring material errors of law in his case to be reconsidered.

Finally in the *Bank Mellat* cases,[227] an Iranian bank which had unknowingly provided banking services to two entities which were involved in the nuclear proliferation programme in Iran was excluded from the financial services markets in the UK by a Treasury direction. The Bank challenged the exclusion as being irrational, disproportionate and discriminatory before the Supreme Court. A nine-Justice

---

[225] *Al-Sirri v Secretary of State for the Home Department* [2012] UKSC 54.
[226] *DD v Secretary of State for the Home Department* [2012] UKSC 54.
[227] *Bank Mellat v Her Majesty's Treasury (Nos 1 and 2)* [2013] UKSC 38/39.

panel held (by 6:3) that despite *Al Rawi*, and in the absence of a statutory provision for the Supreme Court to conduct a closed material procedure (CMP), the fact that they were by statute permitted to hear an appeal from any judgment of the Court of Appeal (where by statute CMPs are allowed) must mean that they could use a CMP themselves. Although this was a procedural win for the Government the victory was a pyrrhic one since the result of holding a 20-minute CMP was to produce a rebuke from both the majority and the minority camps to the Executive indicating that CMPs should only be used in the Supreme Court on very rare occasions where there is absolutely no other option.

The second part of the case related to whether the Treasury direction could withstand challenge. On procedural grounds the Court voted 6:3 to say that the Bank should have been given warning of the Treasury's proposals and the opportunity to make representations. Here the majority was clearly sending a message to the Executive that it had to go about its business, even in the counter-terrorism area, with appropriate fairness. The minority pointed out that the majority's ruling did not accord with the words or the schema of the statute and that therefore the majority on this occasion could not claim to be giving Parliament its position, but rather was re-writing what they had done. The second ground of challenge was substantive, namely that the direction was irrational, disproportionate and discriminatory. The majority (originally by a vote of 8:1 as we saw in chapter five above) said that it was. The minority, originally Lord Reed on his own, but subsequently including the President and Deputy President and the Master of the Rolls as well, said it was not. Both camps claimed to be giving the Executive a wide margin of appreciation and not interfering with foreign and national security policy choices, which were for the Executive. It is easier to see how the minority camp accords with these principles than the majority. After all a choice between the property rights of an Iranian bank and the national interest in avoiding nuclear proliferation seems like a 'no-brainer'. Nevertheless, the majority's robust message for the Executive is that however important the Executive's objective and however central it is to policy fields where the Executive is the appropriate decision-maker, the decision must meet basic standards of fairness, rationality and proportionality and on such matters the final court is the arbiter. It would seem then that the Supreme Court has become more robust than the Bingham Court in its scrutiny of the Executive in its national security jurisdiction, just as it has in immigration and asylum.

Attempts by the Executive to Engage with the Court

The other side of the dialogue—when the Government responds to the rulings of the Court—is equally interesting. As we saw earlier in the chapter, declarations of incompatibility by the final court are not that common and the Executive has usually responded with an adjustment to the offending legislation, as they did following *Belmarsh* with the Prevention of Terrorism Act 2005, which has now been replaced by the Terrorism Prevention and Investigation Measures Act 2011 following the further reverses in *MB* and *AF*. Again the reverse in the Sexual Offences notification requirement case, *R (on application of F) v Secretary of State for Home Dept*[228] has been met with the Sexual Offences Act 2003 (Remedial) Order 2012. On the other hand, as we saw earlier in the chapter, Executive-led legislative responses to decisions of the final court in non-human rights cases have not been that frequent in the last decade.[229]

Even more rarely, on a few occasions the Executive's response to litigation in the final court has been to seek to engage directly in dialogue with the Court. When the *Belmarsh* case was appealed to the House of Lords, the Government wrote to the senior Law Lord (Lord Bingham) to suggest that Lord Steyn, who they felt had expressed a view on the central issue in a lecture,[230] should recuse himself. Lord Bingham, having persuaded his colleagues to refrain from speaking in House of Lords debates precisely in order to head off such challenges, felt compelled to accept Lord Steyn's reluctant recusal of himself. To this day, Lord Goldsmith (then Attorney General) asserts that the Government was right to make the challenge, no doubt in the light of the Pinochet affair. Lord Steyn is equally adamant that the challenge was inappropriate. The challenge was a pyrrhic victory. Charles Clarke, then Home Secretary, was very unhappy when the Lords duly voted 7:1:1 in *Belmarsh* to declare that the indefinite detention of the foreign nationals was a breach of their Convention rights. He felt that he was having to protect the public against suspected terrorists and the Court was being more solicitous of the rights of the accused than of the public. Exasperated, he wrote to Lord Bingham asking for a private meeting to establish what changes to the regime for detaining terrorism suspects might be acceptable in Human Rights terms.[231]

As an example of joined-up government and practical politics, it was a request that appeared to him to make a lot of sense. What was the point in his lawyers drafting a set of control orders for foreign and domestic nationals in the light of the Home Office's understanding of *Belmarsh* only to find that these too might fall foul of the House of Lords? This is a form of law-making which Bentham famously derided as akin to how dogs are trained—you wait until they misbehave and then you smack them, then once they misbehave again you smack them again and so on *ad infinitem*. Mr Clarke felt that if the Court could give him more of a clue, considerable time, money, energy and frustration might be avoided. Lord Bingham seems to have discussed it with his colleagues—at any rate he declined the invitation, probably on the grounds of the rule of law, the separation of powers, a feeling that it would be likely to lead to hostages to fortune, and a concern not

---

[228] *R (on application of F) v Secretary of State for Home Department* [2010] UKSC 17.

[229] See text at n 145 above.

[230] 'Guantanamo Bay: The Legal Black Hole', 27th FA Mann Lecture, 25 November 2003.

[231] See Lord Phillips, 'Introductory Tribute: Lord Bingham of Cornhill' in M Andenas and D Fairgrieve (eds), *Tom Bingham and the Transformation of the Law* (Oxford, Oxford University Press, 2009) xlix and Lord Phillips, 'Judicial Independence and Accountability', above, n 172.

to look as though there has been a fix between the two arms of government. Mr Clarke felt the rebuff badly, since it had been a genuine request for help. Like a dog to a bone he has returned to the matter on several occasions.[232] If the Attorney General could refer cases to the courts in pursuit of a ruling on a point of law, why could he not short circuit the process?[233]

Mr Clarke undoubtedly would have known that Lord Bingham as Lord Chief Justice and as senior Law Lord, like his predecessors and successors, had had semi-regular meetings with the Lord Chancellor—a fellow cabinet minister—to discuss matters of import in relation to the judiciary as a branch of government. Such meetings are not confined to the day-to-day problems of maintaining the final court. In such meetings the consequences of doing X or Y might be discussed. The problem with Mr Clarke's suggestion was not that the Executive was seeking legal advice from a serving judge on an extra-curial basis—that after all happens every time a problem is referred to the Law Commission by the Government, and can occur when a judge is appointed to chair a public inquiry. The difficulty stems from consulting a judge who may be called on to rule on the same point if it is subsequently litigated before the Court. At all events, whatever the seductive attractions of such an intra-governmental meeting, history does not suggest it is a good idea. Thus, Chief Justice Vinson of the US Supreme Court was asked by his friend President Harry Truman as to the legitimacy of occupying the Bethlehem Steel Mills which were about to go on strike during the Korean war. Vinson endorsed the move only to find himself on the end of a 6:3 defeat from his colleagues in the Supreme Court when the inevitable challenge came.[234] Again, in the budget crisis of 1975 in Australia, where the Governor General was considering sacking the Prime Minister (Whitlam) and his Government, he consulted the Chief Justice (Sir Garfield Barwick), who advised him that in certain specified circumstances the Governor General would be entitled to sack Mr Whitlam. The Governor General proceeded to do so, but Barwick's role prompted severe criticism because of the difficulties that could have arisen if the dismissal had been challenged in court.[235] Equally problematic was the coup in Fiji in 2000. It is understood that several members of the judiciary advised the President during the hostage crisis. This is said to have led to a long-lasting schism between those judges who took no part in the political developments and those who did.[236]

---

[232] Including, C Clarke, 'The Role of Courts in a Democracy', Foundation for Law, Justice and Society Seminar, Magdalen College, Oxford, 11 February 2011.

[233] There may be an argument for the introduction of a Home Secretary's Reference, based on the model of the Attorney General's Reference procedure under the Criminal Justice Act 1972 s36. Unlike a private meeting it would be transparent and it could relate to an agreed set of facts.

[234] *Youngstown Sheet & Tube Co v Sawyer* 343 US 579 (1952).

[235] Sir John Kerr, *Matters for Judgement* (Macmillan, Australia, 1978) 342–43.

[236] Sir Thomas Eichelbaum, *Interference with Judicial Independence in the Pacific* (cited in C Das, 'The Threats to Judicial Independence' ch 8 in S Shetreet and C Forsyth (eds), *The Culture of Judicial Independence* (Leiden, Martinus Nijhoff, 2012)).

Even less acceptable are the occasional efforts by members of the Executive to influence the outcome of decisions of the courts. President Eisenhower's not too subtle attempt at a dinner to influence Chief Justice Earl Warren in the seminal case of *Brown v Board of Education*[237]—by telling him that the Southerners 'are not bad people. All they are concerned about is to see that their sweet little girls are not required to sit in school alongside some big overgrown Negroes'[238]—still has the capacity to shock. So too has the cabinet minister who allegedly paid a social call on the swing voter in the Indian Supreme Court at the time of a crucial case to inform him that if he voted the wrong way in the case, he would be 'losing a great opportunity for a higher post'.[239] More recently the Belgian Government came to grief over its efforts to influence the judges in the court of appeal who were determining the legality of the Government's 'bail out' of Fortis, Belgium's largest financial services company, during the global banking crisis, by getting an official to talk on several occasions to the husband of one of the judges in the case.[240] The discovery of this led to the resignation of the Justice Minister, reminding us that some conversations should not take place.

Accountability

The final area for dialogue with the Executive is over power sharing and account-ability. Over the last 40 years, the power of the UK judiciary vis à vis the Executive and the Legislature has grown very substantially. In part there has been a transfer of topics from their 'too hot to handle' in-tray to that of the judiciary—what Dame Hazel Genn calls 'a shifting of reputational risk'.[241] In part also it has been down to the judge-led expansion of the judicial review jurisdiction over this period providing a real and significant check on the way that the other two branches of government exercise their powers. Yet a major element in the enhancement of judicial power was the choice of the Executive and Parliament under New Labour to pursue a purer separation of powers, including the establishment of the Supreme Court, and to incorporate the European Convention of Human Rights into our law through the Scotland Act 1998 and the Human Rights Act 1998. These developments have certainly moved the judiciary, especially at the higher reaches, very much into the political realm with a small 'p',[242] a conclusion shared by the great majority of the Law Lords and Justices whom I interviewed. As Lady Hale observed, it has 'clearly increased the social and "small p" political content of

---

[237] *Brown v Board of Education* 347 US 483 (1954).
[238] See Lord Bingham, *The Rule of Law* (London, Allen Lane, The Penguin Group, 2010) 95.
[239] PJ Reddy, *The Judiciary I Served* (Hyderabad, Orient Longman, 1999) 248.
[240] www.timesonline.co.uk/tol/news/world/europe/article5371351.ece.
[241] H Genn, Hamlyn lecture (2008), 151.
[242] A Horne, 'The Changing Constitution: A Case for Judicial Confirmation Hearings?', Study of Parliament Group, London 2010.

the judging task'.[243] Lord Sumption similarly has indicated that the ECHR often involves the judges in a difficult balancing act to determine what is in the public interest, which is 'an inherently political exercise'.[244] All considered that it had made judicial decision-making at the higher reaches more complicated.

It is surprising how little concern these developments raised in the commentariat at the time. It is easy to forget that the UK judiciary has not always been as lauded in liberal circles as it now is. In *Lawyers and the Public Good* I recalled how Connor Gearty had expressed dismay at the flood of 'dreadful, coercive' public law decisions[245] which emerged from the English courts of the 1980s and early 1990s. Gearty asserted it was not possible to squeeze politics entirely out of a system of entrenched human rights law, pointing to the political debates over the composition of the judiciary which have arisen in most countries that have entrusted judges with the definition and protection of human-rights-based truth on their behalf.[246] Gearty, like Tory backbenchers of today, was uncomfortable at the prospect of democratically elected representatives passing legislation, only to find their efforts thwarted by a bench of 'unelected and unaccountable' judges.[247] However, despite all this he considered the UK Human Rights Act to be a neat solution to the problem, as it retained parliamentary sovereignty since the judges cannot strike down legislation but merely make declarations of incompatibility, and because the Act is not constitutionally entrenched.[248] Yet, as Jack Straw, a former Lord Chancellor, told the Constitution Committee of the House of Lords in 2011,[249]

> It is all very well saying that Section 4 [of the HRA] is very elegant because all it does is provide for a declaration of incompatibility. That is true; legislation cannot be overruled—but, by God, the moment that happens, there is an unexploded bomb in the middle of a Minister's room and you have to work out what to do with it.

For the Scots, however, the position is that the courts can strike down statutes of the Scottish Parliament which they deem to be in breach of the European Convention on Human Rights or because they are thought to have transgressed into a reserved area.[250] Further, as we saw in the previous chapter, since Gearty wrote, a number of Law Lords have spoken openly of the possibility that under

---

[243] B Hale, 'Equality in the Judiciary: A Tale of Two Continents', 10th Pilgrim Fathers' Lecture, 2003.

[244] J Sumption QC, 'Judicial and Political Decision-making: The Uncertain Boundary', FA Mann Lecture, 2011.

[245] His words, not mine.

[246] A Paterson, *Lawyers and the Public Good: Democracy in Action?* 2010 Hamlyn Lectures (Cambridge, Cambridge University Press, 2012) 87–88.

[247] Ibid 92.

[248] Vernon Bogdanor, however, considers that the Human Rights Act only achieved a compromise between parliamentary sovereignty and the rule of law, which might become unsustainable without restraint on the part of the judiciary and Parliament. See *The New British Constitution* (Oxford, Hart Publishing, 2009) 69.

[249] Autumn 2011.

[250] Scotland Act 1998 s 29(2). In *Salvesen v Riddell* [2013] UKSC 22 the Supreme Court unanimously held that an Act of the Scottish Parliament was unlawful—outside the competence of Holyrood.

the new constitutional arrangements parliamentary sovereignty is no longer what it once was. Even leaving aside the recent concerns of the Prime Minister and Home Secretary over prisoners' voting rights—it may be Gearty's concerns were too easily answered.

The Challenge of Accountability

The argument here is that the enhancement of judicial power set out in the last section and the emergence of the judiciary as a third arm of government creates accountability problems. As part of government in a democracy the judiciary have not only to be independent, they also have to be accountable. This is the true conundrum behind the question 'Who guards the guardians?'. For it is not simply who is to guard them, but how is it possible to guard them in the first place, because every measure designed to preserve the judiciary's independence simultaneously makes them less accountable to the community they were appointed to serve. That is what some have described as the democratic deficit that confronts us.[251]

Perhaps not surprisingly, in the interviews the Law Lords and Justices were divided in their attitude to the accountability conundrum. Most saw the difficulty caused by a sharper separation of powers whereby the Parliament and Executive were in some sense democratically accountable but the judiciary remained like 'co-opted' platonic guardians—more at home in an oligarchy than a democracy. Few were prepared to deny that judges ought to be accountable in some sense. Rather more considered the paramountcy of judicial independence to heavily outweigh any need for accountability.[252] This group seemed either (a) to regard the issue as having been resolved in the constitutional settlement of 1688, a view that seems difficult to reconcile with the concept of an evolving constitution;[253] or (b) to consider that most of the increased power for the judiciary (eg under the Human Rights Act 1998) has come from Parliament in the first place and they can take it back. Given that there was a strong judicial lobby in favour of the judiciary taking over more of the running of the courts and that the substantial expansion in judicial review has been judge-led, this cannot be a complete answer. Moreover, for those who think that Parliament cannot now abolish judicial review or reject

---

[251] RB Stevens, 'Reform in Haste and Repent at Leisure' (2004) 24 *Legal Studies* 1, 28.

[252] As Robert Stevens once sagely observed, the judiciary have sometimes not been averse to using judicial independence as a justification for resisting developments which they do not like. RB Stevens, 'Unpacking the Judges' (1993) 46 *Current Legal Problems* 1, 2. Stevens shows how the nineteenth-century judiciary ensured that while every other institution was being reformed by the industrious Victorians—'the franchise, local government, the church, universities, the civil service, the army and navy and even the court structure', the judiciary alone escaped by relying on the mystique of judicial independence.

[253] That said, there remains a vigorous debate in the US as to originalism and the Constitution.

the incorporation of fundamental human rights into our law, another answer is needed.

Those who saw the strength of the conundrum favoured one of four main solutions. The first might be called the Barak answer, after Aharon Barack, a former President of the Supreme Court of Israel. As he has argued, someone has to protect the fundamental rights of the minority in a democracy and independent judges are the best solution.[254] As one Law Lord told me: 'Obviously the greater the discretion that the judges have the more you can say "why should these people be permitted to take policy decisions which nobody can challenge", but what's the answer? Somebody's got to take these decisions'.

The second—epitomised in Lord Sumption's Mann lecture—but adopted by others besides him, is to acknowledge the problem[255] but adopt a strategy of caution when it comes to exercising the enhanced judicial powers such as making declarations of incompatibility, or to give the Executive or Parliament the benefit of any doubt when assessing whether they have acted outwith the limits of their constitutional competence.

> My personal predilection is not to rush into reversing unless I think it's properly justified and I don't start with that as my default position. I would start with the default position that if the Executive has done it, well let's see if it's justified and if it is, don't mess about with it. (Lord Carswell)

> The democratic process is liable to be subverted if, on a question of moral and political judgement, opponents of the [Hunting] Act achieve through the courts what they could not achieve in Parliament. (Lord Bingham)[256]

> You have to be very clear about what matters can appropriately be determined by a court and what the limits are of what is justiciable. So, for example, in the concept of proportionality you eventually reach a stage where you have to make a value judgement and that is when you recognise that other bodies have a legitimacy or expertise, or may not, depending on the subject matter, and they may have what the court doesn't have, and that is where you have to stop and respect that. (Lord Reed)

> In *Axa* there was quite a strong argument that the Scottish Parliament had gone too far in imposing liabilities retrospectively. That was quite a strong example of a court saying, well nevertheless we can't interfere with the decision of a democratic legislature, unless we properly can do so and here it is essentially a judgement on social policy and that is not a matter in which this court can override the view of a legislature. (A Justice)

---

[254] Aharon Barak, *The Judge in a Democracy* (Princeton NJ, Princeton University Press, 2006).

[255] Lord Sumption told me in 2012, 'The Human Rights Convention does create an accountability problem by transferring a number of decisions which are by their nature political to judges in circumstances where judges are rightly not accountable to anyone for what they decide, and in circumstances where the result is incapable of amendment in practical terms.' Several Justices expressed their concerns about the amount of power that had now been conferred on them, finding it quite troubling, not least because it was bringing them into the world of politics with a small 'p' or because it required them make decisions that had political ramifications.

[256] *R (on the application of Countryside Alliance and Others) v Her Majesty's Attorney General* [2007] UKHL 52, para 45.

I think we should be cautious about it ... there are dangers of overstepping the mark. I think the judges in certain times have gone a bit far, but one way in which the judges have been quite conservative is in relation to the power to make declarations of incompatibility for example under the Human Rights Act. On the whole the judges have used that power extremely sparingly. (Lord Clarke)

The third answer, which had a broad measure of support, was to argue that the final court was replete with accountability measures already. These include the requirement to give coherent reasons for judicial decisions, the mechanisms for appeal, the limits which judges recognise to judicial law-making and what should be left to Parliament, and the commitment to openness and transparency through, eg encouraging visitors, providing a user-friendly website, broadcasting hearings and judgments, the use of press releases and supporting television documentaries.

The fourth and final response—which a significant minority of the Law Lords and Justices voiced—was to accept that there was an accountability problem, without necessarily knowing what the solution to it might be. Vernon Bogdanor has argued[257] that whilst politicians can have sacrificial or answerability accountability the same cannot be true for judges. The latter can only be held to account in an explanatory way because of the need for judicial independence. With the greatest of respect to this constitutional scholar, I wonder if he goes far enough. Andrew Le Sueur's further distinctions[258] between probity, process, content and performance accountability seem a more fruitful line for exploration than the acceptance of platonic guardians. In my view, the dialogues which lie at the heart of appellate judicial decision-making which we have discussed in this book (including the ones with Parliament and the Executive) are indeed part of accountability. This is both because of the transparency which they bring, but also because of the link which they provide to the expectations of the wider legal community. Be that as it may, as several commentators have argued,[259] one place where democratic accountability can be introduced for judges in the final court without threatening their judicial independence is at the judicial appointment stage. When judicial appointment in the UK was reformed under New Labour[260] following the Concordat between Lords Woolf and Falconer,[261] the Executive—in the guise of the Lord Chancellor—largely withdrew from the senior judicial appointment process, leaving the field to judicial appointments commissions. Not surprisingly,

---

[257] V Bogdanor, *The New British Constitution* (Oxford, Hart Publishing, 2009) 85.

[258] See A Le Sueur, 'Developing mechanisms for judicial accountability in the UK' (2004) 24 *Legal Studies* 73.

[259] See S Shetreet, 'Creating a Culture of Judicial Independence' ch 2 in S Shetreet and C Forsyth (eds), *The Culture of Judicial Independence* (Leiden, Martinus Nijhoff, 2012), A Paterson, *Lawyers and the Public Good* (above, n 246) ch 4 and A Paterson and C Paterson, *Guarding the Guardians?* (London, Centre Forum and CPLS, 2012).

[260] In fact, the first Judicial Appointments Board was established by a Scottish Liberal Democart, Jim Wallace, in a coalition government.

[261] Itself a clear and significant dialogue between the senior judiciary and the Executive.

the judiciary considered that they were the appropriate people to fill the vacuum left by the Lord Chancellor. They were remarkably successful in this, as *Guarding the Guardians?* showed. Nominally, appointments to the Supreme Court have been in the hands of an ad hoc appointments commission whose Chair and Vice-Chair were the President and Deputy President of the Supreme Court with one representative from each of the three permanent judicial appointment commissions, none of whom needed to be a woman and only one of whom needed to be a layperson.[262] Little has changed under schedule 13 of the Crimes and Courts Act 2013. In practice, the statutory consultations will continue to ensure that effectively the key input to the appointment of Supreme Court Justices will come from 20 senior judges and two or three laypersons.[263] Given that the judiciary and the senior judiciary in particular are the third arm of government, Tom Legg, the former Permanent Secretary in the Lord Chancellor's Department is surely right to express reservations at such a degree of judicial influence over the appointment process. As he has written, 'It is no reflection on our judges to say that this [is] undesirable. No branch of government should be effectively self-perpetuating'.[264]

In short, the current process suffers from an accountability problem. It fails the Tom Legg/Robert Stevens 'self-perpetuating oligarchy'[265] test. Effectively the Supreme Court is choosing its successors.[266] The potential for a cloning effect is likely to be overwhelming. This critique is not personal to the Justices—it is an institutional problem. It is not easy to see how we can best solve some of these problems. The Crime and Courts Bill contained provisions to alter the panel which will select future Supreme Court Justices. Kenneth Clarke, having concluded that his role as Lord Chancellor in the appointment of Supreme Court Justices was reduced to little more than a cipher,[267] proposed that he should give up his veto and become a member of the selection panel, at least for the appointment of the President of the Supreme Court. This was a very clear statement by the Executive that it wished to claw back ground that it had relatively recently ceded to another arm of government. The proposal prompted a frantic dialogue with the senior judiciary which was to no avail—Ken Clarke was not for budging. Fortunately for

---

[262] The Report of the Advisory Panel on Judicial Diversity 2010, p 41 suggested that there should always be a gender mix on the selection panel and if possible an ethnic mix. Curiously the Panel had nothing to say about lay participation in the process.

[263] Ibid, 29. The overwhelming majority of which are white men.

[264] T Legg, 'Judges for the New Century' [2001] *Public Law* 62, 73. See also Robert Stevens, 'Judges do and should have political views. By giving the judges an even greater voice in the selection of their members than they have today, it is unclear why that should be superior from an apolitical point of view. It is replacing one oligarchy with another'. RB Stevens, 'Unpacking the Judges' (1993) 46 *Current Legal Problems* 1, 20.

[265] Robert Stevens, *The English Judges* (Oxford, Hart Publishing, 2002) 177.

[266] The Report of the Advisory Panel on Judicial Diversity 2010, Recommendation 41: 'No judge should be directly involved in the selection of his/her successor and there should always be a gender and, wherever possible, an ethnic mix on the selection panel'.

[267] His only power was to veto a nomination, and only once at that.

the senior judges, a cabinet reshuffle intervened and Ken Clarke was budged—by the Prime Minister, and replaced by Chris Grayling the first non-lawyer politician to become Lord Chancellor since 1673. Doubtless to the relief of the senior judiciary, Mr Grayling concluded that he did not wish to change the role of the Lord Chancellor in senior judicial appointments, after all. However, the relief was short lived. It was gradually dawning on the senior judiciary that a more rigorous separation of powers and the consequent loss of a judicial Lord Chancellor had disadvantages. No longer did they have a voice in the Cabinet. The Lord Chief Justice appeared before the Select Committee on the Constitution to lament the judiciary's loss of power as he saw it.[268] It is even being suggested that some of the senior judiciary now wish to exclude the Lord Chancellor and the Executive altogether from the appointment of senior judges. This, of course, would only exacerbate the self-appointing oligarchy problem. It seems clear therefore that neither arm of government is happy with the balance of powers between them when it comes to the appointment of senior judges. The Report of the House of Lords Select Committee on the Constitution: Judicial Appointments in 2012 took a wide range of evidence, but found little consensus as to how the appointment system should be reformed. The general feeling was that the Lord Chancellor's role should remain more or less as it is at present. The Committee received evidence from Baroness Hale, Jack Straw, Tom Legg and several academics favouring pre-appointment hearings before a parliamentary committee.[269] A majority of witnesses opposed this in part because of a fear that such hearings would begin to resemble Senate confirmation hearings in the United States.[270] Neither the witnesses nor the Committee examined the role of confirmation hearings in the appointment of Justices to the Supreme Court of Canada, which do not run the risk of politicisation, and add a further measure of accountability to the appointment on top of appointment by the Executive.[271] Lady Hale and several other witnesses suggested that as an alternative, some parliamentarians could be included on the appointments panel. This too could provide a dialogue for greater accountability, but once again it was rejected by the Constitution Committee in part because they were unsure how such individuals would be chosen. Instead the Committee's view[272] was that

> The proper role of Parliament is to have oversight of the judicial appointments process rather than to be involved in specific appointments. The Lord Chancellor has ministerial responsibility for the appointments process and is accountable to Parliament for his actions.

---

[268] Annual Evidence session with the Lord Chief Justice of England and Wales, 30 January 2013, Constitution Committee of the House of Lords.

[269] See Mary Clark's helpful article 'Introducing a Parliamentary confirmation process for new Supreme Court justices' [2010] *Public Law* 464.

[270] Those opposed to confirmation hearings did not evidence much awareness as to how they actually operate in the US other than a belief that they are all like the sessions experienced by Bork and Thomas. In truth most Senate confirmations are now pretty anodyne affairs.

[271] See *Guarding the Guardians?*, above, n 259, ch 5.

[272] In para 53.

Disappointingly, the Committee offered no explanation as how Parliamentary and Executive accountability for judicial appointments in which they have had little or no involvement, but the senior judiciary have, provides the democratic accountability that the judiciary needs in an era when their power vis à vis the other arms of government has been growing.[273]

The Lord Chief Justice's recent lament as to the lack of a judicial position at the top table of power with the advent of a political Lord Chancellor[274] is a belated recognition that the old-style Lord Chancellor offered channels of dialogue whose value had been overlooked. Maybe the time is ripe for a more serious dialogue between the final court, Parliament and the Executive. Lord Hoffmann is surely right to assert that 'the development of the law is not solely the province of one branch of government but ought to be partnership between all three'.[275] I would only add that the Law Commission should also be in the partnership. Yet for a partnership to work, the dialogue must work.

---

[273] See Shetreet, above n 259, ch 2.

[274] Lord Judge, appearance before the Constitution Committee, January 2013, available at www.parliament.uk/documents/lords-committees/constitution/lordchiefjustice/CC300113LCJtranscript.pdf. A clear case of 'be careful what you wish for'—the Woolf-Falconer concordat on the new separation of powers—coming home to roost.

[275] '*Fairchild* and After', above, n 24.

8

Final Reflections

THIS BOOK HAS not been an attempt to provide a definitive and objective account of the final years of the House of Lords and the arrival of the new Supreme Court. Other writers have essayed parts of that task with considerable success.[1] Suffice it to say that the record indicates that the Bingham court was probably the strongest in the recent history of the House of Lords, that the new Supreme Court has made a very impressive start on a whole range of fronts, and that the President and Deputy President backed by a settled team of Justices for the first time since the start of the new Court, show all the signs of making a major contribution to collective forms of appellate judicial decision-making in our final court.

Rather this work has focused on the explanatory power of examining the work of the UK's final court through the lens of the dialogues that the judges engage in when making judicial decisions. It has been argued that dialogues are a particularly fruitful line of investigation because of the light they shine on the dynamic nature of appellate judicial decision-making as a social and collective process. We have seen that the dialogue with counsel remains pertinent both for the outcome of cases and the reasoning that underpins that outcome, and also the importance of new dialogues with judicial assistants and with Strasbourg. Most significant of all we have seen how the interaction between the judges and their colleagues on the Court can stimulate reflection and explain changes of mind and vote, even in the later stages of a case—in a way that studies of the attitudes or psychological values of the judges may not.[2] In the remainder of the chapter we will examine these dialogues with a view to offering constructive criticism as to the dialogues of the future.

If dialogues are the key to understanding appellate judicial decision-making in the UK's final court, what do the principal dialogues tell us about the transition from the House of Lords to the Supreme Court? With counsel the dialogue

---

[1] Eg L Blom-Cooper, B Dickson and G Drewry, *The Judicial House of Lords 1876–2009* (Oxford, Oxford University Press, 2009); J Lee (ed), *From House of Lords to Supreme Court* (Oxford, Hart Publishing, 2011); M Andenas and D Fairgrieve (eds), *Tom Bingham and the Transformation of the Law* (Oxford, Oxford University Press, 2009); A Burrows, D Johnston and R Zimmermann (eds), *Judge and Jurist: Essays in Memory of Lord Rodger of Earlsferry* (Oxford, Oxford University Press, 2013) and B Dickson, *Human Rights and the United Kingdom Supreme Court* (Oxford, Oxford University Press, 2013).

[2] See chapter 1 of this volume, above.

has become sharper and more focused. Less time for hearings has placed greater emphasis on the written materials submitted before (and sometimes during and after) the oral arguments, despite oral advocacy inviting greater participation from the judges than written advocacy. Although the power and role of counsel as partners in the decision-making process has also been eroded by the declining strength of the expectations which constrain the arguments that the judges can use to determine cases,[3] both counsel and the judges continue to value the contribution that expert advocates can make to the decision-making process. For counsel and their clients who are interested in playing for rules, a better outcome in terms of the law even if the case is lost can still justify the decision not to settle. For the Justices, effective assistance to achieve better answers justifies the retention of extended hearings. Cost pressures will undoubtedly in time lead to a further reduction in the length of oral argumentation, yet few in the Court consider that more use of judicial assistants and written advocacy from counsel will be an adequate substitute for the flexibility of oral argumentation.

Similar changes have occurred in the dialogue between the Justices themselves. More discussion occurs before the hearing, and more after it, but again there has been a shift in emphasis from oral to written discourse, especially when judgments are being circulated. Which Justices are sitting in a case influences the exchanges which occur in that case, although such variations can be attributed primarily to the Justices' views on team-working, their skills in small group leadership and the links between them (in terms of physical and philosophical geography). Interestingly then, geography matters in appellate courts. Darbyshire adverts to the lack of meeting space in the Court of Appeal[4]—a problem which also afflicted the House of Lords especially when it came to hearings with larger panels. The Supreme Court building resolved the meeting and hearing problems but distributed the Justices on two floors, which has channelled informal exchanges and team-working in unexpected ways.

That said, a notable increase in collaborative team-working and interactive dialogue has been one of the most significant changes from the House of Lords. As a way of working it has much to recommend it. As we saw in chapter four above, short pre-hearing meetings are now held (as they are in the Court of Appeal) to see if collective views exist as to the key issues in the case on which the panel wishes to hear more from counsel. During the hearing Justices, particularly those in contiguous rooms, may work together in an effort to tease a way through to the best available answer. At the first conference Justices are at their most individual: some have detailed notes, some have prepared with their judicial assistant whilst others again turn to their extempore skills from their time in the Court of Appeal. The most junior Justices (who speak first) are no longer encouraged

---

[3] Particularly the convention derived from the adversarial system that the judges should restrict their reasons for deciding the case to points that have been run by, or put to, counsel.

[4] P Darbyshire, *Sitting in Judgment* (Oxford, Hart Publishing, 2011) 430.

to speak for longer[5] and there is greater encouragement for debate at the end of the presentations.

Again, at the stage of the circulation of the judgments, we see that there is more sustained collective engagement than was the case in most appeals in the House of Lords, in part because of the drive by a majority of the Justices for single judgments of the court. By mid-2013 single judgments were running at 55 per cent of the cases determined by the Supreme Court in that year, a level last attained in the mid-1990s,[6] making it probably the most dramatic change from the House of Lords under Lord Bingham. Such a rate of single judgments could be achieved through one of two approaches: either the practice, not unknown in the Privy Council, of letting the judgment writer get on with it and only commenting if something really problematic emerges in the judgment that is circulated, or greater exchanges between the Justices with judgments being circulated and amended or withdrawn.

The Supreme Court's pursuit of single judgments has featured the second of these approaches. The lead judgment will usually be assigned by the presiding Justice but others may choose not to wait for this to emerge, perhaps hoping that a trenchant dissent or an alternative judgment may shake the majority from their original position. As we saw earlier,[7] some task leaders have proved adept on occasions at attracting the lead judgment away from its original 'owner'. Moreover, there is evidence that the potential for engaging in reflective thinking within an ethos that values more collective judgments does not inhibit changes of mind at the judgment circulation stage, as we saw in chapter five above. Suggestions for additions or amendments to the lead judgment were not unusual in the House of Lords: now they are commonplace as the team strives for a 'judgment of the court', albeit one that it is still published under the name of one or more of the Justices.[8] Even in cases where the Justices are fiercely divided there is now pressure, as in *Waya*,[9] the *Bank Mellat* cases[10] and in *Smith v Ministry of Defence*,[11] to narrow the disagreement, if possible, to one majority and one or two minority judgments. Such team-working requires a different skill set in the participants than was once required of Law Lords. The ability to negotiate, to compromise, to persuade whilst robustly defending a position of principle are skills which until a few years ago were more associated with a member of the Law Commission than a member of

---

[5] As they were under Lord Bingham—see chapter 4 of this volume above.

[6] See Table 3.5 in chapter 3 above.

[7] See chapter 5 of this volume, above.

[8] See chapter 3 of this volume, above.

[9] *R v Waya* [2012] UKSC 51.

[10] *Bank Mellat v Her Majesty's Treasury (No 1)* [2013] UKSC 38; *Bank Mellat v Her Majesty's Treasury (No 2)* [2013] UKSC 39.

[11] *Smith v Ministry of Defence* [2013] UKSC 41.

the final court,[12] yet they are now being actively applied in the pursuit of more collaborative judgments.[13]

Nevertheless team-working of this sort can come at a price. It requires greater circulation of judgments and more second case conferences than was the case in Lord Bingham's era, and despite the presider's efforts, such conferences have the potential to reinforce existing tensions rather than contribute to cohesiveness. That said, there are signs that the dissent rate has fallen since its peak in 2011 (when the Court was at its most divided)[14] in part perhaps because dissenting on ones' own seems to have become proportionately less common than in the House of Lords. This too may be a sign of the benefits of greater team-working and that Lord Neuberger's plea for a self-denying ordinance with respect to concurrences and dissents[15] is having an impact.

Team-working potentially has another drawback—a loss of individualism in our Justices. The glory of the common law and its final court has included the individuality and idiosyncrasy of its top judges. The myth of judicial fungibility which sustains the arid judgment style of the European Court of Justice is not a feature that hitherto has attracted many supporters in the United Kingdom. Single judgments representing the outcome of the internal debates within the Supreme Court which are not publicly rehearsed, remove the humanity of individual difference and potentially undermine transparency.[16] For those who believe in the virtues of diversity (including diversity in thought) within the final court this is not necessarily a welcome development. Fewer dissents and concurrences in return for more single judgments mean more judgments devised by a committee and consequently more compromise. At least so thought Lord Rodger of Earlsferry, who wrote,[17]

> If the powers that be have their way, and the new Supreme Court of the United Kingdom adopts more single judgments, then there will be less scope in future for humour or indeed for any other expressions of the judges' individuality. By definition, the author of a composite[18] judgment is not writing just as himself and will alter his voice accordingly.

---

[12] Darbyshire records one Court of Appeal judge as telling her, 'Some judges are easier to disagree with than others: the difficult ones are those (not many) who have poor negotiating skills and defend their position like a dog in a manger.' *Sitting in Judgment* (Oxford, Hart Publishing, 2011) 352.

[13] It may be no coincidence that a third of the current Supreme Court are former members of law commissions.

[14] See Table 3.8 in chapter 3 above. Nevertheless, the overall dissent rate in the Supreme Court at 24% of all cases involving one or more dissents, remains higher than in the House of Lords in its last 40 years.

[15] See chapter 3, fn 174, above.

[16] Lord Neuberger, while in the Court of Appeal considered that where single judgments are taken to extremes 'decisional independence and accountability is lost'. 'Developing Equity—a View from the Court of Appeal' Chancery Bar Association conference 2012, London, 20 January 2012. (Available on the Court of Appeal website). See also L Greenhouse, 'The Cost of Compromise' *NY Times* 10/7/13.

[17] Lord Rodger, 'Humour and the Law' 2009 SLT (News) 202.

[18] By this term he means not simply the relatively rare composite or joint judgment where two or more Justices share the task of drafting the judgment equally, but also the now quite commonplace single judgment of the court.

In *Norris v Government of the United States of America*[19] an offer to write my section of the report in a pastiche of Lord Bingham's style was rewarded with the wintriest of smiles. Indeed, not only humour, but any form of distinctive good writing, is even harder to bring off in a composite judgment than in an individual judgment ... The much touted efficiency savings of a single judgment will be dearly bought if, as a result, we lose individual hallmark contributions of [the] quality [of Lords Macnaghten, Wilberforce and Bingham].

The pursuit of single judgments has one final consequence which had not been addressed by mid-2013. The practice of the Court, as in the House of Lords under Lord Bingham, was for the presiding judge to allocate who was to write the lead or leading judgment setting out the facts. The choice was usually based on the perceived importance of the case (in which case the presider would do it, sometimes even if he was in the minority, because his judgment would be printed first in the Law Reports), or the specialist expertise of the judge in the field, or because someone has volunteered for the task. In Bingham's era when single judgments of the court never rose above 20 per cent of the cases dealt with in a year, and substantial individual judgments or concurrences were the norm, allocating the lead judgment caused few problems. Today, with single judgments of the court running at 37 per cent of cases decided in the court from 2009 to July 2013, and the giving of substantial and concurring judgments no longer encouraged as they were under Lord Bingham, the opportunities for writing are becoming fewer, if you are not chosen to write the leading judgment, and you are not dissenting. Already this has led in some cases to a competition to give the lead judgment. However, in part because Lords Phillips and Hope followed the example of Lord Bingham in choosing to write the lead judgment in many of the significant cases, they were responsible for writing the lion's share of lead judgments until they retired, as we can infer from Table 3.1 in chapter 3 above. As that Table also shows, Lord Neuberger has not followed the example of his predecessors in this regard; nevertheless, it is clear that despite the efforts of the presiding Justices to share the lead judgments more fairly, there are marked differences between the Justices in terms of the percentage of lead judgments given for cases sat in. In the US Supreme Court this problem is dealt with by the convention that each Justice gets around the same number of lead judgments to write a year.[20] Such a solution would not work so easily in the UK Supreme Court given its more specialist caseload,[21] because the UK Court does not sit en banc and, it would appear, because some Justices through their persuasiveness are more adept than others at moving the lead judgment away from the original lead writer. Nonetheless, if the problem is left unaddressed, and the pursuit of single judgments continues unabated, there is a danger that the impression may come to be given, however unfairly, that all Justices are equal but some are more equal than others.

---

[19] *Norris v Government of the United States of America* [2008] UKHL 16; [2008] 1 AC 920.
[20] Approximately eight majority judgments.
[21] Which tends to mean that a Scots Justice will tend to write the lead judgment in a Scots case.

As regards the dialogue with other courts little has changed with respect to the Court of Appeal, the US Supreme Court or the European Court of Justice. However, with Strasbourg the dialogue has deepened, and with it has come greater mutual understanding and respect of the role of each in the political firmament. Yet with Scotland and Scots appeals, incipient tensions remain that may only be resolved with the Referendum in 2014.

With academics the dialogue has remained in the Supreme Court much as it was in the Bingham court. Yet, the discourse with judicial assistants has flourished (partly because of geographic changes—more accommodation has allowed an increase in their number in the Supreme Court, and they have attained a more strategic location nearer the Justices). The impact and involvement of the judicial assistants has grown in the last decade as their role has evolved with different Justices. That was how law clerks started out with the US Supreme Court and now their influence has become substantial. This may be a caution for us.

However, it is with respect to the other two arms of government, Parliament and the Executive, that the Supreme Court has arguably its most problematic dialogues. The geographic split resulting from relocating the final court across Parliament Square, has only served to emphasise the divide between Parliament and the Supreme Court. The seeds of the separation were sown under Lord Bingham when Lord Chancellors were no longer permitted to preside in the top court and the Law Lords were discouraged from speaking in parliamentary debates. The removal of Law Lords from legislative committees caused regret on both sides and a decline in informal channels of communication between the two branches of government. The danger is that whilst the Supreme Court continues to confront parliamentary monologues in the shape of legislation in cases requiring the interpretation of statues, Parliament does not seem to keep abreast of the Court's interpretive rulings, or indeed many of their other decisions. Certainly, the Supreme Court and Parliament are no nearer to reaching agreement on the appropriate role of each institution when it comes to delimiting parliamentary sovereignty or judicial law-making. Indeed, in some respects the Supreme Court has been arguably less transparent in its approach to judicial law making than the House of Lords was under Lord Reid or Lord Bingham. A more effective dialogue between the Supreme Court and Parliament might help to facilitate the mutual recognition of the institutional competencies of each in relation to legislation. For example, could a forum for joint discussion between parliamentarians and/or the parliamentary clerks and the Judiciary be introduced? Topics which might be discussed could include (1) the use of *Hansard* as a tool to ascertain Parliament's intention in an Act and (2) the argument which arose in the *Assange*[22] case as to whether Parliament had been misled by Ministers as to what was a 'judicial authority' and what the implications would be if it was established that Parliament had been so misled.

---

[22] *Assange v The Swedish Prosecution Authority* [2012] UKSC 22. See Lord Mance's dissent.

With the Executive, channels of communication are also a work in progress. As we have seen the Court has remained as robust as the House under Lord Bingham in national security cases and has been even stronger in challenging the Executive in immigration and asylum cases. Nevertheless, Lord Bingham was careful to avoid unnecessary strains in the relationship between the UK's top court and the Executive. Lord Neuberger shows all the signs of understanding the value of this example,[23] but he and Baroness Hale are to be commended for boldly attacking the recent cuts in legal aid and access to justice. The Supreme Court has rightly been successful in wresting the appointment of future CEOs to the Supreme Court away from the Lord Chancellor. However the senior judiciary are belatedly coming to recognise the downside of the Concordat which removed so many of the Lord Chancellor's powers in relation to the judiciary in the pursuit of a purer separation of powers. The recent suggestion in some quarters that the separation of powers be made even more pure by removing the Executive altogether from the senior judicial appointments process is problematic in terms of democratic credibility and accountability. The Supreme Court is more vulnerable to the charge of insufficient accountability for its decisions because the Lord Chancellor can no longer be held to account for the appointments process. Without parliamentary confirmation, or parliamentarians or the Executive on the appointment panel the senior judiciary runs the risk of appearing like a self-perpetuating oligarchy.[24] In a modern democracy the judiciary is required to protect the minority from the excesses of the majority, through the vehicle of human rights, which is one of the real areas of strength of the Supreme Court. However, the Supreme Court may undermine its own legitimacy through an appointment system that lacks parliamentary and Executive accountability and strikingly continues to fail the diversity challenge.

The Supreme Court would doubtless respond by asserting that they are more accountable than the House of Lords was, through the Supreme Court's greater transparency and their consequent willingness to engage with the public. The argument from transparency is undoubtedly a very powerful one. Indeed the Court's strategic objective of a commitment to transparency is commendably manifest in many aspects of the way that it currently functions. It is not difficult for commentators such as Richard Cornes to mount a compelling case[25] that the Supreme Court has completely eclipsed the Appellate Committee of the House of Lords on this front. Welcoming visitors to the new building in their thousands is a far cry from the quiet ways of the House of Lords. The very fact that it has a strong communications section on its staff, with a highly impressive website

---

[23] See Lord Neuberger, 'Judges and Policy: A Delicate Balance' Lecture to the Institute for Government, 18 June 2013. (On the Supreme Court website)

[24] As Paterson and Paterson have argued in *Guarding the Guardians?* (London, Centre Forum, 2012) the current process for appointing Supreme Court Justices is, in practice, overwhelmingly dominated by the senior judiciary. Again it is the guardians who are guarding themselves.

[25] See R Cornes, 'A constitutional disaster in the making? The communications challenge facing the United Kingdom's Supreme Court' [2013] *Public Law* 266.

that far outstrips that of the Appellate Committee is a very clear declaration of intent by the Court that it wishes to engage in a dialogue with the public, which the Appellate Committee had largely neglected. Cornes enumerates a wide range of communications vehicles used by the Court to achieve its objective, ranging from Annual Reports to press releases and from SKY broadcasts of oral hearings to television documentaries illustrating how the Court goes about its business. None of these existed in the case of the Appellate Committee. The Justices believed that by embracing YouTube and Twitter for the delivery of their judgments they would give the Court a higher profile with the public than that of the Appellate Committee without turning themselves into publicly recognised figures. As Baroness Hale told *The Guardian*, 'It's a very narrow dividing line between improving public understanding ... and diminishing the dignity and respect the court should have. We are not politicians'.[26]

Given the great strides that the Supreme Court has taken to heighten public awareness as to its activities it feels churlish to suggest that they should go further. However, that is what will be contended. First, unlike the members of the Appellate Committee or the Justices of the US Supreme Court, the members of the UK Supreme Court have resolutely turned their faces against having a Register of Interests. After the *Pinochet* debacle where Lord Hoffmann unaccountably failed to declare his involvement in a charity which raised funds for Amnesty International (an intervener in the *Pinochet* case) it is surprising that the members of the UK's top court are so opposed to having such a Register. The suggestion that they can be relied on to declare any connections which they might have is exactly the view that Lord Hoffmann took, with such unfortunate consequences. There is a certain irony in the fact that the House of Lords has tightened its provisions in relation to the Register of its members' interests which the Justices who were former Law Lords will have to comply with if they return to the House of Lords after they retire from the Supreme Court. This issue is closely tied to the duty of the Justices to recuse themselves from determining cases in which they have an interest.[27]

The answer to each of these issues, the Register of Interests, recusal and appointment to the Supreme Court is greater transparency in the form of a more effective dialogue with the public. A more effective dialogue with the public may also help to address the enigma which confronts the Court of achieving accountability for its enhanced powers without threatening judicial independence. Greater transparency in the judicial appointments process with fewer statutory consultations and

---

[26] *The Guardian*, 26 October 2010. The Justices' concerns whilst understandable were likely to be misplaced. The experience of the US Supreme Court, a much more overtly political court, is that name and face recognition of Justices by the public averages at consistently below 10% in opinion polls and that it seems to have been declining in recent times. See R Davis, *Justice and Journalists: The US Supreme Court and the Media* (New York, Cambridge University Press, 2011) at 20.

[27] See chapter 3, fn 28 above.

perhaps some form of post-appointment parliamentary confirmation, as exists with the Canadian Supreme Court, would produce real legitimacy gains.

With regard to transparency in relation to judicial law making, we have seen that there has been something of a retreat towards formalism and a down-playing of the creative role of the Court. As Lord Sumption has remarked, 'The declaratory theory is back again in full force'.[28] Overt exercises of the power to depart from their own precedents are fewer than those that go under the radar. Some commentators[29] consider that the Court has become more open in its approach to law making than the House of Lords was. The findings of this work do not point in that direction. Lords Devlin and Radcliffe would feel quite at home with the 'softly, softly' approach of today's treatment of precedent. True the Justices freely admit to making choices but for some of them this is indistinguishable from pursuing the better answer even if there is no single right answer. Justices still give lectures on judicial law making but few that have the bold directness of Lord Reid's evisceration of the declaratory theory 40 years ago—'we do not believe in fairy stories'.

Indeed, one of the curiosities of the Supreme Court's higher visibility through television and social media is that when asked which audiences they wrote their judgments for, the Justices are little more inclined than their predecessors in the House of the Lords to consider that the public is an audience for whom they write. This is hardly surprising in the case of technical matters but many of the public law and human rights cases which make up a major part of the Court's caseload could be made more intelligible to the public. Despite the fact that many of the current Justices work very hard to make their opening paragraph accessible to the wider world, just as Lord Hoffmann and Lord Denning had done before them, on other occasions opportunities are missed. For example, Lord Roger's account of the hopes and dreams of the gay and lesbian population so vividly portrayed in *HJ (Iran)*[30] could have featured more prominently in the communication with the press.

The first big challenge for the new Court in the eyes of the public:[31] the 'unfair bank charges case[32] was arguably an opportunity missed to engage with the public. The public at large, the media and the Office of Fair Trading in its pursuit of consumer protection thought that the case was about whether the bank charges for accidental overdrafts were unfair. The Court did not. Lord Phillips made this abundantly clear in the first words of his broadcast delivery of the judgment: 'This appeal was not about whether bank charges for those who overdraw on their current accounts are fair. It was about a much narrower issue. On what basis

---

[28] Interview with the author, 2013.

[29] Eg R Cornes, n 25 above.

[30] *HJ (Iran) v Secretary of State for the Home Department* [2010] UKSC 31.

[31] Some of the Justices have spoken of the *Jewish Free School* case as being the most significant case that they had to deal with in the first year of the new Court. It is unlikely that the public took that view.

[32] *Office of Fair Trading v Abbey National plc and others* [2009] UKSC 6.

can the OFT investigate the fairness of those charges'. Lord Walker in the leading judgment makes the same observation. The repetition did not make the Court's ruling any more palatable. Assuming that the Supreme Court's analysis was correct on the narrow and determinative point, it does not account for the Court's failure to explain to the waiting public that however penal the charges levied by the banks on the basis of standard-term contracts imposed by the banks, the relevant consumer protection legislation in this country (as opposed to that of some other countries who had implemented the EU Directive) was not couched in a way that would protect them. The correct answer to Lord Phillips' introduction was that there was effectively no basis on which the OFT (or anyone else) could realistically challenge the fairness of the bank charges—in terms of price. Some of the Justices sought to soften the blow by saying that there might be other avenues for challenging the fairness of the charges. Since the OFT had neither the finance nor the backing to return to the fray and in any event the 'other avenues' proved legally illusory, this palliative designed to show that the Court had not missed the point of the case only made things worse. The Court had missed an opportunity to demonstrate that it had grappled as effectively as it could with the aspects of its first big case to touch the lives of millions of ordinary citizens. A bold challenge to Parliament and Executive to address the deficiency in our consumer protection laws might have been apposite. Lord Walker's brief but well intentioned suggestion along this line was too little, too late.[33]

That is more than enough carping. It is clear to all observers that many significant and worthwhile changes have taken place in the transfer of the final judicial authority from the House of Lords to the newly independent UK Supreme Court. We have seen that dialogues lie at the heart of understanding how appellate judicial decision-making works in the final court. The reforms with respect to broadcasting the hearings and the judgments of the Court and the helpful press releases have greatly strengthened the dialogue with the legal profession and the media, and have begun to lay the foundations for significant engagement with the public. So too has the welcoming building and staff. The dialogues with other courts, particularly Strasbourg, have been significantly enhanced with the Court's separation from upper chamber of the legislature. Further, even though the dialogues with Parliament and the Executive are challenging, they are challenging in ways that have the potential to strengthen the unwritten constitution in the

---

[33] There are a few other cases where the Court might also have exhibited some greater attention to public perception, eg *O'Brien v Ministry of Justice* [2013] UKSC 6 (awarding backdated pensions to part-time judges, none of whom when appointed had any expectations of a pension because of the terms on which the post was offered) and *Her Majesty's Treasury v Mohammed Jabar Ahmed and others* [2010] UKSC 5, (the Court, having ruled that the Treasury's confiscation of the assets of alleged terrorists was illegal, then declined to accede to the request of the Government that they be given a short period of grace to rectify the problem so that there would be no danger of funds being returned to an actual terrorist. Somehow only the *Daily Telegraph* seems to have picked up on this story.). It is not that these cases, or the *OFT* case were wrongly decided, rather that they were not couched in terms that might have made more sense to the public.

United Kingdom. Finally, the dialogue between the Justices is being transformed through a commitment to team- and collective-working. Single majority judgments are largely succeeding in sending clearer messages to other courts and the profession as to what the law is, and the greater engagement with each other's judgments in the remaining cases, provides a constructive dialogue with the future by clarifying what the differences between the Justices are. Team-working is also arguably leading to stronger decisions through forensic debate at the stage of the circulation of the judgments. In short, there is much to be admired. The architects and implementers of the transformation have done their jobs well. The debate will necessarily continue over whether all of the changes are for the better or not, or whether some have gone too far and others not far enough but those seem to be the proper questions that arise with respect to institutional change in an ever-changing world. That is surely healthy in a modern democracy.

Index